Leopards and Leaders

Plate 1 The village leader of Bara

Leopards and Leaders

CONSTITUTIONAL POLITICS AMONG
A CROSS RIVER PEOPLE

Malcolm Ruel

TAVISTOCK PUBLICATIONS
London · New York · Sydney · Toronto · Wellington

First published in 1969
by Tavistock Publications Limited
11 New Fetter Lane London E.C.4
Printed in Great Britain
in 12 point Bembo type
by The Camelot Press Limited
London and Southampton
© Malcolm Ruel 1969

SBN 422 73150 1

Distributed in the United States of America
by Barnes & Noble, Inc.

for my father

Contents

Illustrations

Preface

It has become a kind of shorthand to say that political anthropology has moved in the last decade or so from a study of political structures to one of political processes. The influence of *African Political Systems*, as the first book to establish in any systematic way the comparative study of the political organization of traditional societies, was towards the description, analysis, and classification of those institutional structures which served the political needs of a society – above all, the need to maintain order within a territorial framework. More recently, political anthropologists have moved away from a concern with institutional structures as such and have directed their attention to those processes of individual and group action which can be directly identified as political – either because they are concerned with power, or more especially because they are involved in the making or implementation of decisions concerning public affairs. Examples that spring to mind of this latter interest include M. G. Smith's conceptually sharpened treatment of the interplay between 'power' and 'authority' in the government of Abuja and Zazzau, Barth's analysis of the processes producing the bloc power structure of the Swat Pathans, Gulliver's account of how Arusha disputes are settled by a process of reaching group consensus.[1] More recently still, the editors of a new collection of papers, *Political Anthropology*, have made the concern with political process the clarion call to a new theoretical approach.[2]

The present book draws upon both sets of interest. It is concerned to describe Banyang political structure in the sense of how their communities are organized, what principles define their members' co-allegiance, what institutions have a governmental role. It is, however, also and centrally concerned with the political processes that complement these structures. It studies these in two ways. On the one hand it is concerned with the processes which are subsumed by, and themselves

---

[1] M. G. Smith, *Government in Zazzau, 1800–1950* (1960); Fredrik Barth, *Political Leadership among Swat Pathans* (1959); P. H. Gulliver, *Social Control in an African Society* (1963).
[2] Marc J. Swartz, Victor W. Turner, Arthur Tuden (editors), *Political Anthropology* (1966).

maintain, the structures: how 'government' as a process of reaching authoritative decisions about group affairs is indeed effected within these small residential communities. On the other hand, the book is also concerned with those processes that bear upon the constituted organization of the communities themselves: how a village does in fact become a village after a process of political manœuvring and struggle; how a village leader formally acquires this status in competition with others; how descent solidarities are modified, new lineage groups formed in relation to the emerging autonomy of residential groups.

This combined 'structural' and 'processual' treatment relies upon a close adherence to Banyang's own concepts and values concerning what can be understood as 'political'. It is no longer fashionable among political scientists to speak of the 'state' as the subject-matter of their discipline and yet, as Professor d'Entrèves in his *Notion of the State* has shown, theories about the state (its 'might', 'power', and 'authority') have been of central historical importance to the developing political organization of Western society. The present book might comparably be called 'The Notion of the Ɛtɔk', for it is according to this central concept of Banyang political theory that the book is oriented. It may be useful to present here a summary account of the analysis that the book offers and of the descriptive course that it takes.

Starting from a definition of the various senses in which the term ɛtɔk is used by Banyang, Part I ('The Morphology of the Complex Community') describes the form and interrelationship of those groups which are the primary referents of this term, the 'community' as a series of residential aggregates. This part of the book (which subsumes all that follows and was the most difficult to write) faces two major analytic problems. The first of these arises from the indeterminacy or diffuseness of the term ɛtɔk as it is applied to actual residential groups, the named groups 'on the ground'; the second problem concerns the relationship in Banyang society between the principles of descent solidarity and residential association.

The problem of the indeterminate political community is a longstanding and familiar one in anthropological studies of acephalous societies. Radcliffe-Brown refers to it in his Preface to *African Political Systems* (pp. xviii–xix); its clearest statement is perhaps given by Lucy Mair in *Primitive Government* (pp. 104–106); M. G. Smith again refers to it and takes it as his point of departure in his recent article on 'Political Organization' for the *International Encyclopaedia of the Social Sciences*. The problem is indeed a critical one, for although it is not confined to the 'segmentary' societies it especially concerns them and forces us to face the question as to how they can be systematically described or analysed.

For Banyang society, the problem is that, although the concept of the *etɔk* refers to a corporately organized, autonomous 'residential community' (in pidgin English it is usually translated as 'town'), there is in fact in Banyang society no one definite order of grouping to which this term is exclusively applied. The Kenyang *etɔk* (like the Nuer *cieng*, the Dinka *wut*, the Tiv *tar*, the Tallensi *teŋ*) is used of a widening range of residential groups, each of which is able in some situations to act as an autonomous community – a residential group with the authority to govern its own affairs. Studies of segmentary societies have at this point generally discarded the notion of a single political community and have turned instead to examine these contingently autonomous or contingently corporate groupings[1] as a system of groups related to each other in certain definite ways: the 'segmentary system' defined by its relationships of complementary opposition, evidenced in political action by conflict or competition. The range of Banyang residential groups could be presented as a segmentary system of this kind; they fulfil, for example, the criteria that Barnes suggests for such a system (*Politics in a Changing Society*, pp. 49–51), sharing these features not only with the Ngoni but also with the Alur chiefdoms.[2] Such a presentation, however, fails to account for two salient features of Banyang residential grouping: firstly the political action in which these groups are corporately involved is directed inwards rather than outwards – the autonomous handling of the group's own affairs rather than the defence of its rights or property against outsiders – and to this extent each residential group is politically self-sustaining, related to others by the degree of its independence from whatever wider grouping includes it, rather than by its opposition to its fellow groups of the same order; secondly, and following on from the first point, to the extent that any residential group is *dependent* upon the wider group that includes it (again, for the political support necessary for effective autonomous action), so also is it merged in identity as 'one

[1] David Easton, in his extremely suggestive essay on 'Political Anthropology' in the *Biennial Review of Anthropology 1959* (ed. B. J. Siegel), indicates how the segments of a segmentary system are 'contingently' involved in political action. This analysis is further developed by Lloyd Fallers, 'Political Anthropology in Africa' (*European Archives of Sociology*, Vol. 4, 1963). It will be apparent how indebted I am to this analysis, which draws out the element of 'process' in what had earlier been presented with an emphasis on the 'institutional structure' involved, the 'lineage framework'. In the paragraph of the text, however, I am speaking of these 'segmentary systems' strictly as they were presented by Evans-Pritchard and other writers influenced by his account of the Nuer.
[2] A. W. Southall, *Alur Society* (1956).

community' with it. Hamlet, sub-village, village, and village group can each be described situationally as an εtɔk, a residential community with authority to govern its own affairs: as a series, however, they do not form *different* residential communities, different *bɛtɔk*; rather, they are different extensions of the same, single community. In order to retain this idea of a single community, divided though it is into residential groups of different extension, I speak of the 'diffuse community'. It is 'diffuse' in concept – since the same term can be applied situationally and homologously to a range of different actual residential groups. It is also diffuse in operation – since the corporate political actions associated with an εtɔk are carried out at a series of levels by the different groups so identified.

Although in concept and operation the Banyang political community is diffuse, there are certain quite specific criteria which serve to define the relative status of different residential groups. In a classical segmentary society (such as the Nuer or Tiv), these criteria would be genealogical: the accepted relationships between the ancestors whose names now identify the present members of the groups, described as these ancestors' descendants. In Banyang society, genealogical criteria play some part, but more immediately significant are the rights accorded to leaders of certain residential groups to receive on behalf of the community certain reserved 'animals of the community' (of which the most important is the leopard) should they be caught or killed by a member. The right to receive a leopard and to carry out the appropriate ritual concerning it symbolized in the traditional society above all else the independent and superordinate status of the leader of one order of residential grouping: it is this which distinguishes the 'village leader' from the leaders of other less extended residential groups, these rights held by its leader which distinguish the 'village' from other orders of residential group (of greater or lesser extent). The 'village' as one order of residential grouping is universally found in Banyang society and may be said to embody more clearly than any other the conceptual features of an εtɔk as a residential community whose members accept a common solidarity and observe the corporate authority of the group as a whole. (These features are indeed a practical condition of the homage paid to a village leader in presenting a leopard to him.) It is, moreover, in relation to *this* order of grouping that we are able to distinguish others: a 'hamlet' is a component section of a village, inhabited usually by persons who share closer kinties than they do with other members of the village, who also form a corporate residential group (a partially autonomous εtɔk), whose leader is nevertheless obliged to pass forward any leopard or comparable 'animal of the community' presented to him by a hamlet member; a 'village group' is the widest group of people acting together as a single community (and who share associated ties of common descent, distinguishing them from other similar groups) where such a group is composed of a number of different villages. (In two instances the 'village' itself forms the largest politically united residential group.)

The picture that I attempt to draw is therefore of a kind of 'political community' which in one aspect has a 'diffuse' corporateness (since it is embodied in a range of actual residential groups), while in another aspect well-recognized rights, although of a limited kind, serve quite specifically to distinguish different extensions or orders of residential grouping within the overall community. These two aspects of the corporate organization of Banyang communities I distinguish as 'operational' and 'constitutional' respectively. By an 'operationally' corporate group I mean one whose members participate (either directly or representatively) in united action towards a stated end: a residential group is then 'operationally' corporate to the extent that its members combine as an *ɛtɔk* to control the affairs of the group. By a 'constitutionally' corporate group I mean one whose status or identity in relation to others has in some defined way been 'recognized' or 'legitimized': the 'constitutional' status of Banyang residential groups is thus determined by the recognized rights accorded to the leader who represents the group, most notably by the right of the 'village' leader to receive and retain a leopard presented in homage to the 'community'. All Banyang residential groups have a similar 'operational' corporateness: in 'constitutional' status they are sharply distinguished. The same could be said of the territorial sections of the classical segmentary societies (assuming that their 'constitutional' status *vis-à-vis* each other is determined by their accepted genealogical relationships – what Laura Bohannan has described as their 'genealogical charter'). Where Banyang differ from these classical segmentary societies is in the nature of the criteria determining 'constitutional' status: for Nuer or Tiv the defining relationships are genealogical; for Banyang such relationships give way to the rights acquired by a leader in his command of allegiance from the members of one order of residential grouping.

The constitutional identity or status of any group is not accorded by some kind of higher sociological providence, but is acquired as an event in time, or cumulatively over time. We need to distinguish here between the constitutional ordering of a political community which is established by a gradual process of accumulation and consolidation and draws its 'legitimacy' from its continued acceptance over time, and the kind of constitutional ordering of a political community which is established directly, by deliberate political action, and which draws its 'legitimacy' from the authority implicit in this action. The 'genealogical charter' of a segmentary society very clearly exemplifies the first kind: secession from an already existing political community (or, alternatively, the granting of political independence) may be taken to illustrate how constitutional status can be defined by direct action of the second kind. Nevertheless, no political 'constitution' can be *wholly* of one or the other kind. The constitutional ordering of a Banyang community is, perhaps more than most, mixed: the rights which define a leader's status are the focus for constant political struggles, where the underlying issue is one of the independence of the residential group concerned in the struggle, but at the same time a genealogical idiom serves to reaffirm those solidarities deriving a long-term recognition from the past. I try to show how the process of 'constitutional politics' arises when a residential group is able to assert an operational autonomy greater than that formally accorded to it by its present constitutional position, and how this process impinges upon and modifies any statement of political solidarities expressed in a descent idiom. Banyang constitutional politics are centred in the attempt by a residential group to obtain the status and rights of a village, and, as one would expect, stories recording such attempts in the past often involve the presentation of (or failure to present) a leopard. During the Colonial period, a new set of rights served to define the village leader's status and a new authority had been created which was able to sanction them: Chapter 4 describes this new situation and how within it the constitutional struggle of residential groups to achieve a 'recognized' independence was itself modified.

In treating the second major problem of Part I – the relationship between descent and common residence as principles of social grouping – it is again useful to compare the situation in Banyang society with that in the classical segmentary societies. There descent and residence (or territorial grouping) are in some measure equated: lineage and territorial group are identified; the genealogy of groups expresses their political alignments. But, as we have already implied, the genealogical (descent) idiom in Banyang society serves only secondarily to express political alignments: the more important index of a residential group's identity is its members' allegiance to their leader and the relative status which he can claim. It is against this emergence of a form of residential grouping that is operationally autonomous as well as having its constitutional form expressed in the distinctive idiom of corporate allegiance to a leader that the place of descent as a principle of social grouping must be seen. Again, the position of the 'village' as the most distinctive (but *not* the only) order of residential grouping is critical. In relation to Banyang residential groups (and most distinctively in relation to a village) common descent serves a dual role: *internally* it serves to differentiate the members of a residential group into a series of separate descent or lineage groups (*banɛrɛkɛt*); *externally* it serves to 'articulate' residential groups (i.e. to link them as unit members) within a wider grouping with its own shared, if modified, solidarity. To cite only the example of village structure: all Banyang villages are divided into a series of (major) lineage groups, each a corporate group of kinsfolk identified by their descent from a common ancestor; those villages which form part of a wider grouping (the village group) claim also a common descent connection, and the genealogical relationship linking the villages serves both to express and to give evidence of the continuing recognition of their political solidarity. The two principles of common residence and common descent are here not equated (or 'co-ordinate' to each other) but are rather contradistinguished: given the primacy of residential association (which is but another aspect of the corporate autonomy of a residential group), descent disparity differentiates those who are residentially united, residential autonomy modifies (but does not supersede) a wider descent unity. It may be observed that in this interaction between the two principles of grouping, the 'articulating' function of common descent contributes to the 'constitutional' ordering of the overall community, whereas the 'differentiating' function of common descent is relevant to the 'operational' structure of an autonomous residential group, which is divided thereby into a number of separate kin-groups each with an effective solidarity in the face of the wider community.

Part II, 'Processes of Government', does not face quite the same critical problems of analysis. This part is concerned with the concept *ɛtɔk* in a different aspect: it becomes now the source of power and authority in the regulation of community affairs. In this aspect the term *ɛtɔk* does not refer directly to the community as a residential aggregate but rather to those persons drawn from it (elders and leaders) who collectively, by virtue of their status, and corporately, by their joint action, are able to represent the community in any decision concerning its affairs. The 'operational' structure of a residential group consists then of a self-selected body of persons (a 'council') who collectively represent and corporately have authority over the residential group as a whole (i.e. the aggregate of its members). This structure, depicted in *Figure 22* (p. 134), I take as the paradigm for the governmental-cum-political process, which for the overall 'complex community' is repeated at each level of residential grouping. Chapters 6 and 7 examine features of this process in the more specific matters of dispute settlement, policy formation, and legislation. Chapter 7 also gives an account of inter-community fighting in the past.

One of the features which emerges most clearly from Banyang governmental processes is the jealousy with which a community council guards the authority which it corporately controls: council members constantly extol the necessity for united action, and councils will impose the severest sanctions they can command on anyone who is seen to oppose himself (even implicitly) to the order and authority of the ɛtɔk, the corporate community. This feature underlies the direction of the judicial process which (as I try to show in Chapter 6) is concerned to 'isolate the offence, and the offender', who is then required to submit himself to the authority of the group by making a payment (-kwɔ), which is both a punishment and an acknowledgement of his guilt: to refuse to accept the judgement of a council is to run the risk of flouting community authority, of placing oneself 'outside' the corporate group, with which eventually, as a member, one must make one's peace. The same process of mobilizing the corporate community against a miscreant member, who is thereby 'isolated' in opposition, is seen most dramatically in the law of ostracism, which at the present time is the severest sanction that a community council can impose. Nevertheless, if the strength of community authority derives from the power of the corporate group in relation to its individual members, its weakness derives from the diversity of interests contained in the body of persons who collectively decide issues of concern to the community. Radical dissension within a community council renders it powerless to act, and leaves the residential group it represents without a firm authority. Chapter 8 discusses these 'Limitations upon the Corporate Structure of the Community' and points to the differing balance between the formal authority of a residential group and the degree of unity that it can command at the various levels of residential grouping within a village group. This problem which is posed by Banyang political theory, and is implicit in their concept of the ɛtɔk, is then: how can corporate unity (and, with it, strength) be maintained in the exercise of authority while allowing at the same time for the diversity of interests of those who (collectively) embody that authority?

Part III, on 'The Role of the Associations', examines these institutions in the light of that problem. Associations play a very prominent part in Banyang life, serving recreational, economic, and supernatural ends, other than the political which concerns us primarily here. Chapter 9 reviews the general form and range of associations, giving a brief description of two associations (Tui and Basinjom) and the not dissimilar age-groups. Chapter 10 examines in greater detail the important 'Ngbe' or Leopard association, undoubtedly the most effective of the traditional political associations within the whole of the Cross River area. This chapter attempts to show how Ngbe as an association formalizes and thus strengthens the corporate authority of the community: although the association derives its authority from the community – through the fact that its members are indeed the representatives of the community – the presentation of the authority through the constituted and impersonal forms of the association makes its support less subject to diversities of private interest and (as a formal act) more readily the focus for collective support. The widespread Ngbe 'polity', composed of many independent Ngbe lodges all bound to support the formal sanctions of the association, derives from this fact. Yet bound to uphold the *idea* of corporate authority ('Ngbe' as the captive leopard), the association's lodges have also much effective independence: any residential group can acquire a lodge and (while keeping within the general forms of the association) can to this extent develop its own independent interests, and confirm its independent authority as a group.

The role of the Ngbe association relates, however, to the traditional 'diffuse' structure of Banyang communities and to the governmental processes operative in them. More recently a newer, more 'modern' association has emerged, the 'Clan Unions', which are described in Chapter 11, where their radically different organization is related to the problems experienced by Banyang villages and village groups under the Colonial administration. Both Ngbe and the Clan Unions have (as do all associations) their own 'constitution', in the sense of a recognized set of rules formally accepted by their members. In relation to the 'operational' processes of community government examined at length in Part II, I try in Part III to indicate how these associational 'constitutions' become, by extension and on a different level from a village leader's right to receive a leopard, alternative, and, to some extent, competing, political charters – means of explicitly affirming, strengthening, and (hopefully) developing aspects of the same basic processes of government.

The final part of the book, Part IV, returns to examine in a different dimension two of the central themes of Part I. The dimension is now that of the historical processes by which groups develop in Banyang society, and both themes bear upon the central importance of the process by which a residential group develops (differentially, in relation to other groups) an operational autonomy in controlling its affairs, which it then seeks to confirm 'constitutionally'. Chapter 12 examines the interrelationship between descent and residential groups in this process of change. Chapter 13, the final chapter of the book, examines first in general terms and then by a case-study the process of 'constitutional politics' around which so much of Banyang political life coheres.

My first and main period of field research among Banyang lasted from July 1953 until October 1954, the bulk of it being carried out in Upper Banyang country in the two village communities of Tali (now Tali 1) and Bara. I am extremely grateful to the (then) Colonial Social Science Research Council for the award which made this research possible. In 1958 I made a brief return trip of about three weeks to Banyang country. Finally, in 1965, I spent nearly three months (July to September, inclusive) in Banyang (and part in Ejagham) country: this was made possible by a Hayter grant from the Centre of African Studies, University of Edinburgh, and by a number of practical facilities given by the Institute of African Studies of the University of Ife. I am grateful to both these bodies for their support. During this final period of research my aim was to extend my knowledge of the different areas of Banyang country, to explore more fully their relationship with Ejagham, and to test the main conclusions which I had reached regarding the political process and the constitutional structure of the community. Somewhat unexpectedly I discovered that not only had my language of analysis developed in the period that I had spent away from Banyang but that so too had their own political experience. On my first day back in Tali, the word that sounded oddly in my ears, which I could not recognize, was *pɔrrɔtek*: Ta Taboko complained that *'pɔrrɔtek* was spoiling the community'. It turned out that he was referring to the effect of post-Independence national 'politics' on the local communities, which had given a dimension to local factionalism which had not existed under the Colonial administration. I do not attempt to discuss these present-day *pɔrrɔtek*. Nevertheless, when on this revisit the traditional story of how Ndifaw acquired the (constitutional) leadership of Tali (pp. 61–62) was rehearsed once more for me, I was interested to hear that in explaining the manœuvres 'behind' that enabled Ndifaw to become leader, my informant turned to the post-Independence idiom: *Ndifɔ aki pɔrrɔtek*, 'Ndifaw made "politics" '. I was also fortunate on this return visit in being able to consult documentary material in the West Cameroon Archives in Buea and in the Divisional Office in Mamfe.

Language has given rise to a number of minor difficulties, The chief of these has been to know which dialect of Kenyang to use when citing Kenyang terms. I have tried where possible to give both Upper and

Lower Kenyang versions where there is a difference and in actual description to use the dialectal term appropriate to the area referred to in the
description. This means that I have sometimes had to use two terms interchangeably (e.g. *aca* and *acɔ*, Lower and Upper Kenyang respectively for
a leader's house or meeting house). Secondly, the transliteration of names
has produced some problems. The convention adopted has been to employ
a phonetic script when using Kenyang (in italics) and to transliterate
names into the Roman alphabet when not citing them in Kenyang.
Again, this has produced certain inconsistencies (*bɔ Ndifɔ* but the 'children
of Ndifaw', *Mfɔtek* kept as Mfotek) but I hope these are sufficiently
obvious not to be confusing.

I have tried as far as possible to make this an accurate historical record,
as well as a sociological one. This has meant referring to actual places,
groups, and people. Moreover, if I am to describe leadership disputes,
there is no way in which I could disguise the events or participants to
those who have some knowledge of them. I have tried not to betray
confidences, while giving enough information to make the issues of a
case clear. In cases where I have felt that some embarrassment might be
caused by the use of proper names, I have used pseudonyms, marking
these on their first appearance (and in the index) with an asterisk (*).
What I should wish to emphasize is my very great debt to those whose
names (and many whose pseudonyms) appear in these pages.

Among the many Banyang whom I met through my work I should
especially wish to mention the friendship and help given to me by Ta
Taboko, Ta Nyak Ebong, William B. Abange, Richard Eluck, C. T. Bai,
Bai Egbe, Eno Ebi, Johnson Agbosong, Dickson, Chief Nkwa, Chief
Tambe, and Ta Tambe Ebot. I owe a special debt to Tanyi Mbuagbaw,
Tambi Eyong Mbuagbaw, Tom Eyong, and S. T. Tataw. There are
many others whose names would make too long a list to thank individually, although I still owe them thanks. Among my academic colleagues, I
am grateful to Dr John Beattie, Mr G. I. Jones, and Dr Lloyd Fallers for
their criticism of the whole or part of earlier drafts of this book. G. I.
Jones has kindly commented on the chapter describing Ngbe, and Edwin
Ardener on the whole book. Finally, I would wish to take this opportunity
to acknowledge a dual personal and academic debt to Professor E. E.
Evans-Pritchard: this book would not have been written without his
teaching, nor without the personal support which he has given.

Edinburgh
September 1968   M. R.

I

Introductory: The Banyang People

Banyang homeland lies in the central area of the basin of the upper Cross River. It is hilly, forested country with many rivers and streams. Most of the rivers rise in the arc of highland which surrounds Banyang country in the north-east, east, and south, and flow through it, converging on to the main stream of the Cross River, which is formed by the junction of the Mainyu and Bali rivers at Mamfe. At the time this study was carried out, this area formed part of the Mamfe Division of the Southern Cameroons, which was then administered under British Trusteeship. With the coming of independence in 1916, the Southern Cameroons chose to join with the former French Cameroons, and Banyang country within Mamfe Division now forms part of the Western State of the Federal Republic of Cameroon.[1] In 1953 the population of Banyang within their homeland was approximately 18,000, but many others (estimated at 4,000–5,000 persons) were living and working away from their home communities, the large majority in the plantations and towns of the southern coastal area.

Before they became subject to Colonial rule, Banyang were not politically united as a people. Scattered through the forest in many separate small settlements, the largest recognized political groupings are unlikely to have included more than 2,000 people and in many cases certainly fewer. There is an absence, too, of any tradition of common descent or of any story of a common origin. What unites Banyang and distinguishes them from other peoples are the qualities and attributes of 'Kenyang', the language they speak and the culture or (in pidgin English) the 'fashion' they follow. Even this unity, however, is not unqualified and relates them in varying degrees of closeness to those who are their neighbours.

Different writers have variously classified the Kenyang language as

[1] In February 1969 the names of Divisions in West Cameroon were changed, Mamfe Division becoming Cross River Division (HQ Mamfe). At the same time Victoria Division was renamed Fako, and Kumba Division was renamed Meme.

'semi-Bantu', 'Bantu', and 'Bantoid'.[1] Ittmann, in his early grammar, notes the uncertain and wavering connections between Kenyang and Bantu;[2] similarly Richardson, following his investigation of the Bantu borderland, speaks of the uncertainty of relationship between Kenyang and the broader language groups.[3] Part of the paradox of linguistic classifications has been the tendency to align Banyang with their 'Bantu' southern neighbours and thus to dissociate them from their eastern and northern neighbours, the Ejagham (or 'Ekoi') and Anyang, with whom they themselves claim closest cultural affinity.[4] More recently, however, Crabb, working on the 'Ekoid' languages, has sought to demonstrate that these languages can themselves be classed as Bantu, thus moving the Bantu borderline well to the west of Banyang and re-establishing the relationship between Kenyang and Ejagham within the wider category, although presumably Kenyang's distinguishing element of affinity with the other Bantu languages to the south and south-east has still to be recognized.[5]

Within Banyang country – which is itself termed 'Kenyang' – a broad distinction is made between 'Upper' and 'Lower' Banyang. Taking its orientation from the flow of the rivers, this distinction is relative, and the dialectal and cultural differences which are associated with it are gradual. The differences between Upper and Lower Kenyang, moreover, reflect the differences between the cultures lying beyond the borders of the Upper and Lower areas. Thus it is the language and cultural forms of Lower Kenyang which have greater prestige and which are in fact closer to those of the eastern Ejagham (the 'Keaka'), whom Banyang admire and from whom they have acquired many of their institutions, especially associations such as Ngbe and Basinjom, and cult-agencies such as Mfam. Except for that created by successive administrations (which has varied over time), there is indeed no clearly defined boundary between the area of Kenyang culture and *Kɛyaka* (the qualitative *kɛ-* term which for Banyang describes Ejagham language, culture, and homeland, and which

---

[1] P. A. Talbot, *The Peoples of Southern Nigeria*, Vol. IV, p. 88; Westermann, *Languages of West Africa*, p. 114; Greenberg, 'Studies in African Linguistic Classification: III The Position of Bantu', *Southwestern Journal of Anthropology*, Vol. 5, p. 309 (a statement later revised); Richardson in *Linguistic Survey of the Northern Bantu Borderland* (International African Institute), Vol. I, p. 39.

[2] 'Kenyang, die Sprache der Nyang', *Zeitschrift für Eingeborenen-Sprachen*, Band XXVI, p. 19.

[3] Op. cit., p. 39.

[4] E.g. Westermann's statement 'The speech of the Banyangi is . . . a Bantu language, while that of the Anyang . . . appears to belong to the Ekai cluster' (loc. cit.).

[5] *Ekoid Bantu Languages of Ogoja, Eastern Nigeria*, 1965.

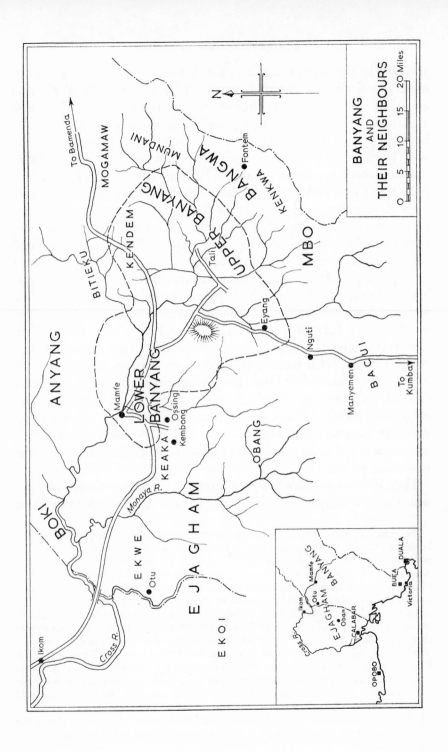

BANYANG
AND
THEIR NEIGHBOURS

0   5   10   15   20 Miles

N

BOKI

ANYANG

MOGAMAW

BITIEKU

KENDEM

MUNDANI

To Bamenda

UPPER BANYANG

BANGWA

KENKWA

Fontem

Tali

MBO

Eyang

Nguti

LOWER BANYANG

Mamfe

Ossing

Kembong

KEAKA

Manyemen

BACUI

To Kumba

Monaya R.

EKWE

Otu

OBANG

EJAGHAM

Cross R.

Ikom

EKOI

BANYANG

BANYANG

EJAGHAM

Cross R.

Ikom

Mamfe

Otu

Oban

BUEA   DUALA

Victoria

CALABAR

OPOBO

was used by the German, and later the British, administration to describe more specifically the eastern Ejagham or 'Keaka'):[1] in the borderland area there is a high degree of miscegenation; most people are bilingual, and in two villages (Ossing and Ntenako) the dominant language varies between parts of the same village.[2] This alignment of Lower Banyang with Ejagham ('Kɛyaka') is recognized both by themselves – who some- times refer to 'Kenyang' as the area of Banyang country to the east which excludes them – and by Upper Banyang, for whom the terms Kɛnyaŋ antɛn (Lower Kenyang) and Kɛyaka (Ejagham) are often synonymous. Upper Banyang, on the other hand, are associated by Lower Banyang with the culturally dissimilar highland peoples (Kɛfiɛt) situated beyond their borders. It was from this area that slaves were obtained in the past, and Upper Banyang are still sometimes spoken of derogatively as 'slaves' (basɛm) or as having a large proportion of people with 'slave' or highland descent in their population. In fact no one is more conscious of the distinction between persons of 'slave' and 'free-born' descent than Upper Banyang. In the past, marriages between Upper Banyang and Bangwa are reported to have been common 'because Bangwa women were cheaply obtained and such Bangwa relationships also led to greater facilities for obtaining slaves'. By 1930, however, such marriages no longer took place,[3] and other signs of Bangwa influence were disappearing. Even the 'Bangwa robes worn by some Eastern Banyang Chiefs' which were then noted as the remaining evidence of that influence[4] had by the 1950s disappeared.

These differences *within* Kenyang form part of a series of scaled changes which include Kenyang but also extend beyond it. Thus among Ejagham

---

[1] The term kɛyaka is in fact cognate with the term ɛjayam used by the people from the borders of Calabar to the boundary with Banyang to describe themselves: kɛ- is a class prefix; the changing of *j* to *y* and the elision of the final consonant are both common features of dialectal changes within Kenyang between Lower and Upper dialects.

[2] It is commonly believed in the extreme Lower Banyang villages that the language of their forebears was Ejagham, a belief supported by the fact that certain village and ancestral names are Ejagham, e.g. Etemetek, bɔ Mfɔtek. The extent of the bilingualism in this area is illustrated by the case of one man in Besongabang who although paternally born to that (Banyang) village was brought up at his mother's home and there learnt only Ejagham. When, as an adult, he returned to live at his agnatic home he found himself unable to speak Kenyang although he learnt to 'hear' it. At a legal case that I attended he was one of the main protagonists and throughout the discussion spoke Ejagham while everyone else spoke Kenyang: there was no translation and no one (other than myself) appeared to have any difficulty in understanding him.

[3] E. H. F. Gorges, *Banyang Tribal Area Assessment Report*, paras. 24–25: 'It is said that the Bangwas object to them because the progeny of such marriages jeer at their Bangwa relatives.'

[4] Ibid., para. 25.

4

themselves there is a difference between those living towards the border with Nigeria (variantly called the 'Ekoi' or 'Ekwe') and those described above as the 'eastern' Ejagham or 'Keaka' who immediately neighbour the Banyang, and who are referred to by the former as *Ngonaya*, those 'across the river' (in this case, the Monaya). The features of language, social organization, and culture which distinguish the 'Keaka' Ejagham from their own western neighbours ('Ekoi') are precisely those which make them closer to Banyang.[1] One is led to the conclusion that Kenyang as a culture has emerged by a process of interaction, differentiation, and spread which probably occurred originally in the area of the Lower Banyang but is likely to have had a related secondary centre in Upper Banyang territory. Relevant to this hypothesis is the distribution of the population, which, while nowhere high, appears in the nineteenth century to have been denser in the eastern Ejagham and extreme Lower Banyang area than further west, a second belt of less densely populated country then lying between Upper and Lower Banyang areas.[2] One factor in the emergence of Kenyang would appear to be the role of Banyang as middle-men in the trade flowing from the highlands to eastern Ejagham and ultimately Calabar: both eastern Ejagham and Upper Banyang held key positions in this trade, the former by their possession of salt-wells which gave them access to one of the most important of the trade items, the latter, by their control of the trade routes from the highlands, bringing in livestock and slaves. A story that illustrates the kind of connection then existing between areas concerns a former Fon of Fontem in Bangwa country who is said, when a child, to have been sold as a slave, finally reaching Kembong; he was recovered through the good offices of the village leader of Tali (whose founding ancestor is believed to have come from Kembong, p. 61) and returned to his father the Fon. It is claimed that in recognition of this service a regular tribute was paid by Fontem

---

[1] The distinction between the 'Ekois' and 'Keaka' and the closeness of the latter to Banyang are made clear by Mansfeld, *Urwald-Dokumente* (1908), especially p. 12.

[2] In the *Intelligence Report on the Kembong Area* (1937), twenty-four 'Ekwe' (Ekoi) villages are listed, with a total population of 1,532 (the largest is Otu, numbering 204 persons); twenty-eight 'Keaka' villages are listed, their total population numbering 7,826 (the two largest are Ossing with 1,541 persons and Kembong with 1,324, and there are eight other villages larger than Otu). Gorges (op. cit., para. 57) notes the gap between Lower and Upper Banyang before the German administration moved a number of villages into this central area. Thus in *Map 2* Mbinjong (a composite village which until 1936 was included as part of the 'Keaka' area) formerly inhabited territory to the south-west of its present position; Mbio and Etoko have more recently come down from the north-east; Bakebe formerly lived to the south, near to the present site of Ashum. The only central village which is now at all close to its former site is the small Mfaenchang.

5

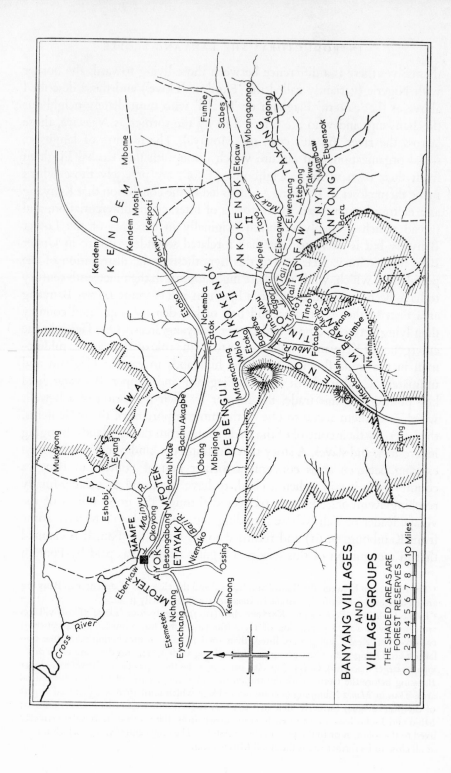

BANYANG VILLAGES
AND
VILLAGE GROUPS

THE SHADED AREAS ARE
FOREST RESERVES

0 1 2 3 4 5 6 7 8 9 10 Miles

to the village leader of Tali and that when he succeeded to the Fonship he gave to it the name 'Fontem' from the great leader and ancestral hero of Kembong.

OBAN	OTU	OSSING	BANYANG
Nucleated villages	Small nucleated villages	Scattered settlements forming dispersed political community	Scattered settlements forming dispersed political community
Village exclusively built in enclosed compounds	Enclosed compounds (? but not for whole village?)	Various modes: some enclosed compounds; other houses in rows or compounds	A few enclosed compounds (often as a minor form behind 'bottom house' of an 'open' compound); most settlements as 'open' compounds.
ɛtɛk (ʔɛtɛɔk) – residentially associated group of kinsfolk and quasi-kin within compound	*ɛtɛk* – village as a body of persons (the group that discuss cases, etc.)	*ɛtɛk* – settlement, village, political community	*ɛtɔk* – settlement, village, political community
mfam – village as a political and territorial unit	*mfam* – village in more general locative and territorial sense		
ntuimfam – village head (*mfɔn emfam* – less commonly used synonym)	*ntuimfam* – village head	*ntuifa* village leader	
mfɔn ɛtɛk – compound head (lit. 'owner')			*mfɔ ɛtɔk* community leader (at any level of *ɛtɔk*) (*mbɔŋ ɛtɔk* – in Lower Kenyang 'owner of the community', a leading member of the village, someone of status)
	ɔkuri – enclosed compound	*ɔkwɛlɛ* – enclosed compound	*ɛkri* – enclosed compound (*mɔɛkri* – 'small *ɛkri*': house behind 'bottom house' of a settlement)
		sɛnta – 'open' compound	*sɛnta* (Lower Kenyang) *kɛnta* (U.K.): 'open' compound where this forms part of a larger settlement

The tracing-through of organizational elements between societies is a hazardous task, especially when these have been subject to change under different Colonial administrations. I have attempted to set out, however, in the table on page 7 a number of related differences for the range of traditional societies between the Ejagham of the Oban hills and the Banyang.[1] The complex of features shown is directly related to the main subject of this book. The most interesting point of the table concerns the Kenyang term *ɛtɔk*, which would appear to be cognate with the Oban Ejagham *ɛtɛk* but has a different reference: whereas the Oban *ɛtɛk* is a residential unit of kinsfolk, affines, and affiliates *within* a village, for Banyang the traditional *ɛtɔk* was both residential unit (the single, small settlement of the past) and the wider 'community' made up of a number of neighbouring settlements. With this change in the meaning of the term goes a change in actual settlement organization: from the sizeable, nucleated villages of the Oban Ejagham to the dispersed and far less clearly demarcated residential groupings of the eastern Ejagham and Banyang. Other features (the falling-out of the term *mfam* and of the status *ntui mfam*; the emergence of a different type of enclosed compound) show a related set of changes. It is as though this central feature of Banyang political organization – the *ɛtɔk* with its leader, the *mfɔ ɛtɔk* – had been picked out from its limited societal context in the larger Ejagham villages, to be expanded and elaborated into the more complex, if also diffuse, set of political groupings characteristic of Banyang society.

If the concept of *ɛtɔk* can be derived ultimately from Ejagham society, a second element, that of secular leadership – where a 'chief' is at the apex of a hierarchical power structure – would appear to owe something to the more developed centralized chiefdoms of the highland peoples beyond the Upper Banyang. The connection here would seem less integral to the basic terms of Kenyang culture: a matter of influence and imitation rather than one of descent or cultural continuity. There is evidence of intermarriage with highland peoples, as we have seen, and also of the assimilation to Upper Banyang communities of a number of persons and descent groups with a highland origin. There would appear

[1] The information for the three Ejagham villages was collected by me in the villages named, but in each case the villages are representative of a larger area. Since, under Mansfeld, an attempt was made to consolidate the dispersed settlements of the Keaka and Banyang, information concerning the exact nature of their traditional settlements is more difficult to obtain and less reliable. The main features noted are however confirmed by Mansfeld (op. cit., pp. 25–26, 32) and Talbot (*In the Shadow of the Bush*, pp. 263–266, see especially the 'Plan of Aking'). Further discussion of the Banyang features, including the slight variations between Upper and Lower areas, will be found below, pp. 26–33. It is notable however that the major difference in settlement patterns occurs within the Ejagham area itself.

to be no evidence, however, of any direct link by way of descent between an Upper Banyang village leader or village group founder and a highland chiefship. On the other hand, it is clear that there was some imitation of the highland chiefs by Upper Banyang village leaders: at its lowest level this may have been a matter of dress; at its highest level it would seem to be evidenced in the concern of the most outstanding of the village leaders to aggrandize their status and to extend their domain (the most notable examples are the village leaders of Tali and Defang).[1] Today there remains a difference in emphasis in the values associated with village leadership between Lower and Upper areas: whereas in the latter the village leader has more of the secular status of an influential man with a strong following, in the former the ritual office of leader has greater prominence (certainly in the case of the traditional 'leader of the community') and the village leader becomes in part a symbolic figure. Two qualifications must nevertheless immediately be added. First, it must be emphasized that this is only a difference of degree. Both types of attribute are present in both areas; the set of rights relating to the 'animals of the community' which define a village leader's status are common to all Banyang areas (and indeed are virtually identical for Ejagham village heads) and it is certainly not only among Upper Banyang that powerful secular leaders have emerged (Fontem of Kembong is one example). Secondly, as I have already tried to indicate, the emergence of powerful leaders in Upper Kenyang in the past is almost certainly in part due to historical factors contingent upon their geographical position which gave them control of the trade routes.

We have spoken of an area of bilingualism and a merging of cultures where Lower Banyang meet the eastern Ejagham or 'Keaka'. A less marked bilingualism and cultural interpenetration occurs also along the northern and southern borders of Banyang territory. Both *Denyā* (the language of Anyang) and Kenyang are spoken in the villages of Nyang and Mukoyong, and during the Colonial period the two villages wavered in their 'Native Authority' allegiance; both now form part of the Takamanda Local Authority and count themselves as Anyang. In the south the village of Nguti has a strong Kenyang element; Mansfeld lists it with Banyang villages but it has since formally become associated with

---

[1] Gorges refers to the rivalry between these two leaders which existed in the past and notes various features of Upper Banyang chiefship which he relates to the highland (especially Bangwa) institution of chiefship, e.g. the sacrosanctness of the chief's wives, filial rather than fraternal succession (op. cit., paras. 23, 24, 173). On the latter point, see pp. 300–301 below. For actions of the Tali and Defang village leaders which give evidence of their imperializing claims, see above, pp. 5–6, and below, pp. 13, 59, 305.

9

the Mbo group. On the other hand, the present-day village group of Awanchi or Kendem (*Awanciɛ, Kɛndɛm*) has been included within the Banyang area. Although in culture the members of this village group are very close to Banyang and speak Kenyang as a second language, they must in fact be regarded as a small, distinctive group, with a dialect of their own ('Kendem') related to *Bitiɛku*, itself a dialect of *Denyã*. Mention should also be made of a small group of Kenyang speakers at Manyemen and a number of neighbouring villages in Kumba Division. They speak of themselves as *Bacui*, their language and way of life as *Kɛcui*;[1] it has many of the dialectal features of Upper Kenyang, but has departed more radically than that dialect from Lower Kenyang. They are now a cultural and linguistic enclave separated from Banyang country by a corridor of both Mbo and Basossi. Wary, for its Local Authority implications, of claiming kinship with Banyang, they claim originally to have come from Manenguba on the borders of Kumba Division and the Eastern Cameroon State and speak of themselves as 'Upper Balong'. Banyang have less hesitation in claiming them as an offshoot from themselves.

By West African forest-belt standards, the overall density of population in Banyang country is very low: approximately twenty three persons per square mile, excluding the present-day large areas of Forest Reserve. Traditionally, Banyang are cultivators, their two main crops being coco-yams and plantains. Except for the initial heavy work of clearing, most of the farmwork is undertaken by women. The ideal in farming is to select a large area of land which is either forest or ground that has been left un-touched for a long period of time, and to clear this land progressively for new farm plots, which are cultivated for a two or three years' sequence before being left to revert to bush and secondary forest. Other plots near to the settlements may be cultivated more intensively, and it is here usually that plantains are grown. There is little or no pressure on land, and land-rights are little developed. In Upper Banyang country general rights to the territory they occupy are held by village groups, and inter-village group boundaries are recognized. Within that territory anyone may clear otherwise unclaimed land and by clearing it establish his rights over it, which continue even after the land is left fallow (*bɛfoko*). All such rights are individually held by household heads and are disposed of by inheritance, allocation, gift, or exchange. Unclaimed land formerly belonging to a member of a lineage group reverts to the head of the lineage group, who will be expected to reallocate it, if and when the need arises, to one of their members who needs land or to someone who has come to

[1] This also is the term used by Anyang to describe Banyang.

live with them, but it is only in such cases that a lineage group is collectively represented in relation to land. As we shall later see, the basis of Banyang political grouping lies in their places of residence – the ɛtɔk as settlement or as a multi-focal residential community. Land-rights are an appendage to residence within a settlement and rarely become a political issue in terms of either individual status or corporate grouping. In the past there would appear to have been little difficulty in obtaining land and there seems to have been a constant process of movement, involving migration and the founding of new settlements. Even today, relatively large settlements have been able to change their sites without difficulty, even where this has meant acquiring territory from a village group other than their own.[1]

Apart from their farmwork, Banyang also engage in some fishing, especially in the many smaller rivers and streams of Upper Banyang country, and a few men go out as hunters. In the past, collective hunting was practised, but it has now become entirely an individual pursuit and, even so, is less followed than the opportunities existing for it would permit. In Upper Banyang country this gap has been filled by professional Bangwa hunters. Numbers of livestock are also kept in the settlements, mainly goats, chickens, and (today) ducks. In the past, a breed of tsetse-resistant dwarf cattle was also kept, especially it would seem by the more influential and wealthy community leaders, but this breed has now entirely died out.

Reference has already been made to the trade routes which passed through Banyang country. The direction of the trade was from the highlands of Bamileke and Bamenda down through Banyang country to the eastern Ejagham, and from there either to the Cross River or more directly through central Ejagham country to Calabar.[2] The most important markets were at Tali, Eyang, and Kembong, each crucially placed in relation to the cultural boundaries of the area, and serving it would seem as much a political function as an economic one in allowing trade to take place between different social and ethnic groups.[3] Certainly

---

[1] The present land of Atebong village (see *Map 2*, p. 6) was, for example, given to them by Ejwengang and Takwa in the two village groups of Ndifaw and Tanyi Nkongo. In 1954 Tali village had also agreed to give land to a section of Etoko village but soon after building had started the leader of the section died and the move was never completed.

[2] Mansfeld, op. cit., pp. 127–129; also *Annual Report on the Ossidinge Division*, 1916, para. 44. (West Cameroon Archives, Ce 1916/2.)

[3] Between Kembong and Calabar there was no further market. Talbot confirms the role of the Ekoi in this trading network (1912, pp. 266–267) but notes the paradox of the absence of markets: 'It is somewhat curious that among a people where the instinct for trade is well developed, there should be no market places throughout the length and breadth

trading transactions were not limited to the context of the markets but operated also through interpersonal ties, especially of kinship and affinity. Throughout the Banyang and eastern Ejagham area, a standard explanation for the secession of kinsfolk in the past is that the ancestral 'son' or 'brother' went off – or was sent off by his father or senior relative – to report back trading opportunities, especially in the purchase of slaves. Such explanations are clearly in part rationalizations of secessions that may have been prompted by a variety of reasons, but they underline the importance of extended social ties to the trading network. Much of this trade appears to have been taken up not with subsistence goods as such (in this respect Banyang settlements were largely self-sufficient) but with prestige or 'status' items. Slaves, livestock, and goods for the European market – ivory, oil, and kernels – flowed from east to west, in return for salt, cloth, guns, and other European products which came into Banyang country from the west. Also involved in these exchange transactions were such purchasable institutions as cult-agencies and associations, the majority of these coming into Banyang country from Ejagham and being passed from Lower to Upper Banyang (e.g. Mfam, Ngbe, Basinjom, Mbokondem, Nsibiri, Eja).

The status of slaves (basɛm) in the traditional society was sharply distinguished from that of free-born (bakwa). Dependent upon their owner, who could sell or dispose of them as he wished, they lived in their own settlements built 'in the bush', at some distance from the settlements of the free-born, from which in other ways they were set apart. The term describing these slave-settlements, kɛsɛm, itself implies their qualitative distinctiveness and the fact that they were outside the political community, ɛtɔk, of the free-born. Slaves and free-born could not marry. Yet apart from their social disabilities and the insecurity of their position, their day-to-day lives seem not to have been particularly hard: the economic task especially accorded to them was the collecting of palm-nuts and making of palm-oil, but they were expected also to give less regular, circumstantial help in farm-clearing, house-building, and other services. (Banyang today refuse to climb palm-trees because of the stigma attached to it, as well as of its danger – the factor which in the past determined that a slave should perform the task, since his life was the more expendable.) Although slaves could be transferred, and at the death of important village leaders might be killed to accompany their owner in his grave,

---

of the land.' Talbot attempted twice to start markets at Oban, but on both occasions the supply of surplus subsistence products to the market dwindled to nothing and the market failed.

most appear to have lived in continuing social dependence, where their owner or 'father' played in relation to them much the same role as to his other dependants. The children of slaves (specifically *bambi*) retained all the disabilities of their parents, but their relationship to their owner became somewhat more secure. In the 1950s, when I carried out my main fieldwork, persons of slave-descent remained an endogamous, inferior class, who still almost entirely inhabited their own settlements and lived a community life outside or peripheral to that of the free-born.

The first recorded entry into Banyang country by a European was in July 1888, when Count Eugen von Zintgraff travelled northwards from the station he had opened at Lake Barombi in Kumba to carry out reconnaisance for a further station which he was to site and open at Bali, in the highland country beyond the north-eastern borders of Banyang territory. Entering Banyang country from the south, he came into the domain of Defang (the pre-eminent leader of the Mbang village group), who succeeded in peaceably holding up the expedition for some weeks and in causing its return to Barombi. When the expedition came back again in December, fighting broke out between Zintgraff's and Defang's followers; some of the latter were killed and a number of Mbang women were taken off by the former to Bali. In 1892, Tinto station was founded. Later this was used as a trading post, but after the First World War ceased to operate. In the final decade of the nineteenth century, German traders began to ply in Banyang country and a series of military expeditions passed through it, but it was not until 1901–1902 that the first civil administrative headquarters were established, situated then at Ossidinge close to the Cross River in eastern Ejagham country. In 1902 Count Pückler-Limburg became first Civil Administrator, assuming responsibility for a district corresponding broadly with what was later to become Mamfe Division.[1]

In 1904 Pückler was murdered when travelling in Anyang country on the 'overside' of the Cross River. His murder sparked off an uprising in which scattered Anyang, Boki, eastern Ejagham, and Lower Banyang villages took part. A number of trading stores were looted, and five traders on the Cross River were killed. Although their occasion and manner suggest that the attacks were in some degree concerted, this was clearly not an organized general revolt and by no means all of these peoples were involved. The action was dealt with severely by a punitive expedition

[1] Zintgraff gives an account of his journey and brush with Defang in his *Nord Kamerun*, Chs. IV, V. Other historical details are taken from Mansfeld, op. cit., pp. 17–18, and from Talbot, *The Peoples of Southern Nigeria*, Vol. I, pp. 362–364.

sent from the south. Those villages which had taken part in the uprising were looted and destroyed, their inhabitants fleeing into the bush. The effects of the expedition in its laying waste of settlements are described both by Mansfeld, who at this time took over the administration of the district, and by Talbot, who visited the area from his neighbouring district in Nigeria.[1] Under Mansfeld the administrative headquarters were changed to their present site at Mamfe. An energetic and resourceful administrator, whose book (*Urwald-Dokumente, vier Jahre unter den Crossflussnegern Kameruns*) gives evidence both of his practical approach as well as his detailed knowledge of the peoples he administered, he remained in charge of the district until the defeat of the Germans in the Cameroons Campaign (1914–1916) when the administration of the district passed into British hands.

Later chapters will examine in more detail some of the changes that have occurred in Banyang political organization under these successive Colonial administrations. It may be useful, however, to summarize here some of the broader changes that had taken place in Banyang society during the half century of Colonial rule that had passed before this study was made.

Colonial rule meant first and foremost for Banyang their subjection to a strong central authority whose political power had simply to be accepted. The punitive expedition of 1904 and other 'strong-arm' actions of the German administration left no doubts as to who was the master. The scale and coercive strength of European rule were unlike anything the Banyang had previously known from their own small-scale community politics; but if its actions were to them sometimes arbitrary, it remained a rule exercised by an alien and distant power which, once accepted, still allowed for a considerable play of interests at the local-community level. Colonial government imposed peace between villages and village groups; it built a system of roads which permitted a vastly extended intercourse; trading in and ownership of slaves were abolished; a series of offences (some new) were reserved for the administration's own punishment, as also was reserved to it the use of the death penalty; a new system of courts was introduced with an extended hierarchy of appeal; such new institutions as schools and clinics were supported by the administration, giving rise, with courts and constabulary, to a new class of government agents and employees. The direct effect of these changes was to remove some important functions from the traditional political system and to deprive it of some of its powers, yet the central institutions of the system were not

[1] Mansfeld, op. cit., p. 18; Talbot, *In the Shadow of the Bush*, p. 152.

abolished, nor yet did they find themselves in serious opposition to the aims and methods of the wider, imposed political structure. To give only one example, civil cases could still be heard and judged at the local village level in the traditional way, the government courts being resorted to only if such judgement were unacceptable, when they had then the *de facto* (but not legal) position of appeal court. This easy relationship between traditional and modern was aided by the British policy of Indirect Rule, which allowed for the pragmatic handling of administrative problems through indigenous institutions. Although local chiefs could not, under Colonial administration, rise to the pre-eminence and coercive power of the former leaders of Tali and Defang, for example, nevertheless their status as leaders continued to be recognized and their traditional role in village politics, although modified, has not been drastically changed.

A second important sphere of change is in economic life: the introduction of new forms of wealth has created new standards of living, and the newly presented opportunities for obtaining money have given rise to new or modified aims in life. These changes in turn have affected the distribution in wealth. European-style clothes, new household goods, from enamel plates to pressure lamps, gramophones, and bicycles, are only some of the goods that have become desired possessions and the present-day symbols of social status. Whereas in the past wealth and political leadership were closely associated, the sources of wealth are now less closely subject to monopoly control and any Manyang has some opportunity of obtaining an income through paid employment. The keynote of life in the traditional communities was the individual acquisition of status through the dispensation of wealth – in bridewealth, in fees for association membership or purchase, in the support of followers. Significantly, in responding to modern circumstances, Banyang have sought to go directly to the sources of wealth, by entering paid employment or by undertaking a relatively large enterprise, rather than by peripheral activity in petty trade or the growing of minor cash crops. Large numbers of men have left home to find work, most with long-term 'career' intentions rather than with the short-term desire of obtaining money for limited objectives. In 1953 over 32 per cent of the adult male population of six Upper Banyang village groups were away from home, the vast majority in wage or salaried employment rather than in trade.[1] The cash farming of cocoa, and more recently of coffee, have also been taken up as suitably large enterprises which have the promise of

[1] These figures and the nature of Banyang labour migration are discussed more fully in the chapter I have contributed to *Plantation and Village in the Cameroons*, E. Ardener *et al.* (1960).

substantial reward. The lure of virtually unlimited land and the model of the southern plantations have encouraged some men to embark on large farms on which they work full-time and employ labourers (mostly non-Banyang). Disease has, however, discouraged many would-be cocoa-farmers. Palm-kernel trading is the less favoured stand-by of someone seeking to raise money in the home society. Nevertheless, in 1953 there was considerable frustration and disappointment in Upper Banyang country that greater means of making an income were not available to the people there. The comparison made was not between the past and the present but between their own thinly populated and poorly developed villages and the richer and commercially developed south.

Migration has depleted the population of the home villages and altered its demographic structure. Most migrants retain contact with their home society, however, especially through their kinship ties, and expect eventually to return home and to re-establish themselves in their home villages. Many older men have already done this, after periods of absence of up to twenty years and more. Elders of the home lineage groups often express their role in this context as 'looking after the lineage group' while their sons are away at work, expecting them eventually to return home and take over their position there.

A direct, imposed change in the forms of the society was the consolidation of settlements enforced by the German administration in the first decade of the century. The features and effects of the change will be discussed more fully in the next chapter: it has made Banyang settlement patterns less fluid and has emphasized the solidarity of wider groupings, but traditional principles of political grouping still operate within and through present-day settlement alignments. Like so much else, the change has been assimilated to Banyang society and Banyang themselves have no wish to go back on it. The past, when they were 'living in the bush', is spoken of disparagingly as a time of ignorance and unenlightenment, the time 'when our eyes were closed'. There has indeed been an immense widening of social horizons. Many factors have contributed to this: education, Mission teaching, the ease of intercourse within the country, and the opportunities for employment outside it. The position of the settlements on the roads, moreover, has given a new value to the traditional orientation of their culture. Antɛn, 'in the lower region', now refers to the areas of modern development in the south and it is here that the roads lead. It is to such development that Banyang look and it is in relation to it that the forms of their traditional society have been adapted.

The Morphology of the Complex Community

PART 1

The Morphology of the Complex
Community

2

The Banyang Community

The diffuse community

The term *ɛtɔk* has a number of distinct, but related, meanings. In its primary sense an *ɛtɔk* is a group of houses, a settlement or place of common residence, especially where the settlement stands by itself. A clear verbal distinction is made between the *ɛtɔk*, the place where people live, and the surrounding area of 'bush', containing farms, fallow land, and forest, and, as we shall later describe, Banyang settlements are indeed always quite distinct as dwelling areas. Closely related to this primary meaning of the term, an *ɛtɔk* in its most general sense is a 'community' or 'residential community', a group of people who reside together and who by their common residence share a solidarity and have a common identity. The members of a physically distinct settlement may be expected to form a community in this second sense of the term; nevertheless, in *this* sense an *ɛtɔk* is not limited to a single settlement: any residentially based group is an *ɛtɔk* if its members do in fact share a common identity and some solidarity as a group. In the traditional society such 'communities' might number a few hundred, or at most one to two thousand persons, inhabiting settlements scattered over an area of perhaps ten to forty square miles, but especially at present the term can be applied to more extensive units. There is indeed no other word in Kenyang to describe political or territorial groupings: the 'country' of Europeans is *ɛtɔk ɔBarek;* the 'land of the dead' (which in stories is visualized as a place one may penetrate to) is *ɛtɔk ɔbarɛm*; the present West Cameroon State is *ɛtɔk ɔ*West Cameroon. Finally, the term *ɛtɔk* is used in a more restrictive sense to describe a body or group of persons who collectively *represent* the wider residential community in the second meaning of the term which has just been outlined. If one enters a house in which the elders and leaders of a village or village group have gathered, the formal greeting is *ɛtɔk ɛcɔko?* 'the community is sitting?', which will be answered in unison by those present, *Ɛɛ!* 'Yes!' Any *ad hoc* group of persons who have status and influence in the community may be spoken of thus as the 'community' in this sense, since they indeed represent it; but the term *ɛtɔk* is also used more directly and consciously to denote the recognized body of persons who, especially in a village, are at the centre of community affairs, wield most influence in it, and are most closely involved in the authoritative actions taken on behalf of its combined members.

These three meanings of the term *ɛtɔk* – 'settlement', 'community', and 'a body of persons representing a community' – are closely interrelated. Together they constitute a concept which stands at the centre of Banyang political theory. The *ɛtɔk* is a group of people (Banyang would say *ncɛmti bo*) who live together and who, by virtue of this fact, are, on the one hand, assumed to share an identity of interest in the regulation of their common affairs, and, on the other, are expected to observe the corporate authority of the group, as it is expressed collectively by those who represent them. This concept defines what I speak of as the Banyang 'political community'. An *ɛtɔk* is a residential group organized to govern itself: one might speak of it as the 'polis' of Banyang political organization.

Nevertheless – and here lies our first and greatest problem – while any group which is an *ɛtɔk* is in some way a corporately organized residential group, the term is not limited to one order of grouping whose extent is clearly defined. The 'community' is an elastic concept, whose extent expands and contracts, according to the situation. The most obvious group which corresponds to the term *ɛtɔk*, certainly at the present time, is the village, that is, the largest residential group whose members recognize a common leader. To outsiders village solidarity is always insisted upon and a Manyang away from his own village but still within Banyang country is most likely to be identified as a person of such-and-such a village, *mu Takwa, mu Bɛsɔŋabaŋ, mu Ebeagwa*, etc. A village however is by no means the largest traditional group which is politically united: most villages belong to wider village groups and when the latter, through their representatives, meet for collective political action or are referred to as a source of political authority, they too are described by the term *ɛtɔk*. In the Ndifaw village group it was, for example, common practice to refer to this, the widest residential group that combined for political action, as 'the whole community', *ɛtɔk ɛnkɔmɛnkɔm*, its two terminal settlements being then specified, 'from Mpomba to Ejwengang'; and when the members of the village group came together, the meeting was described as one of the *ɛtɔk*, the 'community', in the same way as any similar meeting which took place at the lower level of the village. Within a village itself, moreover, there are almost invariably discrete sections or 'centres' (*mantɔ*), which within the context of their own place of residence can each be referred to as an *ɛtɔk*. This is most clearly the case for those village sections which are in fact built as separate settlements, but it applies also to some groups who form only part of a conjoint settlement and to others that are a combination of different settlements.

This elastic or diffuse use of the term *ɛtɔk* is not simply a verbal matter. It is not simply that the Kenyang *idea* of the political community is diffuse, but that the political community itself is diffuse in its operation. The various levels of grouping referred to above (and which we – not Banyang – have distinguished by the names 'village', 'village section', etc.) are linked in their operation and share common features of political form and action. All are residential groups whose members are corporately represented in decisions made about the ordering of affairs within them. A village section, a village, or a village group (to name the three main extensions of the political community which we have distinguished) is each at its own level represented by a body of leading and senior men who by virtue of the fact that they *do* represent the group have the power to make authoritative decisions concerning it.

Figure 1   The diffuse community

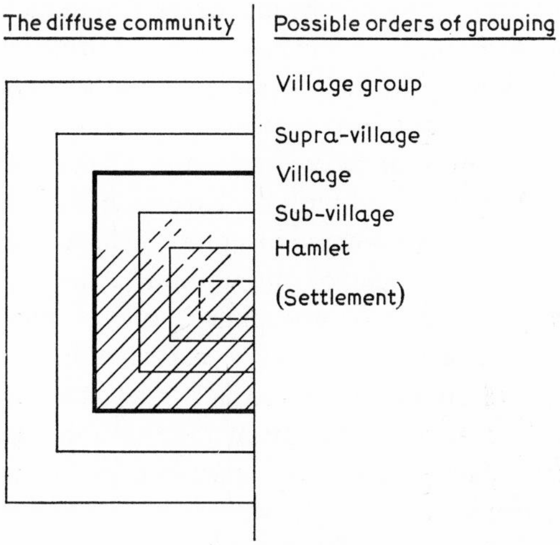

The diffuse community	Possible orders of grouping
	Village group
	Supra-village
	Village
	Sub-village
	Hamlet
	(Settlement)

Figure 1 illustrates the total range of groups which I shall distinguish by name but which all share features of political representation and action as outlined above. Not all these orders of grouping are everywhere present: the 'supra-village' is perhaps the least general, and in two cases 'villages' form the traditionally widest order of grouping. The situation is further

complicated by the settlement consolidation enforced by the former German administration. 'Settlement' has been shown (in parenthesis) as the smallest unit of the series, since this is the position that the small traditional settlements of pre-German days would have occupied, but today settlements of this order are few (they are invariably offshoots of a hamlet or sub-village) and, being defined residually by discrete residence alone, are different in kind from the other orders of grouping in the series. As later described, settlement patterns since the German consolidation of settlements have been irregular, and a hamlet, a sub-village, or in some cases a whole village may now be built as a single settlement. In the diagram the orders of grouping which may now be found as single, extended settlements have been shaded, but the correspondence (like the shading) is irregular. The 'village' has been represented with a heavy line since this is the one order which is universally represented and in relation to which the other main orders of grouping are distinguished. It must be emphasized, however, that nowhere is this the only order of grouping acting with political authority as an *ɛtɔk*: everywhere there are some other orders of residential grouping, either larger or smaller than the village, whose members are corporately represented in political decisions taken in their name and with an authority they must obey.

Two preliminary points should be made concerning the series of groups illustrated in the diagram. First, the basic political principle defining each group and its relationship to the remainder of the series is that of phased autonomous action. In certain circumstances each order of grouping is able to act independently in the regulation of affairs within the group, but in other circumstances (and with the exception of the widest order of grouping) the same group is merged in a more inclusive order of grouping which becomes then the locus of autonomous action. The relationship between the various orders of grouping is one of phased autonomy: each group (other than the largest) has partial political independence; in some contexts it has the power to act independently, but in other contexts it must accept the authority of the wider group in which it is merged. The interplay between these two contextual positions – independence and dependence – is a characteristic and permeating feature of Banyang political processes. We note here, however, only how this principle of phased autonomy distinguishes this system of residential groups from the systems described for the 'classical' lineage-based, segmentary societies, where the corporate identity of segments is established not by their partial independence but by their balanced opposition.

Secondly, these different orders of grouping are different orders of a *single* community: they are not different communities. This point has been implied above, but it is worth making explicit since it is central to the structure and workings of Banyang politics. In certain parts of my description above, I have been obliged to write of a village or village group as having the form of 'a' community, 'an' *ɛtɔk*: it would be more correct to speak of a village or village group as forming in certain situations 'the' community, 'the' *ɛtɔk*. It is here that the diffuseness of the Banyang political community in both concept and operation lies. Membership of a hamlet is not different from membership of the village or village group of which the hamlet is part: a person's position and prestige in the latter are an extension of his position and prestige in the former. So also the authority of the village group is an extension of that of the village, village authority an extension of that of the hamlet. There is no single order of grouping which we can isolate as holding 'sovereign' authority, from which it is delegated downwards: certainly not the village group, which, although the 'community' at its greatest extension, is often weak and ineffectual in its corporate actions. The 'sovereign authority' which should be associated with the political community, the 'polis', is, as it were, refracted in the different orders of community grouping: the 'government' of Banyang society is a combination of 'community' actions made at all levels of grouping.

Two principles of corporate grouping: operational and constitutional corporateness
We have spoken above of community 'sovereignty'. In the traditional society the pre-eminence of the community over its individual members was symbolized most clearly in its corporate claim to certain animals, if killed or caught in the bush by any of its members, or indeed by a visiting stranger. These 'animals of the community' (*nya ɛtɔk*) varied in importance, and while all were required to be brought before the community, or those representing it, not all were brought to the same level of community grouping. The most important of the 'animals of the community' was the leopard, itself the most powerful and most feared animal of the forest. If a leopard were killed it was the overriding duty of the killer to bring it or news of its killing to the person immediately representing him in the community, whose own duty in turn was to carry it forward, until ultimately it was brought to the pre-eminent, most widely recognized community leader. This right of the leader of a certain order of community grouping to receive and to hold on behalf of the community a leopard killed within it I describe as a 'constitutional'

right. It is one which embodies fundamental duties and relationships, serving above all to denote the supremacy of the representative leader who ultimately receives the leopard, and the relative subordination of all those who pass it forward. In the killing and presentation of a leopard are enacted the fundamental relationships between political leaders and their followers: to present a leopard is an act of homage confirming the legitimate status of the representative leader of a community; to fail to present it is to deny his legitimate leadership.[1]

We are brought here to a different aspect of the corporate organization of Banyang communities. Whereas in the last section we were concerned with the *operational* corporateness which characterized a range of residential groups (that is, their ability to act effectively in the political control of their own affairs), the rights concerning a leopard as an 'animal of the community' specify more precisely the *constitutional* status of the representative leader of one particular order of community grouping. That is to say, they specify the formal, 'legitimized' position of one man, the recognized leader of one order of residential grouping. In general, and in the traditional society, this order of grouping would appear to have had an effective operational unity – a clearly established identity as a residential group and a distinctive solidarity shared by its members; the leopard as 'animal of the community' would not otherwise have been brought to its representative leader. It is this order of grouping which can be identified as a 'village', and I speak of its representative as 'village leader'. Formally or 'constitutionally' defined, a village is thus the largest residential group (εtɔk) whose members recognize a common leader. In the traditional society the bringing of a leopard to the village leader was the action which, more than any other, formally betokened this recognition.

A village leader is spoken of as *mfɔ εtɔk*, 'leader of the community', but he is not the only man to be so described. Other 'leaders of the community' (*bafɔ εtɔk*) have a subordinate status in relation to him, but within their own residential group (εtɔk) are formally recognized as its representative leader in very much the same way as is the village leader for the village. Not all villages are divided equally into such smaller discrete residential groups, but where they are, and are formally represented by an *mfɔ εtɔk* subordinate in status to the village leader, I speak of these groups as 'hamlets', their representative heads as 'hamlet leaders'. The hamlet leader has his own rights in relation to the 'animals of the com-

[1] See below, pp. 54, 57, and 59, for stories which illustrate the conscious and deliberate implications of such actions.

munity' killed or caught by members of his hamlet: the most important of these, including the leopard, should be brought to him first, and it is he who should then take them forward to the village leader; the less important 'animals of the community' he is allowed to keep or distribute himself.[1] Nevertheless, as we shall later see, a certain variety of status applies to the hamlet leader and, unlike the village, one of the characteristics of a hamlet is the exclusive descent solidarity shared, more or less strongly, by its members.

Wider than a village, a village group is formally defined by the fact that it is the largest residential group recognizing a common identity and sharing a tradition of common political action – in Banyang's own terms, it is the largest group 'of one voice' (ɛyɔŋ ɛmɔt) even though it lacks a common leader. Like the hamlet and unlike the village (except where, in two cases, villages are themselves the largest political groups), a village group is further characterized by the exclusive common descent recognized by its members. In the present context, however, it is specifically the residential character of a village group which I would wish to emphasize; it is the 'whole community', ɛtɔk ɛnkɔm, which, even if not represented by a common leader, may be invited to take part in the celebration of a leopard's killing.[2]

The residential groups which we are here distinguishing by 'constitutional' criteria have already been incorporated in the diagram of the 'diffuse community' (Figure 1), appearing there in the named identity of different orders of grouping. It is possible, however to abstract the groups differentiated by this single set of criteria and to show clearly a 'constitutional' series of residential groups (Figure 2). In many ways such a diagram gives the simplest and clearest picture of Banyang political organization: the village is the major political unit; a number of villages combine to form a village group; the largest villages (not all) are divided into a number of residentially distinct and partially autonomous hamlets. We should remember, however, that such a picture is drawn by abstracting formal rights of a certain kind from the total, much more confused, behaviour of these groups and from the values underlying their behaviour. Banyang have no separate terms for 'village group', 'village', or 'hamlet'. Nor are these orders of residential grouping the only ones possible: the more contingent and less regularly found 'supra-village' and

---

[1] See below, pp. 49f.

[2] On this point, see pp. 49–53. One would like to be able to say that after a leopard has been brought to a village leader the latter invites the village group to celebrate its capture. Unfortunately, although this is the tradition in most village groups, it does not apply to all.

'sub-village' (see *Figure 1*) are in some cases highly important and effective political groups which exist as well as the village, but lack the formal rights which distinguish the latter. Finally, *Figure 2* suggests a rigidly defined, permanent set of relationships between groups which is at odds with the more fluid, changing pattern of relationship which actually exists.

Figure 2   The constitutional series of residential groups

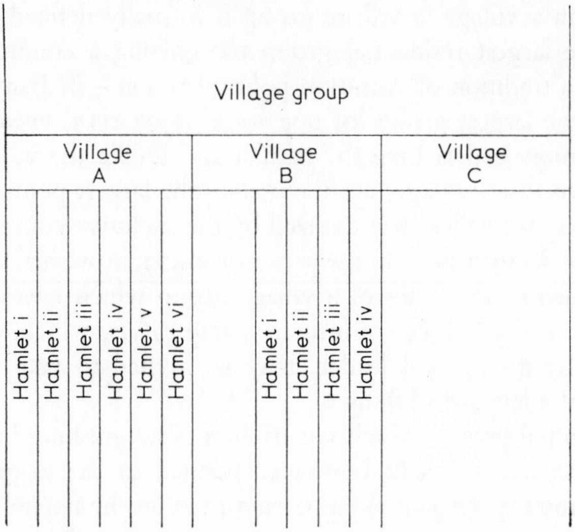

I hope to show in subsequent chapters how operational and constitutional aspects of corporate residential grouping are interrelated both in the structure of Banyang communities and in the political and governmental processes that occur within them. In the remaining sections of this chapter, I describe in greater detail some particular aspects of community organization which the preceding account has referred to only summarily.

Traditional settlement patterns

One of the most tantalizing problems concerning the pre-Colonial organization of Banyang communities is the exact nature and composition of the nineteenth-century settlements. The German consolidation of settlements, which Banyang always refer to as 'the gathering of the community' (*dɛcɛmti ɛtɔk*), and which has been followed by a number of later movements, has made it impossible to observe traditional settlement patterns directly. It is possible, however, to build up some general picture of what traditional settlements were like and by relating this picture to present settlement patterns to show how common principles of organization underlie them both. Three things are clear. First, that 'settlements' (*bɛtɔk*), in the literal sense of discrete clusters of houses, were in fact the central units from which a wider series of recognized residential groupings extended outwards. Secondly, that Banyang shared the pattern of small dispersed settlements with the eastern Ejagham and that both cases of settlement pattern could be represented as the fragmentation or dispersal of the 'nucleated village' settlement pattern of the 'Ekoi' Ejagham. Thus Mansfeld, in instigating the policy of settlement consolidation, saw this move, apart from the practical advantages it gave, as a reversal of the tendency towards residential fragmentation – and so too, in a different sense, do Banyang.[1] Thirdly, one of the key features of both modern and traditional settlement patterns is the relationship evidenced between leadership and residential grouping.

Contemporary accounts by Mansfeld and Zintgraff emphasize how scattered and small were the traditional settlements. Mansfeld writes of 'a complex of six to ten houses, followed by ten minutes of farms, then two single huts, after which farms, followed again by six houses, and so on'. 'One place', he adds, 'often extends for three hours.'[2] Zintgraff similarly notes the smallness of the settlements which consist 'often of only two or three but sometimes ten to fifteen houses'.[3] On the other hand, the settlement of Defang (he refers to it as 'Tok Difang'), where he stayed, was much larger, consisting of four enclosed compounds (*Höfen*) 'as well as a kind of village street with nearly twenty houses, adjoining them'.[4] The accounts I obtained in Upper Banyang territory in the 1950s confirm this picture of generally small settlements, averaging no more than three or four houses, but with the settlements of community leaders larger, going up to as many as forty houses in the case of the leader of Tali.

The layout of a traditional settlement, which is still seen in some of the fragmented settlements today, was then described to me as follows (*Figure 3*). One approached a settlement from a path that led into two opposing rows of houses, which were joined at their far end by a single, usually larger house facing forwards along the path. The point at which the path enters the settlement is its 'head' (*nti*); the other end of the settlement,

---

[1] Evidence for the increasing dispersal of settlement forms is given above, pp. 6–7. For the context of Mansfeld's policy decision, see below, p. 33.
[2] *Urwald-Dokumente*, p. 32. The description refers to the settlement patterns (*Dorfanlage*) of both Keaka and Banyang, which he is contrasting with the Ekoi or Ekwe.
[3] *Nord Kamerun*, p. 122.
[4] Ibid. A third early observer, Staschewski, would seem to be describing the newly consolidated settlements; his account is referred to below, pp. 34–35.

where its main and most imposing house stands, is its 'base' or 'bottom' (*nɛt*). The settlement leader, from whom the settlement takes its name (*ɛtɔkɔN*), lives at the 'bottom' of the settlement, and its axis, from 'bottom' to 'head', forms also a social axis, the position of the houses along this line being determined by the relationship of their occupants to the settlement leader. The houses of the settlement leader's wives were

Figure 3   Arrangement of a traditional settlement

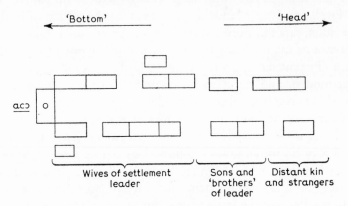

placed immediately next to the 'bottom house' or *acɔ*, the most senior wife being strictly adjacent to it. The leader's immediate kinsmen (sons who have not already gone off to build their own settlements, or close agnates) followed next in the line of houses. Finally at the 'head' of the settlement and in least secure association with its leader were built the houses of matrilateral kin, distant agnates, or strangers who had come to join him. Most houses in the settlement were built directly aligning the path, but occasionally smaller 'bachelor' houses were built behind one of the women's houses in the main body of the settlement. Not all settlements were so large as that illustrated or included such a range of members, but the principles exemplified here were those which governed the arrangement of houses in all settlements, large or small.

This version of the layout of a traditional settlement, given to me by Upper Banyang, does not take account of a variant form which certainly existed in the past but was probably commoner in Lower than Upper Banyang settlements. This is the *ɛkiri* (or *ɛkri*), the 'enclosed compound' formed by a rectangular arrangement of houses opening inwards to a central yard. Mansfeld describes this form of arrangement for the 'Ekois' and adds that it is used also by the 'Bakogos' in the south, but says that 'the Keakas and remaining tribes' have maintained it only in part, in

part converting it (he refers to it as the 'original', *ursprünglich*, form) to
an arrangement where houses are built along the road 'next to one another
in lengthways extension' (*in einer Längsflucht nebeneinander*). It is not clear,
however, from his description or from his photograph of a Keaka settlement (which looks suspiciously newly built) whether by the latter he is
referring to the form described in the last paragraph or to one in which
rows of houses are merely built adjoining a path. He goes on: 'One often
sees both forms wall to wall in a village street. Everywhere one finds that
houses next to each other in a row will be inhabited by poorer people
and that the Ekoi-form has always been enclosed for a well-to-do man.'[1]
Zintgraff's description of Defang's settlement, referring to four enclosed
'compounds' or *Höfen* abutting 'a kind of village street', tallies with
Mansfeld's generalized statement, but this was by all accounts an unusually
large settlement belonging to one of the most powerful of leaders. My
own inquiries suggest that it was only in Lower Banyang and eastern
Ejagham areas that enclosed compounds (called ɔkwɛlɛ by eastern
Ejagham) were found at all frequently and that they existed here alongside
what I have termed the 'open compound' form (*sɛnta*), which is essentially
the arrangement shown in *Figures 3* and *5*, built as part of a larger cluster
of houses.[2] A further, modified version of the enclosed compound, the
mɔɛkri or 'small compound', consisted of a second house built behind the
bottom house or *acɔ* of a settlement as in *Figure 3*, the area between the
two being enclosed by a wall or other small houses. This attenuated and
assimilated form is today more commonly found than the enclosed
compound proper in Banyang country as a whole, but even so is by no
means frequent.[3] I shall however ignore these possible variants, returning
now to the account of former settlement patterns given to me by Upper
Banyang at Tali.

As the leader and his wives formed the core of a settlement, so its
'bottom' house was the scene of most of the settlement's corporate

[1] Op. cit., pp. 25–27.

[2] I shall refer again to the difficulty surrounding the 'open compound', *senta*, as a settlement
pattern. Mansfeld's diagram of an enclosed compound (that of the leader of Ayundep, a
Keaka village, ibid. p. 25) shows very clear similarities with the layout of a settlement as
shown in *Figure 3*. The 'open compound' is an intermediate form, now widely found in
Banyang country, where a complex of houses is built as a U-shaped side extension to the
main settlement (cf. *Figures 8* and *10*): it retains the form therefore of the *Figure 3* 'traditional
settlement' but it has the context of a 'compound', being part of a larger settlement.

[3] Staschewski's plan of what is apparently a newly consolidated settlement shows either an
'enclosed' or 'small' compound (it is difficult to say in what category it would be placed)
behind the house next to the *acɔ*. It is entirely ancillary to the main body of the settlement
which retains on an enlarged scale the layout of *Figure 3*. (*Die Banyangi*, p. 3. See also below,
pp. 34–35 and footnote.)

activities. If members of a settlement met for discussion they would expect to do so here; it was here that guests would be received, wine drunk, offerings to the dead made. The actual form of this house nevertheless varied between settlements, this variation indicating the status of its leader in relation to a wider grouping of settlements. Most of a settlement's houses were built as 'women's houses' (bɛkɛt ɛbagɔrɛ or simply bɛkɛt), containing one or two 'inside rooms', a kitchen, and a main room whose large door opened on to the path and which was mostly filled with couch-beds made of hardened earth (*Figure 4*). In small settlements whose leaders lacked wider status or claim to status, such a 'woman's house' (normally that of the leader's senior wife) might occupy the position of the 'bottom' house. In other cases a different type of house was built, described as an acɔ or acɔ ɛkɛt, a 'meeting-house'.[1] This type of house had a larger main room, with fewer or no couch-beds in it, and was expected properly to contain a 'pole-support' (ɛkwa, L. K. ɛkwap) in the room's centre: this is a stout pole which runs from the floor to the roof-tree and at the base of which earth is packed into a conical shape with a flattened top; at a small hole scooped out in front of this construction (the 'bottom of the pole-support', nɛrɛkwa) ritual offerings are made to the dead (*Figure 4*). The erection of a 'pole-support' was a mark therefore of its owner's wider leadership. Nevertheless today not all acɔ-type houses include a pole-support, and Banyang say that the same was true also of the past. The grading of the 'bottom' houses of a settlement were therefore:

'woman's house' (for leaders lacking wider status or claim to status);
acɔ-type house (for leaders with wider *de facto* influence or claim to wider community status);
true acɔ (for leaders with recognized wider authority).

Figure 5 illustrates one small group of settlements as they were reconstructed for me by the present members of a section of Tali according to their memory of their arrangement immediately before the settlement change. The settlements jointly formed a hamlet and their owners also shared common exclusive ties as a lineage group. (It should be noticed, however, that in two settlements non-agnates had come to join the settlement leaders.) The four settlements were situated separately from each other at distances of up to 200 yards. Mbok was then senior elder and leader of the group and the only man to possess a true acɔ. Both Tanyi Ta and Mbu Esong Ayok had acɔ-type houses (lacking, however,

[1] Lower Kenyang aca. This type of house with a comparable social role runs again through to Ejagham settlement patterns: in eastern Ejagham it is the ɔca, elsewhere ɔcam.

Figure 4 Types of houses

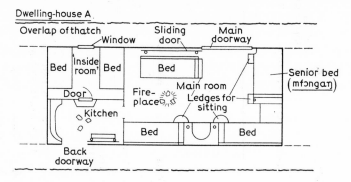

Dwelling-house A

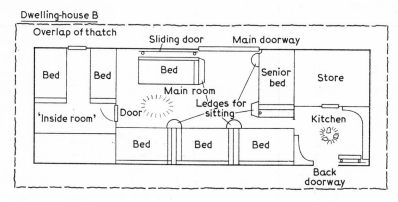

Dwelling-house B

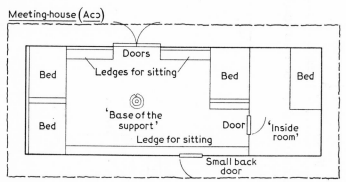

Meeting-house (Acɔ)

the critical pole-support). Some years later Tanyi Ta was to succeed to the leadership of the group, and was also to achieve prominence in wider village affairs. Mbu Esong Ayok was a person of some status within the group but remained subordinate to Tanyi Ta. Nkwainya, a person of more distant kinship whose own descendants in the present lineage

Figure 5   Settlements of *bɔ Mbu*, c. 1900

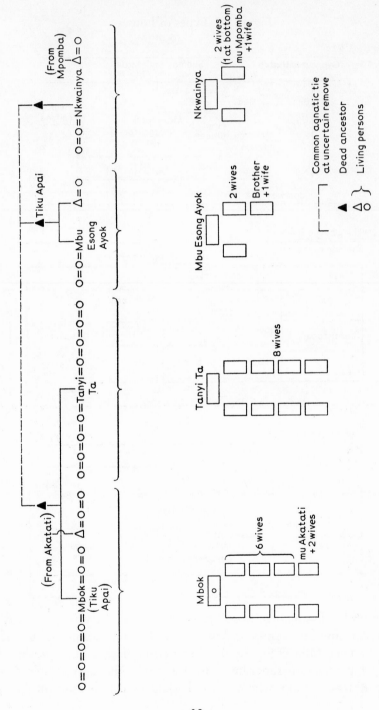

32

group are few, is remembered on the other hand as having only a 'woman's house' (the house of his senior wife) in the position of 'bottom' house of his settlement.

Community status and settlement grouping were then closely associated. A man's name in the wider community became known, it is said, by his building of his own settlement; and the size of his settlement – in wives, kinsmen, and followers he was able to attract – directly reflected his influence and prestige. His formal status in the wider group was further indicated by the character of the focal house of his settlement, which if a true *acɔ* was also the focal centre of the wider residential group. Above all, these settlement patterns, and with them the status of settlement leaders, were fluid: any man with sufficient backing could enter the competition for status; leadership of the wider groupings could move from one settlement leader to another. The fluidity of this interdefining relationship was most likely to be affected by settlement consolidation.

'The gathering of the community' and present-day settlement patterns

When Mansfeld arrived in the district in 1904, one of the first actions that he took as administrator was to encourage those who had to rebuild their settlements to do so as compact groups along the main paths. The reasons for this were in part administrative – ease of access and the better maintenance of the paths – but he was also concerned for the economic advantages that this would bring, and in initiating the change he used as his model what he describes as 'the closed Ekoi-form' of nucleated village settlement that he observed among the Ejagham towards the western borders of his district.[1] The policy, applied first in the Lower region of the country, was supported initially by verbal encouragement and by offering inducements (trade cloths to the leaders who built in this way) but was later applied to all Banyang village groups and was enforced.[2] Much was nevertheless left to the individual settlements. Mansfeld required that the settlements should be built compactly and that they should come to the road: 'at least twenty-five houses along the main path'. But he did not determine who should come together nor exactly how or where they should build. Banyang were therefore left to re-create new settlement

---

[1] Mansfeld, op. cit., p. 32.
[2] The initial implementation is described ibid., p. 20; its later enforcement is made clear from British administrative reports (e.g. Gorges, op. cit., para. 167) but there would seem to have been relatively few cases of actual punishment. (Defang of the Mbang village group – already antipathetic to German rule – and Takwa of Tanyi Nkongo are the only ones named.)

forms which, while accepting the requirements imposed on them, also expressed traditional alignments and some of the features of the traditional settlement patterns. It is significant that Mansfeld's action is described by saying that he 'gathered the community' (*Dr. 'Mamfe' acɛmti ɛtɔk*), a phrase that in other contexts would imply praise since it is in accord with the often repeated need for political unity. *Ncɛmti*, 'Gatherer', is a praise-name of some prestige for community leaders.

In Tali, when the settlements were rebuilt on the path, the form that they adopted was an enlarged and extended version of the traditional layout shown in *Figure 3*. Members from a group of formerly separate settlements now came to align themselves on the 'bottom' house (almost invariably an *acɔ ɛkɛt*) of their recognized leader. Such a very much lengthened settlement was built at right-angles to the path, ideally with the 'head' of the settlement where the path crossed by it. Thus when the members of the group of settlements shown in *Figure 5* came to rebuild on the main path, they did so as a single consolidated unit, with their two rows of houses based on the *acɔ* of their leader, Mbok (*Figure 6*); in this case,

Figure 6   Consolidated settlement of *bɔ Mbu*, initially built on the road, c.1906

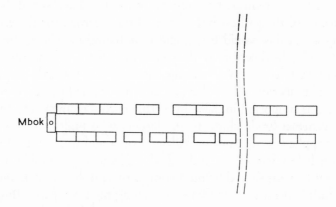

however, the bottom *acɔ* was placed insufficiently far back so that what was traditionally the 'head' of the settlement had to be continued on the other side of the path. Comparable composite settlements were built by other groups parallel to and nearby that of *bɔ Mbu*. A similar form of much enlarged traditional settlement, built at right-angles to the path, is described by F. Staschewski writing at about this time of the Tinto area, and from this and other evidence it would seem that his description refers to the new consolidated settlements then being built.[1] Some settlements scattered throughout Banyang country still retain this traditional but much extended form.

One can only hypothetically reconstruct the kind of development that occurred from this much enlarged settlement form. The fluidity and flexibility of the traditional settlement patterns, in turn related to the continuing play for leadership, have already been noted. An artificially enlarged settlement might reflect, as in the case of *bɔ Mbu*, the relation between a hamlet leader and his followers at one point in time; but by its nature it could not allow for the longer-term processes by which new leaders emerged, and residential alignments were re-formed. The new and characteristic pattern which emerged was one whereby the main body of a settlement – those who held the undifferentiated status of 'followers' – built their houses alongside and parallel to the main path, while the leader or potential leaders of a settlement built their own complex of houses in side extension to the main settlement in a form very similar to that of the traditional small settlements. Such a complex of houses is known as a *sɛnta*, an 'open compound', and is always indicative of the differentiation in status of its owner, either as leader of the settlement or as an influential man within it. *Figure 7* shows a possible developmental sequence, which served to re-establish the fluidity of traditional settlement patterns. All these forms are found at the present day (*7a* being the least common), together with settlements built entirely as two rows of houses adjoining the path, and very small settlements built singly as in the smallest of *Figure 5*. *Plate 3* shows a typical large settlement of the present day; *Plate 2* shows a small, newly established offshoot settlement built according to the traditional form.

One of the unresolved 'puzzles' of Banyang settlement organization which has already been briefly referred to (p. 29 footnote) is the extent to which the *sɛnta*, 'open compound', is an entirely new form, a development of the traditional settlement layout adapted to the context of a larger group, or whether it already existed in the past. It is generally

[1] *Die Banyangi*, p. 2. This book, by Staschewski, was edited and published by B. Ankermann some years after it was written. Although no mention is made of the settlement change, it is clear from his estimated size of settlements – 'forty to one hundred houses' – that he cannot be referring to the older traditional settlements. The plan that he gives tallies very closely with the description and *Figure 6* above, and the fact that he describes it as newly built suggests that he is in fact describing the consolidated settlements built immediately after the change. His account is further discussed in my article on 'Banyang Settlements' (*Man*, 1962). Staschewski speaks of these (enlarged) settlements as small 'villages' (*Dörfer* – I would call them hamlets), five to fifteen of which compose a 'district' (*Landschaft* – my own 'village'), each an 'independent community . . . which comes under a head chief'.

agreed that the term *sɛnta* refers to a U-shaped complex of houses built as part of a larger settlement (*ɛtɔk*). My information from Upper Banyang, together with Staschewski's account, suggests that all traditional settlements, and those newly consolidated, followed this U-shaped layout (the term *sɛnta* being then inappropriate: they were simply *bɛtɔk*): Lower Banyang and eastern Ejagham, at a greater distance in time, say that such 'open compounds' were part of a larger settlement complex which was

Figure 7   Developmental changes in the form of the consolidated
settlements

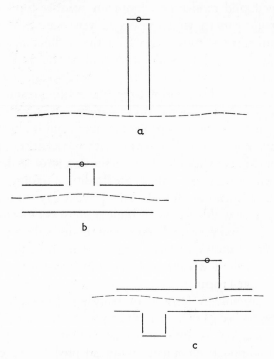

itself the smallest discrete residential group, *ɛtɔk*. However we resolve this discrepancy, and it is possible that both are right, the two elements already distinguished – the body of 'followers' who build in alignment with the path and the 'leaders' or men of status who build a *sɛnta* or 'open compound' in side extension to the main settlement – remain characteristic of all settlements today. The greatest irregularity of present-day settlements is in their size and the degree to which 'open compounds' are found in them. Settlements range from small clusters of two or three houses to larger, straggling groups of sixty houses or more. As a broad generalization, the longer a settlement has remained on the same site often the site it first came to at the time of consolidation – the more differentiated are its groups of houses, the greater the number of open compounds in it.

Three settlements which most clearly illustrate the features just discussed are those of the chiefly *bɔ Mfɔnjo* lineage group in Tali (*Figure 8*). In each of them appears at least one and sometimes two complexes of houses based upon an *acɔ* or *acɔ*-type house, built at right-angles to the main path. Each of these is owned by the leader of the settlement or by someone with differentiated status within it. The main body of each settlement is occupied by those with no claims to leadership, who 'follow' others, and whose houses are built alongside the main path. The simplest pattern is shown in the case of *8b*, the settlement of Baimberi (*ɛtɔk ɔBaimbere*). This was previously owned by the former leader of Tali village, Egbemba, whose many wives were then housed in a side extension which ran back to twice its present length, based on the leader's own *acɔ*. Baimberi (20) succeeded to the leadership of the settlement (although not to the wider village leadership) but with fewer wives had shortened the side extension which he later completed by building his own *acɔ*. He was then in the process of extending his lodge of the Ngbe association which would be housed within the *acɔ*, both combining to enhance his reputation as a community leader. In the other two settlements a slightly greater degree of residential differentiation has occurred. In Tanyi Tabe, the 'settlement of Taboko', the senior elder of Tali village,[1] the group of houses shown on the right of the diagram are those of the settlement leader: they are based upon an *acɔ* which is that earlier illustrated in *Figure 4*. Besides this group of houses there is, however, another, also built at right-angles to the path in a position diametrically opposed to it in the settlement. These two houses (there were formerly three, but one of the owner's wives absconded and her house has since disappeared) include a bottom house of an *acɔ*-type, with all the features of an *acɔ* but lacking a central pole-support. The owner of this group of houses (28) could be described as the secondary leader of the settlement: he had spent many years in outside work and had now returned home where he was seeking to re-establish himself in the community; he was very closely associated

---

[1] Once when I was discussing with Taboko the name of his settlement he complained about its continued identity as 'Tanyi Tabe', the name of its original founder. He claimed that as he was the leader of the settlement it should be known after him. The discrepancy follows, of course, from the fact that, since the change, settlement leaders do not create their own settlements, to be known solely after them, but in the main succeed to the leadership of an already established and identified group.

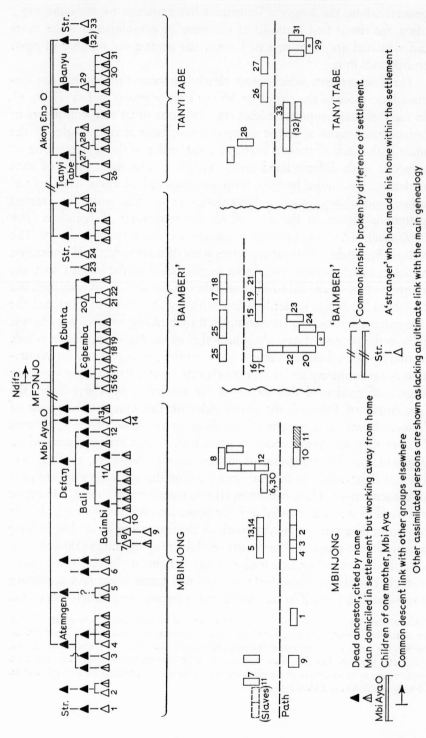

Figure 8 Settlements of the bə Mfɔnjo lineage group

with Taboko in directing the affairs of the settlement and acted as his deputy in wider village affairs; he held a strong presumption to the leadership of the settlement should Taboko, the older man, die. *Figure 8* shows the settlement of the village leader (8), whose own group of houses appears to the right of the diagram. The somewhat anomalous situation then existed whereby the bottom house of this group was not a true *acɔ* but an *acɔ*-type house, the right to a true *acɔ* (i.e. to erect a central pole-support) being held by 7, the senior brother of the village leader who had earlier (and before 8's own succession to the village leadership) succeeded to the limited leadership of this group. He now held the status of elder and was in the process of completing his own group of houses (at the left of the diagram) with an *acɔ*, which would also house the lodge of Ngbe, which he owned. This plan was never completed: 7 was then a sick man and two years later died.

Figure 9 illustrates the much larger settlement of the village of Bara, which stands at the other extreme from the form shown in *Figure 8*. The interesting point concerning this group is that its members moved unitarily as a single corporate community from Tali, whom they had joined at the time of the Mbo wars, some time after the imposed change in settlement organization. Here, except for the gaps caused by deaths and the one house of 2, all the houses of the settlement are built in continuous alignment along both sides of the path. Although in some ways exceptional, this fact accords closely with the tone of community affairs in Bara, where the emphasis was always upon the collective solidarity of the village and where undue derogation of authority was strongly resented. (Cf. the remark quoted p. 188, from a Bara man.) Even the meeting-house of the village leader (20, an *acɔ*-type house and not a true *acɔ*, although his father, village leader before him, had built an *acɔ* on the other side of the path) stands in alignment with the other houses of the settlement. One man only (2) had built a house not in alignment with the rest, standing a little way back from the path; this was of a 'modern' style with a large central room and smaller side rooms off it and with a veranda outside. It was perhaps no accident that this man had also suffered some vicissitudes in his attempts to achieve status: he had earlier been recognized as the minor leader of *bɔ Esɔɲafiɛt*, a section of the village, but had antagonized his supporters with what they claimed was his arrogance or 'pride' and had been removed from the position of leadership; he was then in voluntary exile (living, unusually, with his wife's kin) apparently waiting for feelings to die down before he should return to his place in the village.

39

Figure 9 Settlement plan of Bara village

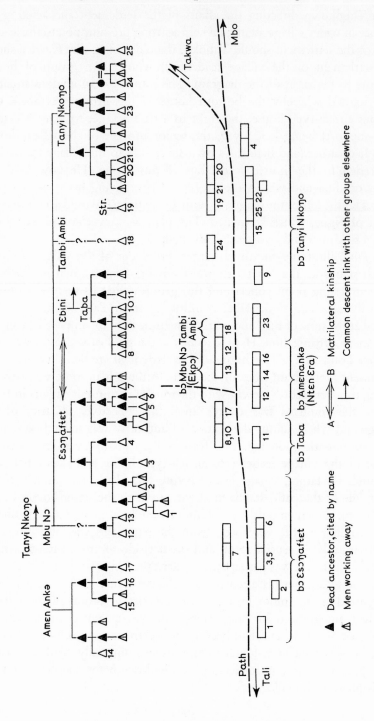

Whereas the members of Bara moved as a group to a new site, those of the composite settlement of Okorobak, Tanyi Ako, Nchemba, and Kembong have continued to occupy, with minor changes, the general site they came to at the time of the settlement change. The plan of the settlement (*Figure 10*) shows how, in the context of the continuing, stable group, individual men over a period of time have rebuilt and re-aligned their houses in response to their personal situation and claims to status. It would be too long and tedious to discuss the personal history of each man who owns a group of houses built in some way irregularly or in side extension to the body of the settlement, the majority of whose houses run parallel to the path. Each case would, however, be a commentary upon achieved status or claims to it. The most notable examples are 26, 32, and 45, each at some time a leader of one of the three sections of the settlement in which they live and all of them leading figures of the wider village community. Two of them, ★Mr N. A. Tataw (26), and ★Peter Esong (45), we shall meet in other roles later. In fact, none owned a true *acɔ*, although Peter Esong was later to build one at the bottom of his own group in Kembong. Mr. Tataw had built what perhaps came closest in Tali to an 'enclosed compound', but this grouping was intended to protect the large 'modern' house which stood as a sign of his well-to-do status and included a small shop, the only one at that time in Tali. This house was frequently the locus for 'community' meetings of varying degrees of extension or exclusiveness.

These examples of present-day Upper Banyang settlements could be matched, almost exactly, with settlements showing similar features from elsewhere in Banyang country. The contrast shown between the long-standing, composite settlement with its individuated groupings of houses (*Figure 10*) and the newly migrated settlement with its two regular rows of houses (*Figure 9*) is one which reappears many times, being associated often in the latter case with a claim to further (constitutional) inde-pendence: Bara itself is an example; others are Etemetek, which moved from Eyanchang, and Obang, which moved from a common site with Mbinjong-Are.

The regularity we have just noted indicates one of the major effects of settlement consolidation: the added emphasis that has been given to wider residential groupings. *Figure 11* shows how the former village community of Tali, widely dispersed over some twenty square miles of bush and forest, became concentrated along four miles of the main (newly established) path leading eventually to Fontem. Most sections of the village built along one continuous two and a half mile stretch of path. but

Figure 10 Composite settlement of Okorobak, Tanyi Ako, Nchemba, and Kembong

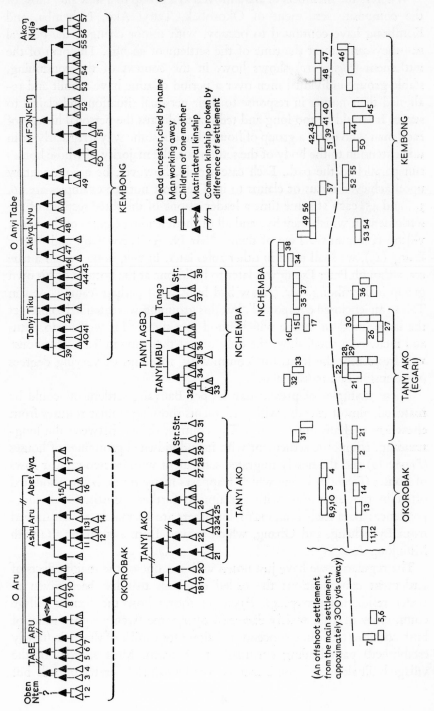

Plate 2 A small settlement, built in the traditional form

Plate 3 The present-day village settlement of
          Ejwengang

Plate 4 Ta Taboko, the senior elder of Tali I

one section (Mpomba) built separately about a mile and a half away near to the river of Mfi. In general, the residential alignments of the former dispersed settlements were retained in the new consolidated settlements, but the 'concertina' had, as it were, been partially closed: the dispersed εtɔk had been 'gathered'. In later years, sections of Tali village moved off, and served in part, and irregularly, to re-open the concertina: Talinchang moved to a point a mile east of its consolidated site; Bara returned to its former territory. Nevertheless, sections of the village continued to occupy the site they had originally come to, and those that moved did so

Figure 11 The change of settlement in Tali

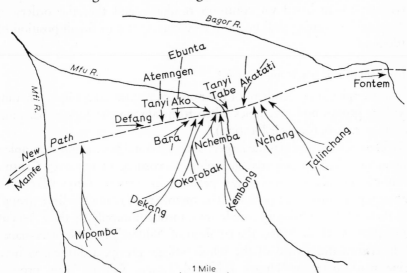

as single united groups. Smaller, individual changes of residence have also occurred, where a household head with one or two followers has gone off to build a separate settlement for himself in much the form of a traditional settlement: the small settlement of 7, shown separately in *Figure 10* is such an example. In the new context of consolidated settlement such a group must, however, always remain a breakaway fragment and is extremely unlikely ever to become the focus for a new wider residential grouping; in fact, most small breakaway groups usually either join with larger established settlements or return (as eventually occurred in the present case) to become reassimilated to the parent settlement.[1]

[1] In Chapter 12 I return to the question of change in the formation of residential groups and examine there the case of a similar small breakaway group which became rather more securely established (pp. 286–289).

These and other movements of residential groups which have taken place since the consolidation of settlements and at various levels of community grouping help to explain why there can be no constant relationship between settlement patterns and specific orders of residential grouping. With few exceptions, all settlements are built along a path or road which usually also links those sharing wider allegiances (always, in the case of villages; mostly, in the case of village groups). The range in size of settlements has already been mentioned. One simply cannot predict whether any single settlement will be a hamlet, a village, the rump of a village, or any other order or residual order of community grouping: all that one *can* say is that community solidarity, at any order of grouping continues to be based on common residence and that the orders of community grouping will in some way correspond to the disposition of settlements.

Two examples of residential grouping

Two examples are given here of the range of residential grouping within a village group, both examples taken from among the Upper Banyang (see *Map 2*, p. 6, for their location).

Ndifaw village group is the largest of the two and has the more complex system of internal residential grouping. According to the 1953 Census, its home population was 1,574 persons, as against Tanyi Nkongo's home population of 603 persons. The members of Ndifaw village group, like those of Tanyi Nkongo, are known most commonly by their descent name (in this case *bɔ Ndifɔ*, 'the children of Ndifaw') but the place-name 'Tali' is sometimes used of the whole village group, a distinction here being made between 'Upper Tali' and 'Lower Tali' or 'Tali' proper. 'Upper Tali' includes the two villages of Ebeagwa (population 371) and Ejwengang (pop. 167), both described as having originally and at different times seceded from the parent community of 'Lower Tali' or 'Tali' proper (pop. 1,076). In 1954 there was a further division of the latter group into two separate villages, 'Tali 1' and 'Tali 2'.

Within the village group, after the division of Tali, each of the four villages had their own recognized leader. Nevertheless, even after this constitutional change, the two parts of Tali continued to insist upon their traditional solidarity as a single community, *etɔk ɛmɔt*, and acted together in matters requiring the assertion of community authority. This somewhat paradoxical situation had been reached only after a very long period of political wrangling and was a condition of the agreement to recognize a separate leader for Tali 2. (An account of the agreement is given in Ch. 13, pp. 311f.) Following upon this agreement, the reassertion of the (operational) unity of the combined Tali was an important factor in the government and politics of Tali and of the village group as a whole, and is expressed in the diagram (*Figure 12*) by denoting the combined group as a 'supra-village'. The two villages composing 'Upper Tali' lacked comparable unity as an operationally united group, but in formal divisions in the village were treated as a unit in contradistinction to 'Lower Tali' or Tali proper.

Varying in size, the four villages vary also in the degree of their internal differentiation. For three of the villages two distinct levels of politically effective operational grouping can be distinguished. 'Sub-village' grouping is illustrated most clearly in the case of Ebeagwa, which is divided into Lower and Upper Ebeagwa, two distinctive residential groups situated some two miles apart from each other (Upper Ebeagwa as a single settlement, Lower Ebeagwa as three separate settlements). The representatives of each separate sub-village met fairly frequently to discuss and decide matters which especially concerned their own group, besides combining to meet more formally (and less regularly) as a village. A similar operational order of grouping existed in Tali 1, whose meetings I frequently had occasion to attend: this was the sub-village composed of Okorobak, Tanyi Ako, Nchemba, and Kembong (i.e. the composite settlement of *Figure 10*) together with the small settlement of Tanyi Tabe (*Figure 8*) across the river. This group lacked the formal identity of a name, but its representatives were easily convened, especially for the judgement of cases, and when they met there was no doubt that they spoke with authority as a residential group representing on that occasion the corporate community, ɛtɔk. The lower order of 'hamlet' is represented most clearly by a number of separate settlements, each of which is a recognized section of the wider village or sub-village but has also some claim to act on occasion and in minor matters as an autonomous community: so, for example, each of the three separate settlements of Lower Ebeagwa is a hamlet in this sense, and other clearly differentiated hamlets are Mpomba, Mbinjong and Dekang in Tali 1, Akatati and Talinchang in Tali 2. In other cases, groups which had formerly some degree of autonomy (and thus the status of hamlets) within the traditional organization, form now only part of a larger, composite settlement and in certain of these cases have lost any claim to independent authority that they may have held before. Thus, for example, in the composite settlement of Okorobak, Tanyi Ako, Nchemba, and Kembong the two sections of Okorobak and Kembong continue each to have the form and authority of a partially

Figure 12 Residential grouping: 1. Ndifaw village group

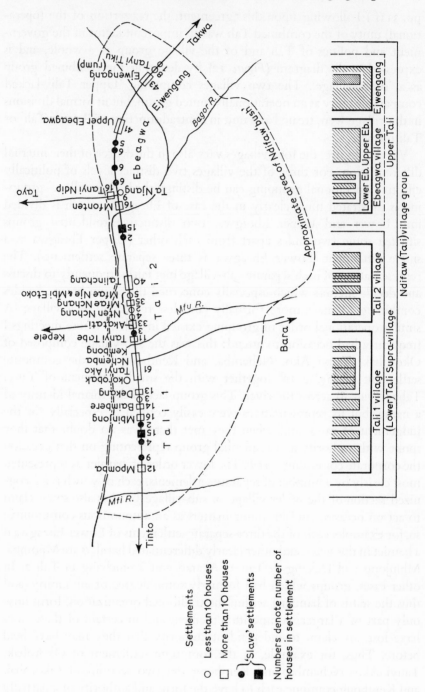

Settlements

○ Less than 10 houses

□ More than 1O houses

⊙ 'Slave' settlements

Numbers denote number of houses in settlement

autonomous community, *ɛtɔk*, comparable in all respects to that of Mpomba or Dekang; on the other hand, the two central sections of Tanyi Ako and Nchemba are described more accurately as lineage groups (*banɛrɛkɛt*), whose solidarity is based upon the norms of common kinship, and whose members do not act separately from the wider sub-village or village in purely residential or community affairs. So similarly Upper Ebeagwa, composed of formerly separate sections, lacks now further political differentiation into partially autonomous hamlets, and in the small village of Ejwengang only one such group is differentiated, the section of Tanyi Tiku. In Tali 1 the two settlements of Baimberi and Tanyi Tabe have the form of hamlets in terms of residential distinctness and the ability to act with some political autonomy, but neither is recognized as a formal section of the village, where they become joined with Mbinjong as the lineage group of *bɔ Mfɔnjo*. Finally, three small breakaway settlements are shown on the map (the small settlement next to Dekang, that between Nten Nchang and Akatati, and the single house built beyond Tanyi Tiku in Ejwengang), whose members, while having some *de facto* independence in their day-to-day affairs, continue to be formally counted with the residential groups from which they have come (respectively, the hamlets of Okorobak, Nten Nchang, and the rump village of Ejwengang) and whose claim to effective political autonomy was so limited and circumstantial that it must be discounted.

The point that I would wish to emphasize is that the corporate residential groups which have here been distinguished are homologous in their form as residential groups and in the way in which they operate politically. There is no formal or fundamental difference in the way a community case (*ndak ɛtɔk*) is discussed and decided upon in, say, the small settlement of Tanyi Tabe, from the way a similar case would be decided by the whole village group. (There are, of course, many practical differences, a number of which will concern us later.) On the occasion that they meet and in relation to the group they represent, the leading and senior members of Tanyi Tabe embody the authority of an *ɛtɔk* and can make decisions in the name of the community just as much as the representatives of the village group as a whole. At the same time the autonomy of each of these groups is partial: neither has exclusive right to act with political authority, to be the only group representing the community. Tanyi Tabe as a residential group is merged in the wider sub-village of Okorobak, Tanyi Ako, Nchemba, and Kembong, this sub-village in the village of Tali 1, this village in the supra-village of the conjoint Tali, the supra-village in the village group of the 'children of Ndifaw', 'the whole community, from

Mpomba to Ejwengang'. Each in some situation acts autonomously as an *εtɔk*: each is part of the total, complex community which includes them all.

Figure 13 Residential grouping: 2. Tanyi Nkongo village group

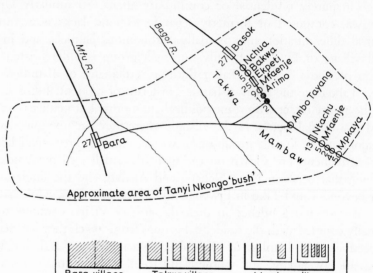

Tanyi Nkongo Village group

The second example, Tanyi Nkongo village group (*Figure 13*), shows a simpler but basically similar pattern of residential grouping. Both Takwa (population 322) and Mambaw (pop. 140) are residentially and politically differentiated, Takwa into a series of hamlet settlements (only Ekpeti and Mfaenje are residentially merged) each with partial autonomy. The most notable of these groups is the relatively large Basok (it has the same size as the independent village of Bara), which in 1954 had a particularly forceful and energetic leader and maintained some independence of action in political affairs, but at the same time observed a formal, 'constitutional' unity with the remainder of the village. The smaller, somewhat fragmented village of Mambaw is composed of similarly distinct hamlet settlements, but in 1954 the more significant operational grouping was the division of the village into two major parts or 'sub-villages', Ambo Tayang being here aligned with Ntachu, Mfaenje with Mpkaya. This division was centred on the issue of village leader-ship, formally held by the leader of Mfaenje but contested by the leader of Ambo Tayang, and while this dispute lasted the two halves of the village maintained an operational independence from each other. The equally small village of Bara (pop. 141) lacked any internal sections able to act with political autonomy (certainly in the sense that Basok in Takwa, Mpomba in Tali 1, or Talinchang in Tali 2 can be described as partially autonomous political groups). Even so, the man who had succeeded the deposed section head of *bɔ Esɔŋafiet* (cf. *Figure 9* and p. 39) was accepted and spoken of as *mfɔ etɔk*, where the residential group (*etɔk*) that he led was composed of the three sections, *bɔ Esɔŋafiet*, *bɔ Taba*, and *bɔ Mbunɔ*. This combined group, potentially a 'sub-village', lacked operational autonomy as a 'community', but formed an important faction within the village, which was reflected in their separate possession of an Ngbe lodge (another lodge was owned by the village leader, from *bɔ Tanyi Nkoŋo*), in the polarized composition of the village's 'inner council' and (inevitably) in claims made to the village leadership at the last succession.

These two examples have been concerned with the political community, as it were, 'on the ground': the actual settlements or series of settlements that combine in political action. I pass now from this emphasis on operational grouping to consider in more detail the rights and duties which determine the 'constitutional' status of certain of these groups and their leaders.

'The animals of the community'

The 'animals of the community', *nya etɔk*, are a series of animals, varying in importance, which if they are caught or killed cannot be disposed of privately, as other animals are, but must be presented to the representatives of one or other level of corporate community grouping. As we have already briefly described, the presentation of such animals, especially of the most important, the leopard, is traditionally regarded as a formal act of homage, due by right to the leader of a residential group, who, if he is himself junior to a leader of higher status, will be expected to repeat the action until the animal, if it is a leopard, has reached the foremost leader, who 'stands in front', i.e. the 'village' leader. The stages of presentation through which such an animal passes indicate, therefore, within a total, complex community, the 'line of leadership', *ndɔŋ kefɔ*, the hierarchical sequence of leaders, each of whose status is relative to the order of community grouping he represents. In their later stages such animals are brought always to the *acɔ* or meeting-house of the respective community leaders, and for this reason they are sometimes referred to as *nya acɔ*. It should be emphasized, however, that the 'leader' who receives the animal does so always as the representative head of a residential group: acting on its behalf, he must either pass the animal forward or send for all its representatives, who then collectively consume or share the animal.

The quality which would seem most to distinguish these animals of the 'community' as a class is their power or strength (*bɛtaŋ*). So, for example, on one occasion when I asked why a leopard should be brought to the village leader, it was this quality that was remarked on. The strength of a leopard was greater than that of all other animals, I was told. The man who had killed the leopard had shown his own strength in doing so. It was then appropriate that the animal should be presented to the village leader so that he, too, and the community, would 'become strong'.

Apart from the leopard, the most important of the animals of the community are the python, the crocodile (in areas where it exists), the elephant (now rare and very heavily restricted by Government), and the 'bush-cow' (also rare, and only infrequently killed). Of these animals, the python is universally the most significant, second to the leopard; it is not infrequently killed. Less important animals of the community include: the baboon (*ɛkurikak*), the harnessed antelope (*nkuwu*), the bush-pig (*njui*), the giant ant-eater (*njensok*), a further species of antelope (*nkoŋo*), a type of ape (*nsoŋnya*, possibly chimpanzee), the civet cat (*mbe*, described as a sibling, *manɔ*, to the leopard) and golden cat (*ɛsa*, also associated with the leopard).

News of a leopard's killing will normally be brought first to the killer's closest senior relative, who will in turn inform the elder of their immediate lineage group, which, we may assume, is the minor lineage group of a hamlet.[1] At this point, these two senior relatives are likely to go to inspect the dead animal before making the further, definite step of reporting the matter, or carrying the animal, to their hamlet leader. Once they have made sure of the reported fact, the animal will be presented to the hamlet leader, being brought from the bush to his *acɔ*. At the time it is brought into the settlement the face of the leopard should be covered by leaves to prevent women and children from recognizing the person believed to 'own' the leopard as his (or her) were-animal. At the hamlet leader's *acɔ* there will be scenes of excitement, guns fired, and in some cases an *ɛnok* dance held. By this time news of the killing will be public and people will begin to crowd around. What action is then taken

---

[1] I have never witnessed the killing or presentation of a leopard. The following description is based on accounts by many elders in many different villages: the topic always aroused interest and, reassuringly to an anthropologist, gave evidence of a high degree of consensus.

depends in part upon the relative status of the hamlet leader and the allegiances he acknowledges. If his hamlet forms part of a sub-village, the leopard may be presented to the foremost leader of the latter; or alternatively a senior elder, to whom formal respect is owed, will be sent for to witness and take responsibility for the leopard in the hamlet leader's own *acɔ*. Finally, with further considerable excitement, dancing, and firing of guns, the leopard will be carried to the village leader. (We describe here the ideal pattern, which does not take account of divisions in the constitutional role of village leaders.) At each stage in this sequence of presentation, the 'leader' who receives the leopard will be expected, either then or later, to 'dash' the person thus honouring him. Relatively large amounts (nowadays in money; in the past, a wife or a slave) will be given by the village leader to the sub-village or hamlet leader, a slightly smaller amount by the latter to his own subordinate; finally, the lineage group elder may be expected to give something like cloth or a gun and gunpowder to the killer (traditionally with the injunction to go out to do the same thing again).

The actions made once the leopard has been brought to the village leader vary in different parts of Banyang country. Among Lower Banyang a relatively simple ceremony is performed which ritually 'appeases' the creature (*-yɛt*, a verb also used for the ritual which 'appeases' or renders propitious a cult-agency): the village leader, seated on a special stool (*ɛruɔ*) and holding the special 'knife of the leopard' (*ngak nkwɔ*) first in his left hand, draws the knife across the skin of the leopard three times, at the end of each stroke touching the ground with it, and then, changing the knife to his right hand, makes four strokes over the skin, each time raising the knife to the sky; finally, at the end of the seventh stroke, the knife is used to pierce the skin and belly (*-te*). The animal is then skinned and butchered. The action of touching the ground is said to inform the dead of the event (who are believed to gather underground just as the living gather above it), and the raising of the knife to the sky is said to be a plea to God (*Mandɛm*, associated with sky and with ultimate good fortune) to 'raise up our right hands' so that all prosperity and goodness should come to the living. At the time of the operation, the whiskers and large canine teeth of the leopard, which are believed to have mystical power and can be used as medicine, are removed, and will later be given to the village leader for safe-keeping. An *ɛnok* dance is held, and there is singing, dancing, and feasting. In Besongabang I was told that the village leader should at this time give a goat to be eaten by the minor (hamlet) leaders of the village; to share in this goat was a mark of one's status in the village.

The meat of the leopard was shared similarly between persons of status representing all the recognized sections of the village. In this village group of Ayok Etayak, portions of the meat were expected to be sent to other villages of the village group, but members of these villages were not especially sent for to participate in the celebration of the leopard's capture.

In Nkokenok I, Tinto, and Mbang village groups a more elaborate action is taken in which the leopard becomes the focus of a temporarily organized politico-ritual association. A place in the 'bush' is prepared to which the leopard is taken, and here, in secret, the ritual 'operation' is performed: this is the 'leopard bush' (εbɔ nkwɔ) or 'secret leopard' (εyu nkwɔ). Since they are secret I could be given no detailed description of actions here: in the main they would seem to be similar to those performed publicly in the Lower Banyang villages, but apparently include also a ritual procedure which serves to 'empower' the village leader by transferring to him some of the quality of the leopard. More important than the actual ritual, however, would seem to be the distinguishing rights of certain individuals to enter the exclusive 'leopard bush'. Women, children, and persons of slave or partial slave descent are excluded, and only those of high status in the community (hamlet leaders and sectional heads) may witness the central operation. The path leading from the settlement into the 'leopard bush' is hung with fourteen palm-frond curtains and those who are not permitted to enter into the central area might be allowed, I was told, to come as far as the third, fourth, or later palm-frond curtain, receiving their share of the food and wine consumed by the others in the central bush. (This typical gradation of status is common to other associations.) The village leader is expected to provide goats and wine, to be eaten and drunk in the 'leopard bush'. The right to enter it is handed down from father to son, but is not entirely automatic since the successor on the occasion of his assuming the rights is expected to confirm his status by the payment of a goat and wine, which are (then or later) consumed by those who have entered the bush. On the conclusion of this first phase of the ceremony, the village leader leaves the bush to enter the 'leopard house' (εkεt nkwɔ) which has been prepared for him in the settlement. This too has something of the form of an association house. Only those who have entered the 'leopard bush' may enter the 'leopard house'. Camwood is rubbed on the body of the village leader and bracelets made of the leopard skin are put on his arms. At the end of fourteen days he emerges, and the occasion then is one of great public celebration, feasting, dancing, and pleasure. If they have not already participated in the leopard bush, members of other villages in the village group ('the whole community') will now come to salute the village leader, will be entertained with wine and food by him, and will themselves give presents to him. As in all Banyang villages and village groups, the public celebration of a leopard's capture redounds to the glory of the village leader.

Finally, in the remaining Upper Banyang village groups (notably, Ndifaw, Tanyi Nkongo, and Tayong) a somewhat abbreviated version of the activities described above is performed, in which the main emphasis is on the 'leopard house' and the activities of the 'bush' are curtailed or omitted. The general form, however, remains essentially the same: that of a type of association, in which the relative status of members of the community is reflected in the degree to which they formally enter the body of persons representative of the community and participate in the activities performed in its name. Birthright helps to establish the right to take part but it has also to be confirmed, and can be acquired, by the giving of a goat and wine, to be shared by those who already hold this right.

As the most important of the *nya ɛtɔk* in the traditional society, the leopard had always to be presented to the highest 'community leader', the ritual response to its killing was the most elaborate, and the celebration that followed involved the most extended orders of community grouping. In passing to the other 'animals of the community', we find that the duty to present them to the highest 'leader' is less compelling, the ritual performed is less elaborate, and only the less extended orders of the community become involved.

Amongst Upper Banyang the killing of a crocodile is celebrated in a way similar to that of a leopard. When in the late 1940s a crocodile was killed in Tali it was taken to the village leader, brought before the *ɛnok* drum, and the village group as a whole was called to celebrate its capture. The animal was ritually 'operated' upon (-*te*) and the 'leopard people' (i.e. the members of the 'leopard house') briefly reconstituted. The crocodile skin remained in the village leader's meeting-house to mark the event.

More commonly, however, it is the python whose killing provides the occasion for a gesture of political allegiance. A python is 'operated' upon in a rite similar to that of the leopard, and its bile (believed to be dangerous as poison) removed and secretly disposed of. In most areas a python should be brought to the village leader, but there is little celebration attached to its killing and no more than the section representatives of the village are likely to be called to witness it and share in it.

For the lesser animals of the community – the baboon, bush-pig, harnessed antelope, etc. – the killer's duties are less clear-cut and more circumstantial. If he is a stranger to the village, or if it is the first animal of this kind that he has killed, it may be presented to the village leader (again, although less formally, being passed through the relevant stages). If these circumstances do not apply, the animal may be taken only to the local (hamlet) leader or to the killer's lineage elder as section head. If the killer is a hunter who regularly kills game he may not wish to send the whole animal but will present then only the 'chest' (the portion formally accorded to a 'leader') to his local head – normally the leader of a hamlet.

As one might expect, stories concerning the presentation of leopards figure in a number of village group histories to account for the present constitutional ordering of the village group. I cite here a text, as narrated to me by Ta Njang (formerly the senior elder of Ejwengang village) which tells how the ancestral founder of the *bɔ Mfɔnjo* lineage group came to acquire the leadership of Tali:

When Ndifaw left Kembong and arrived here he begot Tanyi Takum and made him leader of Ebeagwa. He said: You, Tanyi Takum, now have your own leadership; if a leopard is killed where you are, you can 'eat' it there in Ebeagwa. Then he begot Tanyi Tiku [the ancestral founder of Ejwengang]. He said: When I have died Tanyi Tiku should succeed me. If any of my 'children' [dependants/descendants] kill a leopard they should come and give it to you.

After his death one of his sons, Tabe Aru, went off and killed a leopard. All his 'children' said they should carry the leopard to Tanyi Tiku's place and give it to him. Tabe Aru said no; whatever happened, he would go to tie up the leopard at the head of his father's (Ndifaw's) grave. His children wondered: they went home and he went off. He came to the grave and drove sticks into the ground, one here, one there. He took the leopard and fixed it high up. The leopard became completely putrefied. When Tanyi Tiku was told about it, he had nothing to say – it was a matter for Mandem.

Then father Mfonjo went and set a trap in which he put a kid. The kid cried, maa, maa, maa, and a leopard heard and went to it. The leopard entered the trap, took and killed the kid, and so was caught in the trap. The leopard cried out, hõ, hõ, hõ. Mfonjo came and listened; he was satisfied and went off. He called his 'brothers' [*bɔ ta ji*: fellow agnates – the implication is that they all were of similar status], who came and asked what the matter was. He told them that a leopard had fallen into his trap. . . . [They went to find the leopard, killed it, and brought it to Mfonjo.] They asked him: where will you take the leopard? He said: shall I not carry the leopard to give to my 'father', Tanyi Tiku. Whatever had happened with the other leopard, he would not forget what his father had said. He carried the leopard and gave it to Tanyi Tiku. When they brought it they left it outside [i.e. to be seen and celebrated] and they danced and danced. Tanyi Tiku gave them all presents, every one of them. To Mfonjo himself he gave a slave, a goat, a gun, a matchet; he took a girl, married her, and gave her to Mfonjo as his wife – her name was Akong Eno [the common ancestress of Tanyi Tabe]. Then he called all the children of Ndifaw and told them to observe what he had given to Mfonjo: was this not good? They said: Father, it is good. He asked how many minor leaders (bɔ afɔ) there were in Lower Tali. They told him twelve [the traditionally accepted number of Tali's sections] and he said they should give twelve cows. He himself would give two, a bull and a cow. Altogether there were fourteen. He told them to go with the cows to the former settlement site of his father (Ndifaw) and to keep them there. They wondered, and asked why they should do that. He said, so that anyone who passed by will see how the former settlement of his father is flourishing (-sɔŋ, lit. 'burning').

The cows gave birth to calves, and so multiplied. Then Tanyi Tiku sent for Mfonjo and said: why not take some of the calves and use them to marry with? Mfonjo married ten wives. The others in the bush came out and complained to Tanyi Tiku: Father, where has this youngster got his bridewealth from to marry all these wives? The only work that Mfonjo did was to weave sleeping-mats. Tanyi Tiku told them to go back: every man who had given a cow should take one back. No one should take more than he had owned. In two days' time he would come down there, on Tali's market day. He then called everyone together. They came and gathered and he said this was the reason why he had called them. Mfonjo should now be leader. A chair was brought and Mfonjo was told to sit on it. Tanyi Tiku said that among all of his (Mfonjo's) brothers, if anyone killed a leopard he should come and give it to Mfonjo: he should 'operate' upon the leopard, remove its skin, take off its whiskers and teeth. He was now leader of Tali.

The right of a village leader to receive a leopard killed within his domain appears in the preceding account at two different levels. In the first place it appears as a formal indication of a leader's independence – and thus of the independence of the village that he represents. So in the account, the constitutional status of Ebeagwa, a village within the village group, is briefly stated by narrating that Ndifaw had given Tanyi Takum, its ancestral founder, 'his own leadership': the right to receive a leopard and not to pass it forward (ɔnyɛ nyɛ aga, 'you eat all there') is treated here as synonymous with having an independent leadership. In much the same way, at the end of the account the formal conferring of a village leadership upon Mfonjo is signified by describing how the rights to receive a leopard and to perform the appropriate ritual accrue now to him. The implication of Tanyi Tiku's action here (where Tanyi Tiku is known to be the ancestral founder of Ejwengang) is, moreover, that Mfonjo has become the independent (village) leader of 'Lower Tali', i.e. of Tali proper, with its twelve recognized sections.

In the second place the presentation of a leopard is represented as an act of homage from which the presenter seeks to obtain the maximum capital. We are not explicitly told why Tabe Aru (the ancestral founder of Okorobak) refused to pay homage to Tanyi Tiku; yet the implication is that Tabe Aru was seeking in some way to assert the superiority, and possible independence, of his own leadership. This manœuvre, if as such we may take it, went against him: part of the tradition, which Ta Njang did not give in this text, is that for his failure to present the leopard Tabe Aru and his posterity were cursed by the assembled 'children of Ndifaw' who declared that the men of bɔ Tabe Aru should never marry more than a single wife and that their children would be few. Returning to the text we note that the very failure of Tabe Aru to pay homage gives Mfonjo his own opportunity: he goes out of his way to *catch* the leopard that *he* will present to Tanyi Tiku. What ensues is a stratagem in which Tanyi Tiku and Mfonjo are depicted as being reciprocally involved. Mfonjo makes an ally of Tanyi Tiku who, quite deliberately, lays the foundation of Mfonjo's wealth and prosperity. It is relevant to note here that in another tradition Mfonjo is described as a protégé of Tanyi Ako (the ancestral founder of another of Tali's sections) who spent his time weaving sleeping-mats. It is explained that when Tanyi Tiku made his suggestion to Mfonjo that the calves could be used for bridewealth, he did so 'behind', privately: certainly, as the story is told, it would have been impossible for Mfonjo to achieve the prosperity that he did without Tanyi Tiku's connivance. In the genealogy of bɔ Ndifɔ Mfonjo is always given as Ndifaw's 'youngest child', tancoko mɔ, with the implication again of someone who has arrived late on the scene and who has been treated with some indulgence by his 'father'.[1] Finally, we need to note that the point of the story is not only to commemorate the accession to a village leadership by Mfonjo but to explain how this occurred, what events led up to it. The conferring by Tanyi Tiku of the formal rights of leadership upon Mfonjo is no more than the sequel to what goes before, and it is this that the story is really about: how Mfonjo rose to power by a stratagem; how bɔ Mfɔnjo, by far the largest and most powerful lineage group in Tali, came by virtue of its strength to control the leadership. The story is therefore not only a formal statement of the basic constitution of the village group – three villages each with their independent leader. It is also an account, in one village at least, of the politics leading up to its 'constitutional' status.

There was a sequel to the part of the story concerning Tabe Aru when, early in 1954, a python was caught by a member of Okorobak the day before a meeting of the whole village group (in the form of the Ndifaw Clan Union) was due to be held in their section of the composite settlement. A report of the killing was carried via the leader of Okorobak to Ta Taboko in Tanyi Tabe, who besides being the 'senior elder' of Tali 1 was also informally recognized as the leading representative of this sub-village. Normally a python was taken to the village leader in Tali, who would then call the section representatives to witness it and share in its eating. In this case, Taboko advised that the python should be retained until the following day and presented then directly to the assembled village group. It was hoped that this action would help to make good the legendary error of Tabe Aru and that with the blessing of the village group prosperity would return to Okorobak. This, however, was not the first time that an animal of the community had been presented to rescind the curse placed on Tabe Aru: some years previously a member of Okorobak had shot a crocodile (that mentioned on p. 53), which was presented to the village leader and the legendary curse removed from the hamlet in the presence of the assembled representatives of the village group. A fine of three pounds ten shillings (one 'slave') had at this time been given by the leader of Okorobak to the village group, who was then confirmed by the village group as

[1] The 'last-born' or 'youngest child' (tancoko mɔ) is thought of as the father's favourite. In genealogies the term often euphemistically describes an ancestral founder who has come into prominence some time after those who are now his accorded brothers. During the Tali dispute described in Chapter 13, an attempt was made to turn Mfonjo's 'last-born' status to their own account by Tali 2, who could thereby claim seniority for their own ancestral founder, see p. 309.

its constitutional head. By 1954 the latter man had died: his position had been taken by a successor, who however still lacked formal village confirmation of his status.[1] It was this man who was due to present the python.

So it was that late on the following afternoon, when representatives of Ebeagwa and Ejwengang had gathered in Okorobak for the Clan Union meeting, together with members of Tali 1, including the village leader, the python was brought out, cooked, and shared between those there. At the same time the leader of Okorobak (in the terminology then current, its 'Quarter-Head') presented a goat to the village group in order that his status should be confirmed. Like the python, this goat was divided and shared by the recognized sections of the village group. A brief blessing was given to the leader of Okorobak by the senior elders of Ebeagwa and Ejwengang villages, and a few days later, when the Clan Union meeting had dispersed, Taboko, as senior man of Tali 1, gave an elaborate and more formal blessing, assisted by other senior representatives of the village. The story of Tabe Aru, the misused leopard, the earlier crocodile, and the present python was then recounted to the invoked dead of the village group, who were asked to bring prosperity to the people of Okorobak and its now confirmed leader. 'If anyone in Okorobak has something,' Ta Taboko concluded, referring now in general terms to the duties we have been discussing, 'he should bring it to N—— (the leader of Okorobak), who will bring it to the (village) leader.'

In this sequel to the earlier story, presentation of animals of the community appears again on two levels. The status of the leader of Okorobak is formally confirmed by his position being described in the 'line of leadership': if a 'thing' is found in Okorobak it should be brought to him and he should take it to the village leader. Once more the statement is a formal indication of status, conceived in terms of the rights of presentation. The sequel also shows, secondly, how in the actual presentation of an animal an attempt is made to capitalize on this as an act of homage. Some would say that the capital gained was not wholly to the advantage of Okorobak – for on two separate occasions they were obliged to give extra, to the advantage of the village and village group. Be this as it may, the presentation of the earlier crocodile and of the present python was made in both cases the occasion for confirming the constitutional status

[1] On the confirmation of hamlet and village leaders by a wider community grouping, see below, pp. 302–303.

of the Okorobak leader and for annulling the earlier curse (which was believed still to hold). On the latter occasion, in order to take advantage of the village group meeting to be held in Okorobak, the formal right of the village leader to receive the python was ignored and the presentation made directly to the assembled representatives of the village group, the 'whole community'.

We shall look later in more detail at the ways in which these formal rights become involved in the play of politics. I give one final example of an attempt made to extract political capital from the presentation of a leopard.

In the Mbang village group the story is still told of a leopard killed by one of Defang's subjects while visiting Manyemen, an enclave of Banyang, situated some 25 miles from Mbang.[1] As a gesture of homage, the leopard was brought back all the way to Defang and presented to him. As we have already noted, Defang was then one of the most powerful of Upper Banyang village leaders. He responded with a similar gesture, designed to express his own pre-eminence as the 'owner of the land' (a somewhat grand title, claimed for him by his descendants). He invited people from far and wide: Nkokenok, Bakebe, Ekpaw, Tali, Manyemen itself, besides all the people of Mbang. A great feast was prepared for them and generous gifts were made to the stranger village leaders as they were leaving. In a sense the action was only a matter of prestige, but it served also to establish Defang's pre-eminence among other village leaders. Somewhat ruefully the present villagers of Defang add that 'this is why we say a leopard wastes money'. Ironically, this very pre-eminence of Defang brought him into conflict with Zintgraff and the early German administration, reduced his power, and gave the opportunity to his immediate rival, the leader Mfotabe, to achieve eminence under successive European administrations.

'The things of the community'

Apart from the formal rights we have been considering, there are a number of ritual objects, highly regarded by Banyang, which have similar implications for the constitutional status of those groups or persons who hold them. These are objects which are associated with the traditional unity, authority, or well-being of individual village communities and are normally held by their traditionally recognized leader. In many cases

[1] See Chapter I, p. 10.

they are directly involved in the ritual actions already described. Just as the bringing of a leopard to a leader formally symbolizes his status as village leader, so the holding of the 'things of the community' ideally indicates the person or group possessing a village leadership. One important qualification must, however, be added: the 'things of the community' are more especially ritual in character and they provide in certain cases for a divided leadership, whereby the same village recognizes two leaders, someone who holds the traditional, ritual office, and a second, usually younger, man, who acts as effective leader in day-to-day affairs.

'Things of the community' (bɛnyŋ ɛtɔk) include the 'leopard knife' (ngak nkwɔ) and 'stool' (ɛruɔ) whose ritual use has already been described. They also include a special horn (mbaŋ or mbaŋ ɛtɔk) which in the past was used to summon the dispersed village community to a meeting in the leader's settlement. In Lower Banyang country most commonly, but sporadically in some Upper Banyang villages as well, there is also a variety of cult objects which are the focus for ritual performed on behalf of the village, which serve to symbolize the unity and prosperity of its people, and which ideally in the past were held by the village leader, who also commonly acted as officiant.

Among Upper Banyang the 'things of the community' figure perhaps more in legendary history and in the claims made in village leadership disputes than in actual use. Such objects nevertheless do exist and are cherished material symbols of present or former status.

In Fotabe village I was shown two metal bracelets (ngɔm) which had been passed down through three generations from the founder of the village to its present leader and were said in the past to be used as a gage, which was sent to an enemy to pledge the redemption of a captured prisoner. Handed down from father to son, they could in no circumstances be sold. The attempt of a village leader to sell them would be sufficient cause to remove him from the leadership: selling them, I was told, would be like selling the ɛtɔk, the village.

In Atebong village the 'horn of the community', held by the village leader, had in 1965 become the central symbol of a modern association, the 'Town Men's Council' which was confined in membership to the sectional leaders of the village and which met weekly to discuss village affairs and to drink wine.

One of the clearest examples of the constitutional significance of possession of 'things of the community' is contained in a further, very widely known story of the Ndifaw village group, which tells how Ndifaw acquired village leadership and thus founded the present *bɔ Ndifɔ*.

Ndifaw is said to have come originally from Kembong among the eastern Ejagham. As he was wandering in the forest with his followers, he was seen by one of the slaves of Mfo Dekang, the leader of a community in Upper Banyang country. The slave brought news of the stranger to Mfo Dekang, who gave orders that the stranger should be brought to him. He received Ndifaw and his followers and gave them a place to live.

Mfo Dekang was a stern and oppressive man: 'the community at this time was not well'. In contrast, Ndifaw was a man of good behaviour, who was well liked: he was generous towards people and if a hunter came to present him with an animal he had killed, Ndifaw would take only part of the meat and would return the rest, together with gifts.

One day, at a communal hunt, one of Mfo Dekang's sons killed a son of Ndifaw. Ndifaw therefore brought a case against Mfo Dekang. He claimed that as his son was now dead, so one of Mfo Dekang's sons should die. Mfo Dekang refused, and no settlement could be reached. Some of Mfo Dekang's men then went secretly to Ndifaw and advised him that he held the advantage over Mfo Dekang: provided that he did not insist upon the latter's son's death, he could ask for anything that he wished. (In some versions the whole incident of the killing of Ndifaw's son is said to have been prearranged.)

A new meeting was called and the community gathered to hear the case. (A text continues:) 'They talked of Mfo Dekang's son who had shot Ndifaw's son. Ndifaw said that as Mfo Dekang would not allow his own son to die, what would he, Mfo Dekang, give him instead? Mfo Dekang said he was prepared to give him anything, even a hundred slaves: he should say what he wanted. Ndifaw asked for the "horn of the community" and the "leopard knife". Mfo Dekang was surprised at this and turned to his own people to ask them about it. They replied: "What are these things? He is a stranger and doesn't know that they are things of the community. You should give them to him." And so Mfo Dekang gave them to him.

'With this people started coming to Ndifaw and treating him as their leader. They ignored Mfo Dekang. When Mfo Dekang asked, they pointed out that the horn and knife were now with Ndifaw and these were the things of leadership, so they went to those.'

This story, like the not dissimilar one concerning Mfonjo's accession to an independent leadership, may be read at two levels. At its most obvious level (and somewhat simplistically) it describes how Ndifaw became village leader by acquiring the 'things of the community', i.e. those objects which are formally and symbolically associated with this status. At another level, however, it describes the (more significant) conditions which led up to the change in constitutional leadership: the better 'fashion' of Ndifaw (who responds well to the homage paid to him as leader), the transference of support by the followers of Mfo Dekang, the typical machinations 'behind'. The 'things of the community' both serve to confirm formally Ndifaw's newly won status and are involved in the process by which he gains it. The name 'Tali', which means in Ejagham 'Father has eaten', is cited to support the story.

The story of Ndifaw's ousting of Mfo Dekang implies a simple correlation between possession of the 'things of the community' and village leadership. In some villages such a correlation does in fact hold even today: in these villages the one recognized leader of the village has the right to receive any leopard killed; it is he who should 'operate' upon it, and who also holds the 'leopard knife' or the 'horn of the community'. In many other villages, however, the ritual rights and the effective or secular status of village leadership have become divorced. In recent years this division has often coincided with a distinction that has come to be made between the 'community leader' (*mfɔ ɛtɔk*) – that is, the 'true', traditional leader of the village – and the 'European's leader' (*mfɔ Ndek*) – that is, the Government-recognized village chief. Even before this distinction became common, however, ritual rights and effective leadership would seem often to have diverged. In Bara village, for example, one lineage group (*bɔ Amɛnankɔ*) were described as the 'origin' or 'bottom' of the community (*nɛt ɛtɔk*), around which the village had grown, and which originally held the leadership. This now had passed to another lineage group (*bɔ Tanyi Nkoŋo*), but the 'leopard knife', together with a number of cult stones (*barɛm*, see below), were still held by them. Again, in Tali, *bɔ Tanyi Nga* of Akatati claimed to hold the original 'leopard knife', and advanced this to support their claims to a separate leadership during the Tali dispute. In other villages, similar divergencies occur between the effective leadership and the formal, ritual office.

Many parallels exist in other African societies of a comparable separation of ritual leadership from an office which is more effectively that of political leader. For Banyang the distinction is important since it allows for the formal recognition of what is *de facto* a compromise: the claims of the 'traditional', ritual leader are not overridden, while the status of the newer, more effective leader is also recognized. Such a division of role incorporates within the 'constitutional' ordering of a community what was earlier in discrepancy with it. We shall later see that such a compromise is the not infrequent outcome of the processes we describe as constitutional politics.

A series of cults are found predominantly in Lower Banyang villages which are directly concerned with the unity and prosperity of the community in a religious context, but at the same time serve to express the political unity of the village and, ideally, should be maintained by the village leader. The commonest of these village cults is that of *Barɛm*, a word which in Kenyang normally means 'the dead' or 'the spirits of the dead', but here also denotes the stones (commonly smooth pebbles such as are found in a river-bed) which form the cult-objects. The cult itself is apparently derived from the *Alɛm* cult of the Ejagham, which centres upon nature spirits believed to promote fertility and in particular the birth of children. For Banyang the *Barɛm* are clearly conceived as ancestral spirits but the cult remains essentially one of fertility, concerned with the prosperity of the community through the procreation of children. Although most commonly concerned with community welfare at the level of the village, *Barɛm* or similar cults are occasionally maintained at a lower level, by a sub-village or by hamlets. (The more recently introduced anti-witchcraft cult of *Mfam*, also a community cult derived from Ejagham, has been almost invariably adopted in Banyang country by residential groups smaller than a village.) Three examples may help to illustrate the way in which these village cults acquire both 'political' significance (in relation to the corporate solidarity of a village) and a 'constitutional' role (in determining who is village leader).

In Besongabang in 1965 the village leader owned and officiated at *Ndɛm* (the singular of *Barɛm*), which was referred to as a 'stone', *ntae*, but was possibly a meteorite, a large spherically shaped mass with numerous small pock-marks in it. It was described both as 'a thing of the community' and as 'a thing of leadership', i.e. something that only a leader (normally a village leader) could own. It was kept by the village leader in the corner of his *aca*, meeting-house, where he made regular offerings of food to it, asking for good fortune for the village and himself. Cola broken and thrown in front of *Ndɛm* indicated according to the way it fell possible bad events that might occur, as for example the death of a section leader. If the wives of the village failed to bear children a special supplication could be made to it. Its owner insisted that the cult object had no efficacy in itself: it was 'only a stone', an 'example' or symbol of the dead, from whom all blessings (*afɔk*) come.

An interesting feature of this, as of other *Barɛm*, was its accredited ability to 'flee' or disappear. One day it might simply vanish. Possibly another man would find it, or another like it, and he would then be expected to bring the 'stone' to its original owner. Such a disappearance and later discovery were, however, taken to indicate the *Ndɛm*'s own choice of officiant. So, when the discoverer of the 'new' *Ndɛm* came to the village leader and former officiant, the latter would tell him that he should keep the 'stone' and care for it himself. I was told that once the previous leader had died this man would succeed as village leader. Mfo Tabe, then leader of Besongabang, claimed that this had occurred in his own case. The *Barɛm* of the previous village leader had 'vanished'; he found the present *Ndɛm*, and was told to care for it. It was because of this, he claimed, that he became village leader.

The village cult of Bachu Akagbe, a community situated farther away from the Ejagham border, is *Ngɔm*, whose ritual objects are two pre-European metal bracelets. In 1965 they were kept in the hollow at the base of the pole-support of the *aca* of the Government-recognized village leader. This was the normal place of assembly for the village. The officiant of the *Ngɔm* was the 'senior elder' of the village, who lived in a different section of it and was described also as the (traditional) 'community leader'. All ritual in connection with the *Ngɔm* was however made in the collective presence of the representatives of the village, in which the officiant's role was primarily that of spokesman. The cult was described as 'the heart of the community' (*ntɔ ɛtɔk*), and seems to have represented on the one hand the combined dead of the village and on the other the moral unity and collective authority of its living members. The oblations and sacrifices normally offered to the dead on behalf of the village were made at this shrine, when the dead would be asked to bless and bring prosperity to the living. The cult was also used to curse and ostracize any member of the village who failed to accept the collective decision reached by the village council against him. 'If the mouths of those in the community are set against you, you will not thrive' (*Mbak banyu ɛtɔk anaŋ antɛp wɔ'miɛt, ɔpu ŋwaŋ*).

The 'heart of the community' is a phrase which reappears in many contexts to describe, on the one hand, the small, exclusive, central group of persons in a community which represent it, and, on the other, certain cults or ritual objects which again, but in a more abstract sense, represent the essential life, unity, and well-being of a residential group.

In Bakebe the 'heart of the community', ntɔ ɛtɔk, is a secret cult-object normally kept by the village leader and known only to a small group of persons, themselves minor leaders, who represent the village's seven sections. It is believed to bring prosperity to the village community and its leader: both good order and plenty, especially the plentiful birth of children. Its hiding-place is kept secret and few people have actually seen it. Women and children are expected to know nothing of it. When in the past the village leader died, one of the first actions of this inner group of men was to regain possession of the ntɔ ɛtɔk. It was not given immediately to his successor, but only after he had proved himself capable as a leader. In times of misfortune, when the village leader sees that 'things are turning away from him', rites involving the ntɔ ɛtɔk are performed to restore fortune; at this time the leading officiant is the senior elder of the village, but the rites are attended also by the small group of persons having knowledge of the cult. It is also brought out at the time a leopard is killed, when it is taken into the 'leopard bush' and what was described as a very 'hard' ceremony performed (i.e. a central, important ceremony, which is to be taken seriously, and by implication is known to few persons): presumably this ceremony renews and strengthens the cult in its relation to the community and its leadership.

When I questioned the leading members of the village community where the power of the ntɔ ɛtɔk came from I was told that 'it comes from the voice of people' (bɛfu ɛyɔŋ bo); and then, since like all other village cults the moral and religious association of the cult was with the dead, my informants added that the power 'comes from the voice of those who have died, together with those other seven living men' (i.e. the seven sectional representatives of the village community who are themselves in a different sense 'the heart of the community').

'The leaders of the community'

The link between community 'constitution' as a formal set of rights and the 'operational' structure of the community as an extended series of politically effective residential groups lies in the position of those men who are the recognized leaders of certain residential groups. Two questions that arise here are: firstly, how does a man acquire the status of 'community leader', and, secondly, what procedures are entailed in the selection and succession of a village leader?

There are no clear, definitive answers to these questions. The simple, direct answers are: firstly, that any man may become a leader (*mfɔ*) who acquires his own supporters or 'followers', where these constitute a residential group (*ɛtɔk*) defined in relation to him; and, secondly, that a village leader is chosen and put into office by the collective action of the village. In point of fact, the process of becoming a community leader is more involved than these answers might suggest and emerges, in the first place, out of the complex corporate structure of the diffuse community and, in the second, out of the fluid and ever-important struggle for status that is a concomitant part of community politics. I discuss here some of the more general features of leadership and the fluid status system associated with community structure, returning in a later chapter (Chapter 13) to consider in more detail how succession to village leadership is determined.

Perhaps the most important general characteristic of the position of leader is the leader's dependence in his role upon those whom he represents. *Kɛfɔ*, leadership, is 'a thing of the community': it remains always subject to community control. Its members collectively make a man leader; their continued support is necessary for him to remain one. Banyang are very conscious of the fact that no leader has an innate right to his position and that his position is not one of formal authority. A leader 'stands in front', he is the person 'who has us all', but he remains essentially a representative and should always be aware of this. 'This chair is a chair in itself (literally, in its own body),' I was once told. 'This table is a table in itself. But the leader is not a leader in himself: he is a leader because *we* all call him – leader!' So similarly, in the carrying out of his role, a leader should not act autocratically: he should carry people with him rather than attempt to impose his will upon them. A leader may, according to his circumstances, have a great deal of influence and his word may be much respected, but in itself the office of leadership does not carry formal authority. 'When a leader speaks he speaks with the voice of the community, not in his own voice.' The exercise of authority remains then the collective function of the corporate community; the leader participates in this function, but he does not formally control it.

The relationship nevertheless is not all one way. Community leaders are by no means mere spokesmen of a group whose form or policy is beyond their power to influence. The reverse is in fact the case. While insisting upon the formal equality of all who are members of the community, Banyang also respect and acclaim those whose personal qualities of leadership serve to maintain and enhance the solidarity of the group. The acclamation *mfɔ!*, 'leader!', may be made during a debate to praise someone who has spoken decisively, as a leader should. So also it is said that 'a community cannot exist without someone at its head'. Any residential group relies very much upon the qualities of the man who is the focus of their interests as a group. A forceful leader strengthens the authority and increases the prestige of the group whom he represents.

All community leaders are not of the same status. These differences in status may be related to the corporate structure of the community in two ways. Firstly, the extended series of residential groups forming the complex community is paralleled by an extended, informal hierarchy of leaders with a clearly recognized status relative to each other. Secondly, and in terms of the wider community groupings – village or village group – the measure of a man's claim to political status, however this status may be described, is the extent to which he has penetrated, and has influence over, the central bodies which represent the community and whose decisions are the key ones in the regulation of its affairs. I shall discuss these two aspects of the relationship between leadership and the community structure in turn.

A distinction is sometimes made between the 'big' and 'small' leaders of a community (*mfɔ ngo* and *bɔ bafɔ* or *bɔ afɔ*): in effect this is a distinction between the village leader, the 'major' leader, and the 'minor' leaders of the various smaller residential groups, primarily hamlets, which make up a village.[1] The hierarchy which exists here, and in so far as it is formalized, tends to be seen in terms of the relative status of individuals. Nevertheless, despite its description in these personal terms, the status of the men concerned is clearly dependent upon the sectional groups they represent. Thus frequently a village leader will speak of his 'right-hand man', someone who 'follows him' in order of importance in the village, and such a person is commonly found to represent the most important section of the village other than the leader's own. Hamlet leaders, especially those who are more actively concerned in general village affairs and who keep in close touch with the village leader, are often spoken of as though they were his personal supporters. How a minor leader is described is further dependent upon the context in which he is seen. The leader of a single settlement or hamlet can be addressed as *mfɔ* within it and will be shown then all the respect due to this status. Outside the settlement or hamlet,

---

[1] Cf. the text above, p. 55, in which Tanyi Tiku is represented as asking how many 'minor leaders' are included in 'Lower Tali'.

however, the same person will be seen differently – often simply as a 'person of the community', *mu ɛtɔk* – in terms now which depend upon his closeness to the village leader and upon his active participation in the corporate affairs of the village.

The fluidity and circumstantiality of the status ranking of community leaders gives rise to various, sometimes *ad hoc*, ways of describing their position. It is said that a village leader's main supporters (hamlet leaders in their own right) were called *bakɔm* (sing. *nkɔm*) in the past, but I have never heard this term in actual use and strongly suspect that it has been adopted from the more formal political hierarchy of the Bangwa people, where an *nkem* is a sub-chief, or district head. 'Right-hand man', 'orderly', and a number of terms taken over from modern administrative offices are also used to describe the relative superiorities and inferiorities of status. A word which has been very widely adopted to describe a minor (hamlet) leader is the term *kwɔtahɛd* ('Quarter Head', pl. *bɔ kwɔtahɛd*), the circumstances of its use being frequently to emphasize the subordinate status of the man concerned in relation to the village leader. An example of the way in which foreign terms may be used to denote status may be quoted from Takwa village (cf. p. 48 above), where in 1954 the leader of Basok had written on his meeting-house 'Chief N——', the term 'chief' here translating the Kenyang *mfɔ* in a literal sense but not without provocation. On the other hand, when I discussed the constitution of Takwa village with its leader, the latter was at some pains to point out that N—— was merely 'one of his "Quarter Heads"', even denying to him the status of 'senior elder' of the village, which in other circumstances he might have claimed. While the terms used to describe the individual status of community leaders are varied and circumstantial in any village, the ranking of the dozen or so leading members of a village is clearly known and can be stated, even if conflicting claims are made in some individual cases.

The key to the status system of a Banyang village or village group lies in the corporate activities in which the members of the residential groups are collectively involved. The status of community leaders is in this respect no more than an extension of the general principle that underlies all community status: to the extent that a person is involved in community affairs – is an active, high-ranking member of associations, takes part in community meetings, is a member of the judicial council, or of the 'inner council' of the village – so is he a person with positive political standing and influence. The relevant term here is again relative in its meaning: *mu ɛtɔk*, 'a person of the community'. In a literal sense, any residential member of a community can be described as a *mu ɛtɔk* of that place (*mu ɛtɔk ɛTali, mu ɛtɔk ɛBara*, etc.). More commonly, however, and when the term does not refer directly to a named residential group, 'a person of the community' is someone with positive standing and influence within it, someone who has 'a voice in the community', who participates in the collective decisions of the group, who knows its 'secret affairs' (*ɛyu*), and who by his involvement in such activities forms part also of the network of reciprocities that lie at the centre of community life. The latter point is made in the saying: 'A person of the community, *mu ɛtɔk*, does not go to sleep hungry', i.e. such a person never knows when he will be called to share in the wine or food which is given, on a great many occasions, to be eaten collectively.

The degree of involvement in the corporate, and especially political, affairs of the community serves as the most general criterion distinguishing status. Women and 'slaves' (properly, persons of slave descent) are traditionally placed 'outside the community' and were excluded from its central collective activities; even today 'slaves' enter only on the periphery of community matters, and even then take an active part only usually at the level of a village section or hamlet. Other men who from poverty, lack of support from their relatives, or simply disinclination, take little part in the round of community meetings, wine-drinking sessions, and association activities can be described as *bo ndɛm*, 'people of no worth' or 'of no standing'. These are the people who live restricted lives, who do not often move beyond their own settlements or farms and who learn of what is going on only by hearsay. In this sense they may be said to be 'outside the community', or, more forcefully, to be 'lost in the bush'.

On the other hand, the *bo ɛtɔk*, 'the people of the community', are those persons of status who are collectively and corporately concerned in running the affairs of the community. 'Community leaders' form part of this category (lineage elders are its other most important component). In the past, as we have seen, a man started on the process of becoming a 'person of the community' by building his own settlement, where he was 'leader' of his own group of supporters. It remains, however, the leaders of somewhat larger residential groups – usually of hamlets – who are most centrally involved in the corporate village affairs and from among whose members the 'inner council' of a village is normally drawn. 'Leader' in his own hamlet, he is a 'person of the community' in the wider village. A further term describing the special status of someone who is subordinate to a main leader but nevertheless prominent at the subordinate level is *nɛm mu*: such a man is one who in any residential group supports its main leader, who has acquired status particularly by his own efforts and by representing a section of the wider group. It is a status, however, which is not without ambivalence. One of the commonest sayings of Banyang, which refers to the relativity of political status within their communities, is 'leadership is different: kɛnɛm is different' (kɛfɔ kɛkuri: kɛnɛm kɛkuri), where kɛnɛm is the quality of political prominence, of being a supporter without being a leader, of being, as it were, on the ladder without being at the top.

To give an example of these rather generalized statements: in Tali 1 the key, leading members of the village were: the village leader (whose settlement, Mbinjong, has been shown in *Figure 8*), Ta Taboko, Mr Tataw, Joseph Enaw, and at one time Peter Esong. These men were all members of the 'inner council' of the village and jointly conducted its central strategy. Between them they represented all the most important sections of the village. Ta Taboko was the recognized 'senior elder' of the village, but owed his position as much to his leadership of Tanyi Tabe and to his long prominence in village affairs: as we have seen, he was accepted as the informal leader of the sub-village Okorobak to Tanyi Tabe and in relation to the village leader (whom he followed in importance) represented the other half of the village. Mr Tataw had spent most of his working life away from the village, as a Government employee, and had returned with some capital and with the help of this had established himself in village affairs. He was spoken of in Tanyi Ako as its 'leader', a status which was said to have been formally delegated to him by the senior elder of that lineage group. Within the wider village his position was more clearly that of nɛm mu. Joseph Enaw, a man who had also spent many years working outside, was the combined leader and senior elder of the hamlet of Dekang, who had gained entry into the inner council mainly by his wealth, but in part also by his representation of Dekang: he was a respected man, but did not carry a great deal of weight in village discussions. Peter Esong was a highly articulate man, with a strong personality, who gained his position firstly in one of the sections of Kembong hamlet, became recognized as the leader of Kembong (a position again accorded by the senior elder of the inclusive lineage group, himself from another section of the hamlet), and proceeded to participate very actively in village affairs. In 1953 he had fallen into disgrace by being implicated in some of the actions of 'Tali 2' (then claiming its independence) and had also fallen foul of the senior elder of his (major) lineage group. He had been 'removed from the (inner) community' and his formal leadership of Kembong had been taken from him: he had by no means given up his claims to community status, however, and was then working to restore his standing. Thus on Christmas day of that year (a feast which Banyang have made their own: presents are given by husbands to wives and the husbands, expecting no food, gather to drink and talk) an informal meeting took place in Mr Tataw's house which included, with some others, all the persons named above, and which for the first time for many months Peter Esong entered, giving a bottle of brandy to commemorate the fact that he was drinking once more with the leading men of the community (the *ɛtɔk* in its most exclusive sense). In all, eight bottles of brandy were consumed that morning.

3

The Community and
Common Descent

Two principles of grouping

In the previous chapter we have been almost exclusively concerned with the nature and interrelationship of Banyang residential groups. Many indications have been given there, however, of the importance within the society of a second mode of grouping, that which is based upon the values of agnatic kinship or common descent. Common descent and common residence are the two basic principles of grouping within the society: all other institutions and modes of grouping are in some way dependent upon them.

Neither of these principles is exclusive of the other and the values upon which each is based interpenetrate with each other. *Bɔ ci*, agnatic kin (literally 'children of a begetter'),[1] commonly live together; this, indeed, is one of the features which distinguishes them from *bɔanɔ*, uterine kin (or 'children of a bearer'). Conversely, the people who together form 'one residential group', *ɛtɔk ɛmɔt*, generally also recognize the solidarity of common kinship; in a village council discussion one member may speak of another, for example, as 'child of my father', *mɔ ta ya*, precisely in the sense of being fellow-members of the same group. Again, and unlike some of the other Cross River peoples, this interpenetration of the two sets of values occurs at all levels of corporate grouping. A youth (of whatever relationship) who came in the past to live in the settlement of a man to whom he looked for protection and support, spoke of the latter as his 'father' and became himself one of the settlement leader's 'children'. At the highest level, the unity and solidarity of a village group, 'the whole community', are very frequently expressed in terms of the common kinship they share: all are 'children of one begetter', *bɔ ci amɔt*, descendants of a common ancestor.

[1] I discuss Kenyang kinship terms in more detail in my paper 'Genealogical Concepts or "Category Words"? A Study of Banyang Kinship Terminology,' *JRAI*, 1962.

Despite this overlapping of relationships and interchangeability of terms, the values of residential association are nevertheless different in kind from those of common agnatic kinship and give rise to different modes of social action. One runs the risk of over-simplifying in attempting to characterize each type of value-based action; yet, at that risk: those who live together in a common residential group are associated by their common interests, by their common dependence upon each other, but it is an association based upon a careful reciprocity of interests, where (to employ Gierke's distinction) the 'all' is the all of plurality rather than the all of unity.[1] In Kenyang, a residential community, an ɛtɔk, is an ncɛmti bo, a 'group of people' in the sense of an aggregate – a collectivity who should always *try* to be united, but who always *are* a collectivity. One might speak of a residential group as people bound by a common policy: in Kenyang the criterion of residential unity is their being of 'one voice' (ɛyɔŋ ɛmɔt). The corporate activities associated with residential grouping are governmental, policy-making, 'putting community matters in order'. The sanctions which support these activities are characteristically secular and coercive. By contrast, if a Manyang's residential alignments are his own choice – and, as we have seen, traditional settlement patterns carefully preserved this choice – he has no choice as to the kin-group into which he is born; common agnatic kinship is *ipso facto* a condition of unity, of identity. Perhaps the better contrast with the individualistic and voluntary character of residential association is, however, the extremely strong obligation never to deny one's kinship – this both in the literal sense of not denying the *fact* of the relationship and also

---

[1] Otto Gierke, *Political Theories of the Middle Age*, translated by F. W. Maitland (1900). Maitland himself has made telling use of this distinction in his Ford Lectures of 1897, *Township and Borough* (published 1898), where with special reference to Cambridge he traces how borough communities became 'corporate' in the way that village communities are not. It is central to his argument that the legal 'incorporation' of the borough communities by royal charter (the first being that of Hull in 1439) followed rather than preceded the social processes of developing corporateness. In my own terminology, the granting of a royal charter served constitutionally to 'incorporate' a township that had already acquired the operational unity of full corporateness in its internal government. It is relevant that Maitland takes issue with Maine in the latter's representation of the Family as a Corporation: 'But just in this matter of archaic "corporations", what I think we should demand before we let the phrase pass is some proof that the men who constitute the group are prepared to contrast what Dr Gierke calls the all of unity with the all of plurality, to contrast an "its" with an "ours", or to say that though this land is ours in a certain sense, it is not ours in another sense, for we are not co-owners of it' (p. 22). The same demand could be pressed against many of those social anthropologists who accept the ancestral guidance of Maine in treating descent groups as 'corporations'. In Chapter 8 I discuss further the verbal 'incorporation' of the ɛtɔk, the residential community, in the way Banyang speak of it.

73

in the sense of never refusing to help a kinsman when help is requested. Common agnatic kinship implies, then, a moral bond, an identity which is ascribed, 'given', and which cannot be denied. The 'all' is that of unity rather than that of plurality: in Kenyang a nɛrɛkɛt, a 'lineage group' or corporate group of kin, are mu amɔt, 'one person'. The activities in which kinsfolk are corporately involved are more distinctively long-term in outlook, group- rather than self-oriented, moral in tone: many of them are indeed ritual actions or are based on religious obligations. The sanctions which support these activities are characteristically moral and religious.

There are, as we have seen, occasions when the common descent of members of a residential group is stressed, or when agnatic kinship is equated with co-residence; but for the corporate organization of Banyang society the more significant relationship between these two principles of grouping, each with its associated set of values, is that of contrast, of mutually defining interaction, rather than that of correspondence, of equivalence. As a corporate group, a nɛrɛkɛt, a kin- or lineage-group (as I shall term it), is different in kind from an ɛtɔk, a residential community. In the morphology of Banyang society, common agnatic descent unites those who are residentially divided; it divides those who are residentially united. I shall examine each of these aspects in turn.

If Banyang cannot 'deny' their kinship with others, they can at least go to live somewhere else. Such residential separation weakens the effective, multi-plex, relationship that may have existed when such kinsmen were living together, but it will not sever the relationship as such, which trans-ferred now to a different context has paradoxically a somewhat greater chance to flourish. So in the context of past settlement patterns and in a way we have already described, Banyang refer to agnatic kin who agree to separate, or who are 'sent off' by a 'father', in order to report back opportunities or circumstances they encounter apart. The function served by such 'kinship-at-a-distance' is to provide for a less continuous, more flexible, relationship which is still formally recognized but whose effective-ness is occasional and dependent upon mutual interest. I describe this function as one of 'articulation'. It operates again at all levels of the society: the small settlements of the past (e.g. those of bɔ Mbu, Figure 5) were linked to each other through the descent connections of their leaders; so too the common descent shared by members of a village group, which is traced through the ancestral founder of its constituent villages, serves precisely to 'articulate' them – i.e. to link them as distinct units within a larger whole.

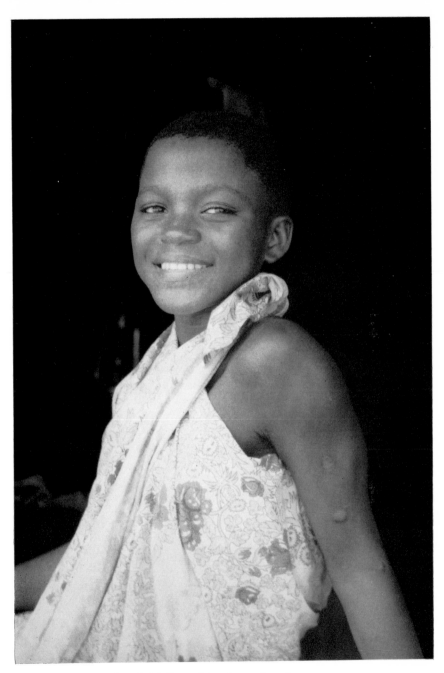

Plate 5 Rose, a schoolgirl from Kembong hamlet

Plate 6
Mbia
association

The articulating function of 'kinship-at-a-distance' blends with what we must refer to as the constitutional aspect of common descent. The point may seem less abstract if we refer back to the text already quoted which describes how Ndifaw village group came to be as it now is:

> When Ndifaw left Kembong and arrived here he begot Tanyi Takum and made him leader of Ebeagwa. . . . Then he begot Tanyi Tiku. He said: When I have died Tanyi Tiku should succeed me. If any of my 'children' kill a leopard . . . etc. (cf. above, p. 54).

The two significant elements of this account for a Manyang hearer are the disposition of the rights to a leopard and the genealogical links between Ndifaw and his 'sons'. The two do not indeed make sense unless they are read together, for they state in constitutional terms how villages became independent while yet remaining united – independent as bɛtɔk, 'communities'; united as a nɛrɛkɛt, a 'lineage group': independent by virtue of their leaders' separate rights to a leopard; united by virtue of their continued identity as agnatic kin. The remembered genealogy for a village group is then 'constitutional' in the same sense but in a different way from the disposition of rights to a leopard: it is the 'recognized', 'received', 'legitimate' account of relationships that unite people, but it acquires this status not by political action (such as affects distribution of rights to a leopard) but by, as it were, historical sedimentation, 'kinship-at-a-distance' become 'genealogical charter'. (But *not*, we would note, the only item of the charter.)

We have described the second aspect of the interrelationship between the two principles of grouping as one where agnatic descent 'divides those who are residentially united'. This differentiating function of agnatic descent within the context of community grouping is one of the most obvious and regular features of Banyang social structure. Whatever common kinship the members of a residential group share (and they are likely to share some links, however distant), differences of descent are bound to exist within the group. Such differences serve to 'precipitate out' (as it were) a series of internal groupings, whose members are distinguished from the wider community in which they are placed by their separate identity as kinsfolk and by the mutual support and solidarity which each such group of persons is expected to exhibit. In speaking of the values of residential association above, I have emphasized the quality of individualism which accrues to action in this context. It would, however, be more accurate to depict a 'community', ɛtɔk, not as an association of individuals, but as an association of kin-groups – either *bɛkɛt*, 'house-holds', at the level of the traditional settlement, or *banɛrɛkɛt*, 'lineage groups', at the higher level of hamlet or village.

It is of some importance to the understanding of Banyang descent groups and of the genealogies which depict their interrelationships that the formative arrangement of 'lineage groups' within a 'community' (or of 'households' within a traditional settlement) is 'segmental' rather than 'segmentary'.[1] Typically, each lineage group is one unit in a series of like units, of equal status, into which the wider community is exhaustively divided. Descent grouping emerges then out of a kind of contrapuntal effect with residential grouping: genealogical relationships must be read in relationship with residential grouping. In *Figure 14*, for example,

Figure 14 Descent and residential grouping

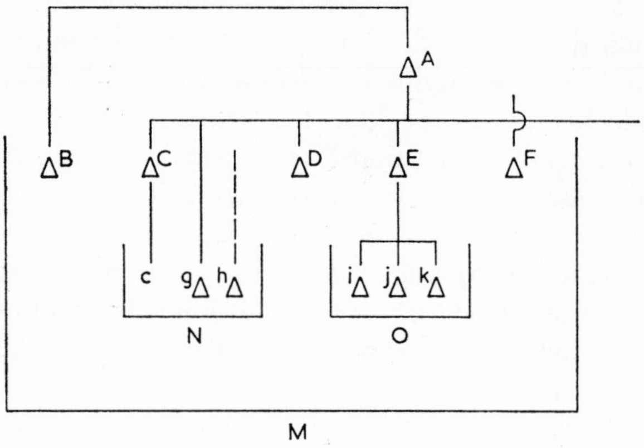

B, C, D, E, and F are each the ancestral founder of a lineage group named after them (*bɔ B*, 'the children of B', etc.), all of them making up the residential group M. The genealogical relationships between these ances-tral founders are unequal and varied: it is not, however, their relative position in the genealogy which determines the relationship of the lineage groups which they founded so much as the fact that each has a distinct genealogical status *in the context of* the residential group M which includes them all.

The same principle applies also where lineage groups are internally divided into smaller lineage groups of a similar form. Again, it is not the purely genealogical context of the division which is significant but the

[1] The distinction between 'segmentary' and 'segmental' units has been usefully made by Middleton and Tait in their Introduction to *Tribes Without Rulers*, p. 8.

residential context of the genealogical relationships. In fact Banyang are often loath to admit that a lineage group, a nɛrɛkɛt, can include further smaller lineage groups, banɛrɛkɛt, which runs against the ideal of solidary identity which a lineage group is expected to exhibit, and here the term 'house' or 'household', ɛkɛt, is sometimes used to emphasize that the smaller groups are of a different order from the larger one. Nevertheless, in a great many instances, lineage groups are so divided, but it is a division which occurs always in relationship to residential grouping. Thus, for example, in *Figure 14* a member of the minor lineage group, bɔ j, will count himself as belonging to a different lineage group from bɔ i and bɔ k only in the context of the hamlet O; within the context of the village M, bɔ i, bɔ j, and bɔ k will see themselves as a unitary group of kinsfolk, bɔ E, in relation to all the other similar groups in the village. This example has been given for lineage groups whose ancestral connections *could* be read segmentarily. Equally if not more frequently, however, the kind of genealogical pattern which occurs is that shown for hamlet N. Here exactly the same set of two-level allegiances applies, but with the additional fact that the name of the inclusive lineage group has itself a double or 'two-level' reference: thus in the context of the village (M) bɔ C are a major lineage group, a segmental component of the village, but the same name (bɔ c) has in the context of the hamlet (N) a more limited reference to what is only one of three minor lineage groups composing the hamlet. Regarding the ancestral founders of the other minor lineage groups, g and h, we should note that (as in the case of B–F in the village) it is not their precise genealogical relationship with C that determines their co-membership of the hamlet but rather that *within this context* each ancestral founder has a distinct status.

One further point must be made. In *Figure 14* bɔ C and hamlet N are the 'same' group, and bɔ E and hamlet O are the 'same'. Where, as in such cases, a lineage group is identified with a residential group (a nɛrɛkɛt with an ɛtɔk), this dualism of identity can be related to the two ways in which such groups face: facing outwards to the inclusive village, bɔ C have the kinship solidarity of a lineage group; facing inwards, they are a 'policy-bound' residential association, an ɛtɔk with partial autonomy. To revert to my earlier distinction, the identification of a descent with a residential group concerns always the 'constitutional' status of the group (it serves thus to 'place' or 'articulate' the group in its formal, 'recognized' relationship to others): 'operationally' the dual identity emerges in two separate sets of activities – *either* as an ɛtɔk or as a nɛrɛkɛt.

It will be clear from what has already been said that the relationship between common descent and residential association as two principles of grouping within Banyang society is radically dissimilar from that which holds in a classical segmentary, lineage-based society, such as the Nuer or Tiv. To give only some of the more obvious differences: in a segmentary lineage-based society there is a formal congruence between the system of lineages and the series of territorial groups, but in Banyang society such a congruence is lacking; there is an all-embracing genealogy for each village group but there is no way of telling *from the genealogy* what residential groupings or relationships are likely to exist. In a segmentary lineage-based society membership of a territorial group is formally equivalent to membership of a lineage, so that a person's relationship to people of different territorial groups will be expressed in lineage terms, but in Banyang society membership of an *ɛtɔk*, a residential group, is different and does not correspond (except incidentally) with membership of a *nɛrɛkɛt*, which is conceived of as a smaller, constituent unit within a residential group, lineage group membership *mediating* membership of the wider group. Nevertheless, in one respect there is an important resemblance between the two modes of grouping described here and the comparable systems of a segmentary lineage-based society: this is the fact that homologous groups appear regularly at different orders or levels of grouping and that the total formation of groups is believed to have occurred as an on-going ever-continuous process.

It will be part of my argument in a later chapter that in the on-going processes by which (in the traditional society) descent and residential groups were formed, the key, determining process was always that by which residential groups acquired the size and strength to assert their own autonomy. Here, where we are concerned rather with the present morphology of social grouping, I would draw attention instead to the critical importance of the *village* as a *constitutionally determined residential group*. As it is in relation to this order of residential grouping that all other residential groups can be distinguished, so it is in relation to the village that we can distinguish different orders of descent grouping. To do so, however, we must turn from our discussion of the general features of the interrelationship between the two principles of grouping to a more specific description of how Banyang lineage groups fit into and complete the formal, constitutional ordering of the complex community already outlined.

Descent grouping and community constitution

Throughout Banyang country the most extended order of community grouping is associated with a named descent group, which in most cases is the widest group of people tracing descent from a common ancestor.[1] In many cases this descent name is that by which the village group is known, e.g. *bɔ Ndifɔ*, *bɔ Tanyi Nkoŋo*, *bɔ Ayok Ɛtayak* etc., but this is not always so: 'Mbang' and 'Tinto' are known more commonly by their names as residential groups and in two other cases the place-name which refers primarily to a village within the village group ('Tali' and 'Etoko') can also be used of the village group as a whole. In two further instances 'villages' do not form part of a wider 'community' and in both cases it is they which are associated with a named descent group (*bɔ Bɛkaŋ* for Eyanchang, *bɔ Ncuɔmbirɛ* for Bachu Akagbe). The ancestral founder of a village group whose present members are described collectively as his descendants or 'children' is not necessarily the 'apical' or the most inclusive ancestor; collateral kin and strangers have in most cases become assimilated to the dominant descent line established by him. It is nevertheless the genealogy stemming from him which serves to express the ultimate, traditionally maintained unity of this, the most extended 'community', and ascribes to its members such common kinship as will distinguish them as a corporate kin-group, *nɛrɛkɛt amɔt*, in relation to outsiders, or to Banyang as a whole.

Villages within a village group are usually linked to this inclusive genealogy through their own ancestral founders, usually 'sons' but sometimes more distant descendants of the ancestral founder of the village group. As in the case of the Ndifaw traditional account already quoted, there is usually a brief and sometimes a more extended statement of how the 'son' or descendant 'acquired his own leadership' (*akwɛn kɛfɔ ki*) or moved apart to 'found his own community' (*ate ɛtɔk ɛji*). So also, when describing the constitution of a village group, Banyang tend to characterize the village specifically as a residential group with its own leader in contrast to the wider village group spoken of now as a *nɛrɛkɛt*: they speak thus of the *bɛtɔk* composing a *nɛrɛkɛt*, or may list the number of 'leaders', *bafɔ*, which are recognized within the *nɛrɛkɛt*. Within the context of a constitutional discussion, villages can be, and often are, identified with named descent groups, the village members being then described as the 'children', *bɔ*, of the ancestral founder and first leader of the village: thus Ejwengang village can be spoken of as *bɔ Tanyi Tiku*, Ebeagwa as *bɔ*

[1] The exceptions to the otherwise general rule are *bɔ Nkɔkɛnɔk* I and II and the two village groups and one village of the extreme Lower Banyang who recognized descent from a distant, somewhat mythical figure, 'Asae', whom they share with other eastern Ejagham villages. According to some elders, however, 'Asae' is 'like God (Mandem)' or was 'created by God', and *bɔ Asae* are nothing less than all people.

79

Tanyi Takum. Such a designation, however, is almost entirely constitutional in reference, serving to relate the village to the wider genealogy, and cannot be taken to imply that the village ever acts in any effective sense as a *nɛrɛkɛt*, a corporate group of kinsfolk. Invariably, also, the descent names applied to villages have a second level reference *within* the village to one of its constituent lineage groups: within Ejwengang *bɔ Tanyi Tiku* are merely one of its major lineage groups, and so also for *bɔ Tanyi Takum* within Ebeagwa.

Every village is divided into a series of sections, spoken of as 'centres' (*mantɔ*, or *bantɔ*) or local foci of the village as residential community. Such sections can invariably be described as *banɛrɛkɛt* and are referred to here as 'major lineage groups'. Major lineage groups are the segmental units of a village: *banɛrɛkɛt* within an *ɛtɔk*. They can always be identified by a descent name, and most elders in a village are able to list without hesitation the major lineage groups composing it. Apart from their form as lineage groups, *banɛrɛkɛt*, some village sections have also the form of residential groups, *bɛtɔk*; these have earlier been described as 'hamlets'. Where a village section has itself the form of a residential group – i.e. is a hamlet – it will contain its own 'sections' (*mantɔ*) which have the form of named *banɛrɛkɛt* and are described here as 'minor lineage groups'. As 'major' lineage groups are the segmental units of a village, so 'minor' lineage groups are the segmental units of a hamlet. We shall later see that most corporate activities of a specifically kinship character (e.g. all formal arrangements concerning marriage, the distribution of inheritance, ritual acts of various kinds) are shared between the major and minor lineage groups, which are similar also in their corporate form and their relationship to the residential group in which they are situated.

As this account implies, village 'sections' do not have a constant or universal form. Some have the form *only* of lineage groups: these are solidary, corporate groups, represented by a senior elder, and lack further internal divisions except of a domestic or interpersonal kind. Other village sections may be identified with a descent group but have more clearly the form of hamlets, residential groups in their own right: these are generally known by a place-name, are represented by a leader, *mfɔ*, rather than by a senior elder, and are themselves internally divided into sections which are minor lineage groups. Size is probably the most important factor effecting this variation in form, the larger village sections (or the sections of the larger villages) tending to have the form of hamlets as well as (major) lineage groups, the smaller village sections having the form only of lineage groups. There are many examples which illustrate the polar extremes of this contrast (e.g. the village sections of Tali versus those of Bara or Ejwengang; the hamlet of Talinchang versus *bɔ Mbunɔ* in Bara), but we should note too the existence of other village sections (e.g. *bɔ Tanyi Ako* or Nchemba/*bɔ Mbu* of Tali 1; *bɔ Esɔŋafiet* in Bara) which are less determinately placed, being more than merely lineage groups but less than full hamlets.

Figure 15 Descent groups within community constitution

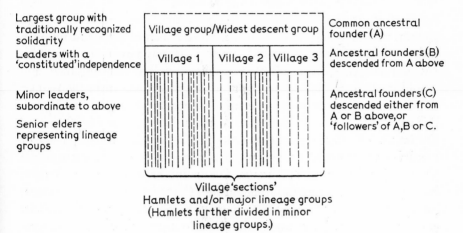

Village 'sections'
Hamlets and/or major lineage groups
(Hamlets further divided in minor
lineage groups.)

Figure 15 shows the way in which the various orders of corporate descent grouping (the 'widest descent group' associated normally with the village group,[1] the 'major' and 'minor' lineage groups) fit into and complement the constitutional ordering of the complex community previously described. Examples of actual genealogies and their relationship to residential grouping will be given in the next section.

Can we speak of these descent groups as being themselves part of 'village group constitution'? I have tried to indicate in the previous section how in an entirely substantive sense the 'received' account of how the ancestral founders of a village group are genealogically interrelated serves precisely to state the 'constitutional' or formally recognized

[1] I hesitate to speak of this order of corporate descent grouping by the term 'clan' since it is characterized by much more than unilineal descent: it is also, and more especially, a residential group, and includes many non-unilineal kin who have become assimilated to it. Although Banyang refer to this order of grouping by the term *nereket* they would never confuse it with the *banereket*, 'lineage groups', within a village or hamlet, and for this reason I hesitate, also, to categorize it with the latter. My way round this difficulty has been to avoid using a category term for this order of descent grouping and to refer to it descriptively as seems most appropriate in the context it appears in.

relationships between the various parts of the village group. Village group genealogies are closely combined in this context with statements of how certain residential groups, or their ancestral founders, acquired the constitutional status that they now have. Such statements do not *confirm* but *qualify* genealogical relationships: the 'son' becomes 'independent leader'. The village group genealogy is then a 'charter' only in the residual sense of having been modified and qualified by later events; or (to make the same point in a different way) its function is not to 'validate' so much as to state what continues to be valid.

Whether or not the lineage groups which correspond to village sections and sub-sections should be described as part of the 'constitutional' ordering of a village group would seem to be largely a matter of definition. I would be inclined to speak of such units as indeed 'constitutional' and would point to the formal recognition accorded to them in the regular divisions of meat or money made at the village or hamlet level to support this view. On the other hand the 'constitutional' status of village and hamlet sections is less critical than that of the residential group – village or hamlet – which includes them, and to a large extent it is the status of the latter which determines *their* status. Two points are relevant here. Firstly, the 'segmental' ordering of lineage groups (*banɛrɛkɛt*) within a residential group (*ɛtɔk*) follows initially as an operational consequence of their social context: they are 'in-groups' within an 'out-group', clusters of near-kinsfolk among co-residents who are only distant kinsfolk. This operational relationship acquires some formal recognition when a lineage group is treated (e.g. in divisions) as a segmental unit of the wider residential group; but this shift of status is not a major one, and rarely threatens the interests of anyone else (especially if their own closest kinsfolk live in *another* residential group). Secondly, although there is some variation in the operational form of village sections (whether they operate as residential groups – hamlets – or as corporate kin-groups – lineage groups), this variation does not affect directly their constitutional position as sections of the village. Inversely, whether a lineage group is a 'major' or 'minor' one (and in many respects the 'major' lineage groups of a politically undifferentiated village have similar operational features to the 'minor' lineage groups of the hamlets of other villages) follows entirely from the constitutional status of the residential group in which the lineage group is situated. To put the point in more practical terms: the best way for a 'minor' lineage group to advance its status is by supporting an advance in status for the hamlet it is in – and if its members are not willing to do this, they ought to go off to join another residential group elsewhere.

Community constitution and descent grouping in two village groups

Figures 16–19 summarize the corporate organization of two village groups. Except for 'Small Mamfe' in *bɔ Ayok Ɛtayak*, constitutional grouping has been given down to village sections in full, but not all hamlet sections have been shown. The genealogical diagrams (*Figures 17 and 19*) show in each case the interrelationship of the founding ancestors of villages, of village sections and of some (but not all) hamlet sections.

The residential grouping of the Ndifaw village group (*Figures 16–17*) has already been described and some account given of the stories which describe how its community constitution came to be as it now is. A summary outline of this constitution was frequently made by referring (before Tali 2 became independent) to the 'three sons' of Ndifaw, Tanyi Takum, Tanyi Tiku, and Mfonjo, each of whom was said to have acquired separate (village) leadership. (Tali 2 in its quest for independence elaborated this story by including a fourth son, Tanyi Nga.) Within each village, the genealogical links between the ancestral founders of the village sections are varied, and the pattern evidenced for each village supports the general account of how the village group developed. Thus in Tali 1 and 2 the ancestral founders of the village sections are in general remembered as the 'sons' of Ndifaw, but include also: a full-sibling (Arak), who is said to have accompanied his brother there; one of the latter's sons (Tangaberi), who is the separate founder of a different section, and two 'assimilated' descendants (Tanyi Aye, the 'child of a daughter', and Mfongwa, more distantly a descendant of Ndifaw through Tanyi Ako, see below). Among these 'sons' of Ndifaw, who are traditionally said to have continued to live close to their father's former place of settlement, Mfonjo is somewhat pointedly accorded the status of 'last-born' (cf. p. 56). In contrast to those of the two Tali villages, the ancestral founders of the village sections of Ejwengang and Ebeagwa are more closely and intricately related, in both cases major lineage groups having been founded by a process of hiving off from the descent line of the village founder. The genealogy shown for Ejwengang supports the picture Ndifaw members draw of Tanyi Tiku with his small group of 'followers' moving off to found the separate community which is now a village. The total genealogy of the village group has thus a one-sided development, a pattern which is repeated within Ebeagwa and is characteristic of many village group genealogies. (One link which it has not been possible to show in the diagram is the full-sibling relationship believed to have existed between Tanyi Mbi of Dekang hamlet in Tali 1 and Tanyi Takum, the founder

83

Figure 16 Constitutional grouping of the Ndifaw village group

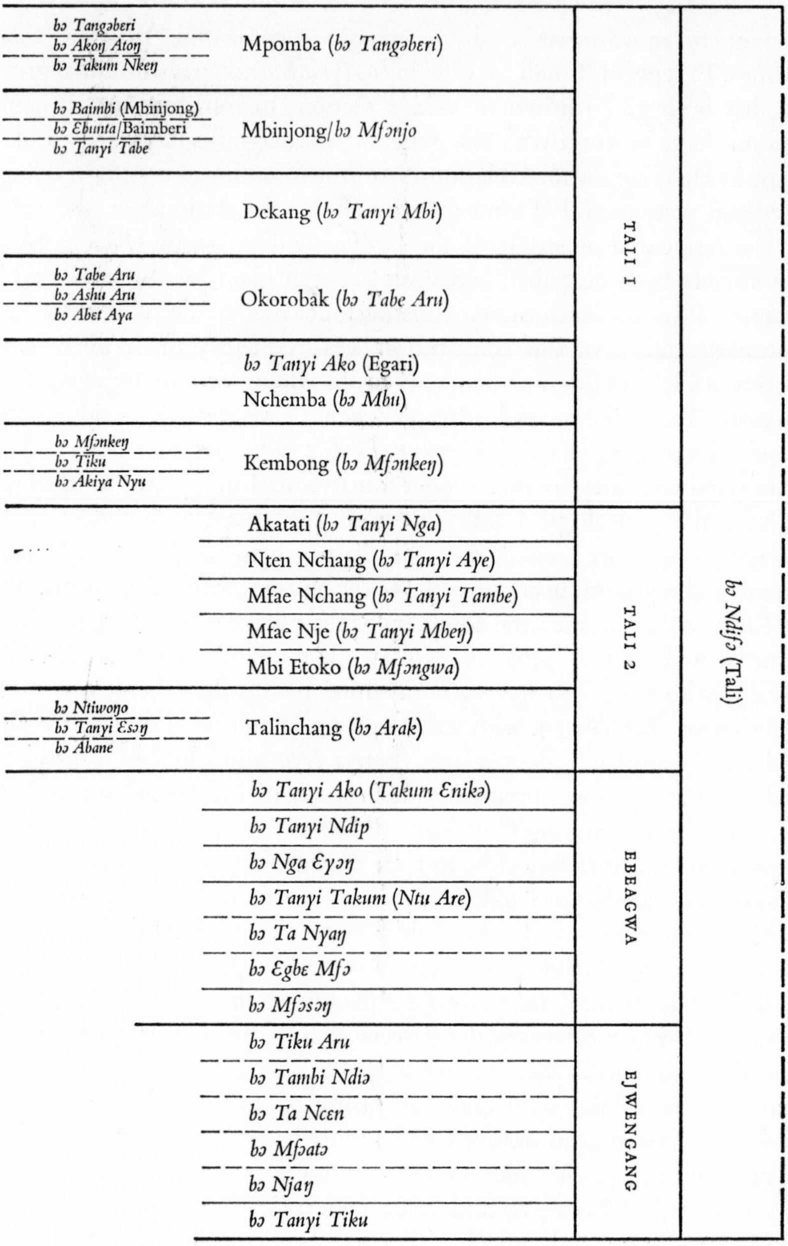

bɔ Taŋgɔberi / bɔ Akoŋ Atoŋ / bɔ Takum Nkeŋ	Mpomba (bɔ Taŋgɔberi)		
bɔ Baimbi (Mbinjong) / bɔ Ebunta/Baimberi / bɔ Tanyi Tabe	Mbinjong/bɔ Mfɔnjo		
	Dekang (bɔ Tanyi Mbi)	TALI 1	bɔ Ndifɔ (Tali)
bɔ Tabe Aru / bɔ Ashu Aru / bɔ Abet Aya	Okorobak (bɔ Tabe Aru)		
	bɔ Tanyi Ako (Egari)		
	Nchemba (bɔ Mbu)		
bɔ Mfɔnkeŋ / bɔ Tiku / bɔ Akiya Nyu	Kembong (bɔ Mfɔnkeŋ)		
	Akatati (bɔ Tanyi Nga)		
	Nten Nchang (bɔ Tanyi Aye)		
	Mfae Nchang (bɔ Tanyi Tambe)	TALI 2	
	Mfae Nje (bɔ Tanyi Mbeŋ)		
	Mbi Etoko (bɔ Mfɔngwa)		
bɔ Ntiwoŋo / bɔ Tanyi Esɔŋ / bɔ Abane	Talinchang (bɔ Arak)		
	bɔ Tanyi Ako (Takum Ɛnikɔ)		
	bɔ Tanyi Ndip		
	bɔ Nga Ɛyɔŋ		
	bɔ Tanyi Takum (Ntu Are)	EBEAGWA	
	bɔ Ta Nyaŋ		
	bɔ Ɛgbɛ Mfɔ		
	bɔ Mfɔsɔŋ		
	bɔ Tiku Aru		
	bɔ Tambi Ndiɔ		
	bɔ Ta Ncɛn	EJWENGANG	
	bɔ Mfɔatɔ		
	bɔ Njaŋ		
	bɔ Tanyi Tiku		

Figure 17 Descent and residential grouping within the Ndifaw village group

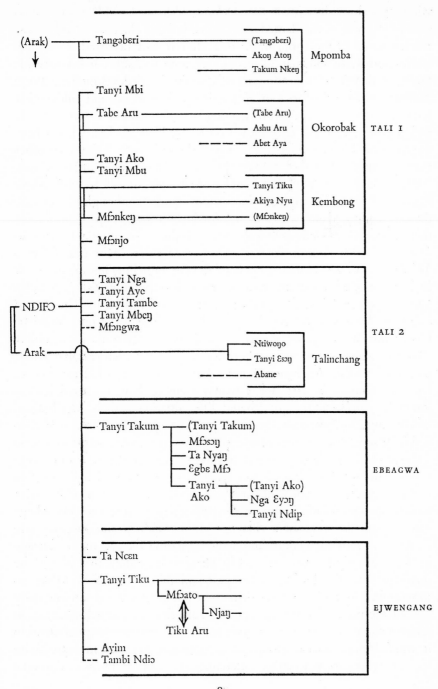

of Ebeagwa village. This relationship is one of the most suggestive of the whole genealogy since it was Mfo Dekang – 'the leader of Dekang' – who is said to have been supplanted by Ndifaw. Ndifaw elders insist when they tell the story of the supplanting that after it had occurred '*bɔ Dɛkaŋ*' became no more and that 'all people are now *bɔ Ndifɔ*'. It is noticeable however that in all the accounts of constitutional development, Tanyi Takum is cited as the first to have acquired independence and unlike other accounts of village origins this gaining of independence is stated briefly and abruptly, as in the text quoted on p. 54. Nevertheless, when I have suggested to Ndifaw elders that Tanyi Mbi and Tanyi Takum are other than the true 'children' of Ndifaw they have always denied it.)

The village sections of Tali 1 and 2 are known mostly by their place-names and most of them have the form of hamlets, although in each case they are associated also with a named (major) lineage group. Traditionally there were twelve sections in Tali, but with the access of independence to Tali 2 a further section has been recognized there, 'Mbi Etoko' or *bɔ Mfɔngwa*, who were formerly part of the (again major) lineage group of *bɔ Tanyi Ako*, who continue now as a rump group within Tali 1. (See also Ch. 12, pp. 295–296, for further discussion of this case.) The special case of *bɔ Mfɔnjo*, who have always held the village leadership, should be noted: this lineage group constitutes a single village section, but unlike all other village sections its members live in separate settlements in different parts of the village (cf. *Figures 8* and *12*) and form there what are in effect separate hamlets. In fact, what would seem to have occurred here is something similar to the growth and differentiation of the village leaders' descent lines in Ejwengang and Ebeagwa, except that in Tali these residentially separated branches have not acquired separate status as village sections and major lineage groups in their own right. (Even so, one of the residentially separated branches of this lineage group, *bɔ Tanyi Tabe*, has within the sub-village of which it is part equal status with the other major lineage groups which compose the sub-village: were this sub-village ever to gain the status of a village, *bɔ Tanyi Tabe* would automatically count as one of its sections and would become then a 'major' lineage group in exactly the same way as *bɔ Mfɔngwa* have done in Tali 2.) The power of the Tali leaders in the past and the ability of *bɔ Mfɔnjo* to monopolize succession within their own lineage group are undoubtedly part of the political advantage gained from their continued solidarity in relation to the wider village. It gives rise however to the unusual situation in which 'minor' lineage groups (as we must call them) are identified with hamlets which are not further differentiated, except in terms of domestic groups and interpersonal relations. The four other village sections whose internal composition has been shown in both *Figures 16* and *17* are by contrast quite regular: each is both a major lineage group and a hamlet, and as a hamlet is further divided into minor lineage groups. In three cases the name by which the major lineage group is known has also in the hamlet context a second-level reference to one of its constituent minor lineage groups.

The three village sections of Lower Ebeagwa (which are hamlets and major lineage groups) have very much the same form as those just described for Tali, although their internal composition is not shown in detail. I am less certain about my classification of the village sections of Upper Ebeagwa, which in their present composite settlement cannot readily be described as residential groups in their own right, although at least two of them (*bɔ Mfɔsɔŋ* and the 'rump' major lineage group of *bɔ Tanyi Takum*) have some of the features of hamlets. In Ejwengang we reach clarity at the other extreme, where most of the village sections have the form only of lineage groups (although lineage groups that continue to inhabit distinct sections of the village settlement) and lack the residential autonomy of hamlets. Nor are these village sections/major lineage groups further differentiated internally, as are most of the village sections in (for example) Tali I. A relevant comparative point is that in their residential and descent structure, and in the genealogical position of their ancestral founders, there is no radical dissimilarity between Ejwengang as a village and (say) Okorobak as a hamlet. Their essential difference is in their constitutional status as residential groups – in one case with an independent leader, in the other a subordinate leader. Certainly, as Ndifaw members see it, Tabe Aru *might* have been successful in his bid for independent leadership; and if Okorobak had obtained (like Ejwengang) the status of a village all that would be required in *Figure 17* would be a certain flexing of the genealogy in relation to the newly ranked residential group, without in any way substantively changing the relationships shown.

The corporate organization of the Lower Banyang Ayok Etayak village group (*Figures 18–19*), is basically similar to that which has been just discussed, but shows a more accentuated 'one-sided' development of the genealogy in relation to residential grouping, a feature which has already been remarked on for the Ndifaw group. Etemetek (its name in the eastern Ejagham dialect means 'former' or 'original settlement') is an extremely small village which suffered considerably, losing much of its population, in the punitive expedition that followed the 1904 uprising. At the time of settlement consolidation, it joined the village

Figure 18 Constitutional grouping of the Ayok Etayak village group

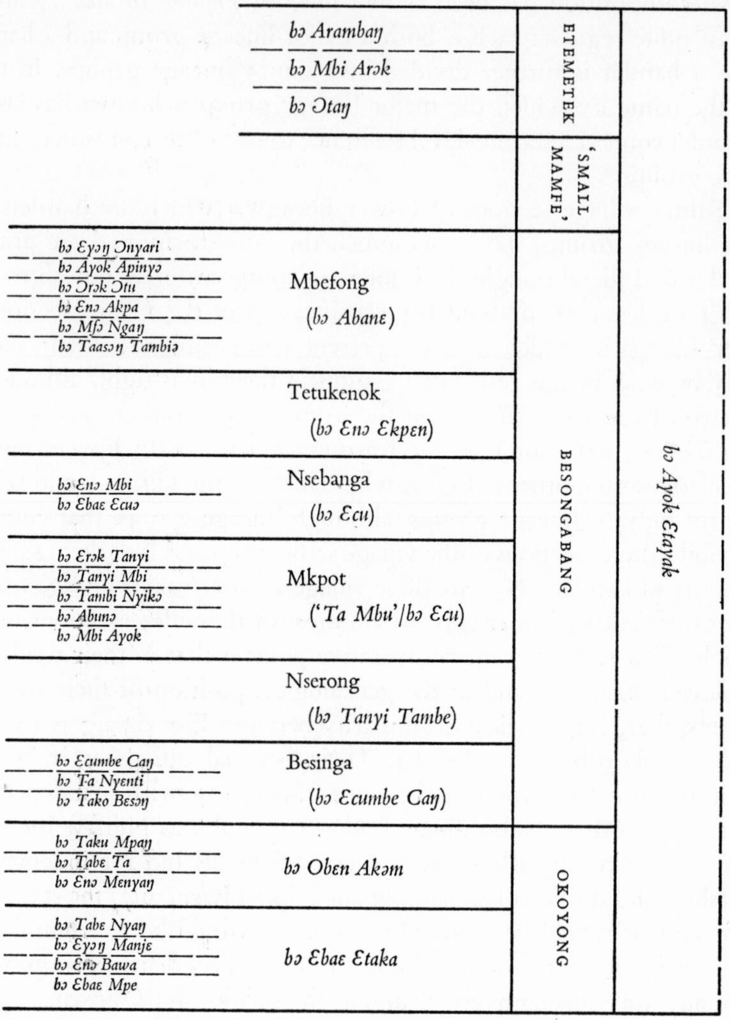

	bɔ Arambaŋ		ETEMETEK	
	bɔ Mbi Arɔk			
	bɔ Ɔtaŋ			
		'SMALL MAMFE'		
bɔ Eyɔŋ Ɔnyari	Mbefong			
bɔ Ayok Apinyɔ	(bɔ Abanɛ)			
bɔ Ɔrɔk Ɔtu				
bɔ Enɔ Akpa				
bɔ Mfɔ Ngaŋ				
bɔ Taasɔŋ Tambiɔ				
	Tetukenok			
	(bɔ Enɔ Ɛkpɛn)			
bɔ Enɔ Mbi	Nsebanga			
bɔ Ɛbaɛ Ɛcuɔ	(bɔ Ɛcu)		BESONGABANG	bɔ Ayok Etayak
bɔ Erɔk Tanyi	Mkpot			
bɔ Tanyi Mbi	('Ta Mbu'/bɔ Ɛcu)			
bɔ Tambi Nyikɔ				
bɔ Abunɔ				
bɔ Mbi Ayok				
	Nserong			
	(bɔ Tanyi Tambe)			
bɔ Ɛcumbe Caŋ	Besinga			
bɔ Ta Nyɛnti	(bɔ Ɛcumbe Caŋ)			
bɔ Tako Besɔŋ				
bɔ Taku Mpaŋ	bɔ Obɛn Akɔm			
bɔ Tabɛ Ta			OKOYONG	
bɔ Enɔ Mɛnyaŋ				
bɔ Tabɛ Nyaŋ	bɔ Ɛbaɛ Ɛtaka			
bɔ Eyɔŋ Manjɛ				
bɔ Ɛnɔ Bawa				
bɔ Ɛbaɛ Mpe				

88

Figure 19 Descent and residential grouping within the Ayok Etayak village group

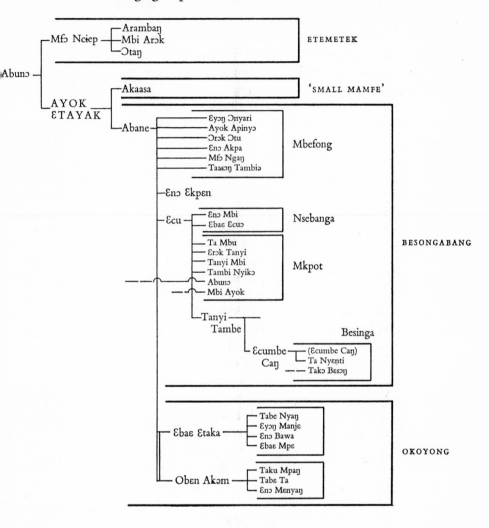

89

of Eyanchang, but under the British administration first moved apart and later regained its formal independence as a village. 'Small Mamfe' – Besongabang elders refer to it by the traditional name 'Kembong' – is again a very small village, which suffered similarly from the punitive expedition and in earlier fighting with Eshobi, and is now absorbed into the modern, largely immigrant, commercial town of Mamfe. By contrast Besongabang is now (after the splitting of Tali) the largest Banyang village, with a population of about a thousand. It is situated four miles from Mamfe and for many years has had a Basel Mission and a large school. Okoyong, a village of perhaps 150–200 persons, was formerly separate from Besongabang, but at the time of the Germans' first arrival returned to build with Besongabang and only later, under the British administration, returned to build near its former site, when it eventually acquired recognition as an independent village.[1]

Ayok Etayak, remembered as the ancestral founder of the village group, is said to have been the son of Abunaw, who lived at Etemetek. The story is told that Ayok Etayak left his father and came to live in the fork of the Mainyu and Bali rivers, where his community grew and prospered. He begot there two sons, Akaasa and Abane. Akaasa continued to live where his father lived, and it is as his descendants that the community that remained there (Kembong, now 'Small Mamfe' and occupying a different site) are known. Abane, his brother, left to build separately, coming then to the present locality of Besongabang: it is said that the reason why he left was because his wives and children were constantly being drowned in the river. Abane became the founder and first leader of Besongabang, whose members can be collectively spoken of as *bɔ Abane*. The fourth village founder is Ebae Etaka, one of the sons of Abane, who has the reputation of having been a headstrong, violent man. Various reasons are given for his going off to live separately. Characteristically I was told on one occasion in Besongabang that Abane sent Ebae Etaka to live at Okoyong to report on slave transactions, but in Okoyong itself a more detailed story was told of how the people of the neighbouring village of Ntenako, resentful of Ebae Etaka's behaviour, ambushed him and his full-brother when they were going to collect tribute from them, and killed his brother. Ebae Etaka wished to conduct a war of revenge, but Abane, his father, refused. For this reason Ebae Etaka went to live

[1] The 1953 Census figures are Etemetek 41, Besongabang 1,046, Okoyong 386. The Okoyong figure includes, however, a large stranger community, built around the Roman Catholic Mission, a mile or so apart from the village. In 1965 Etemetek was certainly larger than 41, but probably not more than 100. 'Small Mamfe' was not distinguished from Mamfe itself in the Census.

separately, and, turning now to Akaasa (of 'Small Mamfe') for help, eventually did make war on Ntenako. Yet another story, told this time in Besongabang, relates the separation to a manœuvre by Ebae Etaka to obtain his share of his father's possessions before the latter had died. Okoyong today remain *bɔ Ɛbaɛ Ɛtaka*, or, more strictly *bɔ Ɛtaka*, where 'Etaka' is the common mother of the two full-brothers.

It will be noticed that it is not the apical ancestor (Abunaw) but Ayok Etayak who has given his name to the village group. When asked why this should be so, Besongabang elders pointed to the proliferation of Ayok Etayak's descendants in relation to the fewer descendants, or 'children', of Abunaw. (A second reason may lie in Etemetek's separation and only later reassimilation to the village group: even today its territory is not continuous with that of the other villages in the group but lies beyond the territory of Nchang village of Mfotek village group.) Today the only remnant of *bɔ Abunɔ* as a named group of kinsfolk is one of the minor lineage groups in the village section and hamlet of Mkpot in Besongabang. Etemetek themselves trace their descent more directly from one 'Mfo Nciep', 'gun leader', who like Ebae Etaka has the reputation of having been a fierce and irascible community leader. (*Nci ɛp* is the name given to a shorter-barrelled, more lethal gun than the common Dane gun.)

Etemetek is divided into three sections, each an undifferentiated major lineage group. Okoyong, still a relatively small village, is divided somewhat unusually into only two sections. which trace their descent respectively from Ebae Etaka, and his full-brother, who was killed in the exploit which led to the founding of the village but whose sons were brought by Ebae Etaka to live with him when he moved. Okoyong elders insisted that each of these sections was a lineage group, *nerɛkɛt*, in its own right and that the sub-divisions within them were merely 'households', *bɛkɛt*, within the wider group. In fact their form is quite consistently that of minor lineage groups. A division within the village is shared firstly between the two sections and then redistributed between their own internal segments.

The internal organization of the very large Besongabang village is complex, but repeats a basically simple pattern of lateral genealogical secession in relation to residential grouping, which is already evidenced by the village group genealogy as a whole. There are six traditionally recognized village sections, each with the form of both a (major) lineage group and a hamlet. (A seventh section, *bɔ Ayok Mbi Awɔ*, has more recently been recognized for tax purposes.) Its founding ancestor, not shown in the genealogy in *Figure 20*, is said to have been junior full-sibling to Abane, who left Abane to live with Tanyi Tambe, to whom he was therefore *manɔ*, matrikinsman. As their designation as 'sections' or 'centres' of the village (*mantɔ*) implies, each of these has equal status with the others. Nevertheless, an intermediate series of linkages is recognized which follows genealogical relationships (although segmentally rather than segmentarily and with multiple-level use of proper names). These groupings are shown

Figure 20 Genealogy relating section founders within Besongabang village

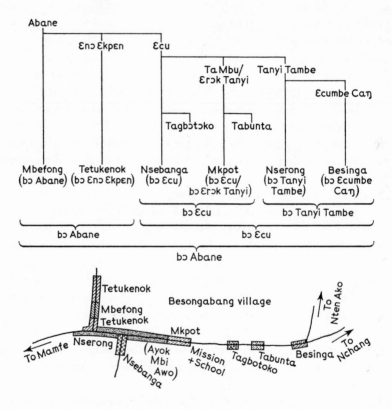

in *Figure 20*. Besongabang as a whole (*bɔ Abane*) is divided into two main descent groups (the separated *bɔ Ɛcu* and the rump *bɔ Abane*), which correspond with 'sub-villages' in terms of residential grouping: each of these two main groups occupies a distinct part of the village and each has its own representative leader, informally responsible for affairs within that part. (These are the two key men in the village, the village leader himself representing *bɔ Ɛcu*, the senior elder and minor leader of Tetukenok representing *bɔ Abane*.) One of these parts is then directly divided into two of the six village sections (Tetukenok hamlet, associated with the separated major lineage group of *bɔ Ɛnɔ Ɛkpɛn*; and Mbefong hamlet, associated with the rump *bɔ Abane*, here a major lineage group). The other part (*bɔ Ɛcu*) is divided into two further intermediate groups (the separated *bɔ Tanyi Tambe* and the rump *bɔ Ɛcu*) which only then resolve themselves into village sections (respectively Nserong and Besinga, Nsebanga and Mkpot, each with their associated major lineage groups).[1] Formal divisions in the village follow the lines of these linked intermediary alliances. The pattern of interrelated genealogical and residential grouping they exhibit may be compared with that of Ebeagwa village (*Figures 12, 15,* and *16*). We shall return again to these examples when considering the processes by which descent and residential groups are formed, but would point here to the existence of two 'break-away settlements' in Besongabang (Tagbotoko and Tabunta, residential offshoots of Nsebanga and Mkpot, respectively) which have not yet the constitutional status of village sections, but which continue the pattern of lateral secession shown so consistently in *Figure 20*. (Further analysis of this pattern and of the breakaway settlement of Tagbotoko will be found in Chapter 12, pp. 286–289, and *Figure 30*.)

Finally, the internal composition of four sections of Besongabang village are shown, which follow the general principles already fully discussed.

The corporate organization of lineage groups

A lineage group, *nɛrɛkɛt*, is an ideally solidary group of kinsfolk, known as the 'children' or descendants of a named ancestor, who maintain a corporate identity in their collective conduct of kinship affairs and in their members' mutual support and collective representation within a wider residential group. As we have seen, there is in fact some overlapping between descent and residential grouping, but the categorical difference between the two types of grouping and the norms defining them is clear and explicit. The axiom which supports this difference states baldly: 'Lineage group matters are different: matters of the community are different.' The distinction implied here is both qualitative and one of group context: the contrast is between the private affairs of kin and the

---

[1] In the case of the hamlet of Mkpot, Ta Mbu is remembered as its founder, but all his descendants have disappeared or died. As a village section, it is occasionally referred to simply as 'Ta Mbu', or by the name of what is now its largest constituent minor lineage group, *bɔ Ɛrɔk Tanyi*; but it is also often (anomalously) spoken of as *bɔ Ɛcu*.

public, political actions of a community. Each type of 'matter' (*ndak*) is conducted at its own level or in its own context, and they should not be confused.

A lineage group is composed, then, of people who are kin to each other, normally agnatic kin, but it is also a group which is corporately organized, with a 'bounded' membership and a specific identity. A lineage group acquires its identity from a lineage (the descendants or 'children' of one man, or occasionally woman) but includes as members persons other than the members of that lineage. In many cases the direct descendants of the ancestral founder form only a nuclear core to the total group to which other more distant kin, or quasi-kin, have become assimilated (cf. genealogies of lineage groups given for Bara or Tali, *Figures 8–10*). Inversely, while the children or children's children of any man can be spoken of as his descendants, *bɔ*, it is not every man's descendants who form (or will come to form) a lineage group, *nɛrɛkɛt*. A Manyang will never speak of his own domestic family as his *nɛrɛkɛt*, which would imply severance from his true lineage group, which is always a wider group and whose solidarity is jealously guarded.[1]

As a corporate group, each lineage group recognizes firstly a senior elder who is its moral head and ritual spokesman. Ideally, this status belongs to the oldest man who is a true descendant of the ancestral founder (or at least of a close agnatic collateral). Age by itself is always given respect. Effective influence in the affairs of the group will depend as well, however, upon the character, wealth, and domestic kin support of the man concerned. Secondly, and of equal importance to the corporate character of a lineage group, are its collective meetings in which matters of common concern to the group members are discussed and settled. These 'matters of the lineage group' (*barak nɛrɛkɛt*) range from the formal negotiation of a marriage contract, through disputes between kinsmen, to any particular enterprise (help for a younger relative, arranging for the purchase of a cult-agency) which the group as a whole may embark upon. The structure of the group is perhaps shown most clearly in ritual actions, when the senior elder representing and in the presence of its living members addresses its dead ancestors (calling first upon its recently dead elders and asking them to call all the dead, 'both those whom I know and those whom I do not know') and informs them of the reason for the lineage group's

[1] For further discussion of Banyang kinship concepts see my paper already cited. I attempt to show in this paper that the 'linearity' of Banyang kinship organization is a function of maintained residence in the male line and of the corporate organization of the *nɛrɛkɛt* and is not directly recognized in the kinship categories as concepts.

meeting, announcing any common action or decision made by them, and requesting the goodwill of the dead in upholding this common action and the living members of the group.

Apart from the arrangement of these internal matters, of specific concern to its own members (their side of a marriage contract, internal disputes, the ritual blessing of a member), a lineage group is expected equally to present a united front against those outside the group, whether in a hamlet or (more markedly) a village context. 'Matters of the lineage group', especially those of central concern, are commonly discussed at a private and closed meeting (sometimes of its most senior members) when outsiders are debarred from entering the house in which it takes place by hanging outside it the *dɛnkwɔ*, or yellow palm-leaf, which is a sign of a closed meeting. So also the internal affairs of the group should not be disclosed to outsiders, who may expect to observe only the final outcome of a decision or the consequence of action. 'If you dive into the witches' pool of *bɔ Mbu*,' it was sometimes said of this (major) lineage group in Tali, who maintained more than most such a solidarity of action, 'you will never get to the bottom' (literally 'you will not see the ground'). When describing how a lineage group should operate within a community, the ideal picture which people often draw is of the senior elder representing the group in a community discussion, with all the members of the group behind him; having presented their case in his own words, the senior elder will turn round to ask his kinsmen 'Is it not so?' to which they in unison are expected to reply *Ɛɛ!*, 'Yes!'

This picture of full participation in the common affairs of a lineage group and the complete solidarity of its members is not often borne out in practice. Some degree of effective solidarity must however be maintained if a lineage group is to continue to exist as one. We may turn here to the actual organization of lineage groups already outlined.

The simplest case is provided by those (major) lineage groups which form part of small, politically and residentially undifferentiated villages (e.g. Bara, Etemetek, Ejwengang). Lineage groups in these villages are usually undifferentiated, exogamous, solidary groups, which sometimes combine in matters of kinship with other groups within the village, but do not recognize within themselves smaller groupings with an effectively corporate form other than the group's component domestic units ('houses' or 'households'). Divisions of interest and differences in proximity of relationship certainly exist in such groups, but they remain primarily inter-personal matters, and the formal corporate affairs of kinsfolk are expected to be conducted on the level of the major lineage group as a whole.

95

In the case of major lineage groups composing larger, politically and residentially differentiated villages, the situation is more complex. Here, as we have seen, there may be 'lineage groups within a lineage group', minor lineage groups within a major lineage group.[1] What this means in point of fact is some fairly recognized division of role and function between the wider and the narrower grouping. The minor lineage groups are each represented by a senior elder and have a closer solidarity as kinsfolk within the wider group. The rule of exogamy tends now to apply to these groups. It is likely that any important matter of kinship will be discussed first within the smaller group before then being taken, rather more formally, to the senior elder of the major lineage group for his approval and action. Formal kinship matters (e.g. negotiation of a marriage contract, the formal distribution of an inheritance) are likely to be conducted in the context of the wider group, but the minor lineage group immediately concerned will probably have made all necessary arrangements and will retain effective control over what takes place. One must add, however, that the balance in corporate form and activity between major and minor lineage group varies between groups and depends upon their particular circumstances: in Tali 1 both Nchemba (bɔ Mbu) and Kembong (bɔ Mfɔnkeŋ) are village sections and major lineage groups, but, whereas bɔ Mbu maintain (as we have seen in the saying applied to them) a very close solidarity of interest and corporate activity, are exogamous, and do not recognize effective internal groupings, bɔ Mfɔnkeŋ as a major lineage group are divided into three very clearly defined, exogamous minor lineage groups, each with its own senior elder, and each with a tendency to conduct its own kinship affairs separately, with but bare recognition of the overall authority of the senior elder of the wider group. Other examples could be quoted of major lineage groups whose features lie between these two extremes.

The attenuation in the kinship solidarity and corporate activities of such major lineage groups as bɔ Mfɔnkeŋ in Tali 1 is, however, directly related to their dual character, for these groups are both ɛtɔk and nɛrɛkɛt, hamlet and major lineage group. I have argued that such a duality derives from the two ways in which all such groups face: outwardly united as a lineage group, inwardly independent as a residential community. Even so, these two contexts are not entirely separate and in practice two kinds of authority are available in the control of social relations within the group: if the moral authority of the lineage elders is not respected, recourse may then be

[1] Note, however, the sense of contradiction that the idea of 'lineage groups within a lineage group' often arouses, p. 77.

made to the secular and political authority of the group as a minor community, a hamlet, sanctioned most commonly at this level by the power of the Ngbe association. It is, moreover, in the nature of Banyang social values that emphasis upon the residential, political nature of social ties at one level is likely at a lower level to heighten the sense of separate identity held by the component kin-groups. The common genealogical tie shared by members of a major lineage group which is also a hamlet takes on here some of the politico-constitutional value that we have seen to apply to genealogical relationships at the widest level of political grouping, village or village group.

Finally, we should note that the range of persons included in the categories of εtɔk and nεrεkεt can never be exactly the same and that this difference is especially important at the level of a hamlet, which as an εtɔk includes *all* its residents (wives, assimilated kin, strangers) but as a nεrεkεt includes only those born into it: it thus excludes wives (who never lose membership of their natal lineage groups) and strangers, and includes assimilated kin only by courtesy; it also includes a number of non-resident members – kinsmen who are living apart, daughters who have married out, and local 'children of daughters' who still actively maintain this matrilateral connection.

Elderhood and leadership

Elderhood and leadership are the two key principles of corporate representation in Banyang society. The qualities and role of each are distinct, and each derives initially from a separate type of corporate grouping. Both, however, are relevant to community organization, where the two roles complement each other and, in part, overlap.

In any comparison of elderhood and leadership (kεsensi and kεfɔ) Banyang have no hesitation in giving priority to elderhood: 'elderhood comes first'. An elder (mu nsensi) obtains his status by the ascribed qualities of age and kinship position. His role as the representative of others is very closely bound up with the moral identity kin are expected to share and with the continuity of the group that he represents. The status of leader (mfɔ) on the other hand is achieved, deriving from personal qualities of character and wealth, and from his recognition as leader from his followers and all others who accept his leadership. A leader's presence within a residential group symbolizes the implicit agreement of its members to continue in political association.

We have described how a residential community is composed of a number of separate kin or lineage groups. So too the corporate body or council representing the community is expected to consist of a leader supported by his elders. Individually, the elders are drawn from the separate lineage groups composing a residential group and serve to represent their kinsfolk in the wider context. At the same time, collectively, as 'elders of the community', *basensi ɛtɔk*, they are expected to act in the general interest, as guardians to the good order and moral welfare of the residential group as a whole. Their stabilizing and traditionalist role thus complements that of community leader, who is expected to act rather more by circumstance, seizing opportunities, taking the initiative, forcing rather than resolving a problematic issue.

This complementarity of roles is often further evidenced in a kind of structural partnership of leader and senior elder. In most villages there is a recognized senior elder of the village; either he is the oldest man, who is then given formal respect and acts where occasion demands it as its ritual spokesman, or (perhaps more frequently) he is one of the most senior of the minor leaders of the village, and represents an important section of it, being second in status to the village leader and an influential figure in the affairs of the village's inner council. One gets the impression that a senior elder of the latter type is often a kind of village leader *manqué*. More especially, a village section which is both a lineage group and a hamlet very frequently has a dual headship, being represented both by a senior elder and by a minor leader. This is often explained by saying that the senior elder is head of the lineage group (formal respect will never be denied to an elder, in the same way that a kinship tie will never formally be denied) but that he has appointed the younger man to 'move with the village leader', representing him and the lineage group in the wider affairs of the village, then coming back to report them to him at home. Yet it is clear that in fact this 'deputizing' of hamlet leader by lineage group elder is often no more than a formal validation of a position achieved *de facto* and on other grounds.[1]

Some overlapping does nevertheless occur in the positions of elders and leaders, and in certain cases the two statuses are merged. An elder's effective influence in the group he represents is strengthened if he has some of the qualities of a leader (wealth, following, personal character); and, with the passing of years, a leader's position may be consolidated by the respect due to his age. As we have seen, the senior elder of a village is very frequently a leader of one of the minor communities composing it. This was the case with Ta Taboko in Tali 1. When in 1965 a senior elder

[1] For examples, see above, p. 70.

of Lower Ebeagwa claimed that he was the oldest man in the whole of the village group (i.e. the senior elder of the widest descent group, the village group as *nεrεkεt*), Taboko's response was characteristically that this was a 'worthless' elderhood: with Ta Njang's death in Ejwengang (the former senior elder of the village, a well-established, articulate, and highly influential man, whose voice in village and village group affairs carried perhaps more weight than the younger village leader's), and with Oben Anyang's death in Ebeagwa (a former village leader, whose deafness caused him to lose his position, although he remained the senior elder of the village and its traditional, ritual head), Taboko claimed that he was himself the senior elder of all *bɔ Ndifɔ*. Even so, the older man by years (the 'worthless' elder) was not an unrespected figure, being both the senior elder and minor leader of one of the village sections of Lower Ebeagwa.

The merging of elderhood and leadership in the representative headship of residential groups is more marked among Lower than Upper Banyang. Among Upper Banyang there is more emphasis upon leadership as a distinctive role: village leaders in Upper Banyang country tend to be stronger, more dominant and domineering men, and there is certainly (as we shall later see) a great deal more competition for, and dispute over, village leadership there. In Lower Banyang country one gets the impression of an ideal of leadership in which the leader stands out less from the group and draws more upon the ascribed virtues of age and ritual ability. (It will be remembered that village community cults are more common to Lower Banyang villages and that traditionally their officiants were the village leaders.) The senior elders of the sections of a Lower Banyang village are equated more closely with the 'minor leaders', *bɔ bafɔ*, of the community: the two terms, 'elder' and 'leader', indeed carry less distinction, and can be avoided by the use of the general term, 'father' (i.e. the person with responsibility for one) or by speaking of the 'head' (*nti*) of a group. Again, in the genealogies of Lower Banyang villages one finds the term 'father' (*ta*) appearing more frequently as the prefix to the names of the founding ancestors of present-day groups, whereas in Upper Banyang villages the common prefix is *mfɔ*, 'leader'. The difference here is nevertheless one of degree and emphasis, and is not a radical difference in mode of organization. Not *all* Lower Banyang leaders are also elders, and the rationale of 'deputizing' by a senior elder is not uncommon. We have noted two 'Upper Banyang-type' leaders in the traditions of Ayok Etayak village group (the irascible 'gun leader' and the violent Ebae Etaka, both village founders), and the founding ancestor of the largest of the Lower Banyang village groups, *bɔ Mfɔtek*, has precisely the name 'leader of the community' (mfɔ and ɛtek, the latter eastern Ejagham). In the latter case a story closely parallel to the story of how Ndifaw became leader is told describing how Mfotek came to be presented and confirmed as 'leader' to the 'ɛtɔk' which is now the village group. Other evidence from genealogies or from stories of the past is not lacking to show the significance of leadership for the corporate formation of residential groups, especially villages. Finally, it is in Lower Banyang villages that the present-day distinction between the (traditional) 'leader of the community' (mfɔ ɛtɔk) and 'European's leader' (mfɔ Ndek) is most clearly and frequently found, a distinction which may be compared with one which operated within the pre-Colonial society between the formal (ritual) leader and the effective one.

To understand the status of the 'European's leader' however, we need to turn to the effects of the Colonial context upon Banyang political system, and in particular to the changes incurred by the introduction of a new 'constitutional' source of authority.

4

Community Constitution and the Colonial Administration

The development of a native administration

One of the first actions of the German administration, established at Ossidinge in 1901, was to acknowledge the status of village leaders and to bring them under the formal protection of their own 'Imperial Government'. Those who applied were given a German flag and a 'Letter of Protection' which was printed on an imposing double-leafed paper, edged with black and red bands, and headed with an eagle crest. The letter ran:

> The chief ....
> Village ....
> District ....

has received the German flag and stands under the special protection of the Imperial Government.

This person is directed *as far as is possible* to *sell* provisions to all caravans travelling through, and in case of disputes or assault by carriers to report immediately to the European in charge of the caravan.

In the event of his affairs not reaching a settlement on the spot, the chief should apply as soon as possible to the appropriate station.

The requisition of carriers and provisions without payment is strictly forbidden.

In unavoidable exceptional cases, a report or notification should be made to the European in charge of the next station or to the Imperial Government.

Kamerun, the .... 190..

The Imperial Governor
(signed) von Puttkamer[1]

[1] Von Puttkamer was Governor from 1895 to 1907. This is a translation of a copy of the

The village leaders, or 'chiefs' (*Häuptlinge*) as they were now called, became the intermediaries between the German administration and the people. For example, when Mansfeld took over the District in 1904, he worked through the chiefs in attempting to restore order and in getting those settlements which had to rebuild to do so as consolidated groups along the main path; a further distribution of flags was made to those chiefs who had not already received them and who complied with Mansfeld's demands.[1]

There would appear to have been no special measure taken to confirm the status of village leaders who applied for the 'paper' (*ɛkati*) which gave them official recognition as chiefs. Latterly it has become commonplace to emphasize the arbitrariness of this process: the British administration picked up the plaint of Banyang themselves that under the Germans anyone could become a chief – he need only apply and was given a 'paper'. In fact, although formally unregulated, the process was far from arbitrary: certain village sections took this opportunity of obtaining separate recognition of their leaders, and no doubt some individuals sought a personal aggrandizement of status, but it would seem that in the main those men who were recognized as chiefs were the accredited leaders of established communities, i.e. the constitutional village leaders. Their importance in these early years of Colonial administration is attested by their listing in an appendix of Mansfeld's book: here under the heading 'Banyang', thirty-seven 'places' (*Ort*) are listed, each with its named chief.

[1] *Urwald Dokumente*, pp. 19–20.
letter given to the village leader of Fotabe and shown to me by his son and successor. The German version runs as follows:

Schutzbrief
Der Häuptling
Dorf
Landschaft

hat die deutsche Flagge erhalten und steht unter dem besonderen Schutze des Kaiserlichen Gouvernements.

Derselben ist angewiesen, allen durchreisended Karawanen *nach Möglichkeit* Lebensmittel *zu verkaufen* und im Falle von Streitigkeiten oder Vergewaltigung durch Träger sich sofort an den die Karawane führenden Europäer zu wenden.

Falls seine Angelegenheit an Ort und Stelle ihre Erledigung nicht findet, hat sich der Häuptling baldmöglichst an die zuständige Station zu wenden.

Das Requiriren von Trägern und Lebensmitteln ohne Bezahlung ist streng verboten.

In unvermeidlichen Ausnahmefällen ist des führenden Europäers der nächsten Station beziehungsweise dem Kaiserlichen Gouvernement Mittheilung zu machen beziehungsweise Meldung zu erstatten.

Kamerun, den .... 190..

Der Kaiserliche Gouverneur

Twenty-seven of the places named correspond to present-day villages.[1] In eighteen of these villages I have collected lists of successive village leaders: in twelve of these eighteen I can locate the 'chief' named by Mansfeld without difficulty; in two cases the correspondence is uncertain; in only four is there no correspondence.

Mansfeld had apparently no very elaborate conception of the political organization of the peoples in his District. He was influenced no doubt by the devastation which had been caused by the punitive war and by the evident disintegration of community settlement patterns that occurred east of the nucleated village communities of the 'Ekoi'. In his book he writes:

> Amongst all the tribes in the District, only for one of them, the Ekois, can one detect some community solidarity (*gemeinschaftlichen Zusammenhalten*). As the separate tribes live unconnected with each other, so for the most part each village community is strictly cut off by itself: no law links it to its neighbour.[2]

Although his account of 'Ewi-Ngbe' ('Ngbe-Law'), which he goes on to give, immediately belies this generalization, his underlying conception of the political organization of the peoples of his District was of a series of small, self-contained autonomous communities, each a more or less clearly defined 'village' (*Dorf*) led by its own 'chief'. These then became the units of Mansfeld's direct administration: the chiefs his agents of administration.

As in the initial stages, so throughout the period of Mansfeld's administration, the village 'chiefs' were responsible for law and order in their villages and for various administrative tasks demanded of them: they were expected to see that the main path was kept cleared, to collect tax (from 1908) and, when required, to provide carriers. If they failed in their duties they were punished or the chiefship was taken from them. For one reason or another a number of Banyang village leaders were sent to prison during this time. One of the last actions of the German administration was the hanging of five village leaders and others suspected in 1915 of helping the British, then advancing from the west across Banyang territory.

The administration of the District was taken over by the British in 1916, and in May was put in the hands of a civil administrator who already had experience of administration in Nigeria. He reports on the general relief

[1] Op. cit., p. 265. Five of the 'places' named are (at the present day at least) not strictly Banyang, and in five other cases the use of Roman numerals (Faitoh II and Eturre II-V) makes their present identity problematic.

[2] Op. cit., pp. 158–159.

felt by the population at being free from German rule, stricter and more pervading than that customary in Nigeria; he appears to have been less inclined to accept the village leaders as agents of administration in the way that Mansfeld used them, but in other respects the *status quo ante bellum* was taken as the basis for the renewed administration. In the first annual report a general account of the peoples' political organization is given:

> All the villages of the Division are independent and their social system patriarchal. There are no powerful chiefs, and in many cases the villages are so small that the term 'chief' is too high-sounding a title for a man who has sometimes less than a dozen men in his village. The old men have the most influence, and the chiefs seem to possess little natural authority, but to have derived what power they had from being the mouthpieces of the Government. Under the Germans the position of chief does not seem to have been eagerly sought after as the office was by no means a sinecure and entailed duties not always commensurate with its privileges.[1]

The departure of the Germans appears to have provided some opportunity for the reassertion of traditional interests, and some cases are reported of villages, formerly consolidated, attempting 'to return to their old settlements, or break up into factions under new chiefs', but these movements were at once discouraged and 'the *status quo ante bellum* made the basis for settlement of disputes regarding the appointment of chiefs, boundaries, and responsibility for the maintenance of roads and bridges. The natives have now realized that settled conditions are once more established and that law and order must be observed as before.'[2]

In the 1920s Mamfe Division, as it now became called, was administered as part of the Southern Provinces of Nigeria and came under the influence of the policy of Indirect Rule, then being extended to these Provinces from the North. In the early 1920s two Native Courts serving the Banyang area were established, one at Tali and one at Mamfe (which also included all Ejagham living in the Division). The Courts were staffed by selected village leaders and were declared Native Authorities. Pending the reorganization of the native administration of the Division, a series of Assessment Reports was written based upon detailed inquiries among its various peoples. The first reports dealt with the Ejagham peoples (Ekwe District 1926, Keaka-speaking area 1928) and were followed first by a

[1] Annual Report on the Ossidinge Division, Kamerun Province, para. 8.   [2] Ibid., para. 10.

'Preliminary Assessment Report on the Banyang Tribal Area' by H. O. Anderson (1929) and then a further 'Banyang Tribal Area Assessment Report' by E. H. F. Gorges (1930).[1]

These two reports give in some detail both general and particular information concerning the organization of Banyang groups: although certain of their conclusions were criticized and their practical proposals were not followed, they provide for us now extremely valuable historical data and appear also to have been used by later administrative officers fairly regularly for reference purposes. The difference between 'Eastern' and 'Western' Banyang ('Upper and' 'Lower') was noted and became the basis for the proposed reorganization of the Native Courts. More importantly, the ties between villages, which up to now had been ignored, were recognized, and fourteen 'Clans' listed according to their component villages. Each of the Clans was visited during the preparation of the reports and something of their histories recorded. Neither Anderson nor Gorges offers a generalized account of the political organization of the Clans, as they see it, and in certain important respects what they do say is inconsistent or ambiguous. The kind of picture which emerges is of a Clan composed of a number of 'Villages', each Village being divided into a series of 'Quarters' or 'Families'. The Clan is ruled by a 'Clan Council' led by a 'Clan Head', the Village by a 'Village Council' led by the 'Village Head'.[2] Individual persons are spoken of as 'Quarter Heads' but in more general description 'Village Elders' or 'Family Heads' are also referred to as supporting the Village Head or as members of the Village Council. Again, the term 'Village Head' is not consistently used, but tends to alternate with the term 'Chief', especially, it would seem, for village leaders who were in fact powerful figures. The very limited formal authority of village leaders was nevertheless clearly recognized, although so also was the fact that the village leader tended to become the main spokesman and negotiator for the village in relation to the administration, or a visiting administrative officer.[3]

Both reports make the same recommendations for a slight reorganization of Banyang Native Authorities, based again on Native Courts and

---

[1] For a fuller discussion of the policies guiding these Assessment Reports (policies which were not always entirely clear) and for their role in the development of a Colonial administrative structure in the neighbouring area of Bamenda, see Elizabeth Chilver, 'Native Administration in the West Central Cameroons 1902–1954', *Essays in Imperial Government: Presented to Margery Perham* by Kenneth Robinson and Frederick Madden (1963).

[2] Here and elsewhere in this chapter, terms taken over from the administration are printed with initial capitals and when printed thus are used in their 'official' sense.

[3] Gorges, op. cit. para. 171.

Court areas. It is argued that the Banyang as a whole are too divergent to be brought within a single Court area, and that two Native Courts should be established, one at Atebong for the five Clans listed as Eastern Banyang, another at Bachu-Akagbe for the remaining nine Clans listed as Western.[1] Specified Clan Heads and/or Village Heads were nominated as Presidents of the two Courts and as the Members of the panel of judges serving the Courts. The two Courts were to be vested as Native Authorities. Pending its approval by the higher echelons of the British administration, this was the system inaugurated in 1930.

The proposals of the Gorges Assessment Report and some of its contents were, however, severely criticized by the most senior officers of the administration, and the whole question of the traditional institutions of authority in Banyang society and its traditional or 'natural' units was re-examined. By this time the Aba riots in south-eastern Nigeria (December 1929) had given a spur to the need for reorganization, had shown the unwisdom of creating large Court areas with officially recognized 'chiefs' acting as agents for the administration (in south-eastern Nigeria, the much disliked 'Warrant Chiefs'), and had suggested that it would be better if the native administration were based upon the smaller traditional units of the society and that, above all, the 'consent of the people themselves' should be sought for any new organization that was created.[2] The administrative officers in Mamfe came in for a certain amount of criticism: they were felt to be 'out of touch', to be relying upon the old, unsound method of Native Courts, to be imposing a system 'from above', and to be 'afraid of self-determination'. The principle underlying the traditional organization was shown to be 'conciliar' rather than 'autocratic', the Banyang according in this respect with the type of organization found 'from Warri to Ogoja'. The 'conciliar' system should therefore be introduced, at a level of organization that accorded with the 'natural units' of the society.[3]

The result of these criticisms and of the further information and

[1] The sharp division between Eastern (Upper) Banyang clans and Western (Lower) was undoubtedly influenced by the rivalry which Gorges noted between the village leaders of Tali and Defang (Mbang), which he was concerned to place in different Court areas. Yet the rivalry itself follows from the attempts towards aggrandizement by both leaders, which in turn is one of the Upper Banyang characteristics.

[2] Margery Perham, *Native Administration in Nigeria*, Chs. XIII–XVI. An example of re-organization effected at this time is Owerri Province, for which 245 Authorities and Subordinate Authorities were in 1934 gazetted by name, and 'which at the time was by no means fully re-organized' (p. 246). In Warri Province 250 Native Courts were established where previously there had been only fifty-two (p. 253).

[3] Correspondence relating to Assessment Report (West Cameroon Archives, Af 18).

consultations that followed from them was the creation of an entirely new structure of native administration, considerably influenced by the south-east Nigerian pattern. In 1934 the 'Banyang Clan Area' was re-organized, the first in Mamfe Division to be so. The 'administrative unit' was now officially recognized as the village, and each Village Council became a constituted Native Authority: forty-seven Native Authorities were thus created. The Village Head in Council was recognized as Executive Authority. The fourteen 'Village Groups' (as they were now called, the term 'Clan' being applied to the wider area of the Banyang as a whole) became the basis for Native Courts of the 'D' Grade, the members of the Court being drawn from the Village Councils of the various villages of each group. The Courts were allowed to hear only civil cases, with full powers in matrimonial or land disputes but otherwise with jurisdiction limited to matters of up to £5. A further Native Court for the whole of the Banyang area was established at Bakebe, which acted partly as a court of first instance (in inter-village group cases and for minor criminal cases) but more importantly as an Appeal Court from the Village Group Courts.[1] Everything thus accorded with the 'natural units', despite some misgivings from the officers within the Division, who quite clearly felt that this multiplicity of Native Authorities and Courts would be extremely difficult to handle.

Initially, however, the system is said to have worked well. The Village Group Courts were 'popular' and the cases heard by them rose from 308 to 788 in the first two years.[2] The District Officer, who must have spent a great deal of time on tour, worked through the Village Councils, although his immediate dealings would seem to have remained with the Village Heads (e.g. in the case of tax collection, or the revision of Nominal Rolls). The same system was not, however, applied to other parts of the Division (when reorganized, the Ejagham area was divided into only three Native Authorities, corresponding to the division between Ekwe, Keaka, and the southern Obang) and over a period of time close supervision of the forty-nine Native Authorities (as they had become by the recognition of two further villages in 1936) seems to have become less strict, the Village Councils being left very largely to run their own affairs in their own way. In his Annual Report for 1937, the District Officer complains of these Native Authorities working at their own instance and not the Government's. Two cases are cited, including one in which an Etoko woman murdered another in the village. 'It was then the duty of the Native

---

[1] Annual Report on the Mamfe Division 1934 (Ce 1934/1), paras. 19 and 46.
[2] Ibid. para. 47. Annual Report 1935, paras. 61 and 65.

Authority to report the matter to Government and bring the offender to justice but instead and as the two women both came from branches of the same family, it was agreed by the prominent persons in the village including the whole village council (which is the Native Authority) to pay compensation for the murder and not to report the matter. A juju was sworn that the matter should not go outside the village.'[1] In 1938 none of the 'Group Courts' were visited (whereas all the other Native Courts in the Division were) and already the possibility was mooted of the reorganization of Banyang Native Administration.[2] Administrative attention seems in fact to have turned from the multitude of village Native Authorities and the Village Group Courts to the 'Clan Court' at Bakebe, which was staffed by the forty-nine Village Heads and which was then under discussion as a possible 'Superior Native Authority'. In 1940 a Treasury for the Banyang 'Clan' was attached to the Clan Court and a process of amalgamation started at the lower level which was eventually to restore the kind of pattern that the Gorges Report recommended in 1930. In this year four Village Group Courts were amalgamated to form a new 'Nchemti Court', and two further steps in amalgamation reduced the now twelve Courts to five (in 1943) and finally to three (in 1947), at Mamfe, Bachu Akagbe, and Tinto, with appeal to the Clan Court at Bakebe.

Throughout the 1940s the Village Council 'Native Authorities' seem to have existed in name only and even so only partially since there is a tendency to ignore them or to mention them only as an afterthought in the Annual Reports, entire administrative attention being given to the 'Superior Native Authority' (which is sometimes referred to simply as the 'Banyang Native Authority'). What seems in fact to have happened is that the administrative officers when on tour would call a general meeting of the village leaders, elders, and other leading men, at which information was passed or requests made in either direction, but this meeting was largely informal and the group that met was the 'corporate community' at the village level, much the same body of persons as met in the past or in more traditional contexts. The 'Village Council Native Authorities' under the British administration were indeed precisely what their name said they were: the difficulty was to link them in any effective way to the authority structure of the administration itself; and this by reason of their smallness and multiplicity seems barely to have been attempted except in the first few years of their existence. The main channel of contact between the British administration and the villages remained

[1] Ce 1937/1, para. 16.   [2] Annual Report, 1938 (Ce 1938/1), paras. 19 and 32.

through the village leaders or the 'Superior Native Authority', itself composed of nominated village leaders selected to represent the fourteen village groups.

In 1952 the Village Council Native Authorities were formally abolished and a single Native Authority was recognized for the Banyang area, with a further Native Authority for Mamfe Town, which two years later was extended to cover the villages neighbouring Mamfe. In 1956 the Banyang-Mbo Group Council was formed; in effect this was a reconstitution and merging of the former two Native Authorities, but the latter term, with its long association with the Colonial policy of Indirect Rule, was dispensed with and the current movement was towards building up a series of local government councils in preparation for independence. Representation to the new councils was by village group, and its members were officially to be elected, but in most villages candidates only up to the number of places available were nominated and these were village leaders. (Ndifaw village group, for example, was represented by the leaders of Tali 1 and Ejwengang.)

The status of village leaders under the administration

The German administration had little hesitation in recognizing the village leaders as 'chiefs' and then using them as agents of their own authority. Under the British administration the position of village leaders was rather more ambiguous: not officially recognized as persons with authority (which accorded with their lack of formal, authoritative office in the traditional society), they nevertheless became the main representatives of their village to the administration, which in itself gave them a new and different status.

It is significant that even after the Gorges Report the question could still be raised whether or not 'chiefs' existed in Banyang society. Thus, in his comments on the Report, the Lieutenant-Governor noted that the term 'chief' was used by Gorges, but asked: to what extent does chieftainship exist? The reply that was forwarded upwards from the Divisional Officer, Mamfe, was that 'chieftainship as defined in the Interpretation Ordinance does not exist amongst the Banyangis'; what existed was rather a 'Village Head' who exercised 'executive powers, whether derived from delegation by the village elders, or in the German time, compulsorily, as the sole responsible authority in the village'.[1] It was in line with this limited conception of the village leader's position, and with the recognition of the importance of the 'conciliar principle' in Banyang political

---

[1] Correspondence relating to Assessment Report (Af 18).

organization, that the structure of 'Native Authorities' was created. The 'Village Head' was given no authority separate from that of the Village Council: the 'Village Head in Council' held merely 'Executive Authority'.

Despite, however, the official emphasis upon Councils as the true Native Authorities and the very limited official recognition given to the village leaders, the position of the latter under the British administration was crucial. Entries in the 'Banyang Touring Diary' for the effective period 1941–1958 make it clear that the initial point of contact with the administrative officers was the village leader, supported as he might be by 'others' or the 'Village Council': 'met the Village Head of N——', 'in the evening usual meeting with the Village Head and others', are the kind of entry which frequently recurs. Again, it should be remembered that it was the village leaders who in the earlier period were nominated to staff the Native Courts and who, after 1934, became the judges of the Clan Court, and later the members of the Superior Native Authority. A number of references in the records make it clear that these positions were sought after and that there was some vying between individuals and groups for them. The most critical problem in the formation of the Superior Native Authority was its membership: should all forty-nine Village Heads be members (as they had earlier been panel members of the Clan Court) or should each village group send only one of their Village Heads? The problem is outlined in the Annual Report for 1938 (para. 28):

The Banyang Clan has . . . been trying to form a superior native authority. The Clan is formed of fourteen groups each of which has its own group court and the proposal is that the fourteen group heads should form the superior native authority. The majority have now selected their group heads from the families of the founders of the various groups. Men who are senior but not senile. All are village heads and it seems to be agreed that when one group head dies or retires the post should pass to the village heads of the other villages in turn. There is however discord in certain groups where there are village heads of comparatively equal seniority and personality competing for the honour of group head. In another case a man of outstanding personality is junior to another village head of considerably less personality and influence.

A briefer, less official, and somewhat wearier note is struck by an entry in the Banyang Touring Diary for 1948, when at Bakebe the District Officer records that he 'meets Banyang chiefs full of disputes about Court membership, Village headship, etc.'.

A slight digression may help to explain the reference to fourteen 'group heads' (i.e. village group heads) above and the 'Clan Heads' which figure in the Gorges Report (see above, p. 105). Both of these positions – if one can speak of them as different – have only a tenuous connection with any traditionally accepted status in the village groups. By definition, there can be no 'leader of the village group' although one of the village leaders may be more powerful and wield more influence than others. It is this *de facto* pre-eminence of a village leader which would seem to underlie the position of 'group head' referred to above, and which accounts both for its agreed circulation between villages and for the competition between village leaders where pre-eminence is in doubt. Gorges's recognition of 'Clan Heads' would appear to derive partly from this but also from another source of misunderstanding: the fact that nominal recognition may be given in the traditional society to a senior elder of the village group (a *mu nsensi* of the *nɛrɛkɛt*, a village group conceived of here as a corporate group of kin). A 'Clan Head' was a logical part of Banyang political organization as it was assumed to exist in the Gorges Report: Quarter, or Family, with Quarter or Family Head; Village with its Village Head; Clan with its Clan Head. The position was also administratively convenient, since 'Clan Heads' provided suitable nominees to the Court Presidentships (very much as in the passage above it has become administratively convenient to speak of 'group heads' as members of the Superior Native Authority). For a brief period (1929?–1933) 'Clan Heads' were administratively recognized as a distinct status, and individuals were appointed to it by the administration. Such appointments provided, however, especially among Upper Banyang, a great source of contention, and, after difficulties had been encountered, any formal recognition of Clan Heads was allowed to lapse at the time of the reorganization of the Banyang Native Authorities in 1934.

To return to the position of village leaders under the British administration: one of their key functions was that of tax-collector. This function the village leaders had fulfilled from the early years of the German administration and continued to do so right throughout the Colonial period. An indication of the continuing importance of this role is a reference made in 1950 to the Village Councils as Subordinate Native Authorities (which they were only on paper) in which it is stated that 'the powers under the Native Authority Ordinance are never exercised . . . apart from duties in connection with tax collection'.[1] As this statement implies, the village leaders did not act alone in the collection of tax, but it was through them that the whole process was channelled. Throughout most of this period the procedure was that a Nominal Roll of taxpayers (all adult men not excused on grounds of physical incapacity) was drawn up by the village leader with the help of the relevant sectional representatives of the village: this Roll was checked each year by the Treasury Clerk together with one or two senior representatives of the Superior Native Authority and possibly later by the District Officer. One copy of the Nominal Roll was held by the village leader; another was held in the N.A. Treasury. Each year, after the Roll had been checked, individual tax tickets were made out and handed to the village leader, who worked through the various sectional representatives of the village (officially the 'Quarter Heads', in fact the hamlet leaders or the senior elders of lineage groups) in dispensing the tickets in return for the payment of tax. The village leader, normally supported by one or two other leading members of the village, then paid in the tax as a lump sum to the N.A. Treasury. If it was paid in within a given time, a '10 per cent Dash' was given to the village leader, nominally to recompense him for his work but in fact for redistribution to the sectional representatives, through whom the tax had been collected. In 1930, when the issue of an alternative method of paying village leaders was put to them, they unanimously supported the 10 per cent Dash. Thus Gorges records:

> A meeting of all Mamfe Native Authorities was held by the Divisional Officer in August, and the chiefs were asked whether they would prefer executive salaries to the present system of Judicial salaries, and a 10% Dash for punctual payment of tax. They unanimously opposed the innovation saying that if they received no Dash for distribution amongst their quarter and family heads for their assistance in tax collecting their aid would cease.[2]

During Assessment the Banyang village leaders confirmed this decision. With some misgivings it was accepted by the administration, and was still in operation at the time of my fieldwork in 1953–1954.

What is perhaps most striking about this process of tax-collection is its

---

[1] Proposals for the Federation of the Banyang, Bangwa, Mundanis, and Mbo Clans of the Mamfe Division, July 1950, from section dealing with 'Existing Native Authorities'. The movement towards this Federation was bitterly opposed by Bangwa and ultimately all that was effected was the residual amalgamation of Banyang and Mbo N.A.s already mentioned.
[2] Op. cit., para. 272.

parallel to the rights and procedures concerning the 'animals of the community' described earlier. The role of Village Head as tax-collector is very similar to the village leader's role as the receiver of a leopard caught by any member of his community. The tax is paid through the 'line of representation' leading eventually to the Village Head. The 10 per cent Dash is a recognition of his status, but is dispersed downwards in the same way as the 'animals of the community', once presented to the community leader, are redistributed among its sectional representatives. It is not surprising, therefore, that tax-collection became an index of Village Headship under the new régime, the paying of tax to one man symbolic of allegiance to him. Instead of the giving of a leopard, the payment of tax came to assume the critical constitutional significance in defining a political leader's status and the relationship of members of a residential community to him. If the village leader in the past was defined by his right to receive a leopard, the Village Head of the Colonial period was defined by his right to receive and pass forward tax.[1]

Although the full implications of this were not recognized by the officers of the administration, it clearly was recognized that tax-collection had this 'constitutional' function in defining formal rights and relationships. So, for example, in an inquiry held in August 1927 to decide a land dispute between Igbeko (Eberkaw) and Small Mamfe, the ruling of

[1] E. M. Chilver and P. M. Kaberry ('From Tribute to Tax in a Tikar Chiefdom', *Africa*, 1960) describe how in the state of Nsaw the payment of tax during the Colonial period was constitutionally reinterpreted in a way not dissimilar to that described here, except that in this small, hierarchically organized chiefdom it became formally assimilated to the relationship of subordinate chief to his overlord, with somewhat different consequences. Mrs Chilver, in her article on 'Native Administration in the West Central Cameroons 1902–1954' which has already been cited, makes it clear in a number of contexts how disputes over tax-collection were in effect disputes over political allegiance or status. As an example of how 'some divisional officers found that their advice in the settlement of domestic political disputes was sought', she describes the progress of a dispute between 'Sub-chief Y' and 'Chief X' which moves in its terms from the usurpation of traditional rights (the 'wearing of the regal necklace of leopards' teeth' and the 'right to the regulatory society, *ngumba*') to the separate collection of tax by Sub-chief Y. 'Chief X wrote "I wish to counted all my people in peace. I no want to separate them, like last year 1934. Please find the tax-list of 1932 and 1933. You will see (my) people are not separate. I wish (to keep) all my sub-chiefs (named). I wish to stay with them in peace as before. Because they are not My Family, they are my chiefs since long time and I wish to join all the total numbers of taxable in one place as before, and I will allow them to get their 10 per cent for tax and I will make list, show how many each chief pay his tax. Because if D.O. separate the tax lists from Bamenda before send them to me to give them, so they will not hear (obey) me. They always said (will always say) D.O. make us free, we are not under chief X again" ' (p. 117). In my own terminology, this is a statement of the constitutional rights and status of Chief X in relation to his Sub-chiefs, which he is asking that the administration may confirm in the face of an attempt by a Sub-chief to assert his independence.

the Divisional Officer was recorded as follows: 'In view of the fact that Besongabang will not follow or pay tax to Besong of Small Mamfe, the Divisional Officer considers that Besong is not of sufficient importance to take tax from and control the stranger town. Besong cannot command tax from his own family, and so how can he expect strangers to pay to him. Moreover it is not definitely proved that Mamfe were formerly sole owners of the land.'[1] The same dispute was brought up again during Assessment, and in his Report Gorges takes a somewhat more critical view of the merits of the two sides. He questions the earlier use of the tax criterion and asks: 'Why should Besongabang pay tax to Mamfe? They have been an independent village for at least thirty-five years. Their present chief is Clan Head as well as Village Head [!]. They live five miles from Mamfe and are a large and independent village. They admit Besong is the representative of the senior branch of the family, but that seems no reason for paying tax to him.'[2] The point here is that Gorges is not denying the appropriateness of the tax criterion, but is using it far more logically to define specifically *village* headship and not merely a vague political overlordship. Gorges's use here accords strictly with that of Banyang themselves.

We have seen that under the British administration village leaders were not given a formal office or formal authority: they became the *de facto* representatives of the village to the administration, or to the organs which had been set up by the administration, but in the eyes of the administration they lacked formal office, except *qua* members of the Superior Native Authority, Court members, etc. Even so, this 'informally official' role has given rise to a distinction in status recognized both by administration and by Banyang: the status of traditional village leader and that of administrative representative for the village. Thus, in their reports, administrative officers refer from time to time to 'official chiefs'. Banyang distinguish, where appropriate, between *mfɔ etɔk*, 'community leader', and *mfɔ Ndek*, 'European's leader'.

It is important to appreciate that this distinction in status refers not to the 'traditional' political organization as opposed to the 'modern', imposed one, co-existing but separate, but to the area *between* traditional and modern (administrative) political structures, an area of interaction where new political forms and relationships have emerged, influenced by both structures but existing in a single, continuous field of political behaviour. Used by administrative officers, the term 'official chief' does not directly make sense. So, in his Memorandum on the Gorges Report, the Divisional

[1] Quoted by Gorges, op. cit., para. 118.   [2] Ibid., para. 125.

Officer writes: 'I do not understand what Mr Gorges means by "Official Chief". There is no such thing in the Division, although certain hereditary chiefs have been allowed, at their own request, to be represented and have their duties carried out by their own nominees. Egbe Mba of Tali is an instance of such.'[1] Yet by the end of the year in his Annual Report the (same?) Divisional Officer writes: 'The principal influence in the district is wielded by four chiefs, the village heads of Etuku (clan head of Nkokenok II), Defang and Bawak of Igbekaw and Takaw of Besongabang. The last two named are not rulers in their own right, but by long and useful service *have retained their official positions with the full confidence of their clans*'[2] (my italics). The key to the paradox of the 'official chiefs' lies in the last sentence: they are 'official' not because they have been put in office by the administration but because they have a special role *vis-à-vis* the administration which is recognized and confirmed by their own village members. Egbemba of Tali is a good example of precisely this. Baimbi was village leader of Tali on the arrival of the Germans and received formal recognition as village chiefs under them. He fell foul of the administration however and was put into prison for slave-dealing. Egbemba (related to Baimbi in the chiefly lineage group) was then appointed as chief. By the time of the British administration Baimbi had returned to the village and his 'hereditary right' to its leadership was recognized by the administration; but by this time Egbemba had become an effective and influential representative, fully accepted by the members of Tali, who did not wish to readopt Baimbi. The position of Egbemba was however legitimized by describing him as the 'nominee' or 'representative' of Baimbi, and not in this sense the 'true' leader of Tali.[3] In 1953, five years after Egbemba's death, there was no doubt about his long and effective leadership of Tali.

From the Banyang's point of view the distinction between 'community leader' and 'European's leader' is similarly a distinction in the nature and context of village leadership as it operates within a single, continuous field of behaviour. In many cases (e.g. Besongabang village) the same man has both statuses. In other cases, status of one type may give way to the other, or the distinction is a formal one, a device to legitimize

[1] Memorandum on Gorges, Divisional Officer, Mamfe, to Senior Resident, Cameroons Province, 6 February 1931 (Af 18).

[2] Annual Report, 1931, para. 43.

[3] Cf. Gorges, para. 36, and Anderson, op. cit., who writes that Egbe Mba was originally appointed to the Germans and 'owing to his personality and great competence he was retained by the present Administration as one of the Presidents of the Tali Native Court . . . all the Clans look to him as their leader and intermediary with the Government . . .'.

the separate roles of two men. In Mbang village group in 1954, a distinction was made between the 'three community leaders' (i.e. the three leaders of the traditionally recognized villages) and the 'five European leaders' (i.e. the three traditional village leaders *plus* two representatives of factional sections of two of the former villages, who had gained effective independence by collection of their own tax but whose separation had not so far been confirmed by their parental villages or by the village group as a whole). In Etemetek in 1965 the 'community leader' was an older man who had formerly been the sole village leader but had lost his position by being put into prison on a bribery charge, his place then being taken by a younger man spoken of as 'European's leader'. In Ebeagwa in 1953, a dispute over village leadership was solved on the suggestion of the District Officer that one man should be 'traditional' community leader, receiving any leopard caught by a villager, the other, younger man, the 'official' village leader (the Village Head, *mfɔ Ndek*), who would represent the village to the administration. This last example shows most clearly the way in which this distinction of status parallels and has a similar function to the distinction between those with 'effective' and 'ritual' status as representatives of the community in the past. Today the 'community leader', if different from the 'European's leader', has usually little more than formal status, acting within the village as its ritual representative and being given formal respect, but lacking the personal influence of the 'European's leader', who remains the more effective representative. But if the latter's role is defined by his relationship to the administration, its 'legitimacy' has still to be confirmed by reference to the 'community leader' who is the 'true', albeit formal, head of the village. As the status of a hamlet leader is legitimized by describing him as the representative of the senior elder of the lineage group associated with the hamlet – someone who 'moves with the village leader' – so the 'European's leader' of a village is often spoken of as the representative of the (formal, traditional) 'community leader' – someone 'who goes to see the District Officer at Mamfe'.

Community structure and administrative authority

The most important change that occurred to the Banyang political communities with the advent of a Colonial administration was that these communities, however diffuse, ceased to hold autonomy in their own right but became part of a wider administrative structure, in which ultimately now all authority lay. Residential groups which before were the sole political communities became now only units of a wider, infinitely expanded political organization, and this gave a new context and a new direction to Banyang political processes.

During the period of British control, one of the main conditions of the wider political context was a concern for and a desire to work through traditional institutions and groupings. This was not the only area in Africa in which the British administrators were greater traditionalists than the people whom they ruled: again and again in the reports which deal with the Banyang people one finds a concern to locate 'hereditary rights', to define the true 'rules of succession', to establish a man's status by 'descent from the eponymous ancestor of the Clan', etc., in situations where the rules are not subject to so clear a definition and where the arrangements arrived at tend to be more circumstantial and open to change than the administrators even seem able to give credit for.[1] This belief in tradition and the 'rule of custom', in the indigenous groupings as the 'natural units' of society, led also to an ignoring of the administration's own role in creating new institutions, in recognizing new statuses, and in sanctioning new arrangements. It is typical that Gorges on his Assessment tour was continually faced with disputes that he was obliged to arbitrate: perhaps ironically his Report was criticized by his superiors for being full of 'petty disputes over chiefships or land tenure' when he ought to have been examining what the institutions of Banyang society really were (i.e. the pure 'customary' forms). What emerged throughout much of the Colonial period was then a process of political shuttlecock: a dispute taken to the administration for settlement is referred back to the 'traditional' authorities, or 'customary' rights, yet ultimately it is only the authority of the administration which can sanction its settlement. It is in this area of interplay that the most significant new political processes developed, new institutions emerged.

Broadly speaking, three main kinds of change occurred. Firstly, there was a greater emphasis upon the wider groupings which accepted a common interest and continuity of purpose in the traditional society. Secondly, a somewhat sharper and more clearly defined constitutional status was given to certain of the traditional residential groups (notably village and village group). Thirdly, the whole focus of the political attempt to gain

---

[1] The following entry in the Banyang Touring Diary speaks for itself. It refers to a meeting at Bakebe between the Superior Native Authority and the District Officer in January 1944. 'Council [the S.N.A.] somewhat disgruntled because it thinks it is ignored in the Tinto Headship disputes. I explain I cannot back them unless they give full reasons for their decisions. They have, I said, a bad habit of deciding for the man rather than for the custom; that is, they decide on a man for reasons known to themselves and not that Banyang custom is such and such, therefore A or B is the right man for the job.'

status, whether as a group or as a person, tended to turn to the administration itself, which was now besieged by an endless series of disputes over leadership. Whether it liked it or not, it was the administration which became the sanctioning, 'legitimizing' authority, which defined the constitutional status of leaders and thus the groups whom they represented, and which was called upon to validate the status of new leaders, new groupings.

Little need be said here concerning the first two kinds of change. Mansfeld's consolidation of settlements, the British administration's use of village and village group in the structure of Native Authorities, the general widening of contacts, have all tended to bring into greater prominence the most extended community groupings, village and village group. 'Nchemti' (a group formed by aggregation, an 'association' or 'federation') is a name which was repeatedly used by the administration for the new groupings it created. Again, the three largest villages, which have resisted tendencies to internal division and maintain a residential consolidation greater than that of most Banyang villages, are all close to Mamfe (Besongabang, Nchang, and Bachu Ntae). On the second point – the more sharply defined constitutional status given to persons and groups – it is relevant to note how a number of the terms used by the administration have come to be taken over by Banyang themselves in describing political status or relationships: occasionally 'Clan' (in the Gorges sense) and 'Village Head', but much more commonly 'Quarter' and 'Quarter Head', both terms which have now become virtually Kenyang words. The assimilation of these two latter terms is significant, for with a greater emphasis on the Village as the administrative unit, with its recognized Village Head, it becomes important to differentiate residential groupings within a village which have their own leaders but which are not of equal status with the Village and Village Head. It is precisely this that the terms 'Quarter' and 'Quarter Head' (*kwɔta* and *kwɔtahɛd*) indicate. (An example of their use in this sense has already been given on p. 68.) Their use begins to turn the diffuse community structure, consisting of a series of homologous groupings, each an extension of the total community, into an ordered hierarchy of categorically differentiated groups (*kwɔta* – *ɛtɔk* (village) – *ɛtɔk ɛnkɔm* (village group) or 'Clan'), each with a defined place and relationship to the others.

In the remainder of this chapter I shall discuss the third kind of change indicated: the role that the administration came to play in defining community constitution and authorizing the changes in status which occurred for individual residential groups.

A number of new villages came into being at the time of the German administration, when 'papers' were given to their leaders and the residential groups they represented acquired in this way independent status. Mfaetok, Ashum, Bakebe, Tinto II, Tinto Mbu are among those which trace their independence to this time. On the other hand, a number of formerly separate residential groups appear to have come together under a common, officially recognized leader at the same time: Etemetek with Eyanchang; Mbinjong with Are with Mfaenchang; Okoyong with Besongabang.[1] At least two residential groups which were then recognized as having independent chiefs no longer exist as independent villages.[2] The present-day Tinto village group provides a good example of how German administrative recognition of sectional leaders is interwoven with more traditional political processes in an account of how the present constitutional grouping emerged:

The members of the village group trace their collective descent from one *Mfɔ Nto* or *Ɛnto*, whose name, apparently misheard by the Germans, produced the present 'Tinto'. (A possible closer derivation is *Ta Ɛntó*, 'father Ento'.) The present-day residential organization and descent grouping of the village group is shown in *Figure 21*. The general genealogical pattern is very similar to those already described: *Mfɔ Nto* is said to have had two sons, one *Cɔ*, who went to build at Kerie, and one *Bɛsɔŋɔ* (literally 'former settlement'), who remained where his father lived. *Bɛsɔŋɔ* had a son, *Ɛntɛbɛ Baŋ*, who at first lived with him at Besinga but later went to build towards the river Mbu. The movements of these 'sons' account for the founding of the separate village communities: Tinto Kerie (founded by *Cɔ*) and Tinto Mbu (founded by *Ɛntɛbɛ Baŋ*).

Neither Tinto Kerie nor Tinto Mbu had acquired a separate leadership before the Germans arrived: at this time all *bɔ Ɛnto* recognized a single leader, Mfo Nkwa (a descendant of *Nkwa Cɛ*), and any leopard

[1] It is difficult to establish how far administrative pressure was used, if at all, to create these amalgamations. In the case of Okoyong it is said they rejoined with Besongabang (whom they had not long before seceded from) since times were harsh and they needed the protection of the larger group. In the cases of Etemetek and Mfaenchang an element of compulsion is claimed (the amalgamation occurring when settlements were consolidated), but one suspects that this claim is at least partly inspired by the later desire of these groups to re-achieve independence. Of these examples, only Mbinjong-Are remain a united village today.

[2] Thus Mansfeld's list of 'places' with their 'chiefs' names 'Eturre' (Etoko) I–V, besides 'Kapelle', 'Tajo', 'Ekbo', and 'Biu'. Under the British administration, however, only seven and not nine villages were recognized in the Nkokenok II village group. (See also below, p. 124.)

killed was brought to him, and it was he who operated upon it. The leopard knife was not held by Mfo Nkwa, however, but by the minor leader of Ɛbɔabɛn, who gave it to the village leader for the operation, and then, after it had been used, took it back to hide it. The story is told of how people from the neighbouring village group of Mbang

Figure 21 Descent and residential grouping, Tinto village group

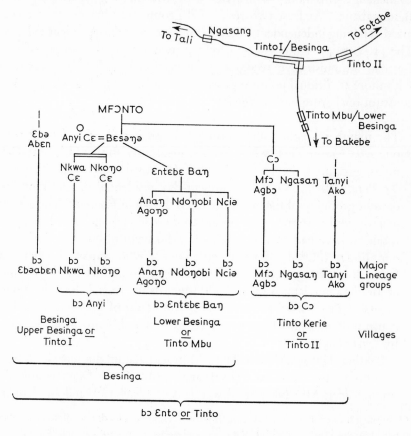

came on one occasion to fight Ta Sim, the leader of Ɛbɔabɛn, in order to get the knife, but Ta Sim had already taken it and had given it to one of his slaves 'so that it should not be the cause of dispute'; the slave had hidden it at the top of a palm-tree. When the fighting had finished and the Mbang people had returned home, Ta Sim asked for the knife, and it was brought to him. Ta Sim then went to Mfo Nkwa, handed it over to him, and gave him his blessing with it. He said it was this which had brought war and danger of his own death: Mfo Nkwa should himself take it and keep it. A meeting was then held by Upper and Lower Besinga (i.e. the rest of Tinto) who said that it was Mfo Agbo, then leader of Tinto Kerie, who had asked the Mbang people to come and get the knife. A case was made against Mfo Agbo and he was asked to pay a fine (*ankwɔ*). He refused. The combined Besinga then made a law that, whenever a leopard was killed in either part of Besinga, the people of Tinto Kerie should not see it. Mfo Agbo went home and established the rule that whenever a leopard was killed in Tinto Kerie he would give it to Tanyi Esong (a senior elder) to operate upon it. When Besinga heard this they made a curse: no one from Tinto Kerie should ever go to the bush and shoot a leopard. This story (which recalls in a number of its features the Tabe Aru story in Tali) is essentially one of an abortive attempt to obtain a separate, constitutional leadership on the part of Tinto Kerie. It was believed that the curse had remained effective, for although three leopards had been killed since this time they had all been killed by visiting strangers and not by the true residents of Kerie. On the last occasion, however, and well after Tinto Kerie or 'Tinto II' had become administratively recognized as a separate village, the right to perform the operation was conferred formally upon their village leader by the person who held this right in Besinga.

When the Germans came Mfo Nkwa had died and his successor, Ta Tambi, was by now an old man. Tinto still had only one leader. As Ta Tambi did not have the strength to do the work demanded by the German administration, he gave the position to Manga. 'Manga was fierce and gave trouple to the community. The minor leader of Ngasang went to report to the German administrator [literally: the German European] that the leader was causing a lot of trouble. The European wrote a paper and gave it to the minor leader of Ngasang. He returned to Tinto II and gave it to the leader there: so he became independent.' (In the words of my informant 'he became "free" in his own right', *aci 'free' ndu miɛt ɛji.*)

Ntantang succeeded Manga as leader. At this time Tinto Mbu were living in the same place as Tinto Besinga. They complained that food was short and the forest was finished. They wanted to go and build separately where they would have more land. Ntantang refused to allow them to move. So they went to the administrator and complained that Ntantang was preventing them from getting food. 'He wrote a paper and gave it to Tinto Mbu: they now became independent ["free" in their own right] with their own leadership.' At first they built close to the Mbu river, but later at the end of the 1920s moved back nearer to the main body of Tinto on the road which was then constructed. Tinto Mbu have since asked to be given a leopard knife (i.e. the authority to operate independently upon a leopard killed by one of their villagers) but when they made their request to their parent village, Besinga, they were told they must give a slave: in fact this was a prevarication, for Besinga had no intention of giving them the knife.[1]

It would follow from this account that the pressures leading to the splitting of *bɔ Ɛnto* into separate communities under their own leaders already existed before the arrival of the Germans, but that it was the action of the German administrative officer which finally confirmed the constitutional separation of first 'Tinto II' (as it was recorded in Mansfeld's list and has continued to be called under the British administration) and later Tinto Mbu. It is significant that the 'paper' having been acquired by Ngasang – itself a potential offshoot from Tinto Kerie – it was nevertheless taken to the superior leader recognized by them, that of Kerie. We may note how in this administratively created village group an attempt has later been made to acquire the trappings of traditional legitimacy for the separate village leaders, namely the right to the independent use of a leopard knife; this was successful in one case, unsuccessful in another.

A further example of a village group created by administrative action during the period of German rule is the group now known as Nkokenok I. Formerly Bakebe, Ashum, and Mfaetok were united with the present-day village of Eyang under its then leader, Atem Akang. Stories (which differ between villages) tell of the latter's autocratic or unjust actions, which provoked the leaders of the now independent villages to apply to the German administration each for their own 'paper'. In this village group, also, there continues to be some discrepancy concerning the collective performance of the leopard ritual: thus Eyang and Bakebe share jointly one 'leopard bush', Mfaetok and Ashum another.

During the first years of the British administration a number of new groupings were recognized. This was aided by the British administrative officers' belief in the arbitrariness of German rule, by their concern to re-

[1] This account was given to me by Mfo Ashu of Tinto I. It was given at first privately, then later again at a general meeting of the village group where all its main details were confirmed.

establish traditional groupings, especially the wider 'Clan' (village group) units, and to work through these in their own administration. At the same time the groups concerned took the opportunity to form alignments which served their own interests.

One of the clearest examples of this process concerns what Gorges refers to as the 'newly recognized Clan' of Debenjui, which came into existence at the time of Assessment. We have already noted the amalgamation of Mbinjong, Are, and Mfaenchang under the German administration. At first Mfaenchang would appear to have had its own officially recognized leader (recorded in Mansfeld's list) but he was later imprisoned for refusing to obey an order, and the people of Mfaenchang were brought under the single leader of Mbinjong.[1] When Native Court areas were first being drawn up under the British administration, Mbinjong, on the strength of an early genealogical link, claimed closer relationship with the eastern Ejagham and were thus allocated to the Kembong Native Court. About 1928 the Mfaenchang leader, who by now had returned home, approached the Divisional Officer for permission to move with his followers away from Mbinjong and to re-establish his own village. It would seem that not all of Mfaenchang were in agreement on this move, but permission was given and, except for one section who continued to live with Mbinjong, Mfaenchang's independence was recognized. This move had the incidental effect of bringing Mfaenchang out of the Kembong ('Keaka-speaking') area and into the Banyang area. This was not all, however, for according to tradition an earlier split had occurred in Mfaenchang, the dissatisfied party migrating to the east, where eventually they were given land and became part of the community of Sabes. During the first years of British administration, this residential group (Fumbe) paid its tax to the leader of Sabes, although, according to Gorges, 'most unwillingly'. In 1929 or 1930 Fumbe petitioned the Divisional Officer 'to be separated from Sabes and the Tainyong Clan and to be recognized as a separate village'. The story of their connection with Mfaenchang was told and was supported by the latter. Finally, a further residential group (Mambat) who were related to Fumbe (and thus Mfaenchang) but who had migrated into Bamenda, were brought back and agreed to rejoin Fumbe if this were recognized as an independent village. Gorges concludes his account: 'In short then, the chequered past of this Clan has led to all its constituent groups being subject to stranger control.

[1] Gorges, op. cit., para. 130.

Fainschang is now an independent village group,[1] and a member of the Badshu Akagbe Native Authority. The recognition of the independence of Fumbe from Sabes and its transference to the Badshu Akagbe Native Authority [where it would not be subject to the dominance of Sabes and the Tainyong Clan] will lead to the return of its hamlet Bamba, and the union of the Clan under one, instead of three Native Authorities as at present.'[2]

The name Debenjui (or Debengui) which was given to this newly constituted Clan appears to have been provided by Mfaenchang: although it is used by them in genealogical accounts as the name of an ancestor, it means 'the mountain of pigs' (*dεbεi njui*) and is associated with their claim that the mountain at whose foot they live and which is inhabited by wild pigs among other animals, is their own ancestral land. Suitably, the group is listed as the fourteenth (and as Banyang would say, the youngest) Clan in the Assessment Report list.

One should perhaps add that Mbinjong later decided to leave the Kembong Native Authority and to rejoin the Banyang Native Authority. (They are earlier listed as one of the Banyang villages by Mansfeld.) Mambat, the offshoot of Fumbe which returned to it as a subordinate hamlet, has since become an independent village. A third unrelated group (Obang), which at one time was part of Bachu Ntae, also joined this village group on becoming an independent village. The group, therefore, which now numbers five constituent villages, is divided into two territorial parts (Fumbe and Mambat; Mbinjong, Mfaenchang and Obang), and its name is subject to some confusion: *bɔ Ɛkuti* or Debenjui (or Debengui).

A number of other realignments and formal separations occurred at the time of Assessment. Bachu Ntae, on the strength of an affinal link with the dominant descent line of *bɔ Mfɔtek*, chose then to be counted with this village group, rather than with its immediate neighbour, Bachu Akagbe, with whom a common ancestral link is also traced. The division between 'Nkokenok I' and 'Nkokenok II' was then formalized: the former is the village group we have described as emerging under the Germans; the latter is a cluster of small, independently-led communities centred on, and often collectively referred to as, Etoko.[3] About this time also, a number of residential groups,

[1] A term Gorges uses synonymously with 'village'.　　　　[2] Para. 142.
[3] According to Gorges, these two Clans are 'each descended from a common ancestor named Nkokenok' but 'neither Clan claims relationship with the other, and if there ever was any family bond between the Nkokenoks all trace of it has been lost' (op. cit., para. 95). Today, at least some descent connection is recognized between the two groups, but priority

which on the pattern of Mfaenchang had been village sections, seceded residentially from their parental group and were recognized as villages in their own right. In 1928 Bara and Okoyong both moved back to their original sites and became independent villages (Bara changing its village group allegiance in the process). Shortly after, Mbanga Pongo moved away from Atebong and was also recognized as a new village.

As the successive Colonial administrations were a primary agent in the creation of new villages and the realignment of established groups, so also the administration became the focus of attempts by individuals to achieve political status. We have already noted how Gorges in his Assessment tour was repeatedly drawn into these disputes and forced to arbitrate in them. In some cases the disputes were directly concerned with Village Headships. The two main foci for dispute apart from these were the matter of Clan Headships, which were then formally recognized by the administration (see p. 111), and responsibility for tax-collecting. Both of these roles were, however, indirectly connected with village leadership and provided a convenient strategy for persons hoping ultimately to achieve administrative recognition as village leaders. The status of Clan Heads was particularly fraught, since, as we have seen, the status had only minor significance in the traditional society but now promised to be the basis of the important appointment of President or Member of the Native Court; moreover, since a 'senior elder' at a village group level is almost invariably in some way a 'leader *manqué*' there was no want of claimants for this newly developed political position. In the Annual Report for 1929 the Divisional Officer refers to a heated discussion on the issue of Clan Headship at Tali and records a remark made by the Ejwengang village leader (the 'Village Head') which 'strikes me as throwing light on the state the clans have arrived at': '"The difficulty is that up to the present [the village leader is reported as saying] the Clan Head does not sit in Court or do anything, but now he is to be made a member, if not a president of the court, it is no use having a very old man or a stupid one, so we now want to choose a suitable man from the proper family, instead of the oldest living descendant of the eponymous ancestor, who was formerly chosen as a matter of right".'[1] The difficulties that arose over Clan

is disputed and within Nkokenok I so too is the name of their founding ancestor, which is claimed by Mfaetok to be *Sɛnɛn Pa*, 'Nkokenok' being a descendant of *Sɛnɛn Pa*.

[1] Ce 1929/1, para. 23. Needless to say, the latter part of this statement, with its deference to 'Native law and custom', springs more from administrative anthropological conceptions than from anything a Manyang is ever likely to say.

Headships came precisely from this positive response to the opportunities it offered.

The most acute of the Clan Headship disputes of this time centred upon one Akuriwa of Ebuensuk, who used this status and the administrative recognition it gave to usurp the position of village leader. Gorges reports as follows:

> The present Clan Head [of 'Tainyong Clan'] is Akuriwa of Ebuensuk, his successors are Defang of Sabes and Nyong of Banga Ponga. [Both Defang and Nyong were at this time the recognized leaders of their respective villages. Akuriwa was the leader of one of the sections of Ebuensuk but appears also to have been a 'senior elder' of some political standing.] Akuriwa is uncle of Arang Takem, Chief of Ebuensuk, and the two, through the fault of Akuriwa, are not on friendly terms. [This dispute, which divided Ebuensuk, extended also into the wider village group, Sabes and Mbanga Pongo siding with Akuriwa, Atebong with Arang Takem, the 'rightful chief'.] Akuriwa came to the front in 1927 when his knowledge of the past was utilized by Mr Denton in a neighbouring boundary dispute. [The dispute was between Atebong and the newly seceded Mbanga Pongo: the final settlement favoured the latter.] After that he made several attempts to have himself acknow-ledged Chief. In this he had the support of his son and one small quarter only.
>
> Arang Takem proved that he was the rightful Chief by producing the Chief's regalia left him by his father. Akuriwa was warned several times that he was the Clan Head only and not Chief of Ebuensuk, but in spite of this attempted through his small following to secure Ebuensuk tax discs where they were being issued at Atebong court. One of his followers was imprisoned for his part in the resulting fight, and Aku-riwa caused no more open trouble. Arang Takem is still nervous of him, however, and says that on his death Akuriwa's son will attempt to make himself Chief . . . (paras 64–65).

Gorges again refers to this case in his general discussion of the problem of Clan Headships as the focus for Upper Banyang village disputes:

> The clash occurred in Ebuensuk (Tainyong Clan) when Akuriwa, who had hitherto passed his days in comparative obscurity, was recognized as Clan Head. He was, or pretended to be, incapable of realizing that he had not supplanted the Village Head, and egged on by his small

quarter and family, attempted to take the chief's place as tax-collector in order to obtain the 10 per cent Dash, and also attempted to have his son acknowledged as future Chief. The result has been a suspicion of Clan Heads throughout the area (para. 175).

So later Gorges writes:

Even if Clan Heads [who are not also Village Heads] have not attempted to supplant Village Heads they are regarded nervously. Defang [of the Mbang village group] on assessment pointed out that his Clan Head was a mere quarter Head, from whom he could not take personal orders, though he deferred to him as head of the consultive Clan Council [presumably as nominal senior elder]. Again, the Awanchi Clan Village Heads complained that the Clan Head never called meetings of the Clan Council nor gave feasts, and thought he could give personal orders (para. 180).

The case of Akuriwa of Ebuensuk also illustrates how attempts to acquire village leadership were frequently made in terms of the tax-collecting role. As Tinto 'constitutional' stories tell of fighting over the leopard knife, as Ndifaw stories tell of the transfer of the 'horn of the community', so Akuriwa and his followers fought over the tax discs. The importance of this 'tax-regalia' is shown in one entry in the Banyang Touring Diary, where the District Officer, after confirming two new Village Heads for Tinto I and II in 1942, continues, 'The Superior Native Authority will recover tax tickets, roll and demand notes from each deposed village head and hand them over to the new men'. The care taken over the due transfer of these administrative impedimenta was no doubt to prevent them from becoming subject to further dispute; yet the effect was to validate a newly acquired status by administrative action just as surely as Tinto II's acquisition of the right to use a leopard knife was to validate their separate leadership ritually. Administrative officers often explained the importance and frequency of these 'tax palavers' by reference to the '10 per cent Dash': as Gorges does above, the attempt to collect tax is seen as a means of reaping the reward in terms of the Dash. The inappropriateness of this purely mercenary explanation is quite clear in the case of Akuriwa; and is completely invalidated by Gorges's own account of how this 'Dash' was *not* retained by village leaders but distributed 'amongst their quarter and family heads' (see p. 112 above). Indeed, in one Village Headship dispute which he was called upon to arbitrate, one of the main complaints against the 'official chief' was that 'over the last six years he has kept the tax dash for himself in spite of protests' (para. 49; the village is Mambaw).

Almost invariably where a section of a village has succeeded in being recognized as a single unit for the collection of tax, the same group has later been recognized as an independent village. In 1942 note was made of 'four new "villages" ... which appear among tax collectors' but 'although they collect tax separately are regarded only as quarters by the Banyang N.A. and not as villages proper'.[1] The four 'quarters' are Etemetek, Onamafong, Ngurefen, and Obang, all of which were later recognized as independent villages with their own officially confirmed leaders. Tali 2's pursuit of independence also led them through a period of separate tax-collection. In the Mbang village group, the residential groups Sumbe and Akriba have both for a number of years petitioned to be recognized as separate villages but have so far only achieved separate status as tax-collecting units.

I have tried to show in the preceding pages how, with the establishment of Colonial rule, the administration came to fulfil an important role in defining the constitution of Banyang communities in the sense of their politically validated grouping. Part of my argument has been that this role of the administration was an inevitable consequence of the fact that ultimate political authority lay (as Banyang had little difficulty in realizing) with the administration. Whereas in the past the constitutional status of a village leader and the village represented by him depended upon the gesture of allegiance symbolized in the presentation of a leopard to him, it now depended more formally upon his recognition by the administration. Under the British administration at least (but probably also under the German) this recognition was not arbitrarily given, but depended upon the nature of the village leader's support from his own village and village group, and upon whatever 'customary' principles could be established by the administrative officers seeking to decide the validity of a leader's case. But if the British administrators were traditionalists, Banyang themselves were political realists and (as the difficulties arising over Clan Heads showed) sought to use the conditions and opportunities of the Colonial régime to their own advantage. As the administrators attempted to get a ruling from a traditional authority, so

[1] Banyang Touring Diary, p. 12. A further note by the D.O. in 1942, in connection with a suit between the leaders of Bachu Ntae and Obang, reads that 'Obang 3-corner, like Ngurefen and Etemetek, though paying tax independently, are not to be looked on as independent villages'.

claimant leaders and their followers turned always to the administration. If the constitutional structure of Banyang communities was altered by the presence of the overruling administration, so also was the process of constitutional politics stemming from a new strategy adapted to fit the administrative framework in which the traditional communities were now placed.

The strongest evidence for the role of the administration lies, firstly, in the number of new villages which came into being during the half century or so of Colonial rule, and, secondly, in the frequency of the village leadership disputes which the administration was called upon to arbitrate. I have mentioned that Mansfeld, writing in 1907, lists thirty-seven villages, of which five would not now be counted as Banyang. In the Register of Chiefs published in 1965, fifty-five villages are listed, each with its 'recognized Chief'.[1] Neither of these lists would appear to be totally accurate,[2] but the comparison gives some general indication of the number of new villages, and new chiefs, that have been recognized during this period. In the Banyang Touring Diary, which effectively covers the period 1941 to 1958, fifteen disputes concerning Village Headship are reported, in which the administration intervened in some capacity or another, most frequently to arbitrate and finally confirm a settlement. Many of these disputes lasted a number of years and produced repeated claims and interventions. We shall later examine, in Chapter 13, how both traditional and modern processes are interwoven in one such case, that of Tali 2.

[1] *West Cameroon Gazette*, No. 10, Vol. 5.
[2] In the more recent list Feitok 'Small and big' have been treated as a single village, and Fumbe is not included.

PART II

Processes of Government

5

The Nature of Community Authority

The authority of the corporate community

The underlying principle of all Banyang governmental processes is that coercive authority is directly or ultimately a function of the community acting corporately. I speak here of the 'coercive' authority of the community to distinguish it from the moral authority of the lineage group, and qualify its functional dependence upon the corporate community as 'direct or ultimate' since associations have also some part in governmental activities but are less directly representative of community groupings than most bodies or councils actually spoken of as 'the community'. This chapter examines some of the more general features of community authority: its operational structure, the values associated with it, the ways in which it is exerted, and the sanctions that uphold it. The two succeeding chapters examine in more detail particular governmental processes (judicial, policy-making, military) and in Chapter 8 are considered some of the limitations that arise from the fact that these processes are so closely tied to the corporate community.

In discussing the concept of the *ɛtɔk*, we have already indicated briefly how Banyang residential groups do in fact operate politically. In its most general terms, the operational political structure of a community can be expressed as in the diagram reproduced on the next page (*Figure 22*). A 'community', *ɛtɔk*, is thus a residential group whose affairs are controlled by a smaller body of persons (a 'council') who represent the wider group and act in its name. As we have already stressed, the key political processes of a Banyang community are those of internal government: the ordering of a group's own affairs. This point is made in a saying: 'A settlement will not burn when people are sitting there', *Ɛtɔk ɛpu sɔŋo bo baci cɔko*, which could also be translated, 'A community will not burn when people are living in it'. Affairs within a residential group will be controlled by it.

Two points must immediately be made about this diagram. The first is that the structure it describes is one of effective action rather than of formal institution. We speak of the body of persons who represent the wider community (the residential aggregate) as a 'council', but Banyang themselves make no such distinction, referring to this body itself as the 'community' or as the 'people of the community' (*bo ɛtɔk*). When we speak, then, of the council 'acting in the name of' the community, we refer to something which occurs literally and in fact, and not to an institutionalized relationship between formally distinct groups. Again, the council 'represents' the community by the fact that it is composed of

Figure 22 The operational structure of the community

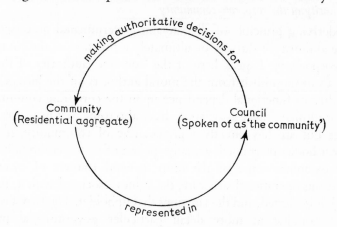

the men who are indeed the prominent, leading, or respected members of a community, who by virtue of their status, individually acquired, *can* speak for others. Even an informal gathering of the leading members of a residential group, met for convivial (rather than political) purposes, can still be referred to as 'the community' in this sense, for it is in and through them that the community is represented. On the other hand, it should be noted that the distinction that we are making here between 'community' as residential aggregate and 'community' as a body of persons who by coming together represent the whole, is one which is fully apparent to Banyang, and is implicit in their use of the term *ɛtɔk*. (On this point, see also the next section of this chapter, which discusses further the relationship between the 'inner council', 'the council', and 'the community', which in practice are quite distinctive bodies, but can all be described in the same terms, as *ɛtɔk* or *bo ɛtɔk*.)

Secondly, the operational structure for corporate community actions shown in the diagram above is an idealized pattern which does not take account of what we have already described as the 'diffuseness' of community organization. Neither the 'community' of the diagram, nor the 'council', can be taken to correspond to any single residential group or body of persons representing it. What occurs is a more or less exact repetition of the pattern at each level of residential grouping that makes up the wider, complex community (*Figure 23*):

Figure 23 The operational structure of the complex community

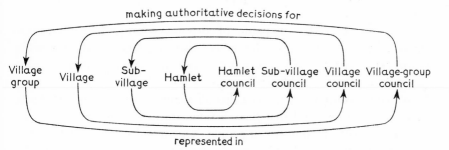

making authoritative decisions for

Village group | Village | Sub-village | Hamlet | Hamlet council | Sub-village council | Village council | Village-group council

represented in

We shall return later to discuss the differences between councils at different levels (which tend to be more formal and exclusive in their membership the higher their level) but the basic repetitiveness of the total pattern should here be emphasized. Whether the persons who have come together are the leader and group of elders of a hamlet, or are the dozen or so leading and prominent men in a village group, if the action they make is concerned with the policy or good order of the group they represent, the action may be described as one of the 'community': it is *ndak ɛtɔk*, a 'matter of the community', having the force of community authority. The government of Banyang society is a function of such corporate actions made at all levels of community grouping; these actions follow a similar pattern, but are also conditioned by the level at which they are made.

Perhaps the most general feature of any corporate action of the community is the fact that it should be respected, obeyed, taken seriously. A basic axiom of political life, which is often referred to in actual discussions is that a member of a community has to accept the authority of the group over him. 'You don't play with the community' (*Mu akɛrɔɔti n' ɛtɔk*). 'What the community says (literally, the voice of the community) is not to be ignored' (*Ɛyɔŋ ɛtɔk mu akɛbiak yɔ*). Sayings such as these show not only the seriousness and authority of community actions, but also the fact that this authority is not to be evaded. 'A matter of community is not left neglected' (*Ndak ɛtɔk bapu giɔ gu amɔk*). Since he is a member of it, a man cannot ignore the authority of the corporate community over him: to do so would be to set himself against the group. If there is a case against him, however reluctant he may be, at whatever cost to himself, he must ultimately make his peace with whatever council is pursuing the case (usually by this stage the village council), resolving the issue in terms that satisfy them. We shall later see that community councils are very sensitive to any action which places their authority in contempt, and have means of 'tying' – constraining by strong pressures – any person who refuses to accept their authority.

The collective, concerted nature of corporate community actions is also stressed by Banyang, especially where they are based upon the wider residential groupings. 'One person does not make up a community: it is an affair of everyone' (*Mu amɔt apu jɛmti ɛtɔk: ci ndak bo bankɔmankɔm*). Many sayings emphasize the fact that *all* a community's members should support its actions, and that these actions are made collectively, by the concerted effort of a number of people. 'One tree does not make a forest' (*Ɛnɔk ɛmɔt ɛpu ki ncuɔt*). 'One hand cannot tie a bundle' (*Abuɔ amɔt apu guɔt nɛkɛp*). Community authority depends, then, upon collective decisions, not upon the decision of any individual, whatever his status. We have already pointed out that Banyang leaders, while they may be extremely influential, lack formal authority: 'When a leader speaks he speaks with the voice of the community, not in his own voice.' Indeed, there are no significant authority-bearing offices in Banyang society: it is always the group that rules the group, whether political, recreational, or religious association, age-group or lineage group.

The following case exemplifies the principle which we are here discussing and serves also to illustrate the more general operational structure of a community already outlined.

A youth of the hamlet of Kembong (Tali 1) had already acquired the reputation of a ne'er-do-well and scapegrace. After a series of minor misdemeanours in Tali he was caught by a travelling European Agricultural Officer after having stolen a sum of £3 1s. from the bag of one of his carriers. The theft was discovered in Ebeagwa at the time that a meeting of the Ndifaw Clan Union was in progress in the 'Lower' sub-village. As a later chapter will describe, these meetings while governed in their particular form and purpose by the constitution of the Union, also operated in a more general way as a representative meeting of the village group, to which any community matter could be brought for debate and decision. The European Agricultural Officer referred the theft, by message, to the meeting. Theft is regarded very seriously by Banyang and the present case was no exception, since it reflected upon the good name of the village group: the youth, it was said, had 'spoilt the community', *acɔŋti ɛtɔk*. After discussion, it was decided that the youth should be debarred from attending any social gathering: wherever wine was being drunk, he should be stopped from entering; no one should be allowed to greet or talk to him. This ruling was announced at the meeting and it applied, by virtue of the extent of the community represented there, throughout the village group. This 'law' was a slightly modified version of the strongest political sanction – the sanction of formal ostracism – that a corporate community can at the present time command. Later, a further punishment was made by the combined young men's associations of the village group, who threw the youth in the nearby river.

About a fortnight later a 'Band' dance was held in Tanyi Tabe settlement near to the youth's own home, as part of the funeral celebrations of a man who had recently died. When the dance was in progress the youth approached Taboko, the leader of the settlement, for permission to join in the dance. Taboko had been one of the leading speakers in the village group discussion and it was he who had announced its decision. When asked for his permission, he refused.

The youth returned to his home in Kembong and obtained the use of the cult-agency, Mfam, from its owner, Kembong's senior elder. (A threepenny fee was paid for this purpose.) The normal use of Mfam, which has the form of a horn filled with medicines, is as a supernatural sanction against the evil of deceit, notably witchcraft, lying, and theft. The youth, however, carrying it through Kembong hamlet, publicly invoked misfortune on any Kembong person who gave Taboko wine to drink. He swore: Should anyone do this, Mfam attack him!

This action was quickly reported and much talked about. It was indeed one of vindictive lawlessness: the youth was quite outside his rights in making it and it was a misuse of the essentially moral and socially integrative virtues of Mfam. It also implied (and this is the point that immediately concerns us) Taboko's personal responsibility for a decision which, although largely influenced by him and finally announced by him, was certainly not formally his. Taboko as an individual stood quite apart from the collective decision of the village group meeting, even although he had voiced it.

A few days later Taboko himself brought the matter to the attention of a meeting which had gathered in the house of Mr Tataw in Tanyi Ako (*Figure 10*, also p. 41). There were about ten people present, representing the various sections of the composite settlement where it was held, together with Taboko himself from Tanyi Tabe. The meeting was one of the 'community', εtɔk, even although only this sub-village was represented, but it was characteristic of the meetings which were commonly held there: it was thus convened circumstantially and without much formality to deal with an issue which, although important, did not extend in its immediate relevance beyond the sub-village. Again, characteristically, Taboko took the leading part in the discussion, but was supported by the others present.

The youth was sent for: he appeared together with a senior relative, the senior elder of his minor lineage group, who in the absence of his father, who had died, spoke on his behalf throughout the case. Taboko then outlined the case against the youth. Expressing himself very strongly on the point, he said that whatever had been decided at Ebeagwa had been decided by the εtɔk and not by himself alone. It was not *his* action but the *community's* action. If the youth wanted to change the ruling he would need to wait for the next meeting of the village group and Clan Union (he referred to it as the next 'Meeting' or 'Gathering') to be held shortly in Ejwengang. What the youth had done by carrying Mfam was completely wrong and unheard of: if he wished to, Taboko claimed, he could have him sent to prison for it.[1] He demanded that the youth produce as a fine a 'goat of the community' (*mεn εtɔk*, see below) and that this very day he should again 'carry Mfam', revoking what he had previously sworn.

The others present at the meeting clearly supported Taboko's view and little more was said. The youth and his kinsman left, and the meeting adjourned to the house of the senior elder of Kembong, the owner of the Mfam concerned. Here three bars of carbolic soap were brought (each with a nominal value of 2s. 6d.), together with 2s., in cash. This was the community's 'goat'; it had in fact been somewhat hastily provided by the youth's (minor) lineage group relatives. It was accepted and shared out among the persons present. The senior elder of Kembong then produced his Mfam and other associated cult-agencies. They were laid out in front of the house and in full sight and

---

[1] This is an interesting indication of the attitude of many Banyang leaders at this time, who saw themselves on the side of authority, without distinguishing too closely between the corporate authority of their traditional communities and that of the Colonial government.

hearing of the settlement, the youth together with the senior elder and Taboko participated in the revocation of the previous 'curse'.

Immediately following on from this case, a second case was discussed, which concerned a theft which had occurred to a visiting stranger the previous night. Suspicion centred strongly upon one person (also a stranger) but no proof was forthcoming and the matter had finally to be left to the supernatural sanction of Mfam. Thus Mfam was invoked for a second time, but on this occasion was carried through the whole of the composite settlement (despite the fact that the theft had occurred in Kembong itself and it was here that the suspected thief was staying).

A number of points emerge from this account: it shows how the community represented in corporate political action may expand or contract according to the circumstances of the case and the issue in hand. The bases for political action however remain the same: it is the community punishing and putting right a misdemeanour which has occurred within it. The village group meeting at Ebeagwa had no special warrant to hear the initial case against the youth but it so happened that a meeting was in progress and the case reported to it: it became then the basis for relatively strong action to be taken against the youth, the 'prosecution' by the community being led by someone from his own village and sub-village who was already familiar with the background. The misuse of Mfam provoked a much less extended meeting of the community and was dealt with at the sub-village level, partly because the case was so clear-cut and the offence so flagrant. Although less formal than a meeting of the village would have been, the sub-village representatives had nevertheless the power to act as a corporate community and imposed their own fine on the youth. This was a fine given to, and shared by, the community as a collective body: Taboko himself received no personal indemnity, although he shared in the fine. The varying bases of community action are also illustrated in the carrying of Mfam: the youth himself, applying a pseudo-legal 'curse', carried it only through his own hamlet (which would be the normal unit for a minor Ngbe law), but in the subsequent case the same Mfam was carried through the whole of the composite settlement of which his hamlet was part.

The case also, and especially, illustrates the principle that authoritative decisions are seen as coming from the group and not an individual member, however respected or influential. It is the community acting corporately (through the councils representing it) which holds authority. A single person as the effective representative of the residential group then gathered may voice the decision, but it remains the group's decision and not his. He himself has no power to rescind it, which can be done only by the same order of residential grouping, again corporately. It is worth noting how strongly Taboko reacted to the use of the Mfam curse which he clearly felt (his threat of 'prison' is an indication) not only placed the community's decision in contempt but also ran contrary to all legitimate order. Nevertheless, not very strong forces were needed to bring the youth to heel, and the settlement of this case, with Taboko lecturing this foolish 'small boy', had a slight domestic air about it: even so, the fine of a 'community goat' was accepted without question and was quickly forthcoming.

As this case illustrates, the authority of the corporate community is most clearly and distinctly expressed in judicial action. This may be of a 'civil' kind: the arbitration and settlement of disputes between individuals. It is, however, of the nature of Banyang governmental processes that the good order and authority of residential groups tend to be implicated in all cases of dispute between individuals, and there is a tendency for all judicial action to focus upon the fact of transgression and to punish it, rather than to seek merely the restoration of social relations. In Durkheim's terms, Banyang law is 'punitive' rather than 'restitutive'. We shall be examining this feature in the next chapter. Community councils also act deliberatively and in making laws. The latter function (*sɪɛ ɛbɛɪ*, 'putting a law') is one of the most important attributes of the corporate community since it serves to sanction decisions collectively (but representatively) made and to extend those decisions to all persons resident in the community. As one might perhaps expect, the corporate community is weakest in its administrative functions, which tend to be made indirectly, by stressing the collective responsibility for its welfare by all of its members, by the 'line of responsibility' that follows the representative heads of different orders of residential grouping, and finally and rather clumsily by a process of legislation which makes it an offence *not* to fulfil a particular task.

In most if not all of these governmental functions, and in the actual running of community affairs, the associations play an important role. Cases are judged, issues debated, and laws made, by or within the associations as well as by community councils. None of these functions are however performed *only* by the associations and in all cases they can be performed by community councils acting independently of the associations. The following pages will refer in many places to the practical importance of the associations in the day-to-day regulation of community affairs, but

for clarity of description and analysis a detailed treatment of their governmental role will be deferred until Part III, when their form, purpose, and
relation to the operational structure of the complex community will be
separately examined.

Community councils

No community council has a formally defined membership but is a body
of individuals brought together by virtue of age and kinship status, by
their representation of sectional parts of the residential group concerned,
or more generally by their involvement in or influence over the affairs
of the group. The two main categories of person composing a council are,
firstly, the senior elders of its constituent lineage groups, and secondly
(and sometimes deputizing for the first), leaders or prominent men within
the residential group, including its major, overall leader, if one is recognized. No one is excluded from any public meeting of a community
council (as distinct from 'inner council' meetings, considered below),
and usually a number of other interested persons – junior supporters of the
senior elders, or persons who have a special interest in the matter to be
discussed – also come along. There is no fixed 'quorum', and it often
happens that some section or person in the residential group is not
represented, but if too many of the key prominent figures are absent, or
if a section especially concerned in the matter is not represented, the
matter is likely to be delayed until a more representative meeting can be
arranged. (It is possible therefore for a person or section who stands to
lose from a decision made by a community council to delay the decision
by a refusal to take part in a meeting; but at the same time he runs the
risk of a harsher decision being made in his absence, particularly if it is
repeated or its motive suspected.)

At the lowest level of residential grouping, a hamlet council is the least
formal of all the community councils, the easiest to convene, and the
most circumstantial in its membership and actions. Most of the affairs of a
hamlet as a residential group are in any case conducted informally by
personal contact between its leader and other prominent household
leaders, who are close neighbours and are likely to see each other frequently
in the day-to-day course of events. A number of the matters concerning
hamlet members are moreover likely to come within the category of
affairs of the lineage group', which are not the concern of a community
council as such but rather of the (major) lineage group, here identified
with the hamlet. Even so, there is a relatively clear category of offence
that concerns the good order of the hamlet as a residential group and

comes within the jurisdiction of its council: this category includes disputes between wives of the hamlet (who are not members of their husbands' lineage groups), disputes between a stranger and the member of a hamlet, especially where the stranger conceives himself to have been injured in some way within the hamlet, and occasionally disputes over property (the ownership of oil-palms or the boundaries between farms). When a case of this kind has been brought to the leader of the hamlet, or to its senior elder, he will call together, often there and then, one or two other of its senior household heads to hear and settle the matter. I cite here an example of judicial action at this level.

The small hamlet settlement of Tanyi Tabe in Tali 1 has already been referred to on a number of occasions (see especially *Figures 8* and *12*, also pp. 37 and 47). One afternoon when a number of women, including some returned prostitutes from the south, had gathered there to mourn the death of one of the hamlet wives, an incident occurred which was to be the subject of a later complaint. A youth who was passing through the settlement had evidently made some insulting remark to one of the prostitutes. According to the youth's statement, the woman had set upon him: she had ripped his shirt, pushed him to the ground, and attacked his genitals, threatening to kill him.

The case was brought to Taboko, as leader of the settlement, about two weeks later when the youth, who was a stranger to the settlement, was again visiting it. He claimed damages from the woman for maliciously attacking him. The case was heard by Taboko and the second leading man of the settlement, the two acting jointly as hamlet council. The meeting was fairly rapidly convened and the case was heard in the late afternoon, in the open, outside Taboko's *acɔ*: although no other men were present besides the youth and myself, a number of women had gathered to watch from the background and to support the defendant; some of these were the latter's friends, others were hamlet wives.

The case was dealt with fairly speedily. The youth made his case against the woman. She denied that she had been the first to attack him: he had no right to sue her; she wished to sue him. In the argument that ensued concerning the fight, the main fact at issue came to be who had in fact started it. The youth, with no witnesses on his own side to support him, had already shown his willingness to swear Mfam to affirm his own account. Circumstantially his account was moreover the more plausible version. The second leading man of the settlement summarized the factual point of disagreement and turned to the woman to ask what she would do now? She said that she ought to have witnesses, but it was said that it was not a question of witnesses. She was thus herself brought to the point of swearing Mfam. A cult-agency was produced (not in fact Mfam, but Kekang, belonging to the second leading man) and her innocence sworn on it. With the case thus made over to the jural action of a supernatural sanction, the matter was concluded and the claim of the youth dismissed.

This case was a rather petty one which was initiated by the youth mainly it would seem to vindicate himself after his loss of face in his tussle with the prostitute. Neither of the two litigants was a member of the hamlet, but, occurring within it, this incident involved the good order of the hamlet and the complaint was therefore brought appropriately to its leader, Taboko, who treated it seriously but as a matter which concerned only his own settlement. To have taken the suit higher (which the youth could have done) would have risked making too much of it. The two men representing the hamlet nevertheless acted with community authority, as an ɛtɔk. Although the youth did not obtain reparation, the trend of the case went against the prostitute and to this extent his purpose in bringing the case was fulfilled.

Community council meetings at the higher level of a sub-village retain something of the circumstantial character of the meetings at the hamlet level which we have just noted: they include a greater number of people, of different (major) lineage groups, but are still convened relatively easily, as the occasion demands. An example of such a meeting has already been given earlier in this chapter and is typical of the kind of meetings that occurred not infrequently there.

At the village level, where the village is of any size, council meetings acquire a greater formality and have usually to be arranged in advance. In Tali 1 it had become the custom for the village council to meet on Sundays if any cases for discussion or judgement had earlier been reported to the village leader or senior elder. The council frequently (although not always) met in the village leader's settlement of Mbinjong (*Figure 8*), and Taboko coming from the extreme end of the village in Tanyi Tabe would collect the various other representatives of its sections in a pro-tracted journey from his own to the leader's settlement. In Tali 2 it was the custom for sectional leaders and senior elders to gather in the house of the village senior elder on market days and it was then that cases for discussion were brought to them as village council.

Except for the somewhat unusual case of the 'supra-village' of the conjoint Tali, for which council meetings were held for a time with a regularity comparable to that of village councils, meetings of the representatives of residential groups wider than the village would seem generally to occur only irregularly when a particular event (e.g. the killing of a leopard) or a particular issue (e.g. an especially recalcitrant dispute, often one centred on a question of leadership) demanded the participation of the widest possible residential group. Characteristically, and in a way that I shall later discuss, the authority of the village group council would seem traditionally to have been reserved for 'constitutional' issues, confirming the election to a village leadership or occasionally being referred to over leadership disputes, and would appear very rarely to have been involved for the general 'routine' matters of government. In 1953–1954 the organization of Clan Unions in the two village groups where I was working provided the somewhat unusual context for a series of village group meetings, which were in effect the conjoint meetings of village councils, supported by Clan Union officials other than those persons normally involved in village council meetings. Although, as I have said, the context of these meetings was unusual, their general form and the conduct of cases at them followed the general principles of community council meetings at other levels of residential grouping. Great point was indeed made of the fact that these meetings represented the community at its greatest extension and held therefore enhanced authority.

Apart from such community councils, there is for certain orders of residential grouping a further, smaller, and more exclusive body, whose meetings are generally held in private, which I have earlier referred to as the 'inner council'. It is generally at the level of a village that the inner council is most operative, but at a lower sub-village level its individual members form an important political core to the residential group, and, beyond the village, meetings between the inner council members of different villages may take place to discuss significant issues of common concern to their conjoint community. Although the terms Banyang use to refer to the inner council of a community are not limited solely to this body, the way and context in which it is referred to leave little doubt as to the persons intended or to their central position within community structure. Perhaps most commonly the inner council is referred to directly and usually somewhat emphatically as the *εtɔk*, with the implication that its members are the leading, most influential persons of a village, in whom are focused the interests, power, and authority of the group as a whole. They are, as it were, both power elite and cabinet rolled into one. So sometimes the inner council or ɛtɔk is in this way distinguished from the general council or *bo ɛtɔk*, 'the people of the community' (the less exclusive but still respected representative heads of a community who meet for the public discussion of affairs), and both of these bodies may, in turn, be distinguished from the 'community at large', *ɛtɔk nɛfi*, or 'people outside', *bo nɛfi*, i.e. those who are merely residents and do not actively participate in community matters. Again, the inner council is sometimes described as the 'heart of the community' (*nɛt ɛtɔk*) or 'the secret (or concealed) community' (*ɛyu ɛtɔk*). The position of the 'inner council' may be shown by extending the earlier diagram (*Figure 22*) thus:

Figure 24 The operational structure of the community: inner council, council, and residential aggregate

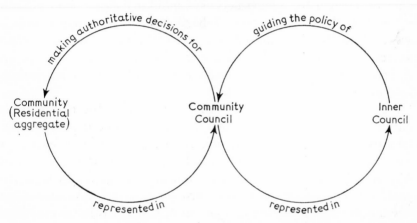

Part of the point of the inner council is the exclusiveness and secrecy which surround its activities. Often its meetings are held at night, in the privacy of a back room, or in a *mɔ ɛkri* where access is controlled. So also any arrangements made by an inner council are not generally revealed to the community at large. In Besongabang I was told how in the past the death of a village leader could be kept secret by the inner council, who at the onset of the leader's illness would take him to live in an isolated settlement (possibly a slave-settlement) and thereafter demand 'food' from the village to aid his recovery. More innocuously, it was said that members of the inner council might meet privately at night or before sunrise to eat and drink together; then when day came they would sit outside in the open: 'People will not know what has happened. They will merely wonder: So-and-so have been sitting and have never eaten: are they not hungry?'

The inner council of a village is unlikely to include more than half a dozen members, drawn from different sections of the village. The members are essentially people who can be trusted, who have a 'strong heart', as Banyang say. The village leader and senior elder (when this is more than a ritual position) are invariably members, together with a number of other prominent 'persons of the community' who are likely to be minor leaders of their own village sections. In the village of Tali 1 the inner council consisted of five men: the village leader, Taboko, Mr Tataw, Joseph Enaw (not very effectually), and (during the period before the settlement of the Tali leadership dispute) *Nyenti, a leading man from 'Tali 2' who had thrown in his lot with the traditional Tali element. These men, drawn from divergent sections of the village, represented the central core of 'established' interest. Joseph Enaw became a member during the time that I was in Tali, giving a goat and spirits to the existing members in recognition of his joining them. Taboko spoke of the group then as an *ako*, the term normally applied to the formal 'associations', and an inner council has something of the character of a highly exclusive club, but within community affairs it is also a body of considerable political influence.

Perhaps primarily the role of an inner council is concerned with the formulation of policy. Membership is thus often associated with knowledge of the 'secret talk' (εyu $k\varepsilon p\vartheta$) of a village, and one educated Manyang compared its role to that of the 'cabinet' in parliamentary government. Any issue likely to face a village community will be discussed first by members of its inner council (not necessarily at a formally convened meeting; it may occur through a process of individual consultations) and a general policy worked out, which can then be tried out at a general council meeting, or will at least guide the actions of the leading members of the village in their general conduct of political affairs. Mansfeld, in describing how a law governing the price of chickens was made for Ekoi villages, describes exactly this process: the main alternatives are discussed in private by a small group of men and then on the next day the chief announces the law at an open meeting, which is acclaimed (especially by those who have earlier agreed to it) and so the law is passed.[1] Very similar examples of the inner council at work in Banyang villages will be given later.

The inner council of a village serves also to co-ordinate the interests and knowledge of the different leading members of its various sections and to give continuity to the governmental actions carried out at different levels.

[1] Op. cit., p. 160.

The kind of mutual consultation and co-operation which is implied here is an important feature of the governmental process and an essential condition of the overall unity of wider community groupings. Thus, for example, Taboko and Mr Tataw in such a sub-village meeting as we have described (pp. 136–139, above) act in this context as the leading members of a relatively restricted council, but they serve also to represent the wider established interests of the village as a whole and will if necessary later report to the village leader or to the village inner council anything that is of wider residential concern. Drawing its members from different parts of the village, the inner council is a recognized means of channelling information to those centrally concerned in its government. Inversely, the very fact that the members of an inner council are the most prominent men, and are drawn from different sections, gives rise to potential tension and conflict within it. Splits within a community are likely to be evidenced first by splits within the inner council: as in British politics, it is the cabinet minister who resigns rather than the rebel back-bencher who is likely to present the more serious challenge. So, for example, one of the members of the Tali 1 inner council in 1953 (Nyenti) was a man who had changed sides from the controlling inner council of Tali 2, and Peter Esong's earlier removal from the inner group of Tali 1 was a further reflection of the same wider split.

Where community councils or inner councils combine, the combination normally occurs according to the status of individual members rather than according to the residential groups they represent. The fusion of groups is 'horizontal' rather than 'vertical'. Thus at supra-village meetings of Tali the two village leaders normally sat together, as did the two senior elders, the remaining 'people of the community' (the body of the combined council) also sitting together and partly interspersed. At the village group (Clan Union) meetings of both the Ndifaw and Tanyi Nkongo village groups there was a similar seating arrangement, by status category rather than by village. Such a 'horizontal' combination determines also the way in which conjoint inner councils operate in relation to a conjoint council or to the extended community: the combined inner council of the supra-village of Tali met to discuss matters of general concern to the conjoint community, and I shall later describe (pp. 175f.) a meeting of the inner council of the whole of the Ndifaw village group which preceded and served to plan the strategy for a meeting of the general council of the village group (in this case, a Clan Union assembly) in a way clearly comparable to similar meetings at a village level. Finally, we should note in this context that the status of prominent men away from their own village community will be recognized in any village they visit and if, for example, a judicial meeting of a community council is in progress (as it may be on market day, when visitors come in from other village groups) they will be encouraged to participate and will do so on equal terms with the elders and leaders of the 'home' village.

Fines and fees

On certain occasions a community council has the right to demand payment, either in acknowledgement of its services (and authority) or in atonement for an offence committed against the community. Such payment is usually referred to as a 'goat' or a 'goat of the community' (*mɛn ɛtɔk*). The main occasions when a 'goat' can be demanded are: when an offence has been committed against the community (e.g. the transgression of a law, acts of violence, failing to respect community authority or a community ruling, acts of contempt); in confirmation of a hamlet or village leader who has newly succeeded to this position; and as payment to a council 'for its work' in witnessing and sanctioning the settlement of affairs within or between lineage groups (see below, pp. 152–156). For the first of these categories the 'goat' has the nature of a fine; for the two latter categories it has the nature of a 'fee' paid to a community council for the exercise of its authority. To an outside observer, concerned perhaps more with principles of equity than with the problems of maintaining a firm authority, community councils give the appearance sometimes of rapaciousness in their demand for a 'goat' on any occasion when this is at all possible. The 'goat' may be either a real goat or a surrogate – a conventionally recognized substitute in money or goods.

Any community council has the right to demand a 'goat', but not all in fact do so. Most cases that are heard at hamlet level would seem to concern relatively trifling matters, where resolution comes from simply airing the grievance or by an arbitrated settlement. (A more serious conflict at the hamlet level is likely to involve Ngbe; its resolution will then be made through the association and usually with the participation of members from a wider order of residential grouping than the single hamlet. See pp. 255–257.) It is at the higher level of a sub-village that the settlement of a dispute or the punishment of an offence is most likely to involve some formal exercise of authority and it is here too that a 'goat' is first likely to be demanded. Even so, the 'goat' here is usually a surrogate and of moderate value: in Tali in 1963 the conventional norm was 10s. in cash or the equivalent in trade goods, such as the soap provided on behalf of the youth of Kembong (p. 138). At the higher level of a village council, there is more chance that a real goat will be demanded, or at least that a more substantial sum be given in cash. At the level of the village group, the demands are likely to be even more stringent, and the unit of reckoning which begins now to appear is a 'slave' (conventionally reckoned at £3 10s.). So, for example, when the hamlet leader of Okorobak was confirmed in his status by a meeting of the entire village group (p. 58, above) there was no question of his providing anything other than a real goat and it will be noted that his predecessor had as well made payment of a 'slave' (£3 10s.). The amounts which have been quoted here are not of course formally fixed: there is some flexibility in whether a real goat or a surrogate will be accepted, and, if a surrogate, how much this will be or what form it will take.

Once a 'goat' has been given to a community council, it is divided between its members, firstly according to certain individual status categories and secondly according to the sections of the residential group represented. The general principles governing this dual division remain the same throughout Banyang country, but its details (mainly concerning the parts accorded to persons of different statuses) vary slightly from village to village. Most of the parts given to persons of a certain status have analogical reference to the role they are expected to play in community affairs. So, for example, the 'head' is given to the leader of the group since he is at the head of discussions (literally, 'carries the head of the talk') or simply because he is 'at the head'; the 'chest' is also given to the leader as 'the person who stands in front' who thus meets 'on his chest' anything which comes to the group;[1] the 'heart' is given to the senior elder, or sometimes to the traditional 'community leader' where he is different from the 'European's leader', since (in either case) he is at the 'heart' of community affairs, or, alternatively, because he is expected to have a 'strong heart' (a phrase describing someone who is not deterred by circumstances, who can be trusted); and so on. The following is a list of the special portions which were given in Tali, together with notes on their significance:

The 'chest' (bɛwat) and 'head' (nti) to the leader of the residential group (village or hamlet). The 'chest' is the most important individual share

---

[1] Whereas both of these parts are accorded to the 'leader' in both Upper and Lower Banyang communities, among the Lower Banyang the 'head' is conventionally the more significant portion, among the Upper Banyang the 'chest'. This is an interesting reflection of the more clearly differentiated role of the leader in the latter communities.

and is the name given to the leader's portion in any division. Even if he is not present at the council meeting concerned, the portion should be reserved and later given to him with information about the meeting. The analogical reference of these portions has already been explained. (In some villages the 'head' is given to the guilty offender, who has brought the goat 'on his head'.)

The 'heart' (*ntə*) to the senior elder. A somewhat less significant portion than the 'chest' but one which is usually given at a meeting at which an influential senior elder was present. Its analogical reference is to a senior elder's position 'at the heart of the community'.

The 'neck' (*ɛmə*) to one of the leading members of the community who acts as an important 'second' or supporter. In Banyang metaphor the neck supports the 'head' and is as well recognized as a figure of speech as that describing a person at the 'head' or 'heart' of matters. The man who regularly received this portion in Tali 1 village was Nyenti, a minor leader of his own section, a close associate of the village leader, a member of the inner council and thus closely concerned in central village community affairs, who was often entrusted with the task of representing the views of the inner council or with other commissions on its behalf. A person who acts in this way as the responsible agent or supporter of others may be described as *ɛmə bo*, 'the neck of people'. In Lower Banyang villages the 'neck' is usually given with the 'head' to the village leader (nowadays usually to the 'European's chief').

When an actual goat is given, the liver and kidneys (*bɛcɛn* and *amaŋabək*) are removed, to be braised and eaten by the elders present. They have no special analogical significance.

The 'throat' (*mbok ngoŋo*) to the spokesman (*ndɛm kɛpə*). The reference is to a person who uses his 'throat' to represent others. This portion was only occasionally allocated, when in the presentation of a case someone had acted notably as an advocate for others.

The 'waist' or 'small of the back' (*ɛbo*) to the divider: this is to compensate the 'butcher' for bending over while making the division, but may also be given in the case of a surrogate.

A 'leg of the animal' (*anə nya*) to the representative of another (usually village) community, who has attended the meeting of the council; this portion is especially due to a visitor who is prominent, either as elder or leader, in affairs of his own community. In fact when an actual goat is divided this portion is very rarely a leg; usually some convenient smaller portion is given instead, sometimes the 'tail' (*ŋgə*).

The term 'leg of the animal' is however always applied to this share of the division, and is an indication partly of the respect due to a visiting stranger from another community, but it also, and especially, serves to associate him with the authoritative action of the community council. By receiving a 'leg of the animal' a visiting stranger becomes party to this action.

The 'back of the animal' (*nsɛm nya*) or simply 'back' (*nsɛm*) went in the past to any slave present (*nsɛm*), to be taken to the other slaves; alternatively it may be given to someone present on a visit to his mother's natal community, his 'back' (*nsɛm*). In both cases there is a pun on words. The latter case applies more strictly to a division of a 'goat of the lineage group', but is occasionally also given for a 'community goat'.

When these individual portions have been removed from the goat or goat surrogate, the remainder is divided, fairly rather than equally, between the representatives of the different sections of the community who have taken part in the meeting. There is no precise general rule here except that all who have taken part should have access to a share, however small. If the initial removal of individual portions indicates the most important individual men within a community council, this concluding division among the body of its members indicates most clearly the internal sectional organization of a residential group and any intermediate alliances between sections. Thus in some cases (e.g. Tali 1, Tali 2, Bara) the division is made directly into the series of major lineage groups which compose the community, but in other cases (e.g. Ebeagwa, Besongabang, Okoyong) there is a 'staged' division, whereby the amount is first divided at one level (usually into two parts) and then redivided, either once or, more rarely, twice, until finally each of the constituent sections or 'centres' of the village have received a share. The pattern of division is very similar at a lower level of residential grouping: in the case of a sub-village the division is normally between those village sections which are represented there (this may include an offshoot from a section established elsewhere in the village); in the case of a hamlet the division is again normally between its component sections or minor lineage groups, but is sometimes made directly between household heads.

One may perhaps abstract the general principle from these various examples and levels of division – which unlike the individual membership of a community council can always be stated in any single community in quite explicit and formal terms – that in so far as an authoritative action of a community council is a collective action of the corporate group, so too the 'goat' which is given in recognition of the group's authority should be divided between all those who have on this occasion participated in the action, according either to the particular role they have played or to their representation of the recognized constituent sections of the community.

Community and lineage group authority

The categorical distinction between *barak εtɔk* and *barak anɛrɛkɛt* has already been briefly considered in Chapter 3. I examine further here not so much the nature of the distinction but the effective relationship between the two types of authority.

We have already emphasized the moral quality of relations between kinsfolk. So also the authority of a lineage group as a corporate body commanding the allegiance of its members tends to be associated with the moral obligations of kinsfolk to help each other, to care for the young, to respect the old, to fear the dead; the authority is focused in the respect that is due to the senior elder of the group, its ritual head, and is supported ultimately by religious beliefs concerning the dead. The authority which controls a community, however, is more strictly coercive in nature: it is the community's power which is feared, its physical command over the life of an individual member in the past, its present power to make the existence of a member unbearable. Thus, in the past, punishment by death or by sale into slavery were the extreme sanctions wielded by a community. At the present the most extreme (but no less effective) sanction is formal ostracism: a law is made by a community council which in some degree restricts the people who may talk or give food or drink to the recalcitrant offender, or which actually confines him to his own house. The exercise of community authority is by no means always dependent upon this threat of physical consequences. Nevertheless, we can contrast the ultimate ability of a corporate community to impose its will (so long as this *is* its collective decision), with the more limited authority of a lineage group, whose senior elder can ultimately do no more than curse an offender, hoping the 'dead' of the lineage group will hear him and retaliate.

In the structure of Banyang society this coercive authority of community grouping surrounds and contains the moral authority of the lineage groups. A dispute which cannot then be settled within a lineage group, or a case which potentially is too strong for it, may be referred to the wider community council. The only exceptions to this concern formal disputes in the lineage group, as, for example, a refusal to give due respect to its senior elder. Such cases are specifically 'lineage groups matters' and cannot form the ground for action in the community. (It is these disputes that give rise to the ultimate moral and religious sanction of the curse.) There is moreover always some feeling of reluctance and/or shame when a case between two lineage kinsmen is brought before a community council, who may send the case back for further discussion in the lineage group before hearing it themselves. There are nevertheless certain cases brought directly to a community (usually village) council, because of the stronger sanctions it controls: the two most important types of case here are the arbitration of the return of bridewealth in a divorce and the allocation among his lineage kinsmen of the possessions of a deceased prominent man (who will thus also have been a man of some wealth, with a large household and a number of wives).

Unlike the bridewealth negotiations at marriage, which are conducted simply by the representatives of the two lineage groups, divorce entails a more complicated reckoning of all that has passed between the two lineage groups over a period sometimes of many years; it is a difficult task which is likely to be punctuated by passionate denials, recriminations, and other outbursts, and the final sum agreed upon is almost inevitably the result of a compromise. Banyang speak of such a case as a 'wild cow' which having run loose needs many hands to recapture it. A community council's role here is to mediate between the parties, to assess the validity of the claims on both sides, and in conclusion to suggest a compromise figure. In the case of inheritance the community council's role is similar, although usually more passive: primarily they act as witnesses to a division which is potentially a source of friction, and will step in to arbitrate only if there is conflict. In contrast, the settlement of the inheritance of all 'ordinary' members of a lineage group will be conducted simply at a corporate meeting of the lineage group without reference to the wider community council.

We have described how an intractable dispute may be transferred from a lineage group context to a community context (most commonly from major lineage group to village): so too in the sanctions available to someone who is both elder and leader within a small residential group which is also a lineage group, a transition is possible from the moral sanctions available to him as elder of a lineage group to the coercive sanctions available to him as the leader of a residential group. In a hamlet settlement such as Tanyi Tabe, for example, Taboko's control of affairs within the settlement is dependent in the first place upon his moral authority as lineage elder, but if his authority in this context is challenged (and if the nature of the challenge is not a formal matter within the lineage group) he may use sanctions of a 'community' type, notably those belonging to the Ngbe association. Thus, if an allocation of land which he has made were abused, or if a minor ruling concerning maintenance of the settlement's washing and water-drawing pool were ignored, he could place an Ngbe sign on the land, or could announce the ruling as a 'law of Ngbe'. This would make any future offence one against Ngbe and liable to prosecution by a meeting of the association, which is in effect a meeting of a community council differently constituted. (For details of the procedure involved here and for further discussion of the equation between Ngbe and community authority see Chapter 10. It is particularly significant that Ngbe can be called upon in a hamlet context, for the association provides just this stronger, coercive sanction which is sometimes needed there.) Taboko made clear that he would employ this sanction against his own son if necessary; in a later case (but slightly different context) we shall see how a village leader employed it against his brother, sitting in the next house (the case of Eyong, p. 238).

The following is a somewhat dramatic example of a dispute between kinsmen which was brought as a case to a community council.

The case followed from a breakdown in the relations between the two most senior members of the *bɔ Taba* lineage group in Bara, *Tambi and *Oben. Both were middle-aged men, Oben being the group's nominal head, formally recognized by the village. Over a period of time, however, and in matters concerning the lineage group, Tambi believed that he had been unjustly treated by Oben. He now claimed before the assembled village council of Bara the return of monies and goods which he had given to Oben in the past; he also demanded that Oben complete the outstanding divisions of inheritance arising from previous deaths in the lineage group (whose benefits Oben had so far merely appropriated to himself). A detailed list of the items to be returned was given: £7 from the marriage of one of Tambi's daughters; £1 for two 'goats' of 10s. which Oben had given to the community when his sectional 'leadership' (*kɛfɔ*, here the status of 'Quarter Head') was confirmed; a piece of cloth; a shirt, and so on. The implication was that Tambi wished to sever his relationship with Oben: what he had previously given because of his moral obligation to a kinsman was now treated contractually, as a loan which had to be returned. The closest parallel to this form of action (which is by no means usual but indeed a highly extreme measure) is the demand for the return of all bridewealth and associated gifts at divorce.

After the claims had been made by Tambi, there was a certain amount of blustering and heated argument by Oben who, however, was pressed by the village council to say whether or not he had received the items mentioned. Incredibly, he denied them all (which he was in a position to do since they were all 'private' lineage group matters and the other members of the village could not be expected to have formal knowledge of them). Since these two men were the only two adult members of the lineage group here in Bara, Oben's denial created an impasse which the community council found it extremely difficult to resolve. As it was pointed out, they had scraps of information which they had happened to acquire about these matters within the lineage group, but this knowledge was highly circumstantial and insufficient evidence. In the heated argument which raged between the two men, the community council were powerless spectators. As the village leader pointed out, 'The community sits like a deaf-mute.'

The issue was nevertheless brought to some kind of conclusion by Tambi's recording, on the instigation of the village leader, a list of all the items he was claiming, which could then be kept until absent members of the lineage group returned home and could give evidence to deny or support them. Tambi swore on Mfam to the truth of his list, Oben being required to pay the cult fee. Oben himself refused to swear and this was held over until such time as he felt himself able to do so (presumably at the time of the re-hearing, when the point would be pressed against him). Tambi finally was called upon to pay a 'goat of the community', which he readily did in bars of soap.

There was a great deal of talk in the village about this case afterwards. The behaviour of Oben was severely criticized for it was quite clear that he must have received at least some of the items named. He was thus spoken of as 'a person of two voices' (mu bɛyɔŋ bɛpai), someone of deceit, and therefore not to be trusted. The fact that this issue between kinsmen had been forced to a swearing on Mfam was also a cause of comment and wonder. As members of a lineage group who traced descent ultimately to a maternal ancestor, they were bɔanɔ, 'matrikin', to each other and shared therefore the closest of possible kinship relations: they were 'one body', miɛt amɔt; how could one swear Mfam against such a fellow kinsman when Mfam could attack either, whoever was guilty?

The following features may be noted from this case: (1) the sharp difference and apparent discontinuity in the two spheres of social behaviour: the community sits 'like a deaf-mute' when faced with events that are normally the private concern of lineage kinsmen; (2) the attempt of Tambi to resolve his difference with Oben by moving from the context of a lineage group dispute, where he had failed to obtain any satisfaction, to the context of community authority; (3) the change in normative reference which accompanied this change in the context of the dispute, items formerly given on the basis of a kinship obligation, now being demanded as though they were a loan from an unrelated person.

One might question how far the exercise of community authority was indeed effective in this instance, since Tambi had by no means obtained anything like his claims. Nevertheless the issue of the dispute was in fact brought to a head: Tambi had shown publicly his refusal to tolerate the conditions of the previous relationship; Oben had been forced to make a definite statement and to adopt a defensive position which later events were likely to prove less than unassailable.

6

Judicial Processes

Hearing a case

Cases brought before a community council for settlement (*banye*, sing. *nye*) arise either from interpersonal dispute over such matters as debt, trespass, damage to property, insult or injury to person, or they arise directly from offences against the community, in particular by transgressing a community 'law' but more generally by acting in violation of community authority or good order. Although this difference in type of case reflects our own distinction between 'civil' and 'criminal' actions, it is not one which is formally made by Banyang and there is a tendency for interpersonal disputes to be taken over into the second category, the 'community' treating the case as an offence against itself.

A case arising from an interpersonal dispute is initiated by a formal complaint made to one of the prominent members of the community council (most frequently leader or senior elder) at the level at which it is wished that the case will be heard. This man will usually indicate when he expects the case will be heard and will make the necessary arrangements. Alternatively, the case may be brought directly before a community council which happens to be meeting, whether formally or, sometimes, at an informal meeting. In interpersonal disputes a 'suing fee' (*nkap nte*) is given either when the case is first reported or when it is laid before the council. The amount varies slightly; in 1954 in Tali and Bara it was two shillings. Any member of the community, however junior, has the right to bring a case to be heard by its council, and will normally conduct his (or her) own case by himself, but with support from others in the general meeting, either as witnesses or (more occasionally) as spokesmen. On the other hand, if a woman or junior person appears as defendant, he or she is more likely to be represented by a senior relative or husband.

Formal respect is always shown to a community council meeting judicially, directed particularly towards its most senior representatives, either the senior elders or the community leader. A person addressing the meeting should always do so standing. On the other hand, anyone who has something to say should be allowed opportunity and time to say it. This applies especially to the defendant and plaintiff, who are allowed to speak fully and without interruptions in putting their case. At the same time the status of the persons present should also be respected. Consequently, although everyone has theoretically the freedom to speak, in effect the judicial conduct of the case depends mainly on the senior elders and leaders present, younger men or men with less status speaking only when they have something specifically to contribute.

In the actual hearing the initial procedure is for the plaintiff, standing facing the senior-most elders at the meeting, to state briefly why he is accusing ('suing',-te) the defendant.[1] The latter, who stands by the side of the plaintiff, on the meeting's left hand, is left to answer the accusation as best he may, which he usually does at some length. This normally brings out further points which require to be answered by the plaintiff, who, indeed, has often to be restrained from forcefully interrupting. By now the case is usually under way in a heated argument between plaintiff and defendant, with restraints and questions from the elders. Otherwise the elders may probe the evidence of either disputant with questions designed to test its consistency, to bring out unstated facts or motives, or to show the acceptance of consequences. In most residential groups, people have close knowledge of their fellows and of the events which happen there. Individuals within the meeting are thus often able to confirm or deny statements of fact made by either disputant, and will do so; material witnesses may be sent for. The actual hearing of a case is not usually long drawn out. During the process of question and statement, the trend of the case usually becomes apparent, whether the defendant acknowledges his guilt, pleads special circumstances, or stands adamantly by his innocence. Further questioning will bear particularly upon this point or, if the defendant maintains his innocence, some attempt may be made to force the issue by recourse to a cult-agency. In the concluding stages various suggestions may be made as to a suitable judgement, but the final summing-up and judgement are left to the senior elder or leader of the community hearing the case. If the weight of the evidence is against the defendant, he will be told to fetch the 'suing fee', which will be used to reimburse the plaintiff. This injunction to 'go and come' is the first indication of the case's conclusion and, if accepted by the defendant, of his willingness to abide by the council's judgement. During his absence there may be further discussion of the action to be taken against him. When he returns and the plaintiff has been reimbursed, the council's

[1] This description of procedure is based upon cases witnessed in Tali and Bara.

decision is announced to him, normally by its leading representative, its senior elder or leader. The 'community has sat' (ɛtɔk ɛcɔko) and the judgement of the case is made in the name of the community: 'the community has spoken' (ɛtɔk ɛrɛm).

Cases of offence against the community, ndak ɛtɔk, follow very much the same procedure as that described above for cases of interpersonal dispute, except that the defendant stands singly before the council to answer the case put to him, usually again by its senior representative. When news of an incident which gives grounds for such an action reaches the ears of one of the senior members of the council, he may discuss it with others, or if he is sure of his case may make his accusation directly at a council meeting. As we have seen in the case of the Kembong youth, and as cases to be later cited show, in a direct confrontation with community authority the wisest policy for an offender is to acknowledge his guilt and to seek what concession he can from the terms of the judgement against him. Failure to acknowledge his offence is likely only to provoke stronger sanctions and ultimately a heavier fine.

Level of council hearing a case

There is no formal requirement concerning the level of community grouping at which a case must be heard. For interpersonal disputes the choice lies with the plaintiff: he may if he wishes take the case to the hamlet council of the defendant, or he can go directly to the representatives of a higher level of grouping, village, or even village group if a council meeting is in session. On the other hand a case taken directly to a higher-level meeting may be referred back to a lower-level residential group if the latter is more likely to know its full circumstances, to be brought forward again only if it cannot be settled there. The relationship between the disputants does not directly determine the level of council asked to hear the case: an unrelated stranger may appeal to the hamlet leader of the person whom he believes to have wronged him; inversely, closely related or residentially associated neighbours may take their dispute to one of the highest-level councils if the circumstances appear advantageous to the disputant. A somewhat more limited flexibility applies also to 'offences against the community', which can be heard by community councils at different levels according to the assessment made by those prosecuting the case as to where the chance of its successful conclusion is likely to be greatest.

In the determination of where a case should be brought, three factors are relevant. The first of these is the ease of convening the council and the degree of formal constraint which it is wished to bring to bear upon the defendant. At the hamlet level a case has often the character of a publicly registered complaint which it is hoped will bring pressure to bear upon the defendant through his immediate seniors. At the higher levels of grouping the degree of formality becomes greater, the circumstantiality of pressures upon the defendant is reduced, and the meeting is less readily convened. A second, related factor is the question of publicity and the solidarity of the smaller residential groups: thus, where a case (especially an offence against the community) *can* be settled at a lower level of grouping, it will often be taken there to prevent too public a debate and to keep the matter in the control of the smaller group. So, for example, the case of the youth of Kembong was dealt with in the sub-village by those who had closest contact with him (despite the fact that broader principles and a wider grouping had been involved), and a number of similarly important although not difficult cases were also heard at this level (e.g. a case in which a member of Kembong had failed to report his killing of a python, which had not therefore as 'animal of the community' been presented to the village leader, and another case in which a member of Okorobak had attempted to commit suicide). Against this disinclination to disclose the internal affairs, or disunity, of the smaller residential groups must be placed a third factor, which is the greater weight of sanction brought to bear by the higher community councils.

The principle involved here is clearly recognized and is implicit in our earlier account of the 'goats' which a community council can demand. When, for example, the member of Kembong in the case just cited was prosecuted for failing to present the python he had killed, the 'goat' that he produced for the sub-village council was 10s. and this was accepted, but the comment was made that if the same case had been taken to the village council (where in one sense it rightly belonged, since it was at this level that the python ought originally to have been presented) the amount demanded would have been greater. In general, the more extended the residential group judging a case, the heavier the sanctions it will impose upon those it finds guilty. This principle has already been in part exemplified and will be by later cases. As a factor deciding at what level a case is to be prosecuted, it is perhaps most clearly evidenced in the case of the village leader of Tali 1, who fought against the 'slaves', which was left until some months after the event when the united strength of the supra-village effectively dispelled the threat of discord between the village leader and the 'slave'-settlement (see below, pp. 165f.).

Since the higher the community council the stronger is its effective authority, the whole series of councils form a kind of hierarchy. The hierarchy *can* become one of appeal: if a disputant does not accept the judgement at a lower level he can declare his intention of taking the case to a higher level. There is nevertheless a tendency to regard this as an act of stubbornness on the part of the dissatisfied litigant, a rejection of the council's authoritative verdict. When a litigant appears dissatisfied (as in the nature of things many must) he is often told that he can if he *wishes* take the matter further but it is likely to cost him more and that the conclusion in the end will be the same. Thus higher-level councils usually give some weight to the conclusions of a lower-level council and as a matter of principle would seem where possible to uphold them. At least, this can be inferred from what Banyang say, and the few 'appeal' cases transferred to a higher council that I have witnessed give every indication of its being so. For example, in a land-boundary dispute heard first in the hamlet of Mkpot in Besongabong and later by the village council as a whole, a judgement which (in my own and my assistant's view) clearly favoured the defendant (it would seem since he had come to take up residence in the settlement, whereas the plaintiff, with stronger formal claims to the land, was no longer living there) was upheld by the village council, and the plaintiff, who clearly felt the verdict was unjust, was warned that even if he took it to the local Court (where one of the leading members of the village council sat on the panel of magistrates) the outcome would still be the same and his money wasted. As the latter circumstance suggests, a relevant factor for this general principle is the overlapping membership of the community councils at different levels: a man centrally concerned in the judgement at a low level is likely to represent the group at a higher level of community council and is able there to exert some influence in the way a decision will go.

We have already said that the relationship between two disputants in an interpersonal case does not itself determine the level of community council at which the case is heard. Most disputes do in fact concern people who share common membership of some order of residential grouping, usually at least of the same village. Where a person has a case against someone of a different village, he can take his suit to that village, to be heard at whatever level of council meeting he chooses, but perhaps most generally at the more formal level of the village council. Members of different villages in the same village group will sometimes take the opportunity of a council meeting representing the whole village group to lay their case before that, and sometimes the councils of neighbouring villages of the same village group will unite to judge a case concerning them both. There is, however, no necessity (and this I would stress) for a case to be taken to the community council at a level of residential grouping which includes both disputants: if plaintiff and defendant belong to different villages of the same village group, the case may still be brought to the village council of the defendant; if they belong to different hamlets of the same village, it may still be brought to the hamlet council of the defendant.

The fact that plaintiffs do not necessarily seek the fullest group support they can obtain (which they would do by going to the council representing the inclusive order of residential grouping) relates to the important ideal of judicial impartiality which is expected to guide a community council. More exactly, perhaps, the 'partiality' of a community council is less a matter of individual interests or the interests of parties than of a committed concern to maintain the authority and good order of the residential group.[1] A case brought to a community council is thus in a sense a challenge to its ability to 'order its own house': if the case is brought by an outsider the challenge is that much the greater. Cases between persons of different villages are in fact often difficult to settle, partly through the lack of corroborative evidence and incidental knowledge that are more readily available when both persons live in the same village. Frequently such cases concern the return of bridewealth, itself a difficult and complex matter. Particularly where the suit concerns bridewealth, the man (or lineage group) laying the case is likely to journey to the other village with as many supporters as he can muster. On the other hand, a more straightforward case of, for example, debt or injury may be presented directly by the one person, who acts as his own advocate and witness. Since this point bears directly upon the autonomy of Banyang judicial processes, which rely much less than other 'stateless' societies upon the pressures of contraposed groups,[2] an example may help to clarify it.

A youth of Takwa village in the Tanyi Nkongo village group was owed money by another youth with whom he had been friendly in Bara. The Takwa youth came to Bara village by himself and reported his case to the village leader, paying a 5s. case fee. (This was more than

[1] The distinction which I have in mind here is between the impartiality which is based upon the 'rational' application of clearly defined norms (and which thus places a minimal value on personal, circumstantial factors) and the impartiality which arises from a concern with broader issues, here the welfare of the corporate group (and which devalues individual interests as of no account in the face of collective interests).

[2] Compare for example, the processes of dispute settlement described for the Arusha by P. H. Gulliver, *Social Control in an African Society*.

required but he was sure of his case, wished to enlist the help of the village, and knew that the defendant would be required to find it.) The sectional representatives of the village were called and met in the leader's house. After much argument, the Bara youth was found in fact to owe the money and was asked to 'go and come' with the 5s. When he returned the question was put to him: when would he repay the debt. He agreed to do so within four weeks. (It was calculated that this would give him enough time to make sufficient sleeping-mats to sell and acquire the money.) The village asked for a surety and another young man, regarded as the leader of the young men in Bara, came forward to add his own word to that of the defendant; as an acceptance of his guarantee, the latter's hand was then taken by the village leader. Then, as an added surety, both youths swore by Bekundi, a sub-association of Ngbe, that the money would be returned by this time. (Thus, if it were not returned, they would be answerable to Bekundi for their vain promise.) In the following weeks the youth was to be seen very busily weaving sleeping-mats, and the money was finally paid.

This case illustrates very strikingly the impersonality of the judicial process: the plaintiff's willingness to submit his case (supported by a large case fee) to a village council not his own; his conduct of the case in his own right and without supporters from his own village; the village council's lack of hesitation in finding one of their own members guilty; the employment of added sanctions, including that of the Bekundi association, to make sure that the undertaking given by the defendant would in fact be honoured. Finally, it is worth noting that if the debt were now *not* paid, it would cease to be an interpersonal case but would become actionable as an offence against Bekundi, that is to say an offence against the community itself.

We may compare this claim by a stranger upon the judicial activities of a community with the acceptance of a *mu ɛtɔk* from a different village by the representatives of a community engaged in judging a dispute (p. 148): in one case an outsider contributes to the exercise of authority; in the other case he benefits from it; but in both cases there is a transference of rights and status, an assumption that the due maintenance of authority overrides party or group allegiances.

Patterns of judicial action

Studies of the judicial process in other African societies have emphasized the element of arbitration, or reconciling the disputants and seeking an agreed settlement.[1] In many cases heard by community councils, the element of arbitration is certainly present (for example, in divorce negotiations and inheritance disputes) but the general tenor of the judicial processes of a community council is less towards the restoration of social relations between disputants than the reassertion of the good order and authority of the residential group, potentially disrupted by an offence committed within it. The direction of a case is then to isolate the offence and the offender: once this is clear, so too is the offender's duty to submit to authority, by reparation or payment of a fine (a 'goat of the community') or both. The relevant term here is the verb *nɛkwɔ*: the person who *ankwɔ* is the person who 'should pay', whose offence has been made clear. *Nɛkwɔ* is to 'pay for one's offence': it implies both acceptance of guilt and submission to authority. The direction of a case is thus to establish who is the offender: who shall *-kwɔ*.

The case that we have just described (the debtor youth of Bara) shows a pattern that is typical of many: a movement in the actionable grounds of a dispute from an issue involving interpersonal relations to one in which the individual offender (actual or potential) is confronted by the collective authority of the group. Most clearly, this is the effect of the use of any association sanction: when, for example, the Ngbe sign is placed upon disputed land, the trespasser is answerable not to its private owner but to the association whose authority he has ignored. But even where a community council does not take advantage of the association sanctions, the same movement can still occur. So, for example, in the case of the land dispute in Besongabang already reported, when the village representatives most directly concerned had indicated where the boundary should be on the spot, their action was reported back to a council meeting at the village leader's *aca*, who in the presence of the disputants publicly re-iterated the verdict: 'The people of the community have been to the place and put *ɛtusɔŋɔ* [a quickly rooting tree often used to mark boundaries]. This is the boundary. Each man should remain on his own side. If either crosses the boundary has he not carried a matter of the community? [A question which received the collective affirmation of everyone there – *Ɛɛ!*] He should come with a goat.' A private dispute is here clinched with the sanction of the community's own authority, so that a further offence

---

[1] For example, *The Realm of the Rain-Queen* by E. J. and J. D. Krige (1943), *The Judicial Process among the Barotse of Northern Rhodesia* by Max Gluckman (1955), *Justice and Judgment among the Tiv* by P. J. Bohannan (1957), *Social Control in an African Society* by P. H. Gulliver (1963).

now becomes one against the community: the offender has 'carried a matter of the community' and must 'come with a goat'.

Part of the reason for so changing the grounds of a dispute would seem to lie in the fact that a confrontation between individual and community presents a clearer issue, more easily dealt with, than an interpersonal dispute, where the circumstances are often complex and (as we have seen in the case of the two kinsmen of Bara) sometimes beyond the competent knowledge of a council. Again, to use Durkheim's distinction, the *conscience collective* of a community is more easily engaged when a direct affront to it is suggested than when it is merely an issue of each man's own rights. Community councils are very sensitive to any implied challenge to community authority, from whatever quarter, and will seek to meet this challenge with the severest sanctions. It is for this reason that, almost invariably, the wisest policy for a defendant accused of an offence against the community is to plead guilty and throw himself upon the mercy of the council. Someone who is 'obstinate', who 'will not listen to what the community says', by implication sets himself up in opposition to the community. As one of my texts records: 'You may think that you are bigger than the people of the community but the community will tighten matters up until in the end you come to plead guilty (-*kwɔ*) in the community; that is to say you come back into the community.' We return here to a basic axiom of so much of Banyang political life, that membership of a group is directly associated with acceptance of the group's authority: if one refuses to accept the authority of one's residential group one places oneself in this sense outside it, and one cannot re-enter it until one has -*kwɔ*, pleaded guilty, which thus becomes a formal act of submission. Such an act is always seen as an eventual necessity: however protracted his case, however he may avoid the issue by going away or by diversionary tactics, if a man has offended the community he must eventually make his peace with it, he must -*kwɔ*, acknowledge his guilt and submit to the decision of the group he is a member of. The proverb quoted to make this point is simple: 'The ground waits for the rain' (*Mɔk anoŋ ci manyɛp*).

This general direction of the judicial process, which entails isolating the offender's guilt and then by his punishment restoring the authority of the residential group, is illustrated in the following case, in which the village leader himself is the offender and his punishment the means of re-establishing the community's corporate authority:

The case arose from a fight between members of the village leader's settlement in Tali 1 and members of its associated 'slave'-settlement, in which the village leader himself became involved. The fighting had occurred some four months before the case was heard, when the Tali dispute still remained unsettled. It had been reported to the police and was then the subject of a police inquiry which could lead to charges against the leader of Tali 1. Few of the details of the incident came out during the hearing. I heard about it the day after it occurred from one of the young men who had been closely involved, and the following account of what actually happened is based upon what he told me then.

The Mbinjong slave-settlement made a law that over Christmas (1953), when they were engaged in their own festivities, no free-born person should be admitted to their settlement. On the afternoon of Christmas day a quarrel arose between the village leader's son in Mbinjong and a young man who was a 'slave'. This quarrel took place in the 'free-born' Mbinjong settlement and led to fighting, which was, however, quickly settled and peace restored. After the fight, however, a group of young men from Mbinjong who had drunk well during the day were incited to go to the nearby 'slave'-settlement. The village leader attempted to restrain them because of the law, but they did in fact go. When they arrived in the 'slave'-settlement its own leader, annoyed at their coming, came out into the path to meet them. There were words and the 'slave'-leader threw down a man who was himself a 'slave', although from a different settlement. At this point the Tali 1 village leader arrived. He attempted to calm matters and to take off the Mbinjong 'free-born' party. I was told that the man who had been thrown down got up, slapped the village leader, and said: 'Why do you tell your people to go back? Let them do what they have to do!' The village leader, who was a big and powerful man, hit back at this man. This started a general fight between the 'slaves' and 'free-born' which during the time it lasted was fierce and resulted in a number of minor injuries.

Nothing had been done about this incident within Tali until April. By this time the dispute which had so long divided Tali had been settled; Tali 2 had gained its formally independent leadership but at the same time the *de facto* unity of the whole of Tali was reasserted and the joint 'supra-village' council, representing all sections of both 'villages', had begun to meet with some regularity. In April, soon after a police investigation of the incident, the leaders of the supra-village, taking advantage of the community's regained strength, arranged for a general hearing of the case. The point was to decide and settle the matter before it reached the Native Court. If the 'community' (here primarily Tali 1, but by extension the whole of Tali) was in agreement, of 'one voice', no case could be made in the Court. On the day that it was discussed most of the sectional representatives of Tali 2 were present, including its own village leader and senior elder, together with the usual representatives from Tali 1, except Mpomba. The case was discussed in the meeting house of the Tali 1 village leader's settlement.

The leader of the slave-settlement was first asked to give his own statement, which he did briefly by saying that the village leader had fought against the slaves. Some questions were asked of him to establish this point clearly. (The village leader himself was not asked to give his side of the case and he remained silent throughout the hearing.) Once the point had been established, Peter Esong got up to say that the village leader, whose duty it was to keep peace in the community, was here in the wrong and that he should be fined.[1] The leader of the slaves hastily pointed out that it was not he who was bringing the Court case against the village-leader: he did not wish to do so; the 'European' had brought it against the village leader. The community council nevertheless continued to discuss what fine the village leader should pay, the main participants in this discussion being the village leader of Tali 2 and its senior elder. It was apparent throughout this discussion that the leaders of the community did not wish to look too closely into the actual circumstances of the case and that it was moving along virtually prearranged lines. No attempt was made by the village leader to defend himself (which he might well have done) or to elucidate the facts. His son, the young man whose initial fight had started the whole affair, tried to interrupt a number of times but on each occasion was told to keep quiet. Finally it was decided that the village leader was guilty and that he should pay £3.10s. (one 'slave') to the slaves, £2 for the Court, and that he should provide a 'goat of the community'.

There was a number of small conferences between the slaves. The senior elder and leader of the Mpomba slave-settlement arrived and the case was re-explained to him. Finally, when the village leader had produced the money (which unlike most cases came forward without hesitation) the leader of the slaves said that they did not wish to accept

[1] By this time the union of Tali 1 and Tali 2 had helped to restore Peter Esong's position and he was now being readmitted to central meetings of the community leaders. (On his initial readmission on Christmas day itself, see below, p. 71.) My evidence that his speech at this point followed a prearranged agreement is only circumstantial but it would have been contrary to all practice and to the general trend of the case for it to have been otherwise.

reparation from the village leader: it was not they who had brought the case against him. The community council accepted this, saying then that the village leader should pay only the £2 for the Court[1] and the 'goat of the community'. The senior elder of Tali 2 demanded that this should be a real goat – 'blood' was wanted, not money or bars of soap. The goat was produced and then sacrificed: the village leader's wrong regarding the slaves was announced to the dead, the fact that this wrong had been righted, and their blessing was asked for him and for the community. The goat was then divided between the members of the community council according to their status and representation of the sections of the two villages.

It was after this case that I was told (by a member of the inner council) to 'See how the community is: the community is strong'. The case thus was potentially a difficult and dangerous one, involving a rift within the community between 'slaves' and 'free-born' which could easily have got out of hand, and had the further imminent possibility of Court action against the Tali 1 leader. That it was brought to a conclusion was dependent upon the effective functioning of the community as a corporate political group, in which a major factor was the concerted action of the community's leading representatives. A number of its features bear comment.

The trend of the case so far as the 'judical process' was concerned was to establish very clearly the village leader's guilt and to demand reparation from him. This point was reached so quickly that a number of people such as the leader's son (and indeed myself) felt that the verdict had been unjust towards the village leader; even although he might finally have been at fault, there was much to be said before this judgement was made, since the large part of his efforts had been to stop or restrain the fighting. Yet the main issue of the case was not really the circumstances surrounding the fight, but the fact that it *had* taken place, precipitated by the village leader's physical retaliation, and that this had given rise to a sectional (one might say, class) rift within the community. The village leader became then a kind of scapegoat, whose acknowledged guilt served to reaffirm the authority and good order of the community. By pinpointing the 'guilt', the authority of the community was re-established (this, it may be noted, irrespective of the fact that it was the leader of the community himself

[1] Which would be used either to settle the case in Court when it arose, or, more likely, as a consideration to stop it arising or to ensure a favourable verdict, strengthened by the fact that it had already been decided in the community.

who was adjudged guilty). In this situation the 'slaves' were themselves forced to retreat, for (although, as it was rumoured, it was they who had in fact originally reported the case to the police) they could not now afford to oppose themselves, even by implication, to the united community. The latter had now a 'goat of the community' for its work and its unity was given the added supernatural sanction of an oblation to the dead.

Some reference should be made to the part played by the members of the inner council of the combined community in this forcing of the issue of the village leader's guilt. The case itself was heard in open council: anyone could be present; anyone (theoretically) could speak. Yet in fact, although the case was judged in the 'community's' name, those who took the leading part were either members of the 'inner council' or were peripherally associated with it. Characteristically it was a man in the latter category (Peter Esong) who voiced the view that was taken up and acted upon by the central leaders. Such direct (and almost certainly pre-arranged) action by members of the inner council does not occur in most disputes but was prompted here by the political implications of the case and the need for its firm settlement.

Finally, we should note the size of the amounts awarded in reparation and fine, and the dependence of the case's settlement on the fact that it was heard at this relatively high level of the 'supra-village', whose effective political unity was at this time especially strong. We shall return later to the conditions underlying this, but would remark here that the speed and finality with which the conclusion was reached were closely dependent upon the role of the Tali 2 leaders in pressing home its issue: if the village leader of Tali 1 remained silent, its senior elder (Taboko), who was normally one of the most vocal members of a community council, made only restrained and limited comments. The leaders of Tali 2 were, however, acting here in the common interest of the inner council of the whole (supra-village) community: if their action had been less concerted, the possibility of reaching a conclusive settlement would have been smaller and the authority of the corporate community thus weakened.

Not all cases can be brought to a definite decision as to the offender, especially in cases of interpersonal dispute. Recourse here is almost invariably made to one of the cult-agencies, on which the innocence of one, or possibly both, parties is then sworn. The most important of the cult-agencies used is Mfam and the swearing takes the form, 'If N—— did so-and-so, then Mfam should attack him; if he did not, then Mfam should be at peace with him'. I have elsewhere tried to indicate how the action of Mfam is always conceived of as protecting the community from the duplicity of its members, notably witches, but also thieves and here liars.[1] Its legal use has the effect of taking the matter out of the 'hands of people' and making the issue one of supernatural judgement. Its use is thus in line with the judicial rule of 'isolate the offence', but the context and potential grounds of the offence have again been changed.

Nevertheless, the employment of a cult-agency remains in the discretion of the community council hearing the case, who will protect its misuse and as far as possible use it in the way that will best serve to locate the offence. Thus someone who attempts to evade his guilt by swearing in circumstances where the council believe that he is responsible, will not be allowed to do so; it is usually argued here that the action of the cult-agency may fall upon a relative and not upon the man himself, and that to protect his relatives he should not swear.[2] Yet if the foolhardiness of a few who are willing to swear their innocence falsely is recognized, for most Banyang faced with the prospect of swearing, the test of conscience would seem to be real enough. The suggestion that a person's case should be made subject to an oath does therefore serve to test the strength of his position: if either disputant refuses to swear, there is a strong presumption of his guilt, which may then serve to bring the case further to a head. In the two cases already described where the conclusion rested with the use of a cult-agency, its use helped in some positive way to clarify the issue of the dispute: thus in the case of the Bara kinsmen (pp. 154–155) the defendant's refusal to swear on the cult-agency considerably weakened his position and provided some future lever for action against him; in the case of the prostitute and the injured youth (pp. 142–143), the accused prostitute was brought to face the contradiction between her own account and the youth's and to accept the responsibility of making what certainly the youth felt to be a perjured statement. The following further example illustrates how the swearing on a cult-agency may be used to force the issue of a case, establishing an 'offence' otherwise in doubt.

Following on from a formal meeting of the supra-village council which had heard cases in the leader of Tali 1's settlement, a few of the leading members of the conjoint Tali, including the two village leaders, moved to discuss a case in rather less formal circumstances in the house of the

---

[1] 'Witchcraft, Morality and Doubt,' *Odu* University of Ife Journal of African Studies, July 1965.
[2] Note that this argument was in fact used in the case of the disputing Bara kinsmen, when there was a strong presumption that one was lying (p. 155).

senior elder of Nchemba. The case concerned the two village leaders of
Tali and one of the members of Nchemba, *Taku Nyang. Some time
previously Taku Nyang had approached the house of Mr Tataw in
Tali 1, in which the two village leaders were sitting: a bottle of brandy
was being presented to them by a stranger of status, a Government
employee, then working in Tali. When Taku Nyang came in, the bottle
of brandy was withdrawn, and he was excluded from receiving any.
He left, and later voiced his complaints about the meeting, saying, 'The
leaders are sitting in secret: they are intending to kill someone' (bafɔ
bacɔko ɛju: bayaŋ ɛwaɛ mu). As they well might, the village leaders had
taken offence at this remark and the present meeting was to clear the
aspersion on them.

The discussion soon brought out the fact that Taku Nyang was
concerned about his son, then working for the stranger. If he was to be
excluded from a meeting with the stranger, this could bear (he argued)
only upon his own son. The discussion ranged around this point: were
the leaders planning to 'kill' his son? When it was pointed out that
Banyang did not kill each other with sorcery (only 'people in the south'
do this), Taku Nyang argued that there were ways and ways of 'killing'.
One might do it by shame: was he, a mu ɛtɔk, to be excluded from a
meeting which included an outsider? Eventually the issue of the case
came to be whether or not the leaders were in some way plotting
against Taku's son.

Two cult-agencies were brought from their local owners, Mfam
and Kekang. Each of the village leaders swore in turn to each of the
cult-agencies: 'At the meeting at Mr Tataw's house when wine was
brought by N [the stranger], if I spoke anything concerning the son of
Taku Nyang, then cult-agency (njɔ) attack me! If I did not, then cult-
agency be at peace with me!' After each man had sworn, his statement
was repeated by the cult-agency owner.

The leaders having denied their guilt, the matter returned to Taku
Nyang. The offence was now his: he was guilty and should pay,
ankwɔ. In reparation, he offered first four bars of soap (equalling 10s.)
but these were said to be insufficient and a further four bars were
produced (totalling a nominal £1). This was accepted by the small
group of persons representing the community as their 'goat', and they
then moved on to a further meeting.

It could be argued that this case served to air suspicions which were
present in Taku Nyang's mind. Yet his suspicions when voiced aloud

became in effect a slander upon the two village leaders. The issue was forced by their own swearing of their innocence: this could not but be accepted as proof of it. The matter then lay with Taku Nyang, whose offence was now clear, and from whom reparation was due. His first offer of a relatively nominal 'goat' was not accepted and only when the amount was doubled was his offence cleared.

Modern influences

The creation under the British administration of a system of 'Native Courts' had, in 1953–1954, only indirectly affected the traditional judicial processes described in this chapter. It is probable that the adoption of a 'suing fee' (certainly in its present form) has been copied from the procedure used in the Native Courts; certain categories of cases, notably those arising from bridewealth or debt, appear to have been taken more readily to the Native Courts; but in other respects the system of Native Courts as it evolved during the period of British rule appears if anything to have lent weight to the traditional judicial processes.

Some account has already been given of the way in which Native Courts formed part of the developing structure of Native Administration under British rule. When in 1916 the German Ossidinge District was taken over by a British civil administrator, a Native Court was established at Ossidinge, presided over by 'chiefs' appointed by the administration. The first annual report notes that 'The work has been very heavy as the Banyang and Keaka tribes are of a litigious disposition', but, after noting the 'encouraging' progress of the chiefs, adds: 'Very few cases have been brought to the District Officer on appeal and in the majority of such cases the judgement of the chiefs has been upheld.' The majority of the cases heard concerned women and marriages, directly or indirectly.[1]

In the reorganization of the 'Banyang Clan Area' in 1934, the creation of 'Village Group Courts' went perhaps the furthest to confirm and support the judicial functions of traditional community councils. In the second year of their existence (1935), the fourteen 'Group Courts' heard 788 cases (all 'civil') of which 207 were classified as 'Matrimonial, including guardianship of children', 507 as 'Debts and other contracts'.[2] What is perhaps most striking in these early years of the Village Group Courts is that only a small trickle of their cases went forward on appeal: thus in the same year only twelve cases were heard in the Clan Appeal Court at Bakebe,[3] and in the following year, although the number of appeals was slightly in-

---

[1] Annual Report on the Ossidinge Division, 1916 (Ce 1916/2), paras. 16-19.
[2] Annual Report 1935, paras. 61, 65.   [3] Ibid., para. 63.

creased, it still represented only 4 per cent of the cases heard at the first instance in the Group Court (32 out of 777).[1] As we have seen, these early units of the Native Administration tended to continue in their own way, and the Village Group Courts came less and less under the supervision of the European administrators.[2] Over a period of time they were amalgamated to serve wider areas.

In 1953–1954 Native Authority Courts Grade D existed at Tinto and Bachu Akagbe, with a further Court serving the Mamfe area in Mamfe Town. Appeal from the two former Courts was to the Native Authority Court at Bakebe, and thence to the District Officer on review. All the judicial activities of community councils which we have described were then in a formal sense illegal. Nevertheless, the vast majority of disputes, certainly in Upper Banyang villages, were still settled at this level and only the more difficult or recalcitrant cases were taken directly to the Native Courts. (The main categories are again bridewealth and debt, both often involving persons from different villages or village groups.) This *de facto* situation was recognized by the administration and its agents, including the police. No detailed study was made of the operation of the Native Courts but both my own observations and the comments of Banyang suggest that the Court members took account of, and where possible upheld, the rulings of the community councils in cases which were brought forward to them. A man involved in a 'community offence' with his own village or village group could not therefore escape his liability to them by appealing to the Native Court. As I shall describe in Chapter 10, this upholding of the traditional authority and judicial processes of Banyang communities by the Native Courts was further extended to cases involving the Ngbe sanction, which received priority and almost invariably were decided in a way that served to protect and support the association.

[1] Annual Report 1936, para. 31.
[2] See above, pp. 107–108, especially the case of Etoko 'Native Authority' (village council), which was acting illegally.

7

Other Governmental Processes

The formulation of policy and making of laws

A community council – notably the council of a village – serves as the most important forum in which any matter bearing on the public interest can be discussed and action advised. Most important issues are not, however, brought directly to the community council, but go through a prior stage of discussion and consultation in which some accommodation is sought between the views and interests of the leading representatives of the community and the main alternatives for action are clarified. The role of the inner council of a village in this process has already been mentioned, and some examples have been given of cases in which prior agreement by the inner council helped to determine their outcome (these examples include Mansfeld's account of a similar process in Ekoi villages, p. 146). Such 'caucus' procedures play an extremely important role in Banyang politics and the conduct of government. The issues, having first been discussed and agreed to 'behind', are then presented to an open meeting; here they may be subject to further discussion but, if those who have achieved agreement are in fact those with influence and power, their agreement must finally become a full and formal decision of the 'community' as a whole.

Inevitably it is difficult to document these processes in detail. Some reflection of them has already been seen in the stories of constitutional changes in the past, notably in the way in which Ndifaw is reported to have obtained the 'things of the community' but also in Mfonjo's own acquisition of leadership (pp. 54–55, 61). One example may be given, however, of a 'caucus' meeting in which I happened to participate and which was a critical incident in the constitutional struggle over Tali 2's independence. The context of these negotiations 'behind' was a Clan Union meeting for the whole of the Ndifaw village group, but despite this particular setting the case illustrates the more general process by which the 'inner council' of a community discusses and reaches agreement upon a policy before this is presented to an open meeting.

When the Ndifaw Clan Union was reformed in September, 1953, its first general meeting was held in the Upper half of Ebeagwa village. Apart from the affairs of the Clan Union itself, the two most important issues concerning the members of the village group were the Tali dispute and the still undecided issue of succession to the Ebeagwa village leadership. On the day that they arrived, the various representatives of the village group were formally received and shown where they would stay: cola was broken and wine drunk. In the evening a 'Band' dance got under way, organized by the young men of the village group. At about 8 p.m. I was called away from the dance to attend a meeting of the 'inner council' (spoken of specifically as the ɛtɔk) which was then being held behind closed doors in one of the houses allocated to the 'Tali 1' representatives. The meeting was conducted in considerable secrecy at one end of the main room of the house, in lowered voices. It consisted of four of the members of Tali 1's 'inner council' (including the village leader and senior elder) together with two other men from the village, one of whom was a junior leader well known to be skilled in debate, the other a close kin-associate of the senior elder. The village leader and senior elder of Ejwengang were also present and later the senior claimant to the position of leadership in Ebeagwa also appeared, together with one of his associates. The house owner (who was on the side of the senior claimant) hovered in the background.

My own part in this meeting was to be presented as the fourth and 'last-born' son of Ndifaw, which was duly accomplished with the presentation of two bottles of brandy.[1] Most of the discussion however concerned (a) the issue of the Tali dispute (b) the central organization of the Clan Union, and (c) the question of the Ebeagwa village leadership. As we shall later describe in Chapter 13, 'Tali 2' were then seeking to obtain separate entry into the Clan Union; their representatives had already arrived and were staying in Ebeagwa. (Significantly, they were quartered in the section of Upper Ebeagwa led by the junior of the two claimant leaders.) It was agreed by those present in relation to the first issue that Tali had only one leader: 'Tali 2' should not then be allowed to make a separate subscription to the Clan Union, but if it wished to join could do so only by paying half of the total contribution due from Tali as a single village, which was the same in amount ($£2$) as that paid by the other villages of Ebeagwa and Ejwengang.[2] It was

---

[1] To this extent I was assimilated to the constitution of the village group. The nickname, MɔNdifɔ, 'Son of Ndifaw', remained with me throughout my time in Banyang country.
[2] See Chapter 11 for details concerning the form of the Clan Unions.

known that this condition could not be agreed to by 'Tali 2' without renouncing their claim to independence. It was further agreed that a letter should be sent to the Banyang Native Authority at Bakebe, signed by the 'Quarter Heads' (minor leaders) of the village group, reaffirming the constitutional unity of Tali and pointing out that the proposed discussion of the question at the next N.A. meeting at Bakebe was unnecessary. As a condition of his acceptance of this combined action, the senior claimant leader of Ebeagwa asked that the other persons present should support his own succession to the leadership of the village: this they agreed to do, and undertook to send a further letter to the District Officer, nominating him as the 'legitimate' leader of Ebeagwa. On the question of the central organization of the Clan Union, it was suggested by the Tali members and eventually agreed to by the others that an 'Executive Committee' should be formed composed of four persons from each village. (These twelve persons, it was understood, would have central control of the affairs of the Clan Union.) The four Tali representatives were named: all were leading members of the village but included neither the village leader nor the senior elder.

The discussion of these issues lasted for some hours. It was notable that 'Tali 2' representatives, although present in the village not many yards from the house in which it took place, were strictly excluded from the meeting, and that the only representatives of Ebeagwa that were brought in were those supporting the senior claimant to the leadership. On the first two issues – the Tali dispute and the organization of the Clan Union – the suggested policy to be adopted came from the Tali representatives and had clearly already been formulated by them in advance of their coming to Ebeagwa. The meeting was punctuated by the departure of the senior claimant leader of Ebeagwa and the senior elder of Ejwengang who each left to consult with their own supporters concerning the agreements they were entering into. The senior claimant leader of Ebeagwa was absent for about two hours and when he eventually returned and the discussion concluded – the Tali proposal concerning 'Tali 2' being agreed to in return for Tali's and Ejwengang's promise to put his own house in order – he presented four bottles of brandy to the meeting in recognition of their acceptance of his succession to the leadership. This secret meeting of the 'inner council' finally broke up at about 4 a.m.

The next morning at an open general meeting of the Clan Union the first issue to be discussed was that of Tali 2's entry into the Union. The agreed formula was put to the meeting and heatedly discussed. As was expected, 'Tali 2' refused to combine with 'Tali 1' in their subscription to the Union: 'Are we slaves,' they asked, 'that we must be under Tali 1?' The point was discounted and the formula insisted upon on the grounds of Tali's traditional unity. 'Tali 2' were thus excluded from the Union and thereafter sat silent, without participating in the following discussions. (Later on the same day they left, having refused to take the food offered to them in hospitality.) The rest of the morning and early afternoon were taken up with other Clan Union matters.

In the evening (after the community leaders had recovered some of their lost sleep) a further meeting of the main representatives of the village group was held, outside the context of the Clan Union, in the senior claimant leader's *mɔɛkri*, behind his *acɔ* or meeting-house.[1] The meeting, described as the *ɛtɔk*, was in effect one of the village group council, including the leading representatives of (the rump) Tali and of Ejwengang (i.e. those who had taken part in the previous night's discussions, plus other sectional heads) and most of the village council of Ebeagwa including now the *junior* claimant leader and his associates. The letter concerning the Tali dispute was composed and signed; it was later given to four prominent minor leaders in Tali (Mr Tataw, Nyenti, and two others) to take to Bakebe. The question of the Ebeagwa village leadership was now discussed. This gave rise to heated debate, particularly on the side of the junior claimant leader. The issue was decided, however, very largely by the forceful speaking of the senior elder of Ejwengang, who declared that the senior claimant should be village leader, 'until he dies'. A bottle of brandy was again brought to seal the discussion. A letter regarding the leadership was written to the District Officer and signed. Finally the 'bottom' of the brandy was poured on the ground as an oblation to the dead by the senior elder of Ejwengang who in calling upon the dead reiterated the decision which had been reached. (In my notes I write that he 'appeared to be informing the present company decisively rather than informing the dead'.) Thus for the moment were these issues settled.

In conclusion it should be noted that the action regarding Tali 2 was for the time being successful, although in the end they were able to gain their constitutional independence. The letter to the Native Authority did not in fact prevent the issue from being discussed there (see p. 311), but the fact that they had been excluded from the Clan Union strengthened considerably the 'traditionalist' case of the rump Tali.

[1] Cf. p. 29.

On the other hand, the issue of the Ebeagwa leadership was by no means concluded. Two days later the junior claimant leader went off to the Native Authority to challenge the decision reached in Ebeagwa, and the matter was not finally settled until the District Officer arrived in Ebeagwa a month later and presided over a meeting of the village, which produced the compromise arrangement which has already been mentioned (p. 116). The decision regarding the 'Executive Committee' of the Union was later modified to include a wider range of persons, less exclusively representative of the established inner core of Tali leaders (see p. 264). The latter were not, however, to know of these later changes and returned home from Ebeagwa well satisfied with what they had accomplished.

The extent of the community involved in this example and the importance of the issues which were to be decided make it in some ways unusual. It nevertheless illustrates the essential process by which a 'policy' is first formulated by a small group of men centrally representative of community interests and then presented in the wider forum where it is hoped that their support will see that this policy is adopted. According to the size of the community involved, the initial formulation of the policy will involve coalition and compromise in order to accommodate the divergent interests of those combining. There may well be an attempt to force the issue through on the strength of the support of those who have participated in the agreement (thus in the later discussion of the Ebeagwa leadership the senior elder of Ejwengang played a prominent part in forcing the decision, which was then announced to the 'dead') but ultimately the adoption of an agreed policy depends upon the representativeness and influence of those who have taken part in the agreement: the policy concerning Tali 2 was successful since it carried the weight of the larger part of the village group; that concerning the Ebeagwa leadership was only temporarily adopted, the size and influence of the junior claimant leader's faction (who were excluded from the 'caucus' agreement) enabling him to reopen the issue and eventually to obtain a compromise more in his favour.

At the lower level of village grouping the processes of policy formation are less contingently dependent upon the particular combination of interests which have been described here. Yet the processes remain essentially the same: a small group of leading men, the 'inner council' of the village, consult privately to formulate a line of action which, if it needs the support of the wider group, will be introduced and spoken to at a public meeting of the village council by those who have already discussed it 'behind'. In terms of strategy such a process has a dual advantage: firstly, in its assured support by a core of influential men and close advocates; secondly, in a certain 'surprise' quality, which leaves its potential opponents uncertain of precisely what issues are involved and in which direction it is heading. In Tali, during the time of the leadership dispute, the inner council of the village was continually preoccupied with the way it should be conducted, various suggestions being put forward and discussed by them. After the dispute had been settled, the combined inner council of the now conjoint Tali met regularly and it was from these meetings that the idea of a 'modern' society, a 'Town Council', was developed.

Not all meetings of an inner council of a village are formally convened: if an issue suddenly arises its members may be sent for (night-time summonses are often cited, somewhat dramatically, to exemplify such close, confidential relationships) but other meetings occur through an interchange of visits, in which the village leader's settlement is often the focal point, although by no means always the meeting-place. Often the exchanging or receiving of 'hospitality' is involved (such as the occasion of the bottle of brandy which caused Taku Nyang's resentment, p. 171). Or occasionally an *ad hoc* consultation of two or three members takes place when a community discussion is actually in progress and the leaders disappear quietly to convene outside or in an adjacent house to take stock of their position and to formulate an approach (to be presented preferably in the open meeting not by those most directly involved but by an associate). By no means all the issues discussed by a village council are subject to an earlier inner council agreement. Most important issues, however, are likely to have been foreseen and discussed by them, so that the general direction of village affairs – its 'policy' in the widest sense – remains very closely dependent upon the role and influence of its central representatives, the inner council.

A community 'law' (*ɛbɛi*) is generally subject to the processes of formulation and presentation which have been described above for all important policy issues. In general, 'laws' are made to ensure conformity in matters of accepted community interest or to enforce the authority of a community when this has been challenged. They are concerned for the most part with particular situations or issues and do not add up to a body of 'law' which can be said to be administered by a community. The circumstances covered by a law vary from the control of everyday activities to more general offences that have become matters of public concern. The following examples comes from the three villages of Tali, Bara, and Besongabang:

> That goats should be tethered in the settlements during the time that the crops are beginning to grow;
> that all members of the village should attend in so many days' time to clear the village paths (both of these being routine, standard laws, administrative in their effect);
> that no one should fight with another person in the community;
> that if a man becomes drunk he should return home to sleep it off;
> that if a man does not own any raffia-palm (used to make roof-mats) he should not cut leaves from a tree not belonging to him, but should seek permission to cut leaves from someone who does own trees;
> that no one should have intercourse with another man's wife;
> that no dog should be allowed to roam freely in the settlement, a hunter who owns a dog being required to keep it on a leash in the settlement and to free it only in the forest (this after two severe cases of biting in Besongabang, including one from which a child later died).

On one occasion in Tali 2 when the food offered to the guests at a funeral celebration was insufficient and gave rise to quarrelling, the leader of Tali 2, acting circumstantially and on his own initiative, announced that 'from today' no one should hold a funeral celebration without preparing sufficient food and wine for it. Finally, a further important category of 'laws' are those, already mentioned, which debar the members of a community from receiving or giving hospitality to a named person.

All or any of these laws may be announced through and supported by one of the community associations. These associations are themselves a further important source of laws, which apply to the community in which they are organized and which bear upon their own aims and interests (for example, the laws applying to prostitutes commonly made by the Clan Unions, see p. 266 and Appendix A). Nevertheless, all laws ultimately rest upon community authority, however this is represented corporately. In fact, the majority of laws probably are announced through and sanctioned by an association, but this is not a necessary procedure and others are announced directly by a leader or senior elder acting in council and with the weight of community opinion behind him. The conventional form in the latter case is the public announcement at a village or other community council meeting that 'From today no one should do such-and-such . . .' concluding with a reiterated 'Do you not hear?', which all present are expected to affirm, *Ɛɛ!*. Sometimes, however, the announcement takes a more circumstantial form, a simple declaration by the community leaders relying upon the implicit support of the community as a whole. The leader of Tali 2's law concerning funeral celebrations was made in this latter way, as also were the laws which will be described in the next section, made by the combined inner council of the Ndifaw village group in their legislative warfare with the members of three other village groups.

But however a law is made, its strength as law depends upon the effectiveness with which it is later upheld, or can be upheld, by judicial action. When, for example, a series of laws were made by a Clan Union Meeting of Tanyi Nkongo village group governing the prices of a number of commodities (animals, sleeping-mats, wine, etc.), some doubt was expressed as to whether these laws would 'become strong' (*cɔŋ ɛntaŋ*). The ways in which these laws could be avoided were too devious and the means of bringing the offenders to book too difficult for any very strong hopes to be held. Laws made in a community that concern general circumstances (for example, fighting or drunkenness) tend in time to be forgotten, and are no longer, or only arbitrarily, referred to. In 1965 the law that had been made some years previously in Besongabang village concerning the free roaming of dogs had by this time been ignored by one or two people who had acquired dogs, and the question then being debated by its inner council members was whether further action should be taken and, if so, what. Community 'laws' are thus limited by the circumstances which produce them and by the judicial processes which strengthen them. On both these counts we shall later see that the role of the associations is important in formalizing and supporting an authority which has only a diffuse corporate expression without them.

Fighting between communities

Sporadic fighting occurred between communities in the past and there were also more extended hostilities between some Banyang and eastern Ejagham communities and the Mbo people to the south-west. Early accounts and present references to these indicate that most of the fighting occurred on an inter-village basis with occasional alliances made between villages for the purpose of particular disputes or in defence against the Mbo. Notable for its absence is any tendency towards a 'segmentary' opposition of groups: like their internal politics, Banyang fighting between communities or with non-Bayang outsiders seems to have been largely factional.

Thus in referring to the 'revolt' of 1903 and the fighting which followed during the later punitive expedition, Mansfeld expresses some surprise about the absence of any general line-up among Banyang or Keaka communities. He writes:

> One would have expected that at least in the common struggle against the foreign intruders, the whites, all village-communities (*Dorf-gemeinden*), would have banded together without exception. But only fifteen minutes distance from their tribal brothers, related to them many times over through marriage, both Banyang and Keaka were much divided in the sides that they took.

He lists then a number of villages, some of which were active in the uprising, while others stayed neutral or helped the German troops by supplying food.[1] Elsewhere Mansfeld records that in the fifty years up to 1904 there had been no warfare between tribes but rather a series of local wars between single villages (*Dorfschaften*). He lists eighteen of those that had recently occurred in Ekoi, Keaka, and Banyang country, including four involving Banyang villages. A number of these wars cut across tribal affinities; often the same village is cited as fighting a different opponent on different occasions.[2]

Today Banyang elders say that the commonest cause of inter-village fighting was the abduction or running off of wives, especially those of leaders (who were more 'at risk' in this respect than others). In retaliation a raid was organized, either a small-scale hit-and-run affair in which a couple of men went by night to kill a selected victim, aided possibly by a 'double-dealer' (*mu bɛnaŋ*) within the stranger village, or a larger-scale operation, with a party of men equipping themselves to go (again by night) to attack the settlements of an opponent community, doing what damage they could to people or property. In the latter case prisoners were sometimes taken, whose return could be obtained by their home community on ransom (together possibly with the agreed settlement of the original offence) or who were otherwise sold into slavery. Such raids might provoke further raids until eventually one community sued for peace and a settlement was reached. These inter-village hostilities did not necessarily bring in fellow-villagers of the same village group and often alliances were made or help was sought along lines which cut across these widest descent groups. Defang of Tali is, for example, described as having

---

[1] Op. cit., p. 159.   [2] Ibid., pp. 16–17.

given assistance on a number of occasions to people outside the Ndifaw group. One such raid was launched against Kendem (of the Awanchi village group) to help a man from Ekpaw (of Nkokenok II village group) whose sons had been captured by them. Other alliances running counter to the widest descent grouping were made between Etemetek and Eyan-chang, and between 'Small Mamfe' and Eberkaw, the latter alliance on one occasion serving to defend the salt-springs of Eberkaw against attack from Besongabang (tracing common kinship with 'Small Mamfe').[1] We may note further that, except in the case of the more prolonged fighting against the Mbo, the 'wars' that are remembered are invariably linked with the names of communities (i.e. not of descent groups) and that almost always these are the names of villages: thus, for example, even if men from other villages of the bɔ Ayok Ɛtayak village group came to help Besongabang in fighting against an outside village, the 'war' (nɛnu) would still be known as that of Besongabang, and not that of bɔ Ayok Ɛtayak.

In some cases (e.g. Ayok Etayak and Nkokenok village groups) fighting within a village group is said to have occurred in the same way as fighting between villages of different village groups, whereas in other cases (e.g. Ndifaw village group) it is said to have taken place only with sticks, clubs, and the flat sides of matchets. In any case it would seem that greater sanction was exerted on whatever fighting did occur in a village group, which was generally settled more quickly than other forms of fighting, with the payment of compensation for the outstanding deaths. Conventionalized fighting also took place between the equivalent age-groups of different villages whereby the members of one challenged their coevals in another as a test of strength.

Fighting against the Mbo seems to have followed very much the same lines as the internal fighting between Banyang villages: a series of raids and counter-raids in which the weakest went to the wall or allied them-selves with their stronger neighbours, whether or not of the same village group. Much of this fighting concerned Upper Banyang, although towards the end of the nineteenth century the Mbo are reported to have pressed as far north as the borders of Lower Banyang and eastern Ejagham country, where a number of villages formed an alliance around Kembong to protect their salt-springs.[2] Among Upper Banyang, Defang of Tali provided the main resistance, organizing counter-raids which seem to

[1] Banyang Tribal Area Assessment Report, para. 18.
[2] Intelligence Report on the Kembong Area 1937, para. 23. The village group so federated adopted the name Nchemti.

have held the Mbo in check. Defang's success in this is especially associated with his possession at this time of a cult association, Eja, by which the young men of Tali were organized and ritually strengthened for fighting. Bara village, close to the borders of Mbo country, suffered especially from Mbo raids and later joined Tali for its own protection. Takwa also at one time obtained protection from the Mbo by allying itself with the neighbouring Bangwa chieftaincy of Fontem. Fighting with the Mbo continued until the German occupation, when it was finally stopped. No equivalent fighting is said to have occurred with the Bangwa, and fighting across the borders of Banyang and Ejagham country appears to have occurred in the same way as fighting between Banyang communities.[1]

The conditions of the terrain help to account for the form taken by this fighting: thick bush or forest country with a sparse population scattered in isolated settlements. In these circumstances the only tactics possible would seem to be those of guerrilla fighting: surprise raids by parties of men who have infiltrated through the forest to attack single or small groups of settlements. Extensive defence is made difficult by the scatteredness of the community, by the speed of the attack, and by the vulnerability of the more distant settlements left by their menfolk. The massing of 'sides' is not possible.

On the other hand, the form taken by fighting in the past also relates to the nature of Banyang political organization. Banyang communities were isolated autonomous groups: as Mansfeld depicts them then (quoted, p. 104), 'for the most part each village community is strictly cut off by itself: no law links it to its neighbour'. Banyang community organization was built out of the internal political relations of group autonomy, where the solidarity of the community unit is not so much dependent upon its relations of opposition to outsiders but upon the need to maintain order within. Fighting was a function of the corporate structure of a community, but an incidental one, whose effectiveness rested somewhat arbitrarily upon the even strength of actual residential groups. 'Villages' (at that time, we should remember, much more residentially dispersed as communities) were the potential fighting units, each under its own leader, but their effectiveness in fighting was conditioned by their size, and by such organizational support as was given by cult associations like Eja: a weak village went not to its extended kinsfolk but to obtain the help of a stronger village under a more powerful leader.

Such fighting no longer occurs. It is relevant, however, to the general

[1] See above p. 182, and Mansfeld, op. cit., p. 17.

point made in the last paragraph to conclude with an account of an incident whereby hostile *external* relations between village groups were characteristically answered by a series of measures dependent upon *internal* political functions: a political affront that developed into warfare by legislation.

The circumstances of the case were in some ways abnormal since it developed out of an invitation which I received to attend the opening meeting of a newly formed 'modern' association, a Federation of the Clan Unions of three Upper Banyang village groups.[1] Shortly before my departure for this meeting, the Ndifaw Clan Union held one of their own general meetings. There (in my absence) it was decided that I should not be allowed to attend alone but should be accompanied by representatives from each of the three villages then in agreement in the Ndifaw group. Our combined arrival at the Federation meeting in Takwa was not, however, welcomed: it was pointed out that the Ndifaw group were not of 'one voice' (*eyɔŋ ɛmɔt*) with the other village groups, except for one issue (the collection of prostitutes from the south, see Chapter 11). The representatives could not then be allowed to attend the meeting. While I stayed on, they consequently were obliged to return, which they did, reporting the matter to their own village leaders.

Within the village group this enforced withdrawal was taken as an affront to the good name of *bɔ Ndifɔ*. A meeting of the leaders of the three villages was convened in Ejwengang to discuss what action should be made in reply. Here, at the combined 'inner council' of the village group, it was decided that, in reprisal for the insult suffered, a law should be made prohibiting any members of the village group from giving palm wine to any members of the three village groups represented in the Federation. This law was not announced through an association but was announced directly by the leaders who had taken part in the meeting and who (in the rump Tali) went from one village section to the next, telling each section leader of the law and obtaining his signature or thumbprint upon the paper which recorded it. The law was nevertheless very strictly observed and had the full weight of community authority behind it.

When the law became known by the three village groups concerned they themselves retaliated by making their own law against Ndifaw villagers. In this case they prohibited members of their own village

[1] Further details of the Federation are given in Chapter 11.

groups from giving palm-wine or selling food to anyone from the Ndifaw group.

This state of suspended hospitality between the village groups lasted for about a month. It was finally concluded at my own instigation when the Ndifaw leaders agreed to rescind their law on the understanding that the three village groups of the Federation would do likewise. (The latter were at first concerned to obtain a 'written apology' but fortunately did not in the end insist upon this condition.)

Administrative functions

A governmental function notable for its extremely weak development in Banyang community structure is that of administration. The administrative tasks are in general met as an adjunct to a community's other activities. Those representing the sections of a residential group at a community meeting are expected to keep their followers informed of any general decision reached by the meeting. Even so, when a general community requirement has been decided upon, it is usually easier to secure its fulfilment by legislation (whereby it becomes a 'community offence' if a person fails to do something) rather than by relying upon any line of person-to-person responsibility. Some such routine laws have already been cited: they cover such standard needs as: finding labour for a given task; preventing the misuse of communal resources (e.g. the muddying of watering-places); keeping domestic animals under control; protecting fruit-trees from too early or random picking.

It might be argued that the rulings made in this context have the character of administrative orders and that speaking of them as 'laws' over-emphasizes their importance. Yet one of the features of these 'laws' is the very cumbrousness of the procedure by which they are made. On certain occasions (where the issue is clear-cut and the need unquestioned), this procedure of obtaining compliance by community legislation is extremely effective: Mansfeld found 'Ngbe law' (Ewi-Ngbe, as he termed the association) a useful instrument of his own administration,[1] and the community or association sanctions which support such laws do indeed guarantee a very highly degree of compliance. On the other hand, not all matters lend themselves so readily to formal legislation, and if any section of the community dissents from the requirement, a collective decision on it is unlikely to be reached, or enforced. The latter difficulty was forcefully illustrated in Tali before the settlement of the dispute,

[1] Op. cit., p. 161. Administrative requirements were thus announced through the local lodges of Ngbe.

when two of the school-houses were due to be re-roofed by the dissenting halves of the community. 'Tali 2', still fighting for its constitutional independence as a village and with a consequently enhanced solidarity, very rapidly produced the large number of roof-mats required and their house was soon re-roofed. On the other hand, the members of the rump Tali, particularly two sections without direct access to the central leadership, were resentful of what they believed had been an unjust treatment of them earlier (when the inner council divided privately, they believed, a fee which they expected to be more widely distributed) and a large number of men refused then to comply with the demand made in the village council that they should complete the work in a certain time; no action could be taken against this collective refusal and the re-roofing was completed only after a long delay, mainly by the immediate followers of the members of the inner council. Again, it happened that the leader of Tali 1 was often requested to find carriers. This request created certain difficulties: it was not something that could be sanctioned by law, nor could he directly order certain groups to provide so many men. He might pass forward the request to the village council, but on at least one occasion he was reduced to pedalling through the village on his bicycle to attempt personally to persuade through their section heads eligible men to undertake this (paid) employment.

Two conditions underlie the absence of any effective administrative structure: the first relates to the hierarchy of leadership in Banyang communities; the second to the strong resentment of any autocratic action which usurps the collective right of a corporate community to make decisions.

We have discussed in an earlier chapter (pp. 67f.) the 'line of leadership', *ndɔŋ kɛfɔ*, which runs from the junior household heads and minor settlement leaders of the past to the most widely recognized (village) community leader. This hierarchy of status reflects the formation and interrelationship of actual residential groups and I have tried to show how it forms part of the 'constitutional' structure of Banyang communities. This hierarchy of leadership is, however, one of 'representation upwards' and is not a series of offices in which authority is delegated downwards. The influence of a leader (which may indeed be very great) derives from the power which he has in fact to hand: in his wealth, in his strategic status as a member of 'inner' community groups, in his knowledge of affairs and his ability to manipulate them. These are personal attributes and not attributes of an office. The sanctions which control a leader stem from his followers, not his superiors. While his status often requires to be

187

confirmed by the wider community of which his residential group is part (village leader by village group, hamlet leader by village), he owes it initially to those whom he represents. A minor leader enters then merely a negotiating relationship with his superiors: his major responsibility lies to those who 'follow him behind'. This being so, the hierarchy of leadership is an extremely flimsy structure when it comes to the downward delegation of administrative tasks: there is indeed very little that a village leader can do to exert pressure upon its section leaders if it is not in the interests of the latter (or if the latter's followers refuse) to accept his requests.

A further condition which limits the effective delegation of authority is the insistence that is constantly made on the collective right of community representatives to make decisions. As I was told once: 'The thing which causes trouble in a community is when one person speaks as though he is the owner of the community, instead of speaking as though it is everyone – "let *us* do this thing . . .". It is so even with the (village) leader. Did he buy the community? It was he who was put in front. If he bought the community, what will he do for the people who are in it?' This was, in fact, said with reference to a village leader who was thought to be becoming too autocratic in his behaviour and who was for this reason deliberately excluded from the central activities of an association that otherwise included all leading members of the village.[1] Decisions affecting a community must (ideally) be collective: but collective decisions are also most vulnerable to the conflicting interests of internal sections.

A case which illustrates the cumbrousness of Banyang administrative procedures concerns a Bara man who, having been asked to do something for the community, failed to.

> *Tanyi Ashu, a section head of Bara, had been asked by the village leader and by the leader of the second most important section of the village (acting here with the force of an 'inner council') to undertake an errand to the neighbouring Bangwa chiefship of Fossung. (The nature of the errand did not come out in the case but it concerned the association Tui, which had originally been acquired from there.) The errand proved fruitless. Tanyi Ashu returned to Bara but failed to report the lack of success of his mission to either of the men concerned. No question was asked by them and they merely waited. After two

---

[1] See also the stalemate that arose at the initial meeting of the Federation of three village groups because of what was felt to be a usurpation of authority by one village leader, pp. 269–271, below.

days a meeting of the village council was called and the question put to Tanyi Ashu: Had he not been sent on an errand by the community? Why then had he failed to report back to the village leader on his return?

Tanyi Ashu admitted his error but pleaded that it was unintentional. In any case there was nothing positive which he could have reported: no disadvantage followed from his failure. The formal offence was nevertheless insisted upon and Tanyi Ashu required to pay (-kwɔ) to the extent of providing a 'goat' of 10s.[1]

The fact that such an omission could be treated as a formal 'offence against the community' illustrates the very limited institutionalization of executive roles within Banyang political organization. The failure is not one of office, but an offence against the state.

[1] This was divided in the following way: the village leader received the 'chest' of 2s. Tanyi Ashu was given the 'head' of 6d. (signifying here the person who had brought it). I received the 'leg of the animal' of 6d. The remaining 7s. was divided according to the sections of the village represented at the meeting: bɔ Esɔŋafiɛt 2s. 9d,; bɔ Tanyi Nkoŋo 2s. 3d.; bɔ Taba 1s.; bɔ Tambi Ambi 1s. One section was not represented and received nothing; the sixth (and last) section was represented only by the defendant.

8

Limitations upon the Corporate
Structure of the Community

The collective basis of community authority forms both its strength and its weakness. Living in Banyang communities one is struck by the degree of potential domination which the 'community' in its various corporate forms exerts over its individual members. One cannot help but also be struck, however, by the limited size of the groups that do in fact accept political unity and by the constant presence of political factions within them. In this chapter I shall try to show how these features are two sides of the same coin: Banyang political structure is based upon the principle of collective action, but is also conditioned by it.

We have already noted Banyang insistence upon the need to respect community authority (p. 135) and the fact that this authority is supported by coercive and not merely moral sanctions (p. 152). An incident in which the village leader of Bara harangued the village for some of its members' failure to respect a village association (Tui), gives some insight into the power wielded by the corporate community. As I shall shortly describe, the association Tui presents through its masked figure an image of destructive violence: when it enters a settlement all its members are expected to flee from it. On one occasion when the masked figure came into Bara, one or two people were bold enough to stand their ground and not (as did most people) hide themselves behind closed doors and windows in their houses. When the figure had retired, the village leader came out and stood in the open centre of the village where he publicly warned its members: It was not a game, he said. When people see an association (*ako*) which has the 'people of the community' (*bo ɛtɔk*) in it, they should respect and fear it. If someone did not flee from it, Tui (the masked figure) could injure him, even breaking his legs. The person himself could do nothing: it was his fault he had not fled from Tui. There would be no way open to him. Even if he went to the District Officer (the 'European') he would have no case.

The point here, of course, is that an individual member of a community, when opposed by all its members collectively, is powerless: there 'is no way' (*mbi apu*). When I have asked Banyang where a community's strength or power (*bɛtaŋ*) comes from, the answer has been quite clear: it comes from 'the hands of people', *amɔ bo*. It is customary after the communal drinking of wine in Lower Banyang villages for various salutations to be made, which reaffirm the status of individual members, or of the group. Especially when the meeting has included representatives from most village sections, including the most prominent men of the village, one of the commonest phrases so used is the reiterated question: *ɛtɔk-a?* 'And the community?' to which the answer, collectively given, affirms the support given to it by its members: 'The community is well grounded' (*ɛtɔk ɛci amɔk*), or 'The community is not uncared for' (*ɛtɔk ɛpu amɔk ndɛm*), all phrases which emphasize that the community is 'in the hands of people'. We have seen also that in the making of laws and in the ritual conclusion of a meeting there is a similar antiphonal response which gives collective verbal affirmation to a decision of the corporate community. The strength of the community stems, then, from the very collective nature of community authority: *ɛtɔk ɛɛtaŋ*, 'the community is *strong*', as Banyang will affirm, citing examples of what a community council by the sheer force of its authority can do: requiring a thief to submit himself to ridicule, another 'to drink water from a basket', and so on. It is the collective support sanctioning a community decision which leaves the isolated offender with 'no way open', as the village leader of Bara pointed out.

Nevertheless, in order to achieve this strength, community councils have to be united in their decisions. The ideal of a united, strong community is constantly invoked at council meetings as the goal which should always be sought: community leaders do not tire in urging people to be of 'one voice' (*ɛyɔŋ ɛmɔt*). The maxim, 'Unity is Strength' (*dɛnyukɛti - ci bɛtaŋ*), accompanies, as we shall see, many newly founded associations. The difficulty is always of achieving this unity. A residential group of any extent necessarily contains a diversity of interests, which include, as a major category, concern over the status of individual leaders and the influence of their following. As fast as individuals seek to improve their status, sectional groups to aggrandize their position, the tendency for the remaining members of the community is to restrain them, to insist that they are only part of the whole, that all action must be collective. It happens therefore in many cases that conflicts between its sections develop within a community which seriously weaken its ability to act effectively.

In all the corporate forms that a community can take, there is this rather uncertain balance between, on the one hand, the unity of the group (for any effective political action depends upon such unity) and, on the other, the diversity of interests which are necessarily to be represented if the group's actions are to remain collective. As I have tried to show in the previous chapter, the refusal to delegate authority is in part attributable to this emphasis upon the collective basis of community authority; yet it is also in the interests of those jealous of their status and influence within the group to restrain any fellow-member who attempts to rise above it.

A verbal device which expresses this dilemma of Banyang political processes is that of reification: the community is spoken of as though it had a material form or personality. In this way a kind of pseudo-corporateness is given to the community as a 'total' group which obscures the more precise organization of persons and groups who do in fact represent community interests and maintain its order.

'The community is a thing that . . . [e.g. will be annoyed if anyone attempts to divide it].' (Ɛtɔk ɛci ɛnyŋ ɛnɛ . . . ɛbe ntɔ mu ayaŋ ɛtakɛti yɔ). The community 'sits', 'speaks', 'makes a law', can be 'angry', and so on. These figures of speech are part of the everyday parlance of those who are concerned in the government of a community. When a mu ɛtɔk visits a different village he may be asked after the health or well-being of his community in exactly the same form as he is asked after his own health: Ɛtɔk ɛci? 'How is the community?' The community is 'well' (ɛcici or ɛci ɛriri) when nothing untoward has occurred in it in the way of illness, death, or mishap to any of its members. More especially a community is said to be 'strong', 'vigorous', or in 'good health' (ɛtaŋ, the verb is also that which is applied to a person's health) when there is no factional dispute in it and when its government is firm and sure. At the first critical meeting of the representatives of all the Ndifaw village group after the Tali dispute had been finally settled, the phrase insistently repeated was that 'the community was sick – but did not die' (ɛtɔk ɛme – ɛbɔk ɛgu). This reification of the community in a political context is even more clearly illustrated in a text which will be later quoted concerning the case of a man who, after failing to accept a community ruling and after being ostracized by an Ngbe law, took his case to the District Officer at Mamfe (who in turn referred it back to the community for settlement there). The man claimed that he had at least the right to take this course:

. . . He said that once a man has fired a gun, whether he has killed an animal or not, it shows that he is a man.

But the community leaders took a different view, turning his suggested analogy to their own account:

> We agreed, but said that he *is* a man and he shot the community. And soon he will have to plead guilty and pay the community as though it were the animal which he shot. (See p. 240.)

Rather in the manner of a similar verbal device in English law, this way of personifying or reifying the community serves (at least conceptually) to 'incorporate' it: it is no longer a mere aggregate of individuals but becomes an entity in its own right, with interests and demands independent of those of all its individual members.[1] This very reliance upon *verbal* incorporation nevertheless leaves undiminished (for Banyang) the collective responsibility of all a community's members for its corporate actions. It is, as it were, as though all members of a group are willing to subscribe to a joint fiction concerning it at one level in order to preserve the element of free play which can continue at a lower level concerning those who on any one occasion will represent the community in its corporate activities. The unity of the group is stated without jeopardizing the diversity of interests within it.

The two linked but mutually reinforcing principles of Banyang political structure – firstly, that the corporate strength of any residential group depends upon the inclusive unity of its members (or their representatives) in decisions concerning it; and, secondly, that any corporate action, by being collective, must accommodate the diversity of interests of the members of the group – of necessity underlie the form and activities of all residential groups, of whatever level of community grouping. The two principles, however, determine in differing proportions the characteristics of these groups: *firstly*, at the different levels of community grouping; and *secondly* at different periods of the same group's history. In both cases the two linked principles operate to give a 'balance in extension': in the first case, over the total structure of 'the complex community'; in the second, over time, as a process of adjustment and change.

Thus, as we have seen, the village group council has the strongest formal authority: it awards the heaviest fines; escape from its authority is the least possible. But at the same time, this, the community at its widest extension, is the most open to opposing interests, in the past was the most difficult to bring together in collective action, and indeed on occasion found its component villages on opposing sides in fighting or

[1] Cf. *Salmond on Jurisprudence* (11th Edn., by Glanville Williams, 1957, pp. 357–362).

lost them through their alliance to outsiders. At the other extreme in the overall community structure, a hamlet is far more united as a residential group, its members accepting a closer and more continuous tradition of co-operation, but by its limitation in size, and thus its inclusiveness in relation to the rest of the community, its formal authority is lessened. (It is less able to close the 'ways to alternative action' which we have seen as intrinsic to community authority.) The village stands midway between these two extremes of grouping and its features show a more even balance between the two factors: in general, village councils have the greatest *effective* authority although not the strongest *formal* authority. In the general processes of government, it is the 'council' and 'inner council' of the village which play the key roles (this we have constantly emphasized), but they do not operate alone (a point we have also emphasized), being supported by the governmental activities of the councils of residential groups at both higher and lower levels.

Nor (must we immediately add) is the balance of factors, at either the village or other levels, stable over time. There are occasions when the leading members of a village, and sometimes of a larger residential group, are brought together in greater accord (usually through the inner council in the first place) to control affairs with greater determination and effectiveness, occasions when the community can be said to 'be strong'. At other times lack of resolution and discord among its members can seriously detract from the effectiveness of a village council, governmental functions then tending to revert to councils representing more limited residential groups, usually a sub-village. On these occasions it is said that the community is 'not of one voice' (*ɛpu ɛyɔŋ ɛmɔt*).

In Tali the period immediately following the settlement of the Tali dispute was one in which the community was notably 'strong'. In the case of the village leader's fight with the 'slaves' (p. 165), which was heard then, the strength of the united Tali was an important factor in the case's conclusion. At this time, indeed, the supra-village council acquired a name for its rapaciousness in judgement and it was said then among the 'ordinary' members of Tali I that if one had a case with a fellow-member one should avoid reporting it to the council.

Two short examples of cases which were heard at that time by the united supra-village council will illustrate the kind of judgements then made.

One concerned the leader of Mbinjong 'slave'-settlement who was accused of tale-bearing, and thus of 'double-dealing' (*bɛnaŋ*), between

Tali 1 and Tali 2. He had in fact taken a report of 'animals of the community' given to the village leader of Tali 1, to Tali 2, where it had reached the ears of its own village leader. At that time if any significant 'animal of the community' had been presented to either village leader he would have certainly been expected to call the other village leader and his followers to share in it. The village leader of Tali 2 had not been called and, having heard the report late one evening, came there and then to face the leader of Tali 2 with it. The latter discounted the story (I do not know with what truth) and it rebounded then upon the head of the leader of the slave-settlement. *Bɛnaŋ*, double-dealing or 'back-biting' as it is most commonly translated in Pidgin, is taken as an extremely serious offence, both moral and political, since it threatens the essential solidarity of all corporate groups. It was this offence with which the leader of the slave-settlement was charged and when his formal guilt was established he was told to bring a goat and a 'slave' (i.e. £3. 10s.). He returned with a (live) goat and £1. This was regarded as insufficient and after two successive increments (bringing the total to £2) he was finally obliged to bring the full amount, £3. 10s. This amount and the goat were a very large fine by all normal standards and were a somewhat heavy price for a mild indiscretion, even though it did concern the village leaders.

The second case arose from the wilful damage to farm crops done by one man against another in vengeance for taking his wife. The matter was brought as an interpersonal dispute, the plaintiff (whose crops had been destroyed) seeking to obtain compensation for the damage done. After a discussion of the amount to be paid in reparation, the sum of £3. 10s. (again a 'slave') was fixed upon, the offender told to bring this amount, together with a 'goat of the community'. He went away and returned with a tin of oil (with the nominal value of 10s.) as the 'goat'. This was completely rejected and the demand made for a real goat, whatever the price he needed to pay for one. In this case, however, the offender simply disappeared: the 'community' sat for some time and, when it was apparent that he did not intend to return, dispersed. I was told that he had 'abused the community' and that the matter would not be left there, but, as I was shortly to leave Tali, I did not learn of its final outcome.

Two final points should be made: the first concerns the way in which the two related principles we have been discussing are evidenced in the form and activities of Banyang associations; the second concerns the part they play in determining the point of relationship between 'operational' and 'constitutional' grouping, according to our earlier distinction.

The role of the associations, certainly in the political sphere of Banyang society, follows the two principles we have discussed very closely. We have referred to the reification of the community as a figure of speech. The associations give precise institutional form to this verbal device: no longer the 'animal' which the Tali offender was said to have 'shot', the community becomes 'Ngbe', the leopard which all should fear. What is projected in this institutional form, is, however, only one aspect of the corporate community as an operational group (its power of domination) which all residential groups can support in the general form and purpose of the association, leaving the diverse interests of particular residential groups to be expressed through the ownership of many separate lodges. The associations provide, then, a way of answering a central political problem: how to achieve a unity of purpose without relinquishing the collective control which is based upon an ultimate diversity of interest. In the following three chapters we shall be concerned to elaborate this theme further.

In an earlier chapter we distinguished between the 'operational' and 'constitutional' features of community corporateness. In discussing Banyang governmental processes we have been concerned primarily with the operational aspect of community grouping. Nevertheless, our finding that it is in general at the level of the village that effective authority lies is relevant also to constitutional grouping, since it is precisely here that the two modes of grouping intersect: the village is not only (in general) the most effective 'operationally' corporate residential group, it is also (by definition) a residential group constitutionally distinguished by its members' recognition of a single, superior leader. We have tried to show, however, that this operational feature of residential groups at the level of the village is not constant, but is subject to the particular circumstances of group solidarity and factionalism. The processes of adjustment and change which occur here must of necessity involve the 'constitutional' features of community corporateness and are focused especially upon the issue of succession to the village leadership. We enter here the field of constitutional politics, whose importance to past changes has already been evidenced and which provides the summating expression of so many of Banyang political processes. This subject will be the special concern of the final chapters of the book.

PART III

The Role of the Associations

9

Traditional Associations

The variety and general features of Banyang associations

There are usually a number of different associations in every village, some representing different sectional interests, others organizing particular activities, some forgotten or moribund, others active and centrally involved in village affairs. The variety of associations within a village or village group is also evident in their regional distribution and in the varying dominance of particular associations over a period of time. Some (such as 'Tui') are limited to a few villages or village groups with occasional outliers elsewhere; others (such as 'Ngbe' and 'Basinjom') extend throughout Banyang country and beyond. Even those associations which, like Ngbe, are common to a wide area often have regional or local diversities, which have arisen either through imperfect copying or through the elaboration of old forms or the assimilation of new. Associations rise and fall in their popularity and effectiveness. These processes of change are especially evidenced in the rise of the 'modern' associations, which will be described later, but the 'traditional' associations would seem equally to have been subject to change, newly introduced associations becoming dominant in the place of older ones, or the form of an established association being extended and adapted by the incorporation of new features.

The term that is here translated as an 'association', *ako* or (in Upper Kenyang dialect) *akoŋ*, has a more precise meaning than the English word suggests. It refers to a certain *kind* of institution, which might be termed a 'secret society' or 'closed association', although neither word is particularly apt. An *ako* is a formally constituted group of persons who have agreed to abide by common rules of membership and who participate in certain formally defined activities. Every *ako* has, then, a 'constitution' (a series of rules defining the status and interrelationship of its members, including their activities within an association context) and consists of one or a number of 'lodges', that is, units of corporate organization, the members of any one unit all living usually in a single residential group (hamlet, sub-village, or village), and having come together in the manner prescribed by the association's constitution. It is possible for an association to be created *de novo* – a group of persons simply come together, decide upon a constitution, and establish themselves as a lodge – but more commonly lodges are acquired by purchase, sometimes by a process of division, less often simply by copying. A feature of all associations is therefore the process by which they spread from one residential group to another by the setting-up of new lodges according to the common constitution of the association. Lodges are linked by their common form, by certain reciprocal rights and duties, and by the general obligation to uphold the constitution of the association, but lodges are not normally linked in any hierarchial organization: each lodge is a fully autonomous unit whose members conduct their own affairs in their own way but along the general lines of the constitution as understood by them. A great many associations are in fact not Banyang in origin but have come from neigh-bouring peoples: Ejagham, Balundu, Bangwa. Such associations may have suffered something of a sea-change in the process by which they have spread into Banyang country but their 'international' aura adds to their prestige, and in certain important cases (Ngbe is undoubtedly the most significant) they provide the basis for reciprocal co-operation which operates across geographical, cultural and linguistic divisions.

Membership of an association is almost invariably dependent upon the payment of fees. These are usually graded in amount according to the various ranks and offices within the association. As such fees, in food, drink, or money, are normally shared among those already of that status, they form in part an 'investment' which the new member hopes to recoup when later-comers seek to acquire the same status. A further rule, which is common to most traditional associations and which is based upon the same principle of reciprocity, is that if and when a member dies his nearest kinsmen are expected to give further 'expenses' (*ncɛ*, the same term as is used for the initial 'fees') in recompense for all that the dead man ate and drank while he was a member.

A rule that applies to almost all associations (and, indeed, to almost all corporate groups in Banyang society) is that nothing which takes place in the context of an association meeting should be repeated outside it. This rule covers any decisions or arrangements made in a lodge, but it applies also and more especially to the constitution of the association itself: the formal arrangement of its parts, the precise activities of its members, the significance of the emblems or regalia belonging to it, and so on. To become a member of an association is, then, to buy knowledge of it; the more advanced a person's status in the association, the fuller, more exhaustive, is his knowledge of it. Indeed, Banyang often speak of 'seeing' or 'knowing' an association (both terms in the sense of 'having revealed to one') as a synonym for being a member of it. The element of formal secrecy as it concerns the constitution of an association is sometimes further elaborated by the use of a secret sign-language. These rules of secrecy (which are discussed further in the case of Ngbe below) act as a means of control over its members and also serve to enhance their solidarity as a group.

All associations have some authority over their members (i.e. according to their lodges) and may fine or punish them. Much of such authoritative activity arises from the plethora of rules governing people's conduct in an association context, and the fines awarded, while certainly evidence of association's authority, provide also the meat and drink essential for the continuance of its activities.

All associations have, then, a very important recreational element: they provide the context in which members of a community can come together to eat, drink, dance, and sing. At the same time there is also an element of prestige in belonging to an association: one enters in this way into a community activity; one learns what is going on; one is not left sitting 'alone' or 'with women'. For a great many associations, especially those which have no more determinate function, both recreational and prestige-giving elements are present in what is often one of their most important activities: a dance held to honour a dead person. Such a dance may form part of the later funeral ceremonies or, when a number of associations have been called for this purpose, may take place on a separate day. In some cases the association (or associations) invited to honour the dead man (or, indeed, woman) may be that of which he (or she) was a member, but an association, or lodge, can also be invited for a non-member, whose kinsmen in this case will be expected to provide rather more in the way of hospitality and gifts.

In this context we should mention finally the 'mask' or 'gown' which is worn at a public dance given by an association and which is very closely linked with its public identity. In most cases no verbal distinction is made between the masked dancer and the association, and the former serves almost invariably to represent or act on behalf of the latter. Thus the name of the association (Nkang, Tui, Basinjom, etc.) is usually given also to the masked dancer, from whom emanate the public actions made by the association (e.g. the taking-off of people for punishment in the case of Tui, the oracular pronouncements of Basinjom). The case of Ngbe is somewhat more complex, since this association has two main masked dancers, and a 'voice', but similar principles of dramatic representation also apply. As one would expect for a dancer who 'images' the association, his personal identity is obscured by the gown or mask he carries and in most cases is not expected to be revealed to outsiders.

For a number of associations their main activity is recreational, or to put on a dance. Other associations are organized to meet political, supernatural or economic needs. There is, however, a certain overlapping of function and the 'same' association which, in some areas, is said to have had a specific political or other purpose, in other areas, is said to have been no more than a recreational, 'dance' association. The following were named as former (pre-Ngbe) associations in the Lower Banyang village of Nchang: *Ncebe, Nsime, Nkaŋ, Nkpɛ, Nsibiri, Mfɔfɔk, Ndise*. All were men's associations and most were ascribed recreational functions. In Tali, among the Upper Banyang, lodges of *Nsime, Nkaŋ,* and *Nkpɛ* are reported to have existed in the past, but whereas *Nkpɛ* is said (as at Nchang) to have been primarily a recreational, 'dance' association (different from, and not to be confused with, Ngbe) both *Nsime* and *Nkaŋ* are said to have had a directly political function, being used as a means of making formal announcements in the community, in the case of *Nkaŋ* the announcement being accompanied by the striking of a double bell-gong (*nkaŋkaŋ*) now used in connection with the Basinjom association. In Tali, *Angbo* is described as an important and powerful association which immediately preceded Ngbe and which could be used to give voice to community decisions: the example given was that it could appear at night to accuse a noted witch and require that he or she should leave the community. In Besongabang village, however, *Angbo* is said to have been part of the Ngbe complex (a 'child of Ngbe') and to have appeared to announce a specially serious community 'law'; it is said also that *Angbo* might appear at the time of an important man's death and then, in mock seriousness, 'divide his inheritance' (*-kɔrɛ nɛgu*), apportioning parts among the notable leaders of the village. The association *Tui*, limited to a number of Upper Banyang villages, also had political functions, being used (it is said) in the past to punish offenders by death. Almost all these associations have today disappeared from the villages for which they are named, or are moribund: remembered, perhaps, as *Angbo* was in 1954 in Tali, for its gown and emblems, which were still kept, and by a few of its members, who were still alive but no longer active, no dance having been held in recent years. Only Tui in Bara had maintained a kind of existence, largely it would seem for the prestige it gave its members.

The one association which has become dominant in the place of these

Plate 7
Basinjom
association

Plate 8 Masked figure of Tui, with attendant

various earlier associations is Ngbe, which without doubt has been in this century the most important association with political functions. This is sometimes described (somewhat anachronistically as far as Upper Banyang are concerned) as being the 'Government' before the Europeans arrived, and part of its success almost certainly lies in its more effective fulfilment of a political role than the earlier associations, most notably that of promulgating 'laws'.

In the 1950s the most important association with supernatural functions was Basinjom, concerned to detect and expose witchcraft activities. A sub-section of Ngbe, *Bekundi*, has also important cult functions, protecting the main association with its medicines (see below, pp. 220–221). *Ɛja*, which we have already referred to (p. 184), and which was used in the organization of fighting to render warriors immune from danger and also to foretell the outcome of a raid, would seem to have been centred primarily upon a cult-agency (*njɔ*) but to have imposed certain requirements as well upon the actual conduct of the fighting. One should mention also in this context Mfam, the most important of the present-day cult-agencies and one which has certain associational features, although it lacks the general social and recreational elements of most associations.

Akaretok and *Bɛjoŋ* are both recreational associations reported to have existed in Tali; only *Bɛjoŋ* had survived into the 1950s. Other associations reported from other villages are *Mancoŋ* (Etemetek), *Eyimane* (Besonga-bang), *Ɔkɔri* (Bakebe).

All those referred to above are traditional men's associations. There are (or were) also a number of women's associations. Almost all of these were recreational but had also some disciplinary control over their members and in certain cases added notably to their prestige. In Nchang village the following women's associations were reported to have existed in the past: *Ɛkpa, Nkim, Ana, Ndɛm, Nɛŋwa.* Of these, the most important and most widespread was probably *Ndɛm*, which was most elaborate and highly organized among Lower Banyang (and eastern Ejagham) but which extended also somewhat fragmentarily into Upper Banyang villages. *Ndɛm* or *Mbɔkɔndɛm*[1] was entered by a girl before marriage: the fees

---

[1] *Ndɛm* is a significant but elusive term in Kenyang: it is the singular of *barɛm*, the 'dead' (spirits, souls), and is thus cognate with the Ejagham *alɛm*, 'nature spirits' (cf. above p. 63, also the cult of *Ndɛm*, or of *Barɛm*). In its singular form *ndɛm* may mean a 'corpse' or 'dead person', an 'ancestor', a 'foetus'. From its name one might surmise that the association was concerned with fertility or procreation, but this was stoutly denied by both my Upper and Lower Banyang informants: they said that its name came from the fact that on initiation its members were given medicines which made them 'unconscious' (i.e. as an *ndɛm*) from which they were revived or 'woken up'. The name *Mbɔkɔndɛm* refers strictly to an individual

were paid by her father and membership gave her higher status; she became, as I was told, like a 'leader' among women. A number of rules applied to members of the association and regulated their relationship with non-members: it was forbidden to shake a member by the hand (if so, a small fine was paid to father or husband), and a member was not allowed to eat beans (*bako*), sweet potatoes (*bɛrɛmɔ*), or fufu (*ɛbaɛ*). (Tali members told me that they ate only 'plantains, plantains' – i.e. that they lived like leaders.) On initiation a series of small cicatrizations were made down the arms, and across the chest and back; a member also took one of a series of special names (*Bɛsɛm, Ɛnikɔ, Ɛbaŋa, Ɛrɛrɛ*). The bridewealth for an *mbɔkɔndɛm* was higher than that for other women; and a heavier fine could also be demanded in the case of adultery. When an *mbɔkɔndɛm* wife had delivered one or two children she was 'washed' with further medicines and was then no longer required to keep to the proscriptive rules concerning food. When appearing at association dances, however, she would wear the distinctive feather in the back of her hair, which was a mark of her status. The association also had its own dance, which was held especially on the occasion of a member's death. Rather more in Lower Banyang and eastern Ejagham communities than in Upper Banyang, a dead member was also commemorated by the building of an effigy (formerly in mud within a protective hut, more recently in cement) to her name. My informants denied any supernatural aim in the association and asserted its primary purpose as giving status to women. This would seem indeed to have been basic to its success, since the association came in this way to reflect indirectly the system of status achievement and competition among the men of a community: community leaders bought status for their daughters (and thus, indirectly, for themselves) through the association; while in turn those men seeking community status sought also to marry these 'leaders among women'. It was not a matter of chance that in both Tali and Besongabang when I inquired about *Ndɛm*, I was sent to the senior wife of the village leader. *Mbia* and *Mɔɛkpɛ*, which I observed in Ejwengang and Bara respectively, would seem to be characteristic of the slighter and more ephemeral traditional women's associations. They were essentially recreational groups, whose members met to provide a dance or to eat together, food having been brought or given for

---

member of the association: among Upper Banyang this was said to be because of the 'feather' (*mbɔk*) worn by a member to denote membership, but among Lower Banyang this was denied and no explanation could be given. Mansfeld in his book makes a number of references to the association ('Mboandem') and shows photographs of a member 'with the typical feather in the hair' (*Plate XXVIII*) and of 'monuments' built to commemorate deceased members (*Figures 124–6*).

the occasion (see *Plate 6*). *Mbia*, which had a short and colourful spell of activity in Ejwengang, also served as the vehicle for showing off the beauty and graces of the young girls of the village, who at its public dance executed singly or in small groups a series of 'steps' which were duly appraised and applauded by the spectators.

Apart from the traditional associations there are a number of associations which I refer to as 'modern' since, although they retain some of the association features, they depart in some significant respect from the traditional associations, a departure which can be related to modern conditions; all also are of recent origin. Of these the young men's associations, which have sprung up very widely and represent a generational division and potential opposition alien to the traditional communities, are closest in their organization and pattern of activities to the traditional associations, (e.g. *Ɛkan*, 'Agency', 'Young Seven'). The modern recreational association, 'Band', also follows very much the traditional pattern. Other recent political associations (e.g. the widespread 'Clan Unions', the 'Chiefs' Council', or 'Town Council' formed in Tali) depart more radically from the traditional form and can no longer be strictly described as *ako*.[1] Instead they are often referred to by the modern general term: *ncɛmti* or *ncɛmɛ*,[2] a 'meeting', 'gathering', 'union', 'association', or 'federation'.

Finally reference should be made to a series of age-groups (*bɛkak* or *baku*) which were organized in the traditional society but have now largely disappeared, their place having in part been taken by the newly formed young men's associations. Except for the fact that their members are drawn from coevals and serve therefore to rank in age-sequence all the male members of a community, these age-groups follow very closely the general form of the associations and might very well be described as 'age-associations'.

This section has tried to suggest something of the multiplicity of Banyang associations (a feature shared with other Cross River peoples) and of the way they pervade all spheres of social life. Children playing in a settlement turn readily to the association form and will organize themselves into a group with defined statuses, salutations, possibly a masked dancer, and other formal features of the adult associations. Throughout his life a Manyang will become a member of a whole series of associations.

---

[1] On this point, however, see a remark by one of the speakers at the inauguration of the Tali 'Chiefs' Council', p. 317 below.
[2] The term *ncɛmɛ* is also used of a co-operative work-group (where a number of men or women agree to work in turn for each of their number) and for a witches' 'company' (believed also to be a kind of association whose members have reciprocal obligations to provide victims for the group's common consumption).

One gets the impression sometimes of associations germinating like mushrooms, overnight and in secluded places. The solidarity, the reciprocities, and the collectivism of the association form are indeed central to the values of Banyang society, as are the associations themselves to the corporate activities of Banyang communities. In the remainder of this chapter a brief account is given of the age-groups and of two traditional associations, Basinjom and Tui, before, in the next chapter, the extremely important political association, Ngbe, is considered in some detail.

Age-groups

A person's *nku* (among Upper Banyang) or his *ɛkak* (among Lower) are in the first place his immediate coevals, his 'age-group' in the literal sense of those born at the same time.[1] Banyang insist that, strictly, people 'of the same age-group' are those born within a few days of each other or, at most, one or two months. As a child grows up his parents are expected to point out his age-equals within the community. Later, however, when an age-group becomes organized, the 'spread' of ages is likely to be greater, extending to one or two years.

The formal organization of an age-group occurred in adolescence or early manhood and was instituted by the youths themselves. The same term (*nku* or *ɛkak*) applies to the formal age-group as to the informal group of coevals. At its first meeting a knowledgeable elder would be invited to witness and advise on the proceedings and to take note of the persons present. Once it was formally constituted, however, an age-group managed its own affairs independently. Ideally, each age-group was composed of three status groups or 'grades', each of which occupied a certain position in the 'house of the age-group' (*ɛkɛt nku*): the senior or 'front grade' (*ɛkɔk ambi*) sat by the door; the 'middle grade' (*ɛkɔk dɛntɔ*) sat at the side of the room; the 'back grade' (*ɛkɔk nsɛm*) sat at the back of the room. Each of these internal divisions was associated with age differences within the group: the 'leader of the age-group' (*mfɔ nku*) was chosen from one of the older members who made up the 'front grade', and who were also expected to be first in providing a goat, wine, and other foods,

[1] This is one of the very few examples of an organizational term which is different in the Upper and Lower dialects of Kenyang. *Ɛkak* means literally 'leg' and is used by Lower Banyang interchangeably with the term *ɛkan*, to refer to the informal (i.e. unconstituted) 'age-group' of coevals. Among Upper Banyang *ɛkan* (an Ejagham word?) is the name of what in the 1950s was the most widespread young men's association. It is worth noting the closeness in form of the Upper Kenyang *nku* to *ako*, the general term for association, the cognate form in Ejagham being *okum*. The description in the text is derived from inquiries made primarily among Upper Banyang (in Tali and Bara), but there would seem to be no major difference, other than name, between the two areas.

which constituted the fees of membership and were consumed by the age-group as a whole. Junior youths seeking admission to the age-group after it was formed were required to pay the appropriate fees and took their place in the junior 'back grade'. Whereas the 'front grade' were the leaders of the age-group, the 'back grade' were its messengers and carriers. The 'middle grade' are said to have been the strength of the age-group: they 'eat on two sides' (i.e. they share in the initial provisions of the 'front' and also in the later fees of the junior members); they were described as the spokesmen and questioners of the age-group, for example in interrogating a stranger to see whether he could be allowed admission. A constituted age-group did not have its own name, but was referred to by the name of one of its members – usually its leader – the 'age-group of N——'.

Age-groups would seem generally to have been formed on a village basis, but some individual members might come in from neighbouring villages, whether of the same or different village group. If he were willing to pay the fees, a man could join more than one age-group, in his own and a neighbouring village. Alternatively, if he were situated between constituted groups, a man might stay outside the age-group organization. Members are said to have numbered between ten and twenty. Women could not become formal members, but they would know which was their age-group by birth and could associate themselves with its members, once it was formally constituted: they would be excluded from its discussions but might provide food for it and could themselves be invited to share in its food or wine. In Tali there seem to have been about fifteen constituted age-groups in existence at any one time.

The activities of an age-group were primarily recreational and centred on eating, drinking, and discussion. The fees in food and wine provided by each of its members in turn formed the basis for its activities. In the past a member could invite his age-group to work on his farms in return for food and wine which he provided. Like all associations, an age-group had the power to make its own laws and could punish any member who went against them. Examples of such laws are: the strict prohibition of adultery with the wife of a fellow-member; the requirement that fellow-members should show respect to each other and in no case refuse wine or food. The solidarity of the group and mutuality of relationship between its co-members were basic norms. Fellow-members were expected to treat each other as equals, sharing in whatever was available. Any offence given by a fellow-member could be reported to the age-group, the case heard, and the offender made to pay a fine (a 'goat' or wine) which would be consumed by the age-group. A public action made by one of the members of the age-group which brought disrepute to it could also be punished by the group. It was said in Tali that a meeting of an age-group might sometimes appoint one man to sleep with the wife of a fellow-member; if (as would be expected) the latter did not wish this, he could 'buy his wife' with a goat. This would seem to be less a claim over the conjugal rights of members (which in other contexts the age-group was concerned to guard) than a way of insisting upon the corporate claims of the group, and of extorting food from those who were thought able to give it.

The term *ntɛ* is used reciprocally between age-fellows, and between a man and his father's (or son's) age-fellows. The latter relationship takes on some of the qualities of mutuality which characterize the former relationship.

If a meeting of an age-group was in progress it was customary to allow a stranger from an equivalent age-group in a different community to enter it and share in whatever food or wine was available. The stranger's status in his home age-group was ascertained before he was allowed to participate in the meeting, and he sat then in the 'grade' position which he held in his home age-group. If he claimed a higher status than was his by right, this might be checked with his home age-group, reported to them, and at one of their own meetings they would fine him.

The period of greatest activity of an age-group was during its early years, when its members were still young men. Age-group loyalties continued to operate, however, throughout its members' life and oc- casional meetings were held until all its members had died out. When a member died, his nearest kin were expected to give to his age-group further fees (*ncɛ*), which reimbursed them for the food which he had eaten during his lifetime. These fees were basically the same as those required for original membership, but could be reduced according to the circumstances or the ability of the person paying. In Tali, where the older age-groups continued to operate, it was only on these occasions that the age-groups met. (In the case of one age-group in Tali all the members had died off and only two remained; death fees had been demanded up to this time. Finally, one of the two died and the remaining man still went along to ask for his fees; he accepted a cock as final payment.)

I have described the organization of age-groups in the past tense since from about the 1930s and in Tali and the surrounding villages organized age-groups have no longer been formed. Those that were formed earlier have continued to operate and something of the structure of the age-group still remained at these upper age-levels of the community. At the lower age-levels the more inclusive organization of the young men's associations has taken over from the age-groups and this has in part filled in the gap created by the absence of youths in school or later in outside work. These 'modern' young men's associations will be described in the next chapter.[1]

Three general points may be made concerning the traditional age-groups. Firstly, their constitution and general form show much in common with the associations (*bako*): their internal division into graded status groups, the payment of 'fees' for membership (including the final death dues), the authority they exert over their members. Age-groups are separately organized for each (village) community, and each is thus a limited group with a restricted membership, but to some extent the transferability of status which is a feature of the traditional associations also applies to them, a stranger to the village being received into a meeting of his equivalent age-group and a network of reciprocal ties being thus created between members of separate communities. The primary function of an age-group is that of a social or recreational club, but besides this they act as a disciplinary authority, and in the past could also be called upon for economic help.

Secondly, in the community at large the organized series of age-groups served to rank all its members by age-status and thus to define the relative seniority or juniority of any man to another. (In Pidgin English the term for age-group is in fact the word 'rank'.) As we have already indicated, age is an important determinant of the formal respect due to a man, although it is not the only factor affecting status in a community. In describing their age-precedence, elders refer readily to their age-group, distinguishing between those who are their seniors, and those who are equal or junior to them.

The organization of age-groups was important, thirdly, in the forum they provided both for general discussion and for the emergence of accepted leaders within the context of a relatively extended residential group (normally a village). It is difficult to document this aspect of their organization when so much of it no longer operates. It is notable, however, that in Tali many of its most prominent men were the leaders of their respective age-groups: for example, the village leader of Tali 1, Mr Tataw, and Peter Esong were all age-group leaders. Particularly in the early years

[1] In Besongabong it was claimed that age-groups were still being formed, even into the 1960s. This may be related to a greater number of youths at home in the village or in close contact with it. Even so, there appeared to be much more interest taken in the young men's association (here, *Nawori*) which met more regularly and was generally more active than any age-group.

of their formation, age-groups would seem to have provided an important field of activity within a village, in which leadership could be achieved and the support of others gained, which helped later to establish a man's general status at the centre of community affairs. Today similar processes occur in the context of the young men's associations.

Basinjom

The Basinjom association belongs to the category of supernatural or cult associations, but is described briefly here since it gives evidence of the general form of Banyang associations and of the way in which these are organized to serve a dominant interest or purpose. During the period of my fieldwork it was also one of the two most active and widespread traditional associations in Banyang country (the other being Ngbe). Like many Banyang associations, it has its origin from Ejagham[1] and its name (*ɔbasi – njɔm*, the cult-agency of God), its titles, formal salutations and most of its songs are in Ejagham (which few Upper Banyang are able to speak). It is 'traditional' in the formal rather than the historical sense, since its introduction to Banyang country occurred after the establishment of a Colonial administration and its first lodges among Upper Banyang were probably not acquired before the 1940s. It has nevertheless had a considerable success and has further spread beyond the borders of Upper Banyang country, and to the peoples of the south; Banyang have themselves taken part in this process of selling the association and setting up lodges among other peoples. The purpose of the association is the detection and exposure of witchcraft, and part of its success probably relates to the prohibition of older methods of witchcraft exposure, notably by ordeal.

A lodge of Basinjom is divided into three main grades, of which the third and senior consists of titled office-bearers.[2] Within the other two grades there are also some other minor offices connected with the carrying

[1] Its gown, general purpose, and procedure would seem to be identical with the association Akpambe, described by Talbot (*In the Shadow of the Bush*, pp. 52–54, 198; also plate facing p. 198, which shows a masked figure identical with Basinjom). Talbot writes that Akpambe invaded the Oban District in 1909 and soon became one of the most widespread associations there.

[2] During my time in Banyang country I became a member of the junior grade of Basinjom and together with its other initiates undertook not to disclose the secrets of the association nor to sell it in any other country without consulting the members of the lodge I joined. My present account is therefore confined to those aspects of its organization which are apparent to or known by outsiders and I omit any detailed description of internal procedures, initiation, its formal emblems and sign-language: I have however permitted myself some

and use of cult-objects at a dance. Each of the grades has its own admission fees, initiation procedures, and duties with regard to the association as a whole; each also has its own position where its members sit in the association house. The grading is further reflected in the degree to which the members have knowledge of the association's internal constitution and procedures. The *bɔ atɛmambi*, who compose the junior-most grade, have the role of 'followers' whose initiation into and knowledge of the association's procedures and emblems is confined to basic facts about the association and its ostensible purpose. They participate in the general meetings of an association lodge, which, despite much formality are nevertheless very largely social or recreational occasions, when wine is drunk and food eaten, accompanied by general discussion and songs. Even so, outsiders are strictly excluded from these meetings, and the air of an esoteric association is emphasized by the many minor rules governing procedure, by the mime language which may be used on such occasions, and by the songs sung which have their own proverbial meanings. At a dance the *bɔ atɛmambi* follow the gowned figure, often carrying guns, and may take part in the drumming, or simply sing the accompanying songs.

The middle grade, the *bɔ ɛbunjɔm*, is composed of those who can wear the gown at a dance. This involves separate initiation and (as will be apparent later) further knowledge of association procedures. There are thus two sections of the association's 'bush', where the central rites of initiation are performed: one, the *ɛbɔ ɛkpɔnɔn*, is used for general initiation, the other *ɛbɔ ɛyantim*, is used for the initiation of the *bɔ ɛbunjɔm*. Within the association lodge there is also a separate meeting-place (*ɛkɛt ɛbunjɔm*) for the middle and senior grades, from which the *bɔ atɛmambi* are excluded. Meetings here are governed by further formalities, but would again seem to be often social occasions, when the fees for this more exclusive grade are shared or consumed.

The third, most senior grade, whose members may be described generically as the 'leaders' (*bafɔ*) of the association, comprise in rising order of status the *ɛsanɛnjɔm*, who at a dance acts as interpreter to the gowned figure, the *ɛbaŋaninjɔm*, who performs the ritual connected with the 'head' of Basinjom (worn by the gowned dancer; it represents a crocodile head and is the central cult object of the association), and the *ɛsɛnɛnjɔm*, who has general charge of the rituals and medicine of the association.

general observations on inner activities which bear upon its general form as an association. I would add that my own knowledge of Basinjom is by no means complete and that (in common with many of the members of the lodge I joined) there was much concerning its central offices and general running which I could only surmise.

The ɛsɛnɛnjɔm is the head of the association and I was told that a prospective initiate to this office must have a 'strong heart'. According to their various duties, the main direction of the association lies with these office-holders.

An association lodge performs its task of divination by means of a dance. On these occasions Basinjom or the 'cult-agency' (njɔ, a term cognate with the Ejagham njɔm, which is often used to refer to the association) is said to have 'come to earth' (asɔp amɔk) and to have manifested itself in the gowned dancer who wears the 'head'. A dance can take place suddenly, without prior warning and often at an unusual time (for example, very early in the morning), or alternatively a lodge may be invited to divine the causes of misfortune that has occurred in a settlement or residential group away from where the lodge is located. In either case the procedure is that a mu ɛbunjɔm is 'seized' by the cult-agency, when in the course of ordinary activities he becomes suddenly 'possessed', becomes stiff and trembles, cries out in a high-pitched voice, etc. Such 'possessions' may occur without a dance taking place, in which case the possessed man is given medicines and placated until he returns to normal. If a dance is to take place, the gown and other cult-objects of the association are quickly arranged outside in the open area of a settlement, the possessed man led to them, and the gown put on him. The quick, rhythmic drumming which is characteristic of the association is started, and the gowned figure, now spoken of as Basinjom or the cult-agency (njɔ) itself, begins a wheeling, gliding dance, followed by its attendants. The gowned figure can move anywhere within the settlement (including inside houses) or its immediately neighbouring 'bush' in its ostensible search for witchcraft or for the places in which witchcraft medicines may be hidden. At various times the gowned figure returns to where the drummers and group of spectators are and halts abruptly: the drummers stop and the gowned figure starts speaking (see Plate 7). The speech is an incoherent jumble of sounds which is listened to and then 'interpreted' publicly by a mu ɛsanɛnjɔm, who carefully observes this role of intermediary, prefacing all his remarks with 'Basinjom (or njɔ) says . . .' and referring back to the gowned figure for further instructions. In this way and with breaks for further dancing the message of Basinjom is conveyed: persons who have suffered from or have been implicated in witchcraft may be called, past events recounted, the cause of misfortune stated, and the procedure to prevent or atone for it prescribed. The occult power of Basinjom to see and speak the truth is always stressed: although the statements of Basinjom are sometimes elliptic, there is little attempt to elicit information by interrogation; the messages of Basinjom are conveyed as statements of what actually happened (to be confirmed by the persons interrogated).

The element of masquerade which is clearly present in the association would appear to be generally recognized by Banyang, although in varying degrees. People also enjoy watching the dance, which is spectacular and, with its accompanying songs and drumming, exhilarating. At the same time I have met few people, even amongst the most educated Banyang, who could be persuaded to doubt the ultimate power of the association to perform what it claims to perform: the discovery and exposure of witchcraft. Between the two alternatives – that it is a staged fake on the one hand or that Basinjom has in fact supernatural powers to speak the truth about witchcraft on the other – lies the organization of the association itself and the fact that those who are members of it share the ideology of witchcraft equally with those who are not. When pressed, persons who are inclined to doubt the reality of the ostensible claims made on behalf of the association tend to emphasize that it is an association – an *ako* – and that the ultimate truth lies with the persons who are within it. In this context it should be noted that the name 'Basinjom' has a complex range of references, which overlap with each other and which, while different, are rarely completely distinguished: the same term refers thus to the association itself as an organized body of persons (one or a series of lodges); it refers to the cult-agency which is at the centre of the association and whose shrine is the 'head'; and it refers to the gowned figure who wears the 'head' and who both represents the association in its public appearances and is believed to be a manifestation of the cult-agency. Full analysis of the operation of Basinjom in relation to Banyang witchcraft beliefs cannot be attempted here, but I would like to stress the comment made by Banyang concerning its form as an association: it is pre-eminently because it is an association, an *ako*, that 'Basinjom' is able to operate as clearly and decisively as it does.

Tui

Tui, an association with political functions, is derived from the Bangwa association of *Ntrɔ*, from which it was acquired directly or indirectly by a number of Upper Banyang villages or village sections some time in the nineteenth century. Lodges are reported to have existed in Ebuensuk, Mambaw, Takwa, Bara, Ejwengang, Tali, and Fotabe (all villages which neighbour each other and are in close range of the Bangwa, with the one exception of Fotabe in the Mbang village group, which is at some distance from the rest).[1] The Banyang version of the association retains many of its Bangwa features as stylized formalities: in the language of its formal titles, the speech of the gowned figure, the dress of its attendants, and the dance-style used.

The accepted description of Tui – both association and the gowned figure representing it – emphasizes its fearsome, evil aspects. In the past it is said Tui could punish a wrongdoer in the community by death. The gowned figure with some members in attendance is said thus to have come by night to the house of the man concerned, where it ordered him to come out and then carried him off to the bush, where he was killed. 'Tui does not like the light,' I was told: 'It comes at night and goes at night.' Again, 'Tui does not stop long in the community.'

Tui (the gowned figure) makes its appearance by entering a community or settlement from outside, as though having come from a journey. When it enters a settlement all the inhabitants are expected to flee, shutting themselves indoors. The gowned figure and its attendants then make a show of destructive power. Nowadays this is restricted to rampaging through the deserted settlement, banging on doors, shouting, and kicking destructively any articles that have been left outside, but in the past it is said that more material damage was done, to houses or to their thatched roofs. The gowned figure (see *Plate 8*) is made completely anonymous by a covering of coarse sackcloth, with slit-holes for eyes, and a further head-covering of netting. Both the figure and certain of the attendants also wear a type of headgear, a circular frame (somewhat resembling a halo) on which is tied a *mambɔp* leaf.[2] After their initial entry into a settlement, the gowned figure and attendants may perform a dance, still with the settlement's inhabitants remaining carefully indoors. Finally, Tui will depart from the settlement, or, if it is to remain, the figure and attendants enter a prearranged house, going in backwards and shutting the door firmly on themselves but leaving their staves outside as a sign that Tui remains in the community. Inside the house its members may again shout and bang loudly on the door, evidently to denote their occupancy of it. Later, the association members will disperse quietly. 'Tui', however, still remains nominally in the community while the staves are left there. These can be removed only when the association members reassemble,

[1] In 1965 I was told of another lodge which had formerly existed in Bakebe at even greater remove, and which was said to have been acquired from Fontem. The gowned figure was described accurately but the association itself was said *not* to have had punitive functions, being used only for dances or at a funeral celebration.

[2] This species of leaf is also used in covering the face of a leopard brought from the bush into the community, cf. p. 50.

the gowned figure reappears (again with attendants, and again moving backwards out of the house), and 'Tui' finally departs from the community.

The main function of the association – punishment by death – cannot of course still be performed, and few of the lodges of the association remain in any way active. The lodge of Tali, for example, was almost completely forgotten and was recalled only when I asked about it. In Bara, the association remained partly active as a prestige group, meeting for the initiation of new members or to receive the death fees of one who had died. The description of it given above is based on one occasion of its meeting in Bara when Tui appeared largely for my own benefit. Even although it had lost all its formal political functions in relation to the community, nevertheless, it was still able to exert a disciplinary authority over its members and potentially had power in relation to the village as well. Thus, one of its members who did not participate in its reappearance in Bara and who was overheard, as a spectator, to say who he thought was wearing the gown was later called before the association lodge and fined by it. And again, in an incident that has already been reported (p. 190 above), when the required formal response to the gowned figure was not forthcoming by all members of the village community, its leader later harangued the settlement in language that made quite explicit the need to respect the association and the power that it *could* wield over those who failed to give it respect.

IO

Ngbe

History, constitution, and activities

The association which Banyang describe as *Ngbε* is found over a wide area, stretching from Banyang country through much of the country neighbouring and within the Cross River bend to Old Calabar, where it formerly had central political importance. Among the Ejagham it is described as *Ɛkpɛ*, 'leopard' in Efik (the language of the people of Calabar); its name among the Banyang, *Ngbε*, means 'leopard' in Ejagham (the Kenyang term is *nkwɔ*). Typically, then, the association is one which has spread through a number of peoples and has acquired its importance partly by means of this assimilation of outside forms.[1] Banyang lie on the periphery of this area and entered the Ngbe 'polity' (if such we can call it) comparatively late: the first lodges of the association were not acquired among the Lower Banyang until towards the end of the nineteenth century and among Upper Banyang it was not until the 1920s, some years after the establishment of a Colonial administration, that the first lodges were bought. This acquisition of lodges, or the addition of further sections of Ngbe to already established lodges, still continued in the 1950s.

The account given here of the association does not claim to be complete, nor is it derived from inside knowledge obtained by membership. What I have attempted to do is to give a general sketch of the formal features of the association, which will serve as the basis for a more detailed consideration of its political role and of its relationship to Banyang community structure. My knowledge of the association is in fact derived from three sources: firstly, from members of Ngbe who have been willing to discuss in general terms the form of the association and the kind of activities which go on in its name; secondly, from witnessing the public appearances

---

[1] Cf. also the term *Nyankpɛ* (or *Nyangbɛ*), literally 'Animal of Nkpe' which in Ejagham is said to form a section of the association, but in the Mamfe area is generally used synonymously with 'Ngbe' as the general name of the association. On the question of the areal spread of Ngbe/Ekpe, and of the variety of forms taken by the association see below, pp. 250f.

of the association and the public activities of its members; thirdly, from the 'inside' knowledge that I have gained of the workings of other associations (most notably of Basinjom) which can in certain important features be either transposed to, or have been explicitly compared with, the form and workings of Ngbe.

One of the first lodges of Ngbe among Lower Banyang is said to have been bought by Obot Egbe Aya, a former leader of Tetukenok hamlet of Besongabang village, some time before the arrival of the Germans, possibly in the 1880s. (Obot Egbe Aya died about 1910.) By the time of Mansfeld's administration (1904 onwards) the association was well established in what he calls the 'Keaka' and neighbouring Lower Banyang villages, although he notes the fragmentation of form which occurs in its eastern extension. Accounts of its use in Mbinjong-Are to sanction early German administrative rulings indicate that it had already been acquired there by this time. Its spread to Upper Banyang villages, however, was not immediate. In Tali, Dekang hamlet was the first to acquire any part of Ngbe but this was a bare semblance of the association, consisting of its drums and songs. Later, about 1925, members of Mbinjong, Tanyi Ako, and Nchemba combined to purchase the first formal lodge, including gowns and preliminary sections of the association. The lodge was bought from an eastern Ejagham village. Later other lodges were established by different sections of Tali: Kembong bought their own lodge from Boki country; Mpomba, Dekang, and Okorobak combined to buy the association from Mbinjong-Are, on the Mamfe road; Tanyi Tabe bought their lodge from Eyang, a village on the southern borders of Banyang country, but close to the Obang Ejagham. In Bara, Ngbe was bought soon after their separation from Tali: bɔ Esɔŋafiɛt and bɔ Taba combined with other members of the village to buy the first lodge, and later a separate lodge was acquired by bɔ Tanyi Nkoŋo. By the 1940s the association had spread beyond the eastern borders of Banyang country, a number of chiefs among the Bangwa people having by that time acquired their own lodges. One of the main reasons given by Upper Banyang for the spread of Ngbe is the loss of status suffered by men from their area when during the early period of administration they visited the Lower area (where the administrative headquarters were and where Ngbe was already established) and were obliged to drink their palm-wine standing, since they were not members of the association. To obtain this right they had to buy their own lodges.

The general spread of the association from the west to the east has been reflected in the main direction of purchase, which is usually (but not invariably) for an 'Upper' Banyang hamlet or village section to seek to acquire a lodge by going to an already established lodge in a 'Lower' Banyang or eastern Ejagham village. The first lodge acquired by Tetu-kenok in Besongabang, later elaborated and strengthened by the addition of further sections, became the model for a number of lodges subsequently bought from its members. The main reason behind this general direction of purchase is undoubtedly the fuller and deeper knowledge of the association's constitution held by those in the relatively 'lower' area, and ultimately by the Ejagham. Since the purchasing group establishes a lodge by being taught its constitution (its rules, the sign-language, the significance of its emblems, etc.) they will be concerned to buy it from an already established lodge known to be expert in matters of the associa-tion. On the other hand, a lodge nearer home whose knowledge is adequate rather than deep may be willing to 'show Ngbe' to them for rather less than what would be demanded by a more distant (and more expert) lodge. Thus, in general, lodges among Upper Banyang are less elaborate in their constitution and include fewer sections than lodges among Lower Banyang, and these in turn are less elaborate than, and do not include some of the recently acquired sections of, lodges of the neighbouring Ejagham. The increasing fragmentation of the association in Banyang country is, however, also related to the nature of the residen-tial groups which acquire lodges: whereas among the central Ejagham a nucleated village of sometimes a few hundred persons owns a single lodge, its meeting-house being the focal point of the village settlement, lodges among Banyang are invariably acquired by village sections (ham-lets, groups of hamlets, or similar units) and one village may have up to six or more different lodges. Thus the very large village of Besongabong contained nine lodges, the equally large Tali (before its division) eleven lodges; the rather smaller village of Ekpaw (1953 Census, population 254) contains four lodges, and even the smaller Bara, occupying a single continuous settlement, has two lodges. We shall return later to this feature of the Banyang Ngbe when considering its position in the wider area in which the association is dominant.

In view of these variations in the form of the association, it is not possible (certainly for Banyang, and I suspect also for Ejagham) to describe the constitution of the association as though it were in any fixed sense uniform. In its general organizations the association is divided into a series of sections, which in the earlier literature are generally referred to as 'grades'. As we shall see, the idea of a ranked series, of a progressive entry into a sequence of stages, runs throughout the association, but the term 'grade' as applied to these main sections is liable to misunderstanding since among Banyang at least the sections are not all of the same kind (in some cases they are main stages of initiation into the overall association, or are a stage in completing the acquisition of a lodge, while in other cases they have the form of sub-associations, operating semi-autonomously in the general orbit of Ngbe): they are not fixed in number, nor, although they may be given an order of importance, are they entered necessarily in the same sequence. Banyang speak of these sections as 'branches', 'parts' of, or 'places' in Ngbe. Sections which have the form of sub-associations are often also described as *bɔ Ngbɛ*, 'children of Ngbe', in the sense perhaps both of being 'offspring' and also of 'dependants'. When I have asked Banyang elders to give me lists of these sections, they have generally given me a few names and then when I have pressed for their completion have added one or two more, less generally present or of minor significance, and have then fallen back upon the general principle that 'one never finishes Ngbe' (*mu apu naŋa Ngbe*): i.e. that there is not a fixed point where one can say that one now knows all the association.[1] Moreover, the lists of sections that have been given have never been exactly the same, although some degree of consensus exists in the initial names.

In a typical list obtained from a Lower Banyang lodge owner, the sections of the associations are named as follows:

[1] On the other hand, on one occasion when I visited Ossing, among the eastern Ejagham, I was given such a list, which was as follows:

Ekpe	*Nkanda*
1. Bekundi	1. Nsibiri Nkanda
2. Esong	2. Ekombo Nkanda
3. Mboko	3. Otongonjum
4. Eti Ngbe ('Stone of Ngbe')	
5. Etem Ngbe (or Orong Ngbe, 'Bush of Ngbe')	*Mutanda*
	Nsibiri Mutanda
6. Oku	

7. Bacung (including Ngeti)

Thus the general association was said to have three main parts, Ekpe proper, Nkanda, and Mutanda, each of these having their own further sections. 'Bacung' (elsewhere *Mancoŋ*) was said to be somewhat separate from the other sections of Ekpe proper and would seem in fact (with its own internal section 'Ngeti') to have been once an important sub-association that has now been reduced in status to that of an ordinary section. This list is more elaborate than those I obtained in Banyang country but I would again doubt whether its apparent exactness did not obscure some arbitrariness of ordering and assimilation of sections (e.g. for 'Bacung'), features which lie more on the surface so far as Banyang accounts are concerned.

Ɛkat
Bɛkundi
Ɛsɔŋ
Ngbɛ ɛbɔ ('Ngbe bush')
Mbɔkɔ
Mutanda
Ntaɛ Ngbɛ ('Stone of Ngbe')

Besides these, however, reference was made to the important major section of *Nkanda*, which again includes within it:

Nsibiri Nkanda and
Ɔtɔŋ njɔm

The following notes may help to explain some of the features of these various sections:

Ɛkat (the usual Banyang pronunciation; the strict Ejagham term is *Ɔkat*). This is the name of the curtained recess in the 'Ngbe house' from which emerges the 'voice of Ngbe' and which is said to contain the 'leopard creature' (see below) which gives the association its name. Entering the *ɛkat* is an early stage of initiation, and initiants are said then to receive scratches on their backs as though from the claws of a leopard.

Bɛkundi has the form of a sub-association which meets separately from the main body of Ngbe and is centrally concerned with the maintenance of certain 'medicines' used apparently in connection with Ngbe. Members of Bekundi are divided into their own status categories and are governed by their own formalities in the drinking of wine and exchange of salutations. The central emblem of the group is a small hollow wooden block spoken of as a 'tortoise' (*dɛwɛn*; whose shell the block resembles). At a meeting of Bekundi the block is placed on a sleeping-mat on the floor as a sign that the meeting is in progress. On entering the meeting, a member must formally greet the block. During the meeting, when a matter is under discussion which is as yet undecided, the 'tortoise' is placed with its flat part, its 'chest', downwards; when all matters have been decided and only food, wine, and song remain, the 'tortoise' is reversed so that its 'chest' is upwards. This block also serves as an instrument which, when beaten with one of its open ends against or away from the chest, emits two tones, and is thus used to give formal greetings or set sayings. Bekundi also has its own form of shield (*nkpa*), a woven mat, with a raffia surround, on which are fixed certain leaves, animal bones, skulls, and horns, and which is usually hung from the central post of its leader or owner's *aca*. These have apparently both the force of 'medicines' (referring to what has been eaten in the sub-association) but also act as a 'charter' for it: knowledge concerning them is said to be especially recondite and held only by its senior elders. There are certain restrictions upon the burial of a member of Bekundi and the death dues payable by his relatives are said to have priority over other claims.[1]

Esɔŋ has probably also the form of a sub-association. Although it is one of the most commonly referred to sections, I have very few details concerning it. It would seem to be a junior sub-association, whose separate meetings are primarily recreational and may possibly be linked especially with the younger men of a community.

Ngbɛ ɛbɔ (or *ɛbɔ Ngbɛ*, 'Ngbe bush' or 'Bush of Ngbe'). This again is a stage of initiation, when initiants are taken at night to a bush or forest grove, outside the settlement ('the Ngbe bush'), and are instructed there – and later in the 'Ngbe house' when they have returned – in certain formal secrets of the association. In any association the time of 'going to the bush' is that of formal instruction. While I have been given some rather heightened accounts of what goes on in the 'Ngbe bush' (for example, that the initiant sees the dead ancestors as though they were living), the 'secrets' that are imparted are likely to be the more matter-of-fact ones of the names and significance of the various emblems that are used to decorate the Ngbe house, the gestures and their meaning in the sign-language (*ɛgbɛ*), and so on.

Mbɔkɔ. My information about this is again limited. It refers to a construction (sometimes said to be like a car; the literature speaks of it as an 'ark') which encloses and conceals the 'Ngbe voice' which is thus brought out into public view.

Mutanda. Apparently a more exclusive sub-association, entered only by the more senior members of Ngbe. We are here in an area of the constituted sections of Ngbe which are most variable. It may be noted that in Ossing, 'Mutanda' was described as a separate major part of the association (see p. 219 fn.) and often *Ɛku* (cf. Ossing 'Oku') is mentioned as a section of about this order: like Mutanda, *Ɛku* would appear to have the form of a high-ranking sub-association, a more exclusive body drawn from the senior or leading members of Ngbe.

Ntaɛ Ngbɛ ('Stone of Ngbe'). This in one sense is a stage of initiation, but is a stage which concerns the acquisition of a lodge, in which the

[1] Most of these details concerning Bekundi were obtained from Upper Banyang sources, but are unlikely to be very different in the case of Lower Banyang lodges.

owner, the 'leader of Ngbe', sets in its place and decorates the stone column or slab which formalizes his right to the leadership and, to this extent, fully establishes the lodge in the residential group of which he is (normally) the leader. The 'stone of Ngbe' (*Figure 25*) is usually placed in

Figure 25 The Ngbe Stone

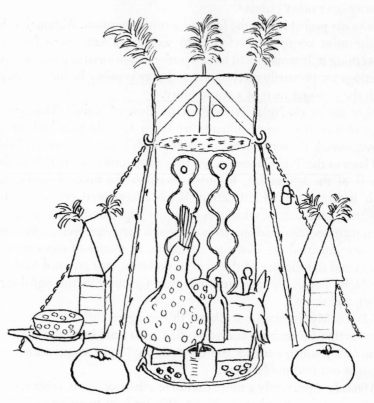

front of the central pole-support (*ɛkwap*, see p. 30) in the *aca* or meeting-house of its owner; when formally set out, a variety of objects cover or surround it, including: an inverted satchel forming a kind of 'head' on which are fixed a collection of feathers, twisted copper or brass rods of the type that was formerly used as currency, two chains with padlocks holding the stone to the ground, a tortoise-shell, decorated calabashes, certain seeds, a white cloth around the 'waist' of the stone in which is fixed a knife, and so on. In general, these objects have emblematic reference to the various sections and activities of Ngbe: the 'stone' then forms a kind of visual 'charter' for the association (of which, however, only its members have exact knowledge, and then only to the extent of their membership). The setting up of an 'Ngbe stone' is one of the most elaborate of all Ngbe procedures. I was told by one senior elder and Ngbe leader how he had previously helped a senior relative (then the formal owner of the lodge) to do this, taking care to provide all the items required and to arrange them exactly; then on completion other Ngbe leaders in the village and neighbourhood were invited to come to 'test' his work and knowledge. He reported, proudly, that they could find no fault with him – he passed his 'test' and no one could surpass him.

Nkanda may be described as a linked association partly separate, partly dependent upon Ngbe. In general form it would appear to be very similar to Ngbe, but is of more recent introduction, is accredited with considerable power, and is said to require a great deal of money to enter it. Banyang speak of it in awed tones. Nkanda, unlike Ngbe, is said to have the power of killing someone. The two sections within it that have been referred to above both have Ejagham names indicating a formal symbolic content: '*Nsibiri*' is a name given to a way of conveying information by a kind of pictogram script (*vide* Talbot, 1912, Appendix G) and *Ɔtɔŋ njɔm* means literally 'showing the cult-agency'.

This list of sections by no means exhausts all the possible parts of Ngbe, especially those which are called 'children of Ngbe' and have the form of attached sub-associations. Thus in Lower Banyang villages and in one context or another, I have heard references to the following sections: *Ɛkwakamɛ, Mancoŋ, Angbo* (but see p. 202), *Ɔkuakaŋ, Makara, Bɛra, Ayikɔ*, and (of most recent introduction) *Ɛkɔ Ɛkpɛ*. Each of these at some time and for some lodges has been bought and so assimilated to the overall Ngbe complex. What is most relevant to note here is that these peripheral, irregularly located, and often half-forgotten 'children of Ngbe' have the same form as the sub-associations most commonly mentioned as parts of Ngbe (*Bɛkundi, Esɔŋ, Mutanda, Ɛku*) but lack their success, are less generally found associated with an Ngbe lodge, and for these reasons have less accepted status as sections of Ngbe. When I have asked why new sections such as these should be bought, I have been told 'so that Ngbe may become strong'. On the other hand, there is also a tendency to disillusionment over the acquisition of such sections; many follow the same pattern of Ngbe without adding anything essentially new to it: 'they spoil money to no purpose'.

Among Upper Banyang the list of Ngbe sections present in one lodge tends to be radically reduced: *Bɛkundi, Esɔŋ*, and *ɛbɔ Ngbɛ* have generally been acquired, but beyond that, other sections are only irregularly present.

Relatively few lodges have an 'Ngbe stone' (in 1953 none of Tali's eleven lodges had an Ngbe stone, but after an upsurge of Ngbe activity three lodges had acquired them by 1958) and in the 1950s I heard of no Upper Banyang lodge which had acquired *Nkanda*.

To return to the general association: formal meetings of an Ngbe lodge are held in the 'Ngbe house', either the meeting-house of a community leader, or some similar house which can be appropriately set out. The house must have two sections: a large main room in which most people sit and most activities occur, and a small inner room, or recess, which is separated from the main room by a curtain. During the time that it is formally occupied by Ngbe, the whole house is open only to members (thus women, among other non-members, are excluded). Within the main room members sit according to three main status-categories: the most senior are the 'leaders' (*bafɔ*), who sit in a position of prominence behind the 'table' (*ɛfeme*); second in rank are the 'elders' (*bɔ tata*), who sit, often on a couch bed (*ɛmbombo*), usually on one or both sides of the table; and finally there are the most junior members, the 'drummers' (*bakoni*), who sit at some distance, facing the 'leaders', often towards the main door of the house. For example:

Figure 26 The 'Ngbe house'

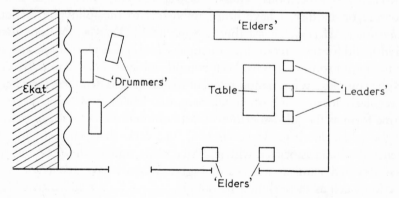

It is in the curtained recess, *ɛkat*, that the 'animal' of the association, 'Ngbe' itself, is said to be contained. This is the central emblem of the association, built up from a number of activities which relate to it: the 'voice of Ngbe', a vibrant, uneven 'growl' which emerges at formal meetings from the *ɛkat*; the scratches received by initiants who have 'entered the *ɛkat*'; various procedures which provide for the fact that

'Ngbe' can 'escape' and return to the bush, from where it must be re-captured; and finally the whole heightened imagery by which 'Ngbe', the 'animal', is described. Thus Upper Banyang, with whom I have dis-cussed this point in greatest detail and whose fragmented version of the association gives added significance to this part of it, speak usually in rather veiled, elusive terms about 'Ngbe': an 'animal' or 'small animal', it is ascribed great power and ferociousness, and is said to be potentially dangerous to any person. Among Lower Banyang, the animal is more explicitly referred to as a 'leopard', but again their references to it are clearly emblematic, attributive. The mechanism which produces the 'Ngbe voice' is one of the most closely guarded actual secrets of the association. Among Upper Banyang the ɛkat was described as the 'heart' (ntɔ) or 'base' (nɛt) of the association and its position compared to that of the inner grove or ɛbɔ ɛyantim of Basinjom (cf. p. 212). Not all initiants were allowed to 'enter the ɛkat' there: a practice which stands in contrast to that among Lower Banyang and eastern Ejagham, where 'entering the ɛkat' is one of the first main stages of initiation.[1]

In the main room of an Ngbe house and at a formal meeting of a lodge, the dominant activities are those of entertainment or pleasure: singing, dancing, drumming, eating, and drinking. There is, however, an under-lying requirement to keep to the rules of the association, including pro-cedural formalities, and discussion may arise concerning these. The occupants of each of the three status-categories have certain rights which differentiate them within a meeting. Most notably the 'leaders' can 'command Ngbe' (-saɛ Ngbɛ in Kenyang; the stricter Ejagham term is -yibɛ) by raising their staff, which is a sign of their status, and calling out a fixed phrase a certain number of times. Once the call is made, all activities within the room must stop – singing, dancing, discussion, etc. – and attention must be given to what is about to be said. Different leaders have, however, the right to call a differing number of times (thus distinguishing each individually within the general category of 'leaders') and in certain instances a leader of higher status can 'out-call' one who is junior to him.[2] Other procedural formalities concern the order in which wine is drunk, the number of glasses allowed to a person of each status-category, whether it is drunk seated or standing, the salutation terms used, the way in which a division of food is made, and other similar items. More general rules

---

[1] In this as in other respects Upper Banyang have made up for the reduced overall form of their version of the association by elaborating further those features which they have.
[2] Among Upper Banyang the greatest number of times a 'leader' can 'command' is fourteen; among the eastern Ejagham it is no more than three. See previous footnote.

include the stipulation that the normal 'praise-names' (*bakoko*) used in inter-personal greeting shall not be used; that European clothes and in particular shoes and trousers shall not be worn; that English words shall not be used to describe the 'table', 'chairs', etc. (which have their own association names); and so on.[1] Should any of these formalities be transgressed, a fine is payable to the meeting (usually as wine, in more serious cases food).

Apart from the general status-categories which cover all members of a lodge, there are also a number of individual offices whose incumbents are charged with special duties. These include: the *ɛkini*, who is the messenger or emissary of Ngbe and who as a sign of his office carries a stick with a Z-like 'crook' in its stem and a satchel slung from his shoulders; and the *dɛkame* (or *nɛkame*), who is in charge of the pouring of wine and division of food (a role whose importance depends upon the detailed formalities that must be observed). Titled positions which bear upon the instruments played include the *mɔtiɛ*, who plays the long drum (*nɔ nko*), and *mɔ rua* who plays maraca-type rattles (*bakacak*). Finally, there is one woman member, *manyaŋarɔŋ*, who sits with the 'elders', shares in the wine and food consumed at a meeting, but is excluded from most other association activities (does not enter the *ɛkat*, is not taught the mime-language, does not use the formal salutation terms, etc.).

Representing the general association in its public appearances are also two types of gowned figure, *ebongo* (which may appear as two or more identical figures, although this is rare among Banyang) and *ɛma Nyankpɛ* (always appearing singly): the former, representing the more 'pleasing' aspect of the association, appears more frequently and may be observed by non-members; the latter presents the more 'fearsome' aspect of the association, and when it appears non-members are expected to flee or hide. A further description of these will be given in a later account of the public activities of Ngbe. Certain of the sections of Ngbe which have the form of sub-associations would appear also to be represented by gowned dancers, but I lack details of these.

Entry into each and every position in the constitution of the association – its main sections, the status-categories of the main association or those of the sectional 'sub-associations', the formal offices – requires the payment of fees. The process of becoming a member also entails a series of minor stages (entering the house, speaking to the leader of Ngbe, etc.) which also have appropriate fees. Basically, the fees are composed of food and wine, together with articles that are to be used in initiation or have reference to the status to be entered; for the more important stages, a

[1] These rules are those observed in Tali. They may vary slightly from area to area.

sum of money is usually also demanded, and in many cases minor items can be commuted for money. One goat and sixteen jugs of wine (each 'jug' equalling two gallons) are a regular requirement for all the main stages.

When discussing my own entry in Bara, I was told that the following would be required for basic membership: *dɛkɔk Ngbɛ*, a yellow powder put on the forehead of a new initiant (or 2*s.*); a jug of wine (or 1*s.*); *ɛkpɛ Ngbɛ* (to speak to Ngbe?) (or 2*s.*); a head of tobacco (or 1*s.*); five cola-nuts (or 3*d.*). Then, following from these items, which as initial payments represent the candidate's first application to the association and show that he wishes to join and to be told how he should proceed, he will be called upon to provide: two pieces of meat; a goat; sixteen jugs of wine; a stem of plantains; oil; a bowl of beans (*bako*); a bowl of melon seeds (*nkwaɛ*); a bowl of peppers; salt; sixteen heads of maize; a bowl of ground nuts. If I wished to proceed to become *tata* I should be required to pay: two sleeping-mats (since one is due to sit on the couch-bed); sixteen chewing-sticks; seven leaves of tobacco; a double-sized jug of wine; a goat.

In Tali, where people were more money-conscious, the following general payments were described for certain stages of admission, given as examples:

Anti mbi, 'at the head of the path'. This is a payment originally made when an Ngbe lodge is bought. The people selling Ngbe stop at the head of the settlement and will not proceed further until given wine and a goat. At his own entry into the association (where his position in entering it is comparable) the new initiant is required to pay his own share of this.

'To come to the leader of Ngbe' the initiant should carry two jugs of wine under each arm and bring two 'heads' of cloth.

'To enter the Ngbe bush': £3, wine, and a goat.

'To sit on the bed' (i.e. to become *tata*): £3, wine, and a goat.

'To enter *ɛkat Ngbɛ*': £7, wine ,and a goat.

To use and raise the staff in 'commanding Ngbe' (three times): £7, wine, and a goat.

The above examples are not inclusive of all the payments required, nor, where money is stipulated, should they be taken as fixed rates. It is probable that, while certain basic items are general for the association as a whole, the extent to which these items can be commuted or extra sums required varies considerably between districts and according to the importance of the lodge or the person seeking entry. People are not usually willing to state the precise sums required in entering Ngbe, partly, it would seem, because these amounts are kept flexible, but also because it is in no one's interest to disclose them unless the person is actually seeking entry. In my own case, for example, it was said that since I was a European I would be expected to bring 'European's wine' (*mem ndek*, spirits) and not palm-wine. Similarly, if I wished to wear shoes within the association this would need special permission, to be obtained by further payments. When the admission fees of the association were being described, it was emphasized that 'Ngbe is things to eat' (*Ngbɛ ci bɛnyŋ ɛnyɛ*).

The admission fees paid in entering an association lodge and its grades are shared by those who are already members of that grade (i.e. who have previously paid comparable amounts). The wine and food is drunk and eaten communally (here including the initiants who have produced them). 'Ngbe cannot be played with a dry throat', as the informant quoted above added, and hence the large quantities of wine required in membership fees. As we have noted, other food and wine can be obtained during the meetings from fines levied upon its members for major or minor offences committed against the rules of the association.

Finally, at the death of a member of Ngbe, other dues, proportionate to those originally paid by him, are required by the association from his relatives. Such death dues are a common requirement for all associations, and for Ngbe, as elsewhere, are said to be in payment for the food already consumed by the dead man as a former member of the association. Here again it would appear to be possible to bargain for a smaller amount or for a token payment, especially when the person is poor and the association has little chance of exacting the full payment. Sixteen jugs of wine and a goat remained (in Tali) the basic fee, to which other amounts were added according to the degree of membership acquired by the dead man.

We have already spoken in brief of the lodge organization of Ngbe and would repeat here merely that each lodge is an autonomous unit, according to the degree to which it embodies the full sectional constitution of the association. Certain lodges entail fuller and deeper knowledge of Ngbe, have more members and greater prestige, but there is no formal hierarchy of lodges or any kind of centralized control. The two basic principles determining inter-lodge relationship are, firstly, the common obligation of all association members to uphold the forms of the association (in particular not to reveal to strangers the esoteric knowledge which defines its constitution) and, secondly, the fact that status (rights and duties) obtained in any one lodge can be claimed, according to the degree acquired, in any other lodge, wherever one is constituted. The latter principle is much stressed by Banyang, for it gives a heightened significance to membership: the initiant may be entering a small lodge in an out-of-the-way Upper Banyang settlement, but by doing so he gains the right to enter any lodge, wherever he finds a meeting in progress, and to assume there his position and rights to food and drink as though it were his home lodge. Alternatively, should he lay claim to *more* than his due, or should he as a stranger commit, in the community he is visiting, an offence against the rules of Ngbe, this will be reported back to his home lodge in his own community, who will be expected to take up the case and punish this man on behalf of the lodge and community where he committed the offence. (This is a very significant reversal of the more usual principle in stateless societies, where corporate residential groups more frequently act to support a member in opposition to an outside group; the point will be discussed further in the context of Ngbe's political role.)

Just as there is some competitive element within one lodge of the association, however, so also is there some competition or emulation between members of different lodges. If one may judge from other associations, a stranger who enters an Ngbe meeting is welcomed but is watched very carefully to see that he makes the right greeting, observes the correct formalities, and, at some time, his knowledge of Ngbe (and thus the degree of his membership) is likely to be tested by means of the mime-language.

Any residential group or combination of residential groups can purchase Ngbe. The procedure of purchasing the association is similar to that of purchasing membership in it.[1] In both cases what is bought is knowledge of the association, of its formal constitution, and of the objects and emblems associated with it. Purchase of the association is undertaken by a group of people, led usually by one man who will himself obtain the most senior position within it. Later he may be spoken of as the 'owner' or 'leader' of the association, which is housed in his own *aca*. The group of people joining with him have each, however, to buy their own positions within the association. Purchase of Ngbe is thus purchase of all its parts by a group of people whose leader expends the most and is shown the

---

[1] 'Slave'-settlements, however, are not permitted to purchase the association (no one would sell it to them) and persons of 'slave'-descent, although allowed to become members, are not normally permitted to rise to any very senior status.

greatest details concerning it. The association is bought from any other lodge (often at some distance away), the members of which come to the purchasing settlement, where its new members are instructed. Sometimes, when a group of people (a series of hamlets, or even a village) have combined to purchase the association, they may later split up among themselves, each of the sectional representatives then forming their own lodge. On other occasions an established lodge may agree to a section of their members setting up their own lodge which they will 'give' to them (on reduced payment). Where a dispute occurs within an established lodge, however, and some of its members retire or are excluded from it, they cannot form their own lodge separately without first going through the process of buying the association, which they will do by going to a completely different lodge, usually at some distance, ignoring thus the 'parent' lodge. In Ejwenang, for example, the dispute which arose concerning succession after the last village leader died precipitated a dispute within the Ngbe of the village, the senior elder with his own party retiring from the lodge; later he purchased the association himself and so established his own separate lodge in the village.

As described, all status within the association is purchased separately by the individual members. We cannot therefore speak of 'inheritance' of status within, or of ownership of, the association in any strict sense. In so far as the association continues within the settlement or community it is handed down by its members as a group rather than by individuals. When the leader or 'owner' of a lodge dies his place may be taken by a near kinsman, or by any other senior member of the group originally combining to purchase the lodge. In either case the assumption of the position, if it involves raising the person's formal status in the association, requires that the person concerned should pay the necessary fees. It would appear, further, that in lodges possessing an 'Ngbe stone', a change in the leadership requires that the 'stone' shall in some way be renewed by the successor. Frequently what would appear to occur is that a successor, in order to consolidate his position, will, once he is able, buy one or more further sections of the association. Thus Baimberi of Tali 1, having inherited leadership of the Ngbe lodge of Egbemba, later added an 'Ngbe stone' by his own purchase to a lodge that did not earlier contain one.

Turning from the constitution of the association to its activities, we may distinguish between those activities which are carried out within the association itself and those more public activities which concern the association's relation to the settlement or residential group in which it is found. I describe here the internal and some of the public activities of the association, reserving description of the association's use as a political sanction for a later section.

As indicated above, Ngbe functions basically as an esoteric club, a highly elaborate one but one which caters primarily for the entertainment and common enjoyment of its members. This fact should be stressed, for the political functions of Ngbe derive as much from its bringing together the leading members of a community in these general activities as from its formal constitution as such. Also, it is for this reason that Banyang enjoy Ngbe. Meetings of the association are thus primarily social occasions when its members eat, drink, talk, dance, and sing together. Full, constitutional meetings of Ngbe, when the Ngbe house is fully set out with its emblems and the ɛkat prepared, are not often held, being reserved primarily for times of initiation or when a senior member dies. Far in excess of these occasions are the many informal meetings of Ngbe, when its members sing Ngbe songs, dance, and so on. At any general meeting of men in a village or settlement, when wine has been drunk and the atmosphere is merry, the men present will usually start 'dancing Ngbe' (dɛbɛn Ngbɛ). Here the forms of Ngbe – the songs, dance, mime, greetings, etc. – are followed even although its material features (the association as formally constituted, with all its emblems) are absent. It is, moreover, because of such occasions that one feels the pervading force of Ngbe rather than because of its formal meetings. This is partly because of their frequency, partly because of Ngbe's closeness on such occasions to social life, but also because with everything implicit and nothing made explicit the exclusiveness of the association, evidenced in its members' knowledge of its forms and outsiders' ignorance, becomes immediately apparent.

Used both at its constitutional meetings and at informal meetings, Ngbe has its own songs, instruments and drums, also its own secret language (ɛgbɛ). Many of the songs are in Ejagham; others are in Balundu. The instruments include: maraca-type rattles (bakacak) which are shaken in each hand, a type of bell-gong (ɛbok) beaten with a stick against or away from the chest, and a series of drums including the long, deeply resonant nɔ nko, two medium bɛkpiri drums, and the small mɔkpɛŋ. These instruments are played with a rhythm particular to the Ngbe association. The songs themselves are proverbial in form; they can be used after particular incidents at the meeting, implying some criticism of a person present or that some action is required from him. Ɛgbɛ, the secret language, is a gesture language consisting of a series of signs having reference to the constitution of the association, including the stages of initiation, what has been learnt there, knowledge of the emblems of the association, knowledge of ɛkat, and so on. Ɛgbɛ is performed by two people as a kind of prolonged mime, usually when dancing. It takes the form of question and answer, each of the two testing the other's knowledge, and thus, implicitly, the stage that that person has reached in membership of the association. The first sign of the series is thus made by passing the right forefinger across the eyes and corresponds to the question 'Have you seen Ngbe?' (i.e. 'Are you a member?') The series then continues with more elaborate gestures concerning what exactly the person has seen until one of them is shown to be superior and has vanquished the other.

It will be apparent that 'dancing Ngbe' has much of the charade element that has been described for Basinjom. In the case of Ngbe, however, this element would appear to be mainly innocent, having as its primary purpose the amusement of the persons concerned, although it is also linked with the constitution of the association and serves to heighten the sense of esoteric knowledge which surrounds and defines it. A further aspect of the charade element is also found in connection with the central symbol, 'Ngbe' itself. Here we may turn to the public activities of the association in its relation to the community.

When formally constituted meetings of an association lodge take place, the presence of the association in the settlement is signified by the 'voice of Ngbe' emerging from the Ngbe house: 'Ngbe', the leopard-like creature, is then said to be 'crying' (aadi). These meetings take place, and 'Ngbe' is heard, at times of initiation, on the occasion of the purchase of a lodge or of a new section, or when a leader or senior member of the association dies. (When initiants are taken to the 'Ngbe bush', 'Ngbe' is heard crying from the bush, and is later brought back into the settlement, and into the Ngbe house. On such occasions 'Ngbe' is said to be particularly strong.)

The formal appearance of Ngbe on the death of senior members would seem both to be a way of honouring the deceased[1] and of exerting the force of the association's claims over its members vis-à-vis non-members. The accounts I have obtained of the exact procedure in the case of a death vary in detail, but all suggest that the association in some way 'takes over'

[1] On one occasion in Besongabong when an important man who did not belong to Ngbe died, the association was brought out to honour him. As the village leader remarked, people coming to the 'death' from other villages would think that something was wrong were Ngbe not in evidence.

the deceased, allowing access to the 'death' only on its own terms. Thus in one community I was told how news of the death was kept secret (the women who had attended the dying man being restrained from public wailing, the most usual way a death is made known) until 'Ngbe', the 'voice', made it known by its crying; in other communities it was said that relatives coming to mourn the dead man would be required to make some payment before being able to see the corpse. In another case I was told that, if the man's son came from the south wishing to see his father, he might be told that he must first join Ngbe before he could see him; by this time, however, the dead man would have been buried and the son could only be shown his father's grave (but by now it would be too late to turn back, for he would be already within Ngbe). Whatever the procedure immediately following a senior member's death, Ngbe 'comes out' – i.e. is formally constituted – for a period of time after it; the time varies according to the occasion and the status of the member, but is said to be fourteen days for a senior 'leader'. A draped cloth or banner is hung from a long pole set up immediately outside the house of the dead man, and the emblems of the association (presumably those signifying the extent of his membership) are formally arranged outside the house. During this time the members of Ngbe meet to eat and drink in the constituted association house and the voice of Ngbe is heard intermittently. Informal dances, in which one of the masked figures appears, may take place in the evenings during this time. The period of ceremonial mourning is concluded with a larger, staged dance in which *ɛbongo* and *ɛma Nyankpɛ* appear, and possibly the masked dancers which represent sectional sub-associations.

Ɛbongo and *ɛma Nyankpɛ* have essentially similar costumes, a tight-fitting, multi-coloured netted fabric, covering the head and body completely and leaving only hands and feet uncovered; various objects are attached to the costume or carried by the dancer. First *ɛbongo* appears, and, according to accounts given to me, shows his (and thus the association's) concern in the death: the figure takes part in the formal destruction of property which helps to signify the death, and the widows of the dead man are brought to the figure, who is expected to chastise them if their mourning is insufficient. The material of which the *ɛbongo* costume is made is softer, more attractive, than *ɛma Nyankpɛ* and the figure would appear to represent the more pleasant, publicly tolerant aspects of the association. This dancer then disappears and *ɛma Nyankpɛ* reappears, whereupon all non-members are expected to flee; the figure demonstrates its fierceness and, if it sees any non-member, may make to attack him (or her). The 'power' of the association (or possibly of its central symbol, 'the animal of Ngbe') is apparently figured in such mock actions.[1]

On any occasion when 'Ngbe' (the leopard-like creature) is manifest in the community, no noise or outbreak must occur in the settlement. A violent quarrel, a sharp report (such as a gun firing), or the carrying of a cult-agency (taken here to be a potential threat against Ngbe) will cause the 'animal' to 'escape' back to the bush. The 'crying' of 'Ngbe' will now be heard coming from the bush, and while 'Ngbe' is at large women and other non-members will not be allowed out in the settlement. Whoever caused the disturbance will be asked to provide a piece of meat, a white fowl, and cola. With these the members of the association will set about recapturing 'Ngbe'; it will then be brought back into the settlement and association house, its presence there being once again signified by its 'voice' emerging from it.

Finally, status obtained through Ngbe membership is reflected in general social activities, notably in the communal drinking of wine. A non-member must drink wine at a public meeting (i.e. when other members of Ngbe are present) standing; only an 'elder' (tata) or 'leader' of Ngbe has the right to drink wine sitting. Men of the two latter status-categories have the further right to multiple glasses: two in the case of tata and for a 'leader' of the highest status (among Upper Banyang) as many as fourteen. (Not all these, however, need to be filled: after the first two or three glasses have been drunk, later glasses are likely to be given only in token gesture.) Among the Lower Banyang, after wine has been drunk and the pouring completed, someone may compliment the pourer by giving him the half-jocular Ngbe salutation, Dɛboɛ! to which he replies (if he is a member) Ngbɛ! Another person present may then repeat the compliment, Dɛboɛ! and the pourer, if he is able to, will answer with the name of any Ngbe section he is a member of, thus: Nkanda! (Dɛboɛ!), Esɔŋ! (Dɛboɛ!), Bɛkundi! (Dɛboɛ!), Ɛtɛm Ngbɛ!, until finally his repertoire of membership is exhausted or there are no more persons present willing or able to make the salutation.

[1] I have never witnessed the appearance of ɛma Nyankpɛ, which among Upper Banyang is an event more talked of than one that actually occurs. The gown as it has been shown and described to me is almost identical with the illustration of an 'Ekpo Dancer' in D. M. McFarlan's *Calabar*, facing p. 26, and tallies with descriptions by other writers for the Ejagham (e.g. Talbot, op. cit., p. 44): a large raffia ruff is worn around the neck with smaller ruffs on the ankles and wrists; a sash is tied around the waist on which a bell is fastened at the back; in the right hand is carried a whip or stick, in the left a bunch of leaves; other attachments are worn on the head (mɔsukul) and the back (ɛkwɛti).

Plate 9 Nbge emissary, announcing a law

Plate 10
A play-group
association

Ngbe as a political sanction

In its primary form a recreational association providing the context for communal fellowship and conviviality, Ngbe has also an important political or governmental role. It operates here essentially as an authoritative sanction which can be used to protect the rights of individual members of the association or to uphold a community decision, in this case announced as an 'Ngbe law'. In comparing it to the 'Government' of Colonial times, Banyang would seem also to be indicating the extent of its range, the formal respect due to it, and the inviolacy of its ultimate authority. Despite their anachronism in certain cases, I have heard in different villages similar stories of how the effectiveness of Ngbe was demonstrated to early European administrators. Nevertheless – and the point is an important one – the legal or governmental processes which are in this way taken over by the association are rarely, if ever, initiated from within it. The rights which Ngbe protects are not Ngbe rights, but the rights of any individual member of a community: 'Ngbe laws' are laws which originate from decisions of a community council but which are given the added formality of being announced through Ngbe. Once the association has been used in this formal way to sanction individual claims or community laws, any challenge or transgression becomes, however, automatically an association matter. Someone who has defied the sanction of the invoked association is said to have 'broken the neck of Ngbe', 'struck Ngbe', or simply to have 'carried a matter of Ngbe'. He is then answerable to the association for his guilt.

The individual rights which Ngbe may be invoked to protect are most commonly those to land or property. An 'Ngbe sign' (*ɛrɔŋ Ngbɔ*) is placed on the property by its owner or claimant owner, especially where he fears trespass, theft, or misuse. A number of 'signs' are used for this purpose, including: *dɛcɔŋ Ngbɛ*, a plaited and spliced loop of fibre cord, fixed to the top of a stick; a square lattice woven from a palm frond (a sign especially associated with the *Bɛkundi* sub-association and referred to by its name); two joined horns of a goat (*babaŋamɛn*, also known as 'Bekundi'). Any member of the association (or of the sub-association Bekundi in the case of the two latter signs) has the right to make use of such a sign, although if he is a junior member it is likely that he will consult a respected senior member before doing so. An outsider cannot use the sign, even if he makes a request to do so through a member. Misuse of the Ngbe sign (by someone not entitled to do so, or on property which does not belong to the person concerned) is itself an offence, punishable by the association.

As we have seen in the example of the case of the youth from Takwa (p. 163), Bekundi as a sub-association of Ngbe can be invoked in formal support of a pledge; certain other sub-associations are also invoked for the same purpose. In Lower Banyang villages a further procedure is recognized by which a man who believes himself to have been wronged by another (for example, by someone who has consistently refused to return a debt) can constrain him by making the Ngbe salutation over him (*Dɛboɛ*!), then pronouncing that unless he rights the wrong (e.g. by returning the debt) he cannot leave the house in which he now is. To this may be added various other possible constraints, for example, that he cannot go to the latrine, cannot eat food prepared by his wife, and so on. This formal constraint effected by an individual member in the name of the association may be compared with the law of ostracism which is one of the most powerful of the more general sanctions of the association. In this case its use has the effect of forcing the issue in an interpersonal dispute which might otherwise become extremely protracted. The person so constrained has no choice but to call upon the leading members of the relevant Ngbe lodge (normally that of his own settlement) to hear and judge the dispute, and so release him from the imposed constraint. On the other hand, to ignore the latter would be to offend directly against the association; he would then be 'breaking the neck of Ngbe'.

The formal sanction of Ngbe can be applied to any community decision, or 'law of the community', which automatically becomes a 'law of Ngbe'. The range of such 'laws' corresponds to those already cited as 'community laws' in Chapter 7 (p. 180), any or all of which *could* have been promulgated through Ngbe. One of the most significant of the laws generally made through Ngbe is that of formal ostracism, whereby it is declared that a named person shall not be given food or wine, or received in any social group. (There are a number of minor variations here which alter its stringency.) It may be noted that the form taken by such laws places the obligation of conformity not on the person named but on all the remaining law-abiding members of the community: the punishment of the offender, placed thus 'outside' the community, assumes the solidarity of its remaining members.

An Ngbe law is announced by one of its junior members going through the settlement or settlements of the community concerned carrying the small *ɛkpiri* drum which he beats, declaring what the law is (see *Plate 9*). As we have implied above, a law may be made at any order of residential grouping, provided that it has a lodge or lodges, and provided that the representatives of all the lodges, if there are a number, have agreed to the law. Lodges may therefore combine in promulgating an Ngbe law; where this has been done, Banyang sometimes say that the punishment for any consequent offence requires equivalent amounts to be paid to *all* the lodges involved. In fact, this would seem to be more a threat than an actual statement of procedure. Where lodges do combine in promulgating a law this combination normally follows from the order of community grouping whose council has determined the law rather than from any joint action of Ngbe lodges *qua* lodges.

An 'Ngbe case' is judged in very much the same way as other community cases, except that certain formalities appropriate to the association must be observed, and that only association members are formally allowed to participate. An *ɛkpiri* drum placed on the ground is the sign that an Ngbe meeting is in session: it should remain there until the matter is settled and during this time no one should leave the meeting. In Tali and Bara such meetings were not closed to outsiders, but it was only the Ngbe members who spoke judicially at them, others speaking as witnesses. The formal respect due to statuses in Ngbe is observed, 'leaders' in particular exerting their right to 'command Ngbe' and thus to assert their authority. In the initial calling of the case a 'bottle of wine' and a 'head of tobacco' must be provided and at its conclusion other formal items may be requested (money to 'quieten Ngbe', something for the 'spokesman' appearing for the defendant), besides the 'goat' (again, a real goat or its surrogate) that will be demanded from the person judged guilty. In other respects, however, the conduct of a case by accusation, defence, and discussion follows very much the pattern we have already considered.

Nevertheless – and here we come back to the importance of Ngbe as a sanctioning agent – Banyang emphasize the effectiveness of Ngbe as a political sanction and the seriousness of attempting to challenge it. The effective authority of Ngbe is greater than that of a community council acting alone. The fines levied by Ngbe are said to be much heavier than those levied simply by a community council, a fact which is confirmed by those cases I have witnessed. If an Ngbe case is brought to the Native Courts, the case is given priority and the verdict, I was told, would be most unlikely to go against the association. In the two remaining sections of this chapter we shall be discussing the conditions underlying the effectiveness of the Ngbe sanction. Before doing so, however, it may be useful to examine two actual incidents in which Ngbe became involved that illustrate the relationship of Ngbe to community authority and the way in which Ngbe may be used to support it.

The first is a comparatively minor incident which occurred in Bara. The leader of this village was becoming annoyed over the attitude and behaviour of his younger brother. This annoyance, shared also by other members of the village, arose from what was later described by the young men of the village as his 'pride', his independence, and his show of superiority in village life. The matter came to a head when the young man advised a Bangwa hunter, who was then staying in the village, not to give the whole of an εso antelope he had killed to the leader (whose right it was to receive this as an 'animal of the community') but to give only half, retaining half for himself. The hunter attempted to do this. He was questioned about it and the other half was demanded. When the case was settled (the whole animal was brought, laid before the village council, and half was in fact returned to the hunter) the leader's brother, the young man, was called to appear before the village council to account for what he had advised the hunter. The young man refused to come. This was a direct affront to the authority of the council, and of the village.

After a short wait, the εkpiri Ngbε, the small Ngbe drum, was taken down from the wall of the leader's house and a messenger was sent to beat it through the village, announcing the law that no one there should receive or entertain the young man, whom we may call *Eyong. This action was instigated by the village leader, but it had the support of the other members of the community present. The εkpiri Ngbe was returned, and placed on the ground, and those present awaited events. The meeting of the community had now become automatically transformed into a meeting of Ngbe: apart from the placing of the Ngbe drum on the ground, however, there had been no other change in its form or membership. In a short time Eyong appeared. (He had, in fact, been staying in the adjacent house.) The case was discussed and the seriousness of his action in contempt of community authority pointed out to him, both in relation to his advice to the hunter and his refusal to appear before the village council when summoned. One of the young men of the village gave further support to the council's action by complaining about the 'pride' of Eyong in relation to the young men, which has already been mentioned above. Eyong himself, represented in this context by a 'spokesman', was apologetic and appropriately contrite. (He could not be otherwise.) An Ngbe fine was made, including initial dues and a 'goat' of 10s. (a comparatively small sum since the law had not stood for any length of time). The εkpiri drum was taken up from the ground and once more beaten through the village, this time removing the law.

This example requires little comment. Perhaps its most striking features are, firstly, the very close association of Ngbe and community authority which it shows, and, secondly, the ease with which, in this clear-cut case of refusal to accept the village council's authority, the Ngbe sanction was imposed and obtained its results. Once the Ngbe law had been passed it was virtually impossible for the young man to do otherwise than appear before the village council to answer for himself. The longer the delay, the more serious would have been its implications.

The second incident arose out of the political factions that formed during the time of the Tali dispute and concerned a man whose refusal to accept the combined authority of the (supra-village) Tali was more obstinate and prolonged than the case of Eyong above. We have already referred to Nyenti, the leader of the village section of Nten Nchang in Tali 2 and formerly one of its leading members, who changed sides during the progress of the dispute, ending up as a supporter of the 'traditionalists' in 'Tali 1'. His defection gave an opening to a fellow-member of Nten Nchang to claim the leadership of the village section by remaining loyal to the leader of 'Tali 2', then seeking status as an independent village leader. This support (which is said to have included monetary aid) was not in fact recompensed (for reasons we shall give later) when finally the formal independence of the Tali 2 leadership was agreed to. *Tanyi Ndip (the claimant section leader), extremely annoyed at what he regarded as his betrayal by the leader of Tali 2, spoke against him publicly. This was reported, and at a council meeting, strengthened by Tali's present unity, Tanyi Ndip was fined as a *mu bɛnaŋ*, a 'back-biter'. Tanyi Ndip refused to pay the fine, maintaining that he had spoken the truth and that it was he who had been wronged. The Ngbe drum was then beaten against him. Believing that this action was unjust and that he had a case against it, Tanyi Ndip took his complaint to the District Officer at Mamfe. He became thus the person 'who sued the community to the European'. Partly because of the necessary journey across Banyang country, made both by Tanyi Ndip and by the leading members of Tali, news of the case spread very quickly. In Bara, on the eastern borders of Banyang country, I heard about this 'suing of Tali' as it was happening. A young man who was then working for me but was living in Besongabang on the western borders of the country heard about it at about the same time and said that it was also much discussed there.

The District Officer heard the case from both sides and, finding the members of Tali in agreement against Tanyi Ndip, ruled that this was a matter which concerned themselves alone and should therefore be settled within Tali. The following text was written by the young man mentioned above, who met the leading members of Tali in Mamfe and here writes about the case it was described by them:

Tanyi Ndip sued the community to the European that they caught him and said that he should give a goat and three pounds. He unsettled the foundations of the community (literally: he lifted the community up from the ground) and we travelled yesterday so that we could say how Tanyi Ndip had acted with the Ngbe of Tali.

Earlier it was wanted that he should plead with the community (i.e. to apologize and accept their verdict) but he only lifted the bottom of the community from the ground, to wrangle over it at Mamfe. But when we go home, then we shall see the place he is going to. The community will sit and will be watching what he does. If a person thinks that he has a head which is higher than the community let him remain until the community knocks him to the ground. He said that once a man has fired a gun, whether he has killed an animal or not, it shows that he is a man (i.e. it is good to try even if one fails). We agreed, but said that he is a man and he shot the community. And soon he will have to plead guilty and pay the community as though it were the animal which he shot.

In fact even on his return Tanyi Ndip still refused to accept his guilt in the face of the community. Life became impossible for him in Tali and he left to stay with relatives in the south. He died there a year or two later.

Features of this case will be referred to again later, especially as it shows one of the characteristic processes of governmental action in which Ngbe is also involved: the isolating of the guilty individual against whom is opposed the solidary, corporate community. One should also add that while it lasted this case became a nine-day wonder, with repercussions outside Tali. Tanyi Ndip and the leading members of Tali 1 and 2 thus passed through many other villages on their way to Mamfe. It is reported that Tanyi Ndip obtained little or no support from them. Generally he was spoken of as a person to be distrusted: he had 'sued Tali to the European'. If he entered any meeting in a community, Ngbe or otherwise, might he not do the same thing again?

Community authority, the constitution of Ngbe, and the effectiveness of the Ngbe sanction

The undoubted power of the 'Ekpe' association (as its name becomes) in Ejagham villages and the Efik communities of Calabar has been linked by some writers to the cultic control of a forest 'spirit' or similar super-natural agency.[1] Whenever I have suggested to Banyang that the power of Ngbe was supernatural this has been strongly denied. Association activities include a ritual or supernatural element, as do most aspects of Banyang life: the blessing of the dead may be asked for in an association context; 'medicines' are used to protect the rights of association members or as a test of truth. But the central purpose or power of Ngbe is in no way supernatural. 'Ngbe', the leopard-like creature that gives its name to the association, is a secular and not a religious symbol. So for example, when discussing the effectiveness of the *dɛcoŋ Ngbɛ*, the coil of rope that is placed on property to safeguard it from trespass, I have been told that it is not an *njɔ*, a 'cult-agency': it is merely a 'sign' (*ɛrɔŋ*), effective because 'the people of the community are watching' to take action if the sign is ignored. Once during a council discussion, when the subject of associa-tions was under debate, the leader of Bara village insisted with hard-headed rationalism, 'An association does not come down from the sky: it is the people of the community who sit down to buy it.'

The question which then arises is: what gives Ngbe its authority to issue pronouncements for, or make demands on, the members of a residential group in which a lodge is established? Banyang answer this question equally clearly: it is because the lodge contains the 'people of the community', the elders and leaders of a residential group who collectively hold authority over it. 'Ngbe *is* the community' (*Ngbɛ – ci ɛtɔk*).

In the next section I discuss in greater detail the extent of the corre-spondence between community membership and membership of Ngbe, also the relationship between lodge organization and community group-ing: here it can only be asserted that lodges of Ngbe are very widely distributed throughout all Banyang villages, and that the majority of men within any village are members of the association, the most influential tending usually to occupy the highest status. The political operation of the association depends directly upon this fact of overlapping member-ship.[2] Nevertheless, if we grant this fact, a further question arises, which

[1] For example, P. A. Talbot, *In the Shadow of the Bush*, pp. 38–40.
[2] The importance of a similar feature to the operation of Yakö associations has been pointed out by Daryll Forde, *Yakö Studies*, p. 190.

is, if the authority of Ngbe lies not in the association itself but in its members, what is it that the association adds to the government of Banyang communities? If the members of a lodge are 'the people of the community' (and we have seen in the case of Eyong, p. 238, how easily a community council can transform itself into an Ngbe meeting), what advantage is to be gained by operating in this way, in the name and under the guise of Ngbe? It is this question that I discuss in the present section.

In a previous chapter I attempted to show that the corporate structure of a Banyang community was dependent upon two linked but opposing principles: firstly, the necessity for political action to be based upon the united agreement of the members of the group concerned; secondly, the need to accommodate within such collective action the diversity of interests of the persons who make it. In Banyang's own terminology, a community must be 'one', but any action concerning a community must also be made by everyone, 'all the people'. The role of the associations, and in particular of the Ngbe association, is closely determined by these two principles. Thus an answer to the question, what advantage does Ngbe offer?, is twofold: firstly, that the association provides a way of organizing people in which all the emphasis is upon solidarity, and through which solidary action is more likely to be achieved; secondly, that Ngbe represents a common idea or set of values which can be upheld by many diverse groups, irrespective of their local interests.

In contrast to the simple and relatively unelaborated rules which determine the 'constitutional' ordering of Banyang communities, the constitution of an Ngbe lodge is both elaborate and highly formalized. Most associations have this elaborately formal element according to which the status, procedures, rights, and duties of members are carefully defined by rules that are sanctioned by fines should they be contravened by members. The elaborate code of rules serves in a number of ways to emphasize the solidarity of the association or lodge as a whole and to minimize the chance of any individual member obtaining a disproportionate personal influence. In the first place, the constitution of an association is always impersonal and 'respect for persons' is systematically minimalized. Thus, although many of the rules do in fact define the prerogatives of those occupying particular status-categories, none of them concern individuals as such, and the Ngbe rule prohibiting the use of everyday salutation names (which are closely linked with a man's personal identity within the community) further indicates the desire to leave personal status outside the Ngbe house. Moreover, the rules of an association apply to all members alike and whoever breaks one, whatever his status, is liable to be challenged and fined. (Indeed, in this respect more senior members are often more vulnerable than the junior.) Again, where an association gives certain advantages to those of a higher status-category (e.g. the 'leaders' and 'elders' of Ngbe), it is well recognized that the persons who hold this position have reached it only after a period of time (by 'climbing the ladder' as it were), that they have paid for their positions, and that those who are now junior have all an equal formal opportunity to 'reach the top'. An association is entered deliberately (knowingly, as Banyang say) and there would be no point in becoming a member if one were not willing to abide by the rules. At the same time, the existence of the elaborate code of rules serves further as an ever-present reminder of the general authority that an association has over its members. Most associations require on entry some definite action on the part of the candidate by which he places himself under the authority, and in this sense on the mercy, of the group, and this constraint once established is constantly maintained by the code of rules. Banyang treat the need to keep to the rules partly as a game; many of them are formalities for formalities' sake, and one watches to catch out one's neighbour in the hope of gaining an extra jug of palm-wine or a bottle of spirits. At the same time the very elaborateness of the rules means that should any individual member overreach himself – by personal arrogance, by flaunting his wealth, by seeking undue influence – he can be made the target of constant fines until he learns to temper his behaviour. This disciplinary effect of association membership is well illustrated by a case in Besongabang where a particularly headstrong youth of one section of the village was purchased membership of one of the best-run lodges in another section of the village especially to quieten him down: it did precisely this – *apɔp* (a term which refers to physical tiredness after exertion, perhaps here: 'no more fight was left in him').

If the 'constitutional' authority of Ngbe is impersonal and is exerted over its members in the general name of the association, within the association there are nevertheless many different 'levels' or 'grades', which differentiate members. This is one of the most remarked-on characteristics of Ngbe, the comparison which is most frequently made being that 'Ngbe is like a school: you enter in the first class and move upwards until finally you reach the top'; one man (Baimberi of Tali 1, who was then in the process of buying the 'Ngbe stone') even said that he had 'left school' and was now 'going to the university'. The graded structure of Ngbe is characteristic of all parts of its constitution: its division into sections, the status-categories of the main association and of its various sub-associations, the progressive step-by-step sequence of initiation rites. We have also noted the tendency for such grades as exist to become further ramified (p. 225), and the general reluctance of Banyang to admit to any definite number of stages or grades in the organization of Ngbe: 'a person never finishes Ngbe'. This graded structure – which is flexible, and can respond to the situational needs of a particular community – gives to each association lodge a Chinese-box-like form. A small, highly exclusive inner group of persons have effective control over the formal activities of the lodge, but their position and the kind of influence they exert will to outsiders or to persons less close to them tend to be obscured by those around and supporting them. To A (in the simplified diagram, *Figure 27*) it is the overall association which wields power. B, the junior members of Ngbe (the 'drummers' or those who have obtained membership of only the initial sections), will be perfectly aware of their own peripheral position and limited influence in the affairs of the association, but in relation to outsiders (A), it will be in B's interests to identify themselves with the association as a whole, even although they lack detailed knowledge of affairs in the more exclusive intermediate group (D and C combined). A similar but more critical choice exists for C, who have the advantage of higher status than B (and A) while still being excluded from the most central group (D): again it must be in their interests to align themselves with D in maintaining their prerogatives over B. This whole structure is further supported by the reciprocities involved in membership: D are the persons who have invested most in purchasing their rank and who will therefore be most concerned to maintain the formal constitution of the lodge intact; B are the most junior members but may look in time to further advancement and to replacing their seniors. The elaborately differentiated rank-sequence of Ngbe gives then to each member a clearly defined position in relation to others, but also ensures that this position has no value except in relation to the whole, and that in order to pursue his own interests the individual member must maintain the solidarity of the whole. One may suggest perhaps that the organization of Ngbe has something of the form of a large modern trading corporation in which a great many people have invested capital and whose combined shares establish the (economic) power whose control is concentrated in the hands of very few.[1]

The rules of secrecy which are a second major characteristic of Ngbe's constitution further serve to heighten the collective solidarity of its members while formally distinguishing their status one from another.

[1] David Lynch, *The Concentration of Economic Power* (1946).

These rules of secrecy are essentially designed to preserve the in-group exclusiveness of the association, and are effective at all stages of its graded structure. The association itself is of course *not* a 'secret' organization (in the sense that its existence is secret): what is secret is its formal constitution, the way its sections and offices are organized, and in particular the emblematic representation of these in material symbols (the 'Ngbe stone')

Figure 27 Simplified diagram illustrating graded structure of associations

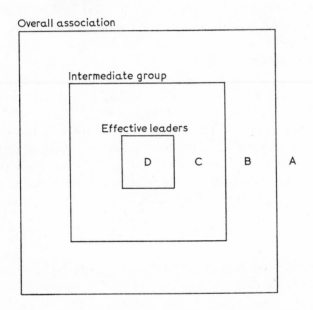

Overall association

Intermediate group

Effective leaders

D   C   B   A

and the sign-language. As we have seen, membership of Ngbe is synonymous with 'seeing' Ngbe or 'knowing' Ngbe: to become a member of Ngbe is to be taught, in some degree, the formal knowledge of its symbols and thus its constitution. Ngbe, like many other Banyang associations, are groups of people organized in relation to the shared understanding of an object. On many occasions when discussing the nature of association, I have been told: 'An association is when people meet and agree to call this a "table", this a "chair", this a piece of "paper" ' (in each case a different object being indicated and a name specified for it). But since membership of Ngbe is graded, so too is the formal knowledge associated with membership. Its most dramatic expression is the sign-language which is used to ascertain the extent of a person's membership and his knowledge of the things which occur in Ngbe.

These rules of secrecy are nevertheless significant not so much for what they hide as for what they define. The veil of Ngbe secrecy does not serve to cloak political machinations on the part of the leaders of a residential group. What it does do is to unite them in the common observance of a form of behaviour, which is then protected from adoption by outsiders by their 'legal' claim to exclusive knowledge and use of it. Moreover, once a member has obtained *any* status in Ngbe it is in his interests to observe the formal rules of secrecy relating to the whole of the constitution, even though he may be ignorant of a large part of it. To return to the diagram already used (*Figure 27*), a person in the most junior position stands outside the majority of the more exclusive, inner groups, but to a non-member these internal divisions will be less significant than the fact that B *is* a member, and he in turn will certainly wish to align himself with the association as a whole *vis-à-vis* the outsider, despite his very limited influence within it. C is in a similar, if modified position: here concerned to uphold the forms of secrecy which distinguish him from B, and from outsiders, while himself debarred from the full knowledge held by D. The operation of the formal rules of secrecy is, then, similar in effect to the graded constitution discussed above: while they limit and define each individual member's status, all members have equally a vested interest in upholding them, and above all in maintaining the inviolability of those features which define the association as a whole. We turn here to the central symbol of the association: 'Ngbe' itself.

As it appears in the constitution of the association, 'Ngbe' the purported animal has three leading characteristics: firstly, its power and ferociousness are always stressed (these follow from the very idea of a leopard, the most powerful animal of the forest); secondly, the creature is depicted as being held within the association under duress (contained normally in the inner recess, the veiled εkat, it can 'escape' on occasions when there is a threat either to it or to the order of the community which it dominates, and it then 'returns to the forest', where it has to be recaptured); thirdly and finally, the material form of 'Ngbe' – i.e. what exactly it is that produces the 'voice', scratches the initiants, and so on – is the central and most guarded secret of the association.[1] These three characteristics can be related each to a different level at which the 'Ngbe' symbol operates and which combine to give it its complexity.

[1] For example, I learnt in more than one village where I stayed that the villagers had been warned by outsiders that whatever else I was shown in their village, I should *not* be told about this.

Most straightforwardly, 'Ngbe' the leopard or leopard-like creature symbolizes the power of the association as a corporate group – or, more correctly, as an indefinite series of corporate groups (i.e. all its lodges). This conceptual reference of 'Ngbe' as a symbol of power ($b\varepsilon ta\eta$) is to some extent blurred by the other levels at which the symbol operates, but is nevertheless consciously recognized and has been explained to me in just these terms by senior members. We may note however that the *actual* power that the association (or a lodge) holds flows not from the symbol but from the association as an organized body. The power which 'Ngbe' the animal symbolizes emanates in fact from Ngbe as an associated group of persons. At this, the second level of reference, 'Ngbe' is more than merely a symbol with conceptual content but becomes the focus for those very activities which serve to 'constitute' the association – which bring it formally into existence. In this context we need to note that the metony-mous usage of the name Ngbe (the association is called after the 'animal' it contains within it) allows precisely for the ambiguity concerning the actual source of Ngbe's power (when a Manyang says Ngbe is extremely powerful, does he mean the 'animal' or the 'association'?) and is further taken over into the organization of the association so that where the 'animal' demands respect, makes its mark on initiants, etc., the action is in effect conceived as relating to the association as a constituted group of persons. But it is just *these* actions which are required by the rules defining the association. At this second level, then, 'Ngbe' is not merely a symbol, but is 'enacted symbol', one whose force depends upon those activities which give credence to it. The flow here is two-way: the power of the association as an effective body (a power metonymously represented through the symbol of 'Ngbe' the animal) depends in its turn upon the due enactment of the procedures concerning this animal, for it is these centrally which define the association as an organized body. Similarly, if its mem-bers did not support the ostensible reality of 'Ngbe' the animal (as a thing to be feared, appeased, etc.), then the association would lose the very basis of its formal organization. In this regard it is entirely appropriate that the leopard-like creature is said to be held in constraint by the association, for the power attributed to it lies in the organization of the association based upon the enacting of procedures concerning it. We are not, I think, unduly extending the symbolism when we say that the concept of a leopard outside the association ('escaping' to the bush) represents diffuse and unregulated power, while within the association, constrained and directed by and through the 'constitution', the same con-cept comes to represent effective authority, the regulated 'power' of the organized group.[1] The effective organization of a group cannot rely, however, merely upon the charade-like enactment of a putative symbolism, and it is here that the factual and somewhat prosaic secret of the material nature of 'Ngbe' has relevance. Again, it is not the content of the secret which is so important (although certainly this has some significance) but what it defines, and the way in which the maintaining of the secret further supports the solidarity shared by members of the association. We have already quoted the leader of Bara's statement that 'an association does not come down from the sky: it is the people of the community which sit down and buy it'; ultimately the hard fact of what is brought is the prosaic truth of how the 'voice of Ngbe' is made, along with similar, if less important, items of information.

I have so far discussed the question posed earlier (what advantage is to be gained by operating in the name of and under the guise of Ngbe?) by considering how the formal constitution of the association helps to achieve the type of solidarity which is a prerequisite to all political action in Banyang society. The success of the association is however closely related to the effectiveness of the Ngbe sanction used as a legal device. The effectiveness of this sanction derives only in part from the formal organization of the association; it depends also upon the conditions which make it particularly appropriate to the governmental needs of Banyang society.

In the first place, use of the formal Ngbe sanction serves to accelerate what has earlier been described as one of the essential processes in dispute settlement, that by which an interpersonal dispute is converted to one in which the overriding issue is the individual's acceptance of group authority. By invoking this sanction in a private case, the person who does so converts it from a personal and particular issue, to an impersonal and general one directly concerned with the acceptance of group authority. In this sense Ngbe always serves to 'force the issue': it lays down the criterion by which the offence can be isolated. Once the sanction has been invoked, *someone* must always be found guilty: there can be no dismissing the case, and even prevarication is unlikely to give much succour. If the defendant is not himself found guilty, then the plaintiff *is* and will be

[1] Other examples concerning leopards illustrate the same principle by which 'power' is transmuted to 'authority' by actions incorporating the 'leopard' into the formal organization of the group: the most notable concerns the leopard as 'animal of the community' which when killed in the bush must be brought to the community leader and ritually consumed by the leading 'people of the community'. As earlier chapters attempted to demonstrate, it is this action above all else that defines the authorized constitution of Banyang political groups; it is this which, on the one hand, makes the community and its leader 'strong' and, on the other, 'legitimizes' the status of one man as overall 'leader', one order of residential grouping as a 'village'.

required to pay (*-kwɔ*) for wrongful use of Ngbe. In fact, the person invoking Ngbe is unlikely to do so unless he is sure of his case. All this contributes to the apparent inviolability of the sanction: Ngbe does not take sides and is impersonal; it does not engage itself with regard to the substantive claims at issue, but merely sanctions the behaviour of those who are so engaged. Whereas individuals can put themselves in the wrong, it is rarely possible for Ngbe, the reified and incorporated community, to do so.

Closely related to the first point is the second, that Ngbe as an association representing the community serves by its political and judicial use to demonstrate to an offender his potential isolation *vis-à-vis* the group, the community to whom he owes his status. We have noted above how the essential process implied by the sanction of ostracism reaffirms the solidarity and law-abiding unity of the residential group over against the individual who is thus 'removed from the community': the confrontation is not between political groups as such but between the political group and an individual member who threatens its good order. This vital relationship between the group and its individual members, which is at the basis of all Banyang politico-residential grouping, is clearly expressed and given unequivocal support by the constitution of the Ngbe association and the judicial processes in which it is involved.

Thirdly, the support which is thus given is not limited to a single village or even village group, but comes from all communities owning an Ngbe lodge. If a man is ostracized through Ngbe in one village no other village will receive him (cf. especially the case of Tanyi Ndip, pp. 239–240). In the 'closing of alternatives' that Banyang judicial sanctions effect, the Ngbe sanction by implication closes the alternatives open to an offender not only in his own community but in most others that he may have access to, since by failing to accept the authority of one Ngbe lodge he has failed to accept the authority that all seek to preserve. In the next section we shall return to this aspect of Ngbe as a polity, loosely linking autonomous communities in the common support of certain values.

Finally, we may point to the way in which the internal activities of an Ngbe lodge, like most associations, impose a discipline on its members which emphasizes throughout the need to accept authority, to observe the rules of the group; such a discipline moves without discontinuity from the more relaxed, recreational context of 'playing Ngbe' to the context in which entirely serious, central political issues are in question. Many Banyang have learnt to their cost the danger of not treating seriously an apparently frivolous injunction made by or within the association. Taking an association (such as Ngbe) seriously is the same as taking the community seriously: what is learnt in one context applies equally to the other.

The Ngbe polity

Accounts of the origin of *Ngbɛ* or *Ɛkpɛ* all indicate its spread from people of one culture or language to another and the fact that by this process of adaptation and use it gained in importance. In origin the association is almost certainly Ejagham, but it appears first to have spread to certain of the more clearly Bantu south-eastern neighbours of the Ejagham before being adopted by the Efik of Calabar and from them returned to the Ejagham of the hinterland.[1] Its adoption by the Efik of Calabar had a considerable significance: firstly, because in the eighteenth and nineteenth centuries Calabar was one of the major centres of West African trade and because it gained considerably in prestige from its success among the wealthy trading chiefs and lineage heads there; secondly, because the trade routes which the Efik controlled became the avenues for the further dispersal of the association. In an area of small autonomous communities lacking any general authority, Ekpe became one of the means by which traders' rights were safeguarded and the passage of persons between communities protected.[2] Indeed, Ekpe as an instrument of authority and guarantee of protection would appear to have become one of the major 'exports' of Calabar to those hinterland peoples who supplied them in turn with slaves, ivory, and oil. So Waddell describes a 'grand and rare Egbo ceremonial' which was the occasion of the purchase of a lodge:

> Some persons of consequence had come from a far country to purchase the honours and authority of that institution, that they might introduce it among their own people, and become the founders of a new branch. This was the equivalent to entering the confederation of which Calabar

[1] Accounts of the origin of *Ngbɛ Ɛkpɛ/Egbo* are given by P .A. Talbot, *The Peoples of Southern Nigeria*, Vol. III, p. 780; H. M. Waddell, *Twenty Nine Years in the West Indies and Central Africa*, p. 313; and G. I. Jones, 'The Political Organization of Old Calabar', in *Efik Traders of Old Calabar*, p. 136.

[2] Most writers comment on the importance of Ekpe to the flow of commerce: see, for example, Waddell in his account of the origin of the association, loc. cit.; Talbot, op. cit., p. 784; Charles Partridge, *Cross River Natives*, p. 37; J. Parkinson, 'A Note on the Efik and Ekoi tribes of the Eastern Province, *JRAI*, Vol. 37, p. 264. The benefit that membership gave to trade would appear also to have prompted certain European traders to join it. Thus Holman (*Travels in Madeira, Sierra Leone, etc.*, quoted by G. I. Jones, op. cit., p. 141) reports that 'Capt. Burrell of the ship *Heywood* of Liverpool held the rank of Yampai and he found it exceedingly to his advantage as it enabled him to recover all the debts due to him by the natives'.

was the head, and they were consequently treated with distinguished respect (op. cit., p. 265).

By the end of the nineteenth century the association had spread over a large area stretching from Calabar to the Cross River bend, from the easternmost Ibo and Ibibio to the Balundu and Mbo of the Cameroons, an area roughly corresponding to that whose immediate trading connections were with Calabar.[1]

Although our accounts are fragmentary and lacking in detail, there were clearly many variants in the form of the association over this area. The number and names of the 'grades' or main sections of the association, the amount required for entry, the name and duties of the main office-bearers vary between areas and at different times. Some of this variation must be due to the processes by which new forms gained prestige and were purchased by others. Thus, for example, Talbot in his account of the Ejagham Oban Ekpe notes how certain of its (most important) 'grades' had been acquired from the Efik, these grades replacing older equivalents.[2] Despite these variants the main ostensible features of the association – the 'leopard' voice; the 'stone' set in a palaver or assembly house and arranged with various emblems; the masked figure (or figures) who may whip or beat those not fleeing from him – would seem to be common to its appearance over most of this area, and so, too, would its main political use as a santioning agent for community laws or for the protection of individual rights. At least, this is so in the central and southern part of the area demarcated: the association's less significant political role among some of the peripheral peoples of the area can be related to the weakening of some of its features there.

I have tried to show in the account of the association among Banyang that, despite its political and governmental importance, its primary role is as a sanction, a means of formalizing and enforcing community authority, and that it is not itself a source of authority. This point is also made by

[1] In view of their key position in the hinterland trading network it is interesting to observe that the Aro Ibo, together with their neighbours, the Ututu and Ihe, are reported by Talbot to have had 'the Ekpe Club in all its seven grades and its full ceremonial derived from Calabar'. The entrance fee there, unusually high for a peripheral area, is quoted as 180s. (op. cit., p. 782).

[2] Op. cit., pp. 41–42. Two of these defunct sections named by Talbot for Oban in the first decades of this century (Isong and Mutanda) were still being referred to by Lower Banyang in the 1950s and The 1960s. 'highest and final grade' which the Oban people had then acquired from Calabar was Nkanda, which by mid-century had reached the eastern Ejagham and Lower Banyang but had not been acquired by Upper Banyang (cf. above, pp. 223 and 224).

M. H. Swabey, an administrative officer writing of the association in the 1930s as it existed then amongst the eastern Ejagham of Mamfe Division. He writes:[1]

The Nyankpe Society [a common Europeanized synonym for the association] has been universal in the area for some time. Full details are difficult to obtain as many of the ceremonies are secret. It is quite certainly not in the least harmful, however, and is primarily a society for feasting and playing. It has seven grades and to pass through all and become a full member requires a considerable outlay. But it is money well invested as members receive fees from new members. It has become associated with the administration of the village council. For instance if the village council makes a law, it is announced by Nyankpe drum and is often called a Nyankpe law. It is not that, however, but an order from the council promulgated through Nyankpe. In the same way any infringement of these laws is called a fine to Nyankpe but it is not really that but a fine for disobeying the council. The fine however is generally in livestock and the livestock is kept and killed at Nyankpe feasts. It is the laws of the council made through Nyanke that are almost invariably obeyed or, if transgressed, the fine to make amends is paid without complaint or reference to the Native Court or Administrative Officer. All the village belongs to Nyankpe and public opinion is behind it. Christians may belong if they wish. [The writer then cites examples of laws made through the association.]

In the more complex situation of the nineteenth-century Efik communities of Old Calabar, it is difficult to establish the same principle with equal certainty. Most of the accounts of the association there place emphasis on its role as sanctioning agent, the upholder of established authority, but since for the Calabar communities as a whole the association provided the context for the widest joint discussions as well as the means of promulgating the few laws that all groups occasionally agreed to, it is not easy to distinguish whether the authority so invoked emanated from the circumstantial meeting of the representatives of the independent communities concerned, formalized and sanctioned by the association, or whether in some sense such laws were truly imposed by the association, of an authority inherent in it. G. I. Jones remarks on the function of 'Egbo' in bringing 'together into a single disciplined organization all the

[1] Intelligence Report on the Kembong Area, Mamfe Division, Cameroons Province, 1937, para. 56.

leading men in each local community', but goes on then to write of the distinctive identity and authority of Egbo. 'Egbo, not a general assembly of lineage elders, was the body that made the laws . . . Egbo again was the supreme judicial authority. . . .' (op. cit., pp. 140–141). Nevertheless, a close reading of Hope Waddell's account of the law made in 1850 to abolish human sacrifices at the death of a chief (which G. I. Jones cites as an example of Egbo's supreme authority) suggests that it was the representatives of the independent communities *by virtue of this status* who agreed to this law, giving it *then* the sanction of announcing it formally through the association. After an account of preliminary negotiations initiated by Mr Anderson, a missionary, involving 'Archibong ['king' of Duke Town], Duke Ephraim, and the other native rulers [presumably of Duke Town]', 'the river gentlemen' (i.e. the European traders), and 'King Eyo and his counsellors' (of Creek Town), Hope Waddell continues:

On the 12th February that important meeting, of all native authorities of the two towns with the Europeans, was held, and, after much discussion of the great question under consideration, the two kings and twenty-six of their principal men signed an engagement to abolish for ever, by Egbo law, the practice of human sacrifice in Old Calabar. Three days after that meeting the law was proclaimed, with all due solemnities, in Duke Town by a procession of Creek Town Egbos, and in Creek Town, the day after, by a similar procession from Duke Town. Thus the two towns became guardians of each other, and guarantees for the observance of their engagement (op. cit., p. 422).

This passage suggests that collective political action of a circumstantial kind was agreed to by the representatives of independent communities and that this collective decision was then sanctioned by joint announcement through their various 'Egbo' lodges, the common values of the association allowing for the reciprocal action whereby each main community (Duke Town and Creek Town) promulgated the law in the other's settlement and held thus a watching brief over its observance there.[1] The fact that 'Egbo' was not a superordinate authority but served rather to support the independent authority of each community's own representatives is shown by an incident which followed the joint proclamation of

[1] Goldie, in *Calabar and its Mission*, records that it was 'the custom in weighty affairs' for this reciprocal proclamation of an 'Egbo law' by the two communities to occur. We may note, too, Hope Waddell's use of the plural when referring to 'Creek Town Egbos', implying the participation of more than one lodge.

this law. Thus it became known that at Old Town (a minor community, loosely associated with the two main communities of Duke Town and Creek Town but formally independent of them), a number of killings had occurred in violation of the law. Hope Waddell writes:

> When Captain R——, our president,[1] told King Eyo about the Old Town murders, we learned with astonishment that the Egbo law was not in force there, not having been proclaimed. Its chief, Willy Tom Robins, being at his farm for a long time, had not been consulted, and, of course, had not consented; and without his consent the law could not take effect there. *Otu George*, his second, the very man suspected of having made the sacrifices, had declared that the law did not reach him, and he could still do as he pleased. That seemed a very extraordinary state of matters; and we all felt not a little indignant that Old Town should have been exempted from the operation of the law, which was designed to reach the whole country. King Eyo pleaded that he could not control the affairs of that town, as its chief was independent. *Any usurpation of his authority would be a violation of Egbo principles, and be repelled by Egbo penalties.* Willy Tom and his chiefs must consent before Egbo could be sent to their town with the law (op. cit., p. 423, my italics).

This latter case, including what Hope Waddell reports of King Eyo's statement, exemplifies what I take to be the essential nature of the Ekpe (or Ngbe, or 'Egbo') polity. The association, by its reduplication of lodges in different communities, provided the common forms by which joint action could take place; it expressed common values (the need above all to respect the community's authority) which each community could accept and would support; but at the same time it allowed for the continued independence of each community with its own separate authority.

The Ekpe polity nevertheless and within the terms described above showed some flexibility, operating somewhat differently in the different areas of its dominance. As we have seen above, it became in Calabar the means by which otherwise independent communities could act jointly in matters affecting their common interest (and since almost all were trading communities, the conditions of trade and their relationship to the traders occupied a central position in this interest). Again, in Calabar, Ekpe

---

[1] The missionaries and the 'river gentlemen' had formed themselves into a 'Society' to watch over the operation of the law they had collectively pressed for. It would seem that they had not only entered into the local political system but had been 'acculturated' by its forms.

appears to have been turned to a special problem that threatened those of established status: the protection of the rights of the free-born *vis-à-vis* the large class of subservient 'slaves'. Both Professor Dike and G. I. Jones have shown how the clash of interests between these two classes was expressed through the formation of another association, the 'Blood Men', which sought to assert the rights of the 'slaves' in the face of the oppression that 'Egbo' until 1850 served to enforce.[1] Away from Calabar the common possession of Ekpe lodges by different communities was politically important rather as a means by which individual rights could be transferred from one community to another, so that a person passing between communities was given some protection. We have already noted the relevance of association membership in this respect to the trading network centred on Calabar.[2] In some cases the Ekpe lodges of individual villages made laws preventing the molestation of traders.[3]

To return to the place of Banyang within this wider polity. The most notable difference in the organization of the association as it is found in Banyang as against Ejagham communities is its greater fragmentation in the former – the fact that its lodges are owned by smaller residential units, that fewer sections are incorporated in a lodge, that the forms of the association are less clearly followed or indeed known about. I have already tried to relate this difference to the difference in politico-residential grouping between the two peoples: the nucleated village settlements of the central Ejagham, each with its unitary, highly organized association-lodge based upon a single, central 'palaver-house' contrasts with the traditionally dispersed, small settlements of Banyang, each settlement with its variable 'bottom house' or *aca*, but none so large or impressive as one of the Ekoi 'palaver-houses'. This difference in organization can be further related to a difference in process, arising from the greater degree of competitive factionalism in Banyang politics.

I start again with the point that Ngbe is not itself vested with authority but acquires its authority, which it serves to formalize, from its members who are the effective representatives and leaders of a residential group. A small residential group seeking to consolidate its status will wish to acquire its own lodge of the association, both for its prestige and for the formal Ngbe sanctions thus made independently accessible to the group. As we

[1] *Trade and Politics in the Niger Delta 1830–1885*, pp. 156 et seq.; G. I. Jones, op. cit., pp. 148–157.
[2] Page 250 above and footnote, citing references.
[3] For example, by 'Keaka and Ekwe villages along the main trading routes' (Swabey, op. cit., para. 57).

have seen, the purchase of a lodge proceeds automatically; as a matter of courtesy the village leader may be informed, but in order to purchase the association the residential group acquiring the lodge does not formally require the permission of the wider community of which it is part, and the purchase itself is often made from an entirely different village group. In slightly different circumstances – where two or three small residential groups (hamlets or settlements) have combined to purchase a common lodge – this may later be divided between them when they desire some independence of action, each group then setting up its own lodge. The lodge distribution of Ngbe in Banyang country tends therefore to follow the lowest order of residential grouping operating in a political context as an independent community (usually a hamlet but occasionally a section of a village or a sub-village if the village is small). The correspondence, however, is not fixed or formal, and very frequently recent acquisition of a lodge gives some informal indication of a move towards independence of the group concerned.[1]

While the constitution of Ngbe allows this reduplication of lodges, it provides also for common action should the members of separate lodges wish to undertake it. The pattern here is very similar to that which apparently existed in Old Calabar in 1850. Each lodge has separate access to its own formal Ngbe sanctions; in accord with the basic political principle of autonomous rule, these sanctions can be applied only *within* the residential group associated with the lodge, or only with the agreement of that group's representatives; if the representatives of a number of residential groups (usually hamlets of a village, but it may be villages of village group, and it can be a wide series of *ad hoc* groupings) agree to common political action (usually the enactment of a law), such action can still be promulgated through Ngbe, despite the fact that different lodges are involved. Either the law will be announced by a single emissary, jointly commissioned (as, for example, occurred in the Bara case described above, p. 238) or it will be agreed to announce the law separately by each lodge or set of lodges in their own residential group. If such a jointly promulgated law is violated and a case brought against the offender, the consequent fine should be divided according to the lodges involved and represented at the hearing. This expansion and contraction of

[1] For examples of the distribution of lodges, see above. It may be noted how the polarity of Bara village politics is clearly represented in the two lodges there; also how acquisition of further lodge sections in the Tali settlements considered on pp. 37 and 41 was associated with their leaders' attempt to improve their own status and that of their residential groups. In Besongabang village the most newly acquired lodge belongs to Ayok Mbi Awo, the seventh and most recently recognized of the village sections (cf. p. 92).

Ngbe as a sanctioning agent was well illustrated by two cases which occurred in Tali in 1954:

In one of these an Ngbe law was made in Mpomba, protecting ripe palm-nuts from being collected by someone who did not own the tree. In another case in Talinchang the Ngbe sign had improperly been put upon some plantains. In both cases, when the offenders had been found, Ngbe representatives from the wider village were called to help in the hearing and to lend weight to the verdict, which they did in return for a share of the fine.

There are very few occasions when lodges can come into competition with each other, and when this does happen it means that the interests of the members of the lodge have overridden their formal rights and obligations according to the association. The underlying principles determining the relationship between lodges are, firstly, respect for another lodge's autonomous authority, and, secondly, within a lodge's own sphere of authority, the acceptance by that lodge of the status and rights of any Ngbe member, whatever the lodge in which these were acquired. According to the first principle, Ngbe members should never act so as to detract from the authoritative action of another lodge (e.g. by harbouring an offender formally ostracized, by repeating information that could be construed against another lodge). The second principle needs no example. Both these principles of action operate reciprocally between lodges, and it is perhaps this more than anything else which safeguards them. The only case of which I have record of a dispute between lodges (when the lodge of one village sought to protect its boundary with another village by placing the Ngbe sign on it) was resolved by a joint meeting of the lodges concerned.

I have tried to show how the factional nature of Banyang politics and political grouping is taken up and expressed through the lodge organization of Ngbe. Much of the strength of the association lies in the accommodation that it gives to this diversity of local interests while at the same time offering a set of common values and procedural forms that allow the unity of occasional joint action, or of limited reciprocal recognition of political rights. Yet if this is the strength of Ngbe as a polity it is also its weakness. The factionalism which allows for the acquisition of different lodges of the *same* association also opens the way to the purchase by competing residential groups of lodges of *different* associations. The factional emulation of residential groups at the lowest level of Banyang political organization here underlies the competition between associations as polities within the society as a whole.

Inevitably it is difficult to document this process, yet all the evidence points to a history of the rise and fall of associations: this history Banyang share with other peoples of this general area politically organized into small autonomous communities.[1] It is impossible to make any valid comparison concerning the rate of change for these associations, especially as Ngbe itself did not reach Banyang country until the turn of the last century. Among Upper Banyang and in Tali the politically dominant association at the end of the last century was probably Tui, and before that it had been Nkang and Nsime. None of these, however, had been as universal as Ngbe was to become; nor were they, Banyang say, as effective as instruments of government.

As Ngbe replaced these earlier associations, so for a brief period in the 1950s a new form of association, the Clan Unions, spread rapidly through Banyang country and seemed to provide the effective answer to their political problems. It is to these associations that we now turn. If Ngbe is to be seen against the traditional political structure and sources of authority of Banyang society, the Clan Unions and other 'modern' associations like them must be seen against the changed forms of political grouping and the divided sources of authority that characterized the Colonial period.

[1] E.g. Yakö, Mbembe, Ibibio, and others. The obvious contrast is with West African peoples whose associations have shown a marked stability – the Mende *Poro* or the Yoruba *Ogboni* – whose political organization is more centralized. The stability of Ekpe among the Ejagham and Efik may appear to be an exception but, as I have tried to indicate, sectional change of an 'axe-head-and-handle' kind did occur for Ekpe. Talbot is quite explicit about the proliferation of other associations for the Ejagham (*In the Shadow of the Bush*, p. 48).

I I

Modern Associations and the Clan Unions

Modern associations

The 'modern' associations are characterized not so much by the fact that their introduction and spread are recent (which is true both of Ngbe and Basinjom) but by a form or purpose which shows some adaptation of the traditional pattern of the association to meet specifically modern conditions. They are as varied as the traditional associations.

In the 1930s an association which had a considerable success and spread rapidly through a large number of Banyang villages had the English name 'Band'. In purpose recreational, its members bought and played European instruments to put on a public dance. At the same time it had an elaborate constitution according to association principles: a series of offices, fees for membership, procedures to be followed by members, an elaborate set of rules punishable by fine by the collective group. A missionary report of the time describes how its outwardly modern appearance (' "There is nothing harmful in it," we were told. "Everything is from you Europeans." ') belied an organization which retained all the laws and proscriptions of the old 'secret societies'.[1] A plethora of young men's associations had been formed by the 1950s and included then among Upper Banyang such names as Ekan, Young Seven, Sɛmɔ Sɛngɔ (lit. 'let us try and see'), and Ɛjɛnsi (properly 'Agency', but with an accent on its second syllable: the formal greeting on entering a meeting was Ɛjɛnsi! Ɛjɛnsi! – response: Transport!). Various 'Town Councils', a 'Chiefs' Council', and 'Women's Councils' had been formed. Thus in 1964 I met in session the 'Town Men's Council' of Atebong, which had as its members the leading men of the village (the 'Quarter Heads' of all the village sections)

---

[1] Jahresbericht 1937 von Rev. E. Peyer, Fotabe, p. 2871, X/1. Archives of the Basel Mission, Basel. I am grateful to the Rev. A. Trub for this reference. Accounts of 'Band' were also given to me in Tali and Bara.

who met to drink wine provided in turn, and to discuss issues of importance to the village; these might then be presented later to an open meeting.
Held in the large *acɔ*-type house of the village chief, the meeting was closed
to outsiders: the emblem of the group and a sign of its being in session was
'the horn of the community', *mbaŋ ɛtɔk*, an old carved ivory tusk; this,
together with the (English) name of the association, was depicted on the
banner placed outside the meeting-house.[1] We shall return later to
comparable groups elsewhere. In the remainder of this section I describe
two modern associations of Tali to illustrate how such associations develop
circumstantially to meet new needs but nevertheless retain in their form
and operation certain of the essential traditional features.

The Tali 'Bank' or 'Meeting' was started in 1951 by two returned
migrants who for this purpose had adapted the idea of a reciprocal
lending or contribution club which they had experienced in the south.[2]
The aim of the Meeting was to collect and save money, the money
saved being used to provide loans on interest; all the money saved,
together with proportionate interest earned, was returned to the
original contributors at the end of the year, before Christmas. A secondary aim was to help a member in difficulty, especially serious illness,
and to this end all members were required to contribute 1*d.* per week
towards a special 'Trouble Bank'. Apart from this, the amount members
could deposit with the Meeting was not stipulated: the more a member
paid in, the higher his eventual return in interest.

In its first full year of operation (1952) it obtained only a few members
and was treated with caution. By 1953 suspicions were quieted and in
Tali 1 it gained a very large measure of support: a total of £527 was
then collected and paid out. Also in that year various imitation 'Meetings'
were established in separate small sections of Tali 1 (Baimberi's settlement, Peter Esong's section of Kembong, for the 'strangers' in Tanyi
Tabe) and in Tali 2.

The regular Sunday meetings of the main Meeting had only partially

[1] The 'sign' element of this group was extraordinarily heterogeneous. The 'horn of the
community' was straight from the past (cf. above, pp. 59–60); the modern-sounding name
'Town Men's Council' translates into English exactly what its members would be called
in Kenyang (*ako bo ɛtɔk* where *bo ɛtɔk* = 'people of the community' in the sense of those who
collectively hold authority in a community, cf. pp. 69 and 134); finally, and in accord with
the modern village constitution, its section representatives (properly lineage heads or minor
leaders) were spoken of as 'Quarter Heads', *bɔ kwɔtahɛd*.
[2] For a description of such clubs, see Shirley G. Ardener, 'The Social and Economic Significance of the Contribution Club among a Section of the Southern Ibo' *WAISER Conference
Proceedings*, Sociology Section, 1953.

the form of an association. The main business was taken up with the collection of subscriptions (pennies for the Trouble Bank) and deposits. The dɛnkwɔ, yellow palm-leaf, was used to exclude non-members, and the senior men who participated used their own authority to keep the peace and prevent disturbance: at the final, paying-out session, strict rules to prevent disturbance were imposed. Behind the general session, however, there was a smaller inner 'Committee' which was organized on association lines: drawing its members from those who were primarily responsible for running the main meeting, it met privately, had its own emblems (a banner bearing the words 'Committee Friendly Society No Entrance'), its procedures, officers, and rules, infraction of which was punishable by fine. Serving partly to prearrange and regulate the activities of the main Meeting, the group-also served as a social club; food and spirits were provided by its members in turn. Much of the success of the wider meeting (with its substantial bank and elaborate accounting) depended upon the direction, confidence, and means of checking that came ultimately from this inner group. At the end of 1953, after its successful year's running, the inner 'Committee' reconstituted itself even more elaborately, with specific fees for membership and further rules to exclude strangers.

Finally, certain of the political implications of this group should be noted, since one of its two leading members was a man who, after a long time working away from home, was concerned to build up his status within the home community and belonged to what might be described as the opposition faction in the central settlement of Tali 1. It was in this section of the composite settlement that all meetings were held and although other 'established' members of the settlement took part in the main meetings, almost all the members of its inner 'Committee' were drawn from this group. The imitative spread of this form of modern association also draws attention to certain of the political alignments and pretensions then in existence in Tali: the isolation of Peter Esong and his followers; the attempts of Baimberi to enhance his status and develop his settlement; the split between Tali 1 and Tali 2.

Ɛkan, a young men's association, was first formed in Tali in 1952. In Chapter 9 we spoke of the disappearance in Upper Banyang villages of earlier forms of age-organization owing to the absence of many of the young men (p. 209) and the taking-over of some of the functions of the earlier age-groups by young men's associations, which have become very popular in Banyang villages. Through their representation of a wider age-section of the community there has been a tendency, however, for these young men's associations to come into conflict with those representing older and more established community interests.

The name *Ɛkan* is Ejagham (where it means 'age-group') but the form of the Tali Ekan probably owed more to young men's associations already in existence in Lower Banyang villages. It was nevertheless formed independently by the young men of Tali 1 and not 'bought'. As always, it included a large recreational element, but in its early days served also to organize work-parties and later developed as a channel by which suggestions and grievances could be put to the Ndifaw Clan Union. While it operated thus in a modern context, its form and procedures followed traditional patterns very closely. It had its own officers, formal procedures, punishable rules. Its members were divided into three categories, each with their appropriate place in the meeting-house, which was closed to outsiders. Membership fees were payable according to the category and office entered. A smaller inner group (also termed a 'Committee') was formed from the leading members of the main association and served to regulate its main activities. There were interminable discussions at the main meetings over the forms to be observed and the rules to be made. One's impression nevertheless was of an ultimately genuine attempt to exert control over members by the association and to express their legitimate interests and views to the older, established leaders of community opinion. The following list of rules was confirmed at a meeting held in October 1953.

- Members should not steal from or abuse their parents.
- Members must not leave the meeting 'under their own power' or in anger.
- Members must not be familiar with others' wives. (This covers both adultery and such private encounters as may lead to adultery.)
- Members must obey an order before complaining about it.
- If work is done by Ekan then some money must be put into the bank.
- Members must not speak against Ekan either inside or outside the meeting.
- No member must be 'proud' with the meeting or flaunt his money.
- A member must not ask another 'Who are you?' (*W'ɔci ara?* – a question implying abuse.)
- Meat must be divided in the presence of all members.

Most of these rules were given stipulated fines, and there were minor rules concerning conduct at a meeting. We shall return later to the way in which the association, together with the young men's associations of the other villages of the village group, presented their views to the Ndifaw Clan Union.

Clan Unions[1]

Clan Unions were first formed by some Lower Banyang village groups in the late 1940s, the initial idea apparently being derived from the Mamfe Town Union which was set up at this time by S. A. George, a Manyang migrant who had spent many years working in Lagos and who on his return to Mamfe constituted this association on the model of the tribal unions he had observed there. The Mamfe Town Union was centred in Mamfe town itself but it drew its main membership from migrants outside the Division. Like the tribal unions of the urban areas, it was intended as a mutual aid society and was also concerned with the development of the Mamfe area. At about the same time that the Mamfe Town Union was founded, and probably stimulated by it, some of the village groups in the immediate neighbourhood of Mamfe started their own Clan Unions, also initially concerned with general aims of development in each of their own village groups. The movement was successful and rapidly spread by imitation to other areas. By 1953, when I first arrived in Banyang country, most of the village groups in the area away from Mamfe had either already organized their Unions or were in the throes of doing so.

Thus, in January of that year, the Ndifaw village group called a meeting of the leaders and section heads of the three villages of (the rump) Tali (the Tali dispute was still at issue and 'Tali 2' did not take part), Ebeagwa, and Ejwengang, in order to organize the Ndifaw Clan Union.[2] There was some discussion as to the form of the Union: what offices should be created and who would fill them; what laws should be enacted. But the

[1] I speak throughout of 'Clan Unions' although they were not always known by this name. The English term was frequently used ('clan' had already become familiar by administrative usage) but in Kenyang they were usually referred to by the term *ncemti*. Tanyi Nkongo referred to itself as a 'Clan Federation' (see Appendix A): I speak of it here, however, as a 'Clan Union', reserving the term Federation for the union of Unions effected by three Upper Banyang village groups.
[2] I describe in some detail the history and structure of the Ndifaw Clan Union since this was the one most closely known to me. Other Upper Banyang Clan Unions were very similar in their general form, aims, and activities. Lower Banyang Unions (which were the first established) had the same general form but on the whole became less actively concerned with the issue of migrant prostitutes.

meeting was broken up by a fight which took place between the young men of Ebeagwa and Ejwengang over a dispute which the meeting was called upon to settle but was unable to. After this, it was not until September that a fresh meeting was called, this time in Ebeagwa, and the Union finally got under way.

Perhaps the most significant feature of the Union was that all members of the village group were regarded as members of it. It therefore formed a means by which the leading representatives of the village group re-organized themselves in order to achieve closer political unity and thus a more effective pursuit of their common aims. In its constitution the Union, like many other associations, operated on two levels: there was, firstly, the general assembly, which was open to all members of the village group but from which outsiders were debarred, and which initially met in monthly rotation at the three villages taking part; secondly there were the more exclusive village 'Committees' or 'Councils', from among whose members was elected a further 'Executive Committee' to act for the village group as a whole. Each village had its own officers (President, Banker, Secretary, Messenger, Spokesman, each with an Assistant, except the last) and these, together with formal representatives from the various village sections, made up the village Committee.[1] The village Committees discussed issues which were to be taken to the general meeting, or to the overall Executive Committee, which at first met immediately prior to the general assembly (again, primarily to decide its agenda) but later met instead of the entire Union, when monthly general meetings had become too cumbersome. Whereas the assembly was an open, public meeting (at least for members of the village group), both village Committee meetings and the central meeting of the Executive Committee were held in private, as 'closed' or exclusive bodies. For the Executive Committee in particular a number of formalities were established, including the use of a ship's bell, which became the emblem of the group and was rung on formal occasions at the entry or departure of a member or to presage an important statement.[2] A monthly subscription was levied at the rate of £2 per village, which was raised within the villages themselves, either on a head-to-head basis or by village sections: it was collected and held by the Banker in whose village the meeting

[1] In the case of the rump Tali, Peter Esong had first been appointed President but was then withdrawn after he had been removed from the inner council. (His appointment was also attacked by the young men.) His place as President was taken by Joseph Enaw; Nyenti was Assistant President. Mr Tataw was Banker.

[2] Ships' bells have a wide dispersal in the hinterland of Calabar and seem to have become assimilated to the formalities of associational usage early on.

took place, each village Banker thus receiving £6 in three-monthly rotation. In this respect we may note that while the Union (and village group) were represented singly by two *bodies* – the main assembly and more exclusive Executive Committee – it was not represented singly by one *office*: each village had its own set of officers, who acted jointly but on equal terms.[1] Normally at a general meeting the officers of the same status – the three Presidents, Bankers, Secretaries – sat together and, in relation to the meeting, shared a common role, occasionally and if necessary the most senior taking precedence.

The Tali Secretary recorded the Union's aims as follows:

– for Social Unity.
– to lead other clans to realize the importance of unity.
– for the improvement of Education in helping to train boys in Colleges.
– for the extermination of prostitutes.

A slightly different version of the Union's aims was recorded by the Ebeagwa Secretary (Appendix A) who again stresses the need to promote village group (or 'clan') unity, but who sees the political function of the Union more in relation to the Colonial administration. The Union is thus intended (Aim 2):

– to provide a channel through which all matters affecting the clan can be presented constitutionally to the Government;

and while fostering the spirit of unity *within* the village group it is also meant to promote '... sympathy and understanding between Government and the Clan as a whole' (Aim 3). The two final aims are added:

– 4. To strengthen the financial background of the clan.
– 5. To settle disputes, other than criminal, arising between members of the clan.

As is so often the case with Banyang associations, many of the activities of the Union were concerned with establishing what form it would take or with dealing with disputes its very existence tended to throw up. There were endless discussions regarding constitution and procedure, and the usual series of laws were made on this score. Other laws were made to exclude strangers from the meeting (fine £5), to prohibit *bɛnaŋ*, 'double-dealing' or 'back-biting', between members of the village group (fine £5), to prevent fighting at a meeting (£3 fine for the person who starts it), to punish adultery between a member and another's wife (fine £1). A number of general issues came up for discussion: help to be given to

[1] Cf. the dispute which made abortive the first meeting of the three-village group Federation, which was on this issue, pp. 269–271 below.

265

members if they fell sick away from home; the regulation of prices of goods sold in the village group; possible scholarships for the education of children. On all of these issues difficulties arose; little effectively came out of the discussions and the matter was allowed to drop. The issue of the Tali split loomed large in the progress of the Union, which became involved in the strategy of the two sides and their allies.[1] The diffuse aim of helping in the development of the village group, which was certainly present in the Union's formation, rarely gave rise to a viable project: thus, characteristically, everyone supported the usefulness of creating a 'bank' or common fund, but agreement was never forthcoming on how this money could be used. (For example, the possibility of educational scholarships, which was championed by the Tali Secretary, did not obtain the support of the older men, who did not see how this would give them any return for their money.) Never called upon, this money eventually gave rise to the discord which broke up the Union.

The one issue on which agreement was forthcoming and which gave the Union its 'teeth' concerned the 'prostitutes': migrant women who had left the village group for the plantations and urban areas of the south and who in doing so had walked out of the complex set of rights and monetary arrangements that depended upon their due fulfilment of their roles as wives and daughters. There was considerable bitterness felt against these women, in part rationalized in the accusation that they were thus diminishing the future numbers of children that could be born into the home society.

From its inception a number of laws were passed against prostitutes who were temporarily in their home village – those who, perhaps, had returned to visit relatives, often to carry out the second funeral celebration which is incumbent on close kin. They were debarred from attending any Union functions, including the dance which accompanied its general meeting. They were forbidden to wear certain types of dress, shoes, hats, or to carry umbrellas. They were prevented from organizing a funeral celebration. Most of these laws carried a fine of £5. These laws made by the Ndifaw Clan Union were similar to those already made by Clan Unions of other neighbouring village groups. They could apply, however, only to the home area. The issue was debated in the Banyang Council Native Authority throughout the latter part of 1953 and it was agreed that five village leaders from different village groups should go, with the backing of their Clan Unions, to the main areas of the south in which the prostitutes were then living, in an attempt to repatriate them. There they

[1] See the incident described above, pp. 175–178; also Chapter 13.

collected about two hundred women, put them on lorries, and so brought them back to their home village groups. At home the women were put in charge of their own lineage kinsfolk who were made responsible to the Union for their behaviour. Between thirty and forty women were re-patriated in this way to the Ndifaw village group. New laws were now passed preventing them from leaving the village-group area, except by special permission of the Union; and at one of its general meetings these women were called and admonished, being told of their duty to return to their true role as wives and mothers.

In its initial phases this campaign by the Clan Unions to deal with the problem of the prostitutes was very largely successful. Many, if not all, had been brought home, and the various pressures exerted on them persuaded some to enter marriage again, when the disabilities of their status as prostitutes were formally removed. It was at the height of this campaign and spurred by their common interests in the matter that the Clan Unions of three neighbouring village groups among the Upper Banyang united to form a Clan Federation which we describe below (pp. 269–271).

We have seen that one of the aims of the Ndifaw Union, recorded by a village secretary, was that it should provide a channel of communication between the village group and the Government. This aim in the case of the Ndifaw Union did not give rise to any very effective action[1] but it was nevertheless felt desirable that 'official' sanction should be given by the administration to the Unions' activities. The expedition by the village leaders had already the backing of the Banyang Native Authority. This party of village leaders were also careful to work through the (European) administration, and received supporting letters from the District Officer, Mamfe, to the D.O.s in Kumba and Victoria Divisions. The attitude of the administration was, however, later to change and instead of sanction-ing – somewhat neutrally – the village leaders' activities, all active support was withdrawn from them. (The District Officer, Mamfe, had himself changed in the meantime and the new District Officer took the view that this large-scale operation against the prostitutes was an infringement of basic liberties.) The Clan Unions were left to carry on their campaign as best they could, without administration backing.

The withdrawal of formal administrative sanction, together with the

---

[1] An attempt was made to 'register' the Union by writing to the Federal Government offices at Lagos, who informed them however that such registration was unnecessary. In the case of the Clan Federation an attempt was made to involve the Colonial administration more directly.

fact that the Unions by now were rather overplaying their hand, led to the eventual foundering of the campaign. Some of the women who had been given permission to return to the south to get their belongings and settle their affairs failed to return home. A second and more extensive expedition that took in Duala met with only partial success: it was reported that in one place the prostitutes, now forewarned, jeered the party of village leaders off. In the home villages there were recriminations against some leaders who had accepted bribes and against those who had failed, it was claimed, to repatriate their own erring kinswomen. In any event, by the end of 1954 and in 1955 those women who had been brought back to their home villages were steadily escaping back to the south, many of them being smuggled across the border which then existed between the French and British Cameroons. By 1955, although the discussions concerning the problem still continued, the effectiveness of the Clan Unions' sanctions against the prostitutes had become minimal.

In a minor way the Ndifaw Clan Union also ran into difficulties over its relation to the young men's associations of the village group. We have referred to the fight between the young men of two villages at the formation of the Union: this arose over who would supply the music for the public dance after the meeting – the 'Band' of Ebeagwa claimed to have been officially asked, but this was disputed by the young men's association of Ejwengang, who in this respect were led by the young village leader, who was also one of the main originators of the Union. On this as on other occasions the young men of the village group took the Union meeting as an opportunity for their own social gathering and celebration. Despite the initial conflict, the young men's associations later took the opportunity when the Union finally got under way to hold their own meetings at the time of the Union meeting, although separately from the main assembly. Proposals connected with the prostitutes or on such matters as the enforcement of pit-latrines were regularly put by them to the general assembly. They also claimed the right to separate representation in the village Committees and ultimately in the general Executive Committee. Eventually, however, their arrogation of authority and separate rights to themselves aroused the hostility of the established representatives and leaders of the village group. There was always much talk at general meetings of the Union that here was represented the entire village group, that the meeting embodied the full, undivided authority of the community, the ɛtɔk. At the same time the young men's associations were claiming that they too represented the community (individually the villages, conjointly the village group): the term ɛtɔk was bandied also in their own meetings. The question was eventually put: can the *ɛtɔk* sit in two places? If the Clan Union represented the community could the young men's associations do so as well? The threat was then made of outlawing the young men's associations by making an Ngbe law against them. This threat seems to have been sufficient to curb their more extreme claims, and while the relationship continued to be uneasy it never gave rise to open conflict.

By 1956 the Ndifaw Clan Union had passed into rapid decline. In common with other Upper Banyang Clan Unions, its action against the absconding women of the village group had proved ineffective. On no other important practical issue was agreement reached. Village group 'development' was an elusive ideal. Initially involved in the strategy over the Tali dispute, the non-Tali members of the Union found that with the settlement of this dispute, the combined Tali 1 and 2 now dominated its affairs and were in any case represented in a new association, the 'Chiefs' Council' (see Chapter 13). Finally the suspicion arose that the Union's funds were being put to private use by the Bankers, and it was ultimately because of a dispute over this issue that the Union broke up. When I returned to Banyang country in 1958 the Ndifaw Clan Union had been disbanded and, as far as I was able to ascertain, the Clan Unions of other neighbouring village groups were also moribund or defunct. In the two villages where I had worked – Tali and Bara – a new interest had arisen instead in the traditional Ngbe association, of which three lodges had had sections added to them and one lodge had been newly acquired.

The Ncɛmti Federation

A further development of the Union form occurred in the latter part of 1953 with the formation of a Federation comprising the three Clan Unions of Tanyi Nkongo, Nkokenok II, and Tayong village groups. These Unions were then collaborating in the matter of collecting prostitutes from the south. The suggestion now was that a more formal Federation should be constituted, to be called the '*Ncɛmti* Federation', to further the course of development for these, somewhat isolated, village groups. It is significant that the political grouping so created went beyond the largest political groupings of the traditional society (the village groups). Much of the initiative for the Federation came from the village leader of Takwa (a prominent member of the Banyang Native Authority and active in the representation of Upper Banyang affairs) and it was in Takwa that a large inaugural meeting took place in December 1953. The following account is concerned with this one meeting.

269

Before its assembly, a series of laws had been made governing the meeting, with the usual fines for fighting, abuse, failing to obey the meeting's ruling, philandering with wives, for strangers entering the meeting, and so on. At the opening of the meeting the precaution was taken of carrying a cult-agency (*Kɛkaŋ*) around it, invoking misfortune upon anyone who attempted to do evil while the meeting was in session; a second cult-agency (*Ɛkongaŋ*) had been prepared and was fixed in the centre of the area in which people assembled; this also was addressed at the opening of the meeting. The Agenda had been prepared for the meeting by the village leaders of Takwa and consisted of the following topics:

Improvement of the Road
Request for a Primary School
By-laws of the Union
Development of the Area
Proposals for a new market
Registration of the Union

The first hours were taken up, however, with settling cases which had arisen because of the meeting itself. Two fights had broken out (one a large one involving the representatives of two villages); a man's wife had gone off with another man; a drum had been broken; the Secretary of one of the Unions was accused of withholding a case, having been bribed. Judgement of these cases (which was given in the name of the *ɛtɔk*, the 'community' there represented) took up most of the morning. The main agenda then was proposed. At this point, however, a representative from the Tayong Union stood up to ask why the leader of Takwa had signed himself as 'Acting President' in the letter giving notice of the meeting. (This letter had been circulated to the participating Clan Unions and also the Native Authority, the District Officer, and myself.) The Federation had as yet no President; who had nominated the leader of Takwa? This gave rise to an extremely long and heated discussion. Finally, the village leader agreed to give written apologies to the two village group Unions other than his own, which he did. He was then asked to send similar written apologies to the Native Authority and District Officer; the representatives of the two other village groups threatened not to continue with the meeting unless this was done. The village leader refused. The meeting therefore came to a halt, and it was adjourned for 'refreshment'. (Vast quantities of palm-wine had in fact been prepared for the meeting.)

Further negotiations then continued 'behind'. Finally, on the basis of an agreement reached there, the meeting was recalled at nine o'clock in the evening; (it had started originally at about 9 a.m. and had adjourned at 3 p.m.). The difference in temper was very apparent. In seating arrangements, for example, all three Clan Unions now made separate, self-enclosed groups with their members standing up in the middle to address their own circle as much as the general meeting, whereas in the morning the Unions had combined at their respective levels – officers sitting together, senior men together, and the remainder as general spectators. Composed thus of what were virtually three separate discussion groups, the meeting now developed into a kind of warfare by discussion. The items of the agenda were taken point by point but in each case parochial interests arose, each village group insisting upon its own needs. If the Tali road was to be extended into Tanyi Nkongo village group, then Tayong demanded their own road to connect with the Mamfe–Bamenda road. Villages away from the road refused to give help in preparing it. The site of the proposed school was similarly disputed: was it wished, it was suggested, to build it along the new road? Some interest came to the meeting, however, with the discussion of its by-laws. In particular the laws against the prostitutes were reiterated and passed. Finally, before the meeting was adjourned to complete its business on the next morning, an eloquent speech was made regarding the aims of the Federation. It was made by the leading representative of Tayong (who were the main cause of the meeting's disintegration) and extolled the virtues of unity: the aim of the Federation was to create unity, for 'Unity is Strength' (*dɛnyukɛti – ci bɛtaŋ*).

On the following morning, which was the day that people were due to disperse, a hurried meeting was held to finish the agenda. Here it was decided that there should be no further general meeting of the Federation. An initial meeting of single representatives from each of the eleven villages involved should first be held to settle an agenda; then a Committee would be formed of eight representatives from each of the three Clan Unions, who would meet three times a year, their meetings rotating round the three village groups. In connection with 'Registration of the Union' it was suggested that the District Officer should be informed of its existence and that copies of its proceedings should be forwarded to him and to the Native Authority. This first meeting did take place, but later nothing was heard concerning the Federation and its activities appeared to be in abeyance.

The form and effectiveness of the Clan Unions

In form the Clan Unions (and Ncɛmti Federation) retained many of the features of the traditional associations: the emphasis on internal solidarity that goes with the closure of the meetings to outsiders and the secrecy concerning discussions; the series of formal 'offices' set in a constitution in which the main body (the Union itself or general assembly) contained within itself more exclusive 'inner' groups (the village Committees and overall Executive Committee) which had their own rules of procedures, insisted upon the formal 'secrecy' of their affairs, and – in the case of the Executive Committee – were even represented emblematically (by the ship's bell) in a way not dissimilar from the formal concrete symbols of the older associations. The members were well aware of this continuity in form with the traditional associations and, while on the one hand they welcomed and wished to incorporate 'modern', Europeanized forms (sometimes one felt for a kind of magical efficacy that was associated with such names as 'Executive Committee', 'President', 'Banker', and the rest), they would on the other and in certain circumstances insist that in its operation and form the Union was still an *ako*. In Tali the Executive Committee was often referred to as *ɛju ɛtɔk* (the 'secret community', a term also describing the 'inner council') and when representatives of the young men's associations were allowed to join these more exclusive groups (the Tali village Committee and later the village group Executive Committee) 'fees' were demanded from them in spirits, palm-wine, and money. One should remember also that while the associative principle may be described as inherent in Banyang society, the actual associations adopted have invariably come from outside Banyang country: the difference then, is, not in the adoption of foreign forms but in the direction from which these forms have been adopted.

In their governmental role the Clan Unions also bear a close similarity with such traditional associations as Ngbe. As Ngbe is described as the *ɛtɔk*, the community, so too were the Clan Unions. Indeed, at the general meetings of the Ndifaw Union, the meeting carried out many of the normal governmental functions of a body representative of the community: in hearing cases brought before it, in general discussion, even on occasion in receiving the tribute of an 'animal of the community', and in validating the succession of a minor leader (pp. 57–58). The leading men of Ndifaw village group when speaking at the Union meetings made much of the fact that the entire village group was represented there, that these meetings indeed contained the whole of *bɔ Ndifɔ*, the whole *ɛtɔk*, with all its solidarity and authority as a group.

Yet here too is probably the most significant difference between the Clan Unions and Ngbe as political institutions. Whereas Ngbe as an association represents the values or *idea* of community authority, the Clan Unions represented actual communities and in themselves embodied the authority of those communities. In one case the constitution of the association, repeated in the organization of many different lodges, establishes the common values and grounds for reciprocating political action that we have termed a 'polity': in the other case the Clan Unions themselves provided a new constitution for the village groups. The indirect, overlapping, symbolic relationship between Ngbe and Banyang politico-residential grouping has given way to a direct and mutually exclusive relationship. Thus *each* village group had its *own* Union and the structure of the Union (each village with its own Committee) corresponds to what we have earlier called the 'constitutional' grouping of the village group. Again, *all* members of the village group were counted as members of the Union, and people from other village groups (whether or not they had their own Union there) were excluded from its meetings. This condition is very different from that of Ngbe membership. With this direct, exclusive representation of the village groups and their authority, the Clan Unions avoided taking on some of the more diffuse social and recreational functions that Ngbe has. The Clan Unions were not recreational clubs but were formed explicitly for a political purpose. For a short time, indeed, the members of Banyang village groups such as Ndifaw, reconstituted themselves politically: the Clan Unions were new, village group constitutions.

Moreover, within these constitutions (since there were a number, although they followed a similar pattern) certain significant changes of emphasis had occurred. Thus it was the largest political groupings that were emphasized: the effort was to consolidate the village groups or 'Clans') as united groups. With the Ncɛmti Federation an even larger (and unique) political grouping emerged. This emphasis given to the largest groupings (strongly contrasting with the generally hamlet-based lodges of Ngbe) can be related to modern conditions in which it is felt that only the largest groups can command the support and resources necessary for development or indeed any political action. At the same time, their relationship to the then Colonial administration was also relevant: the 'Clans' were indeed administrative units, a number of them (as I tried to show in Chapter 4) created by the administration. It is significant that those who helped to establish the Unions were aware of the need to have them formally sanctioned by the Colonial administration, sought where possible directly to involve the local administration, and had visions of the Union acting (in the words of the Ebeagwa Secretary) as 'a channel through which all matters affecting the clan can be presented constitution-ally to the Government'. To this extent the Unions were an attempt to bridge the gap between the two political systems then existing within the Division, each with its own authority, that of the Colonial administra-tion and that of the indigenous communities.

Why finally did the Clan Unions fail? If we put aside the one issue in which they *were* successful, the story is one of too diffuse or too ambitious a series of aims, which when brought down to practical proposals (educa-tional scholarships, even pit-latrines) foundered for want of agreement. The need for general agreement before political action could be taken, coupled with the divisions of interest in the traditional communities, provide one reason for failure.[1] Where the Unions were successful, at least for Upper Banyang and initially, was in the campaign they conducted against the prostitutes. On this score there was no difficulty in obtaining agreement and the sanctions available, of legislation and fine within the home communities, served at first as an effective means of control. When, however, the Clan Union leaders moved outside the sphere of authority of their own communities their relationship with the Colonial administra-tion, holding its own superior authority, was put to the test. The failure to obtain continued administrative support led eventually to the collapse of the campaign. The second reason for the Clan Unions' failure lies then in the constitutional link between the two authorities, the two political systems, which they sought to create: this link simply did not hold, and the village group communities were thrown back upon their own too limited resources, divided as they were by divisions of interest and factional rivalries that could not be put aside for very long in the pursuit of these charters for unity and effective action, visions of a brave new world which needs only the right constitutional code to bring it into existence.

[1] One may compare in this regard the Banyang Clan Unions with the improvement associa-tions described for the Afikpo Ibo. The latter were much more successful in realizing their aims, but represented only sectional interests in the community, largely those of educated young men and similar progressives, whereas the Clan Unions were organized on the basis of 'total' communities and had that much more difficult task in securing agreement (S. Ottenberg, 'Improvement Associations among the Afikpo Ibo,' *Africa*, 1955).

PART IV

Processes of Group Formation

12

Genealogical Growth and the Formation of New Residential Groups

In this and the following chapter I shall examine the regular on-going processes by which new groups (communities or lineage groups) are formed in Banyang society. While I am concerned primarily with how these processes occurred in the traditional society I shall attempt also to show how they have been affected by the changed circumstances of Banyang society during the Colonial period. The main point which I seek to establish in these two chapters is the overriding importance of what I have described as 'constitutional politics', the process by which operationally corporate residential groups seek to obtain formal recognition of their status by the acquisition of an independent (village) leadership. This chapter seeks to show how the interrelationship between descent and residential alignments in time is governed by the growing political autonomy of the residential group (*ɛtɔk*) as such. The following chapter examines, especially in relation to the long-drawn-out Tali dispute, how the constitutional sanction which an effectively autonomous residential group must acquire is the last but sometimes the most difficult task of its development.

Processes of development: the prototypal explanation

As in other societies where descent ties and residential or territorial alignments coexist through all levels of corporate grouping in the society, Banyang are very ready to account for the present organization of groups by a generalized statement of the kind of processes by which groups are formed, processes which include both genealogical or lineage expansion and residential dispersal. Whereas, however, in a classical 'segmentary' society these two processes are normally presented in parallel as part of an even, regularly expanding process of ramifying growth, Banyang tend to depict both processes of genealogical expansion and residential dispersal as an uneven, one-sided movement of secession whereby a newly-established group hives off from a parent stem or place of residence, coming eventually to have a status equal to that of the rump, parental group it has left behind. We shall see also that the explanation of growth by such a process of hiving off tends to assume the interaction and not merely the equivalence of the two principles of grouping; the separation of a residential group as such is likely to be qualified by the continued maintenance of descent ties; the separation of a lineage group from its stem is likely to be affected by the context of residential grouping in which this occurs.

In its simplest versions, the kind of explanation offered runs like this: A man (A) has his own settlement (εtɔk a) and a number of sons (B, C, and D). For D, his eldest son, he marries a number of wives and sends him out to live in his own settlement (εtɔk δ). For C also he marries wives and he too goes out or is sent out by his father to build and live in his own settlement (εtɔk γ). Other sons are less fortunate (B only is shown in the diagram, *Figure 28*) and with fewer wives or dependants continue only to

Figure 28 The paradigmatic process of genealogical expansion and residential secession

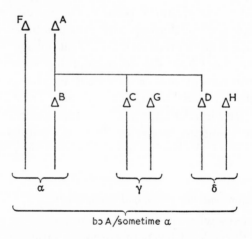

occupy the settlement that their father established: they help to perpetuate its existence but do not change or add to its identity.

Offered thus in its simplest and briefest form, this account can be elaborated in a number of ways. Firstly, the inequality in the status achieved by the sons is a fact well recognized and commonly attested to by present circumstances. One man may have many wives and children who all survive and who are thus distinguished by the name of their common ancestor. Another man who leaves few survivors will not be remembered by name, his children being merged in the wider group he himself belonged to. It is well recognized that not all men achieve the distinction of founding a group known by their own name. Secondly, it can be made explicit that the descent line that is here being described is closely associated with the status of leadership: A is a 'leader' (mfɔ) in his own settlement; C and D both become leaders of their newly founded settlements. Thus, thirdly, we may add a feature as well recognized and as general as the first: this is the attachment of 'followers' to persons of some standing who in return for protection and help are willing to subordinate themselves and their individual interests to the 'leader' who represents them, who 'stands in front'. For consistency, such 'attached' persons are shown for A (F), C (G), and D (H). Although no actual link is shown (the most significant fact is their bond of common interest evidenced by residential association) a wide variety of links are possible here: close or distant agnation, a matrilateral connection, simple protection of a stranger.

Such a 'model' of how new groups are formed (*Figure 28*) is drawn from what Banyang themselves say and is used by them to account for the organization of residential groups at all levels of corporate grouping: the processes of change occurring at the level of the smallest settlement are merely extended in scale and continued in time to account for the present constitution of a village group. On the basis of this diagram – the 'proto-typal explanation' – three separate features of on-going group formation may be distinguished.

1. The 'dominant' or organizing descent line. This is the line established by the effective founder (it may not always be the earliest ancestor) of the widest group of people continuing to recognize a common political solidarity. This line may be indefinitely extended or unevenly ramified, but it is always maintained and provides the point of reference ultimately linking all members of the largest continuing corporate group, which has the character both of an ɛtɔk and nɛrɛkɛt, a community and a descent group.

2. The formation by secession of new residential groups (bɛtɔk, settlements or communities) which come to acquire equality of status with the parental group from which they have seceded. We shall find that the founding leaders of such separated groups are frequently remembered as 'sons' (including a high proportion of 'first sons') to the founders of those groups they have seceded from and that such 'staged' secession often occurs in the line of succession to a village leadership.

3. The formation of new lineage groups by serial assimilation to an established residential group, where a change in status of the residential group often helps to precipitate the lineage group's independent recognition.

In the remainder of this chapter I elaborate and discuss examples of these various features.

The dominant descent line

It is a striking fact that, with the one exception of Ndifaw, all the ancestral founders of the largest politically corporate groups (village groups or villages) are claimed not to have come from elsewhere but to have lived always where the community associated with their name has continued to exist.[1] Insistence upon this fact (and in many cases elders have insisted somewhat tenaciously upon it, sometimes in the face of contradictory evidence) would seem to be based upon each group's claim to independent status and implies an ultimate link between residential and genealogical continuity. Were one to admit that an ancestral founder came from elsewhere it would imply that the community now associated with his name was *not* independent, but was linked to and merged with another group elsewhere. Inversely, it is by membership of or attachment to the descent line of the ancestral founder that all the sections of the widest community grouping can confirm that they are ultimately united, ultimately *bɔ ci amɔt*, descendants of a common ancestor.

We should note here that for Banyang the idiom of common descent is the idiom of unity. To describe two people as agnates (*bɔ ci*) is to ascribe a common bond between them: such a bond may be more or less effective, their common, uniting ancestor more or less distant; but while the relationship is there and is recognized it is expected that the persons so related should act in common cause one with another. The dominant descent line of a village group asserts this ultimate solidarity of its members while allowing for change to occur in the arrangement of its parts: the descent line may become ramified (by the emergence of 'sons' who found their own groups) or non-agnates may become assimilated to it (by coming as 'followers' to those already established), but the ultimate solidarity of the overall group is not questioned and continues to be asserted in descent

---

[1] The Ndifaw exception is an interesting one and accounts partly, I believe, for the weight put on the story of how Ndifaw gained the community leadership. Even so, we may note the insistence that all people became *bɔ Ndifɔ*, his 'children', to the extent indeed that the lack of 'attached' persons, in Tali at least, is unusual. This unwillingness to admit that an ancestral founder has come in from another place contrasts with the very elaborate histories of village migration that I have obtained in Ejagham country.

terms. Evidence of the kind of flexibility that is allowed here has already been given in earlier genealogies (*Figures 17, 19, 20, 21*).

Not all members of a village group (or village) are true descendants of its ancestral founder, even although the group as a whole is spoken of in general terms as *bɔ N——*, 'the children of N——'. Banyang descent idiom again allows this kind of assimilation to an established (named) group by those who are not strictly members, whether they are patrilateral kin, matrilateral kin, or strangers. The subtly differentiating term which is often used to distinguish such residentially assimilated persons is *batɔ bɔ ci*, a phrase meaning, as far as one can literally translate it, 'fellow-patrikin', but which in its inclusion of the term 'fellow' (*batɔ*) implies that they are not quite 'patrikin', *bɔ ci*. (In another, wholly kinship context, one of the bridewealth payments is made to the *batɔ bɔ ci*, and the phrase here refers in a direct, straightforward way to the collateral agnates of the bride, fellow-members of her lineage group.) Otherwise the more exact link between assimilated and true descendants of the ancestral founder can be stated. In the present context the point to emphasize is that such assimilations do, and are known to, occur without affecting the ultimate claim of descent solidarity, that all are *bɔ N——*.

I have spoken above of the 'idiom' of common descent. In the total genealogy of a village group this idiom remains formally the same, but the effective relationships it denotes change considerably. Thus the solidarity of the widest group known as the descendants of a common ancestor (e.g. *bɔ Ndifɔ, bɔ Ayok Ɛtayak, bɔ Ncuɔmbirɛ*, etc.) is based far more on their continuing political solidarity – upon their acting on occasion as a single, united community – than upon any effective kinship that they share; but at lower levels of the village group genealogy (e.g. the major lineage groups forming a village or the minor lineage groups a hamlet) the same idiom, *bɔ——*, covers a relationship that is more effectively and fully one of kinship solidarity. This change in the content of the relationships in structural depth is one which can also occur in time: the relationship between agnates which is one of kinship solidarity can be transmitted to their descendants unchanged, or it can (without changing the idiom) become rather the solidarity of political associates. The commonly given reason for residential separation in the past – a father sending off his 'son' to give him information about slave transactions – implies just such a process of change: as we have previously expressed this, it is kinship become kinship-at-a-distance. Such changes in the context of genealogically expressed relationships, which occur constantly and cumulatively within a village group, are part of the general process by which the total genealogy is gradually formalized: it gathers to itself, as it were, over time the residual form of events, and presents in small range what has taken place over a much longer time-span. It is indeed precisely this accruing of significant relationships to it which gives the dominant descent line its importance.

The genealogies already evidenced and later given below are not then 'history' in the unqualified sense of a true account of what has occurred in the past, but they do show, it is claimed, in a limited way some of the stages by which present groups were formed. Clearly, there has been a continuing process of genealogical simplification – the telescoping of names, the assimilation of non-kin to quasi- or full-kinship status – but many of the relationships shown can have no structural or constitutional significance *except as* a factual, genealogical account of how people are related to the on-going, dominant descent line of a village or village group. The genealogies cited in this book are presented therefore not as 'rational-izations' of existing structures, but as 'partial histories' of present groups, where the genealogical links do indeed refer to the past but explain how past processes of change have produced the present constitutional ordering of a residential group. Regularities within these genealogies may refer, therefore, as much to regularities of historical process as to regularities of present organization.

The genealogies already cited give evidence of the kind of 'historical' regularities of process here at issue. It may be useful, however, to give a further example which illustrates this point especially clearly. The regularities in the genealogy recognized by members of Bachu Akagbe village (one of the two politically unallied villages of Banyang country) recall similar features of other village and village group genealogies (*Figures 17, 19, 20*) and of the 'model' genealogy of *Figure 28*, in particular the pattern of 'one-sided' growth and of variable 'attachment' to the dominant descent line within the context of a residential group. What is important here is that these 'recurrent' features have to be understood in the context of the historical processes of growth and change: they simply do not make sense as an account of the present *constitutional* ordering of the village, *unless* this is seen as the outcome of such historical processes.

Bachu Akagbe (*Bacuɔ Akagbe*) is centrally situated in Banyang country and may at one time have been related to its neighbouring village of Bachu Ntai, although this is now denied by them. It is highly regular in its constitution as a village, and the genealogy linking its various sections also gives evidence of a regular process of growth.

Thus the village as a whole is composed of three sections, each of which is both a lineage group (bɔ Ncuɔmbirɛ, bɔ Ɛbaɛ Ɛfaŋ, bɔ Ɛyɔŋ) and a residentially distinct hamlet (respectively, Nsebanga, Nti Mbi, and Tanyi Eyong – the last lacking a true place-name, but called after its founder). It is said that bɔ Ncuɔmbirɛ at Nsebanga are the oldest section, the 'stock' or 'origin' of the village (nɛt ɛtɔk), but in any division carried out within the village each section has equal status and should receive a third-part share. Each section as a hamlet is divided internally into a further series of smaller lineage groups (four in the case of Nsebanga, three for Nti Mbi, four for Tanyi Eyong). The genealogical status of the ancestors by whose names these groups are known varies considerably, even within their respective hamlets (note, for example, the three lineage groups of Nti Mbi – one tracing descent from a separated son, one from the rump of the father's descendants, one from an assimilated stranger), but again all are treated as having equal constitutional status, and in a division in the hamlets these separately named lineage groups should each receive their own share.

Turning now to the genealogy linking these various sections of the village, the most striking fact concerning it is the lack of any direct correspondence with the regular constitutional grouping we have just described: the three village sections have ancestors at different generation depths, giving the whole genealogy a lop-sided appearance; in two cases lineage groups at different levels of organization and of differing extension are identified by reference to the same ancestor (Ncuɔmbirɛ and Ɛbaɛ Ɛfaŋ); in other cases where hamlet sections of equal status trace their descent from ancestors of some genealogical equivalence the nature of the links between those ancestors varies. These 'irregularities' in terms of the genealogy's formal correspondence to the corporate constitutional organization of the village become 'regularities' when the genealogy is taken as evidence for the way in which this corporate organization has emerged.

Thus the members of the village trace their collective origin from Nchuombire and all are linked to the descent line which he established: all are bɔ Ncuɔmbirɛ (even although when we examine detailed origins more closely we find that some members of the village are not directly Nchuombire's descendants). In fact Nchuombire is not the earliest ancestor who is remembered, but rather Mfɔ Ṣɛparɛ (or Mfɔ Hɛparɛ), who is said first to have 'cleared the bush' and to have begotten Nchuombire, the founder of the village. Two of the three sections are said to have been founded by sons who each in turn inherited the leadership of the village from their father and established their own separate residential groups. Ebae Efang inherited the leadership from Nchuombire and established the section now known as Nti Mbi (literally, 'the head of the path'); Eyong Eta inherited the leadership from Ebae Efang and established the most recently formed section, Tanyi Eyong. In each case of residential hiving off, a 'rump' group was left who retained the descent name of the originating ancestor: bɔ Ncuɔmbirɛ (now a major lineage group and village section: the descendants of Nchuombire less those of Ebae Efang) and bɔ Ɛbaɛ Ɛfaŋ (also a major lineage group and village section: the descendants of Ebae Efang less those of Eyong Eta). Needless to say, the present constitutional leadership of Bachu Akagbe is still retained by bɔ Ɛyɔŋ, the third village section, although a complementary village elder, who is given respect as a formal traditional leader, is also recognized, coming from the oldest section, bɔ Ncuɔmbirɛ.

Figure 29 Descent and residential grouping of bɔ Ncuɔmbirɛ of the village of Bachu Akagbe

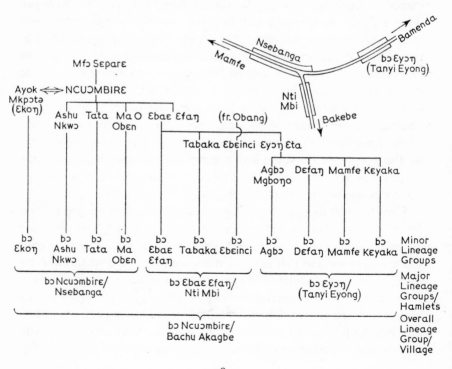

Within these three village sections, thus linked through their founders to the descent line established by Nchuombire, the component minor lineage groups are themselves related to this line in various ways. At greatest genealogical depth, Ayok Mkpoter is said to have been a matri-lateral kinsman (manɔ) of Nchuombire, from Ayok Aba (a village on the borders of eastern Ejagham and Banyang country), who was sent for by Nchuombire to live with him and to cohabit with his wives when he himself was suffering from venereal disease. In fact, Ayok Mkpoter's descendants grew greatly in number and threatened at one time to absorb bɔ Ncuɔmbirɛ. It is for this reason, it is said, that they became known as bɔ Ɛkoŋ, 'the children of termites', since termites 'spoil the house that they enter'. (Again, this story describes what is essentially a historical process of possible absorption – a change in the dominance of a descent line – which there is no reason to doubt was actually threatened; in other cases, e.g. Ndifaw, such a process of absorption did occur.) Two other minor lineage groups in Nsebanga trace their origins from sons of Nchuombire, a fourth from a daughter (Ma Oben). I have already commented upon the variable links between the minor lineage group ancestors of Nti Mbi, the second village section. The genealogical links between the minor lineage groups composing the most recently established village section of Tanyi Eyong would appear to be the most regular but I strongly suspect some genealogical glossing when these were given to me: certainly the names 'Mamfe' and 'Keyaka' suggest assimilated outsiders; these were said at first to be the names of two of Eyong Eta's wives and only later to be his sons. Whatever the case here – and I am inclined to think that closer acquaintance would have revealed a variety of assimilated links – in other Banyang villages lateral assimilation of distant kin and strangers is usually most marked in the settlements or hamlets of village leaders.

We have been concerned in this section with the simple fact that a single, if complexly extended, descent line when seen in time–depth serves to link, and thus to express the continuing solidarity of, the widest group of people who recognize themselves as one community. The following two sections examine in more detail some of the processes of change which occur in relation to this descent line and which have already been indicated in the example just given.

Residential secession: the hiving-off of 'sons' who become equal to their 'fathers'
There is a great deal of evidence that the kind of lateral or one-sided

secession illustrated in *Figure 28* has in fact occurred in the formation of present-day villages. Much of this evidence is genealogical: the lop-sided or 'staged' pattern is very clearly evident in the genealogies for *bɔ Ncuɔm-birɛ (Figure 29), bɔ Ayok Ɛtayak (Figures 19* and *20)* and (less regularly but still clearly present) *bɔ Ndifɔ (Figure 17)*. In present circumstances, where formerly dispersed small settlements have been consolidated and where in any case large numbers of young men are away from home, evidence as to this continuing process is difficult to obtain, and clearly it cannot be expected to occur in the same way as in the past. Nevertheless, such small-scale residential secessions as do occur would seem to follow the principles already described and establish on a small scale the residential and genea-logical patterns which are 'writ large' in the genealogies and residential grouping of the wider communities.

In Besongabang village two new small settlements have been established by residential secession since the village was first consolidated at the beginning of this century. Both settlements were first established in the mid-1920s when touring British administrative officers informed Banyang that they were free to build where they wished. Both settle-ments are named after their founders, who have since died, and they are very similar in their general circumstances and composition: 'Tabunta' was founded by secession from the hamlet of Mkpot, 'Tagbotoko' by secession from the hamlet of Nsebanga. The latter is examined here in detail (*Figure 30*, see also *Figure 20*, p. 92).

When Agbotoko (the 'Ta' is the prefix of respect for an elder) first came to build his settlement he brought with him his two younger full-brothers. He himself is said to have been the eldest child (*mɔ mbɔ*) of his father Abunaw, who continued to live at Nsebanga. The separa-tion is described as taking place with his father's consent and because of his own 'many children'. The descendants of Agbotoko, now into the third generation, do in fact form the largest element of the settlement, but his two younger brothers are also represented there. The youngest of the three, the only one still alive, is away working in the south but owns a large modern-style house which is now let out to a schoolteacher. Descendants of the second brother continue to live in the settlement, but one of his two sons (not shown in the genealogy) has returned back to the parent hamlet of Nsebanga. This group of close agnatic kin have been joined by a number of others who are permanent residents in the settlement or are domiciled there: a more distant agnatic kinsman, now dead (described as *mɔ ci Abunɔ*), whose two migrant sons have begun to build another modern-style house in the settlement; an in-law who has come to live here after spending some time in another hamlet of Besongabang (Nserong); a matrilateral relative of Agbotoko (10) who as a boy came to live with Agbotoko's eldest son and was brought up by him. Despite this diversity of actual relationships, a common kinship is asserted for all members of the settlement: collectively they are bɔ (T)Agbɔtoko, 'the children of (T)Agbɔtoko'. The formal leader of the settlement (mu nti, the 'head man') is Agbotoko's own grandson (2) but since he too is now working in the south his role has been filled by Agbotoko's second son (3).

Figure 30 The breakaway settlement of Tagbotoko, Besongabang village

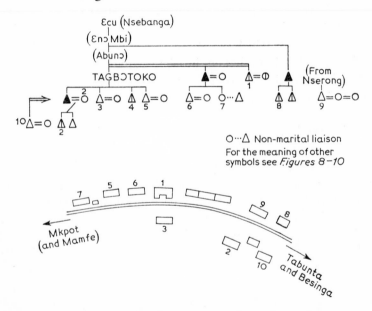

This man, the acting head, was quite clear about the status of the settlement members in relation to the group they had left. Despite their residential separation from Nsebanga, they were still nɛrɛkɛt amɔt, common kinsfolk, with those who lived there: they were still members of bɔ Ɛnɔ Mbi (one of the two minor lineage groups of Nsebanga) and of bɔ Ɛcu (the inclusive major lineage group). On any matter of importance he would consult with the senior elder of bɔ Ɛnɔ Mbi and bɔ Ɛcu (the same man) and would call him to officiate in major activities here. The settlement could be described as a nɛntɔ, a 'centre' or section of the village, but he as its head could not go directly to the village leader: he would always go first to the senior elder of bɔ Ɛcu at Nsebanga. He was responsible through him for tax. If a leopard or python were caught he would send for this man and it would be the latter who would carry the news to the village leader. (When I asked what would happen if he took a python directly to the village leader anyway, he said at first that the leader would not accept anything directly from him, and then that if a python *were* taken, the village leader would send word to the senior elder of Nsebanga who would say that he knew nothing about it; the latter would wait a day or two and if then he had still been told nothing he would bring a case before the village leader – Why had a python been caught and he had not been informed of it?)

Nevertheless, in most everyday practical activities bɔ Tagbɔtoko had clearly far closer relations between themselves and managed these activities independently of those at Nsebanga, half a mile away. To pursue a metaphor which we have earlier implied: the kinship connection has stretched but it has not broken; if anything, what has occurred is a slight vulcanization of the rubber – a formalization of the ties linking the two groups and a careful insistence upon defined rights and duties.

Tagbotoko have not yet equal status with Nsebanga. What they do have as a separate settlement is the opportunity to acquire effective autonomy in practical matters which can then by constitutional sanction (formally recognized direct access to the village leader) raise their status to that which would be equivalent to Nsebanga's. The acting leader of Tagbotoko denied his wish to do this: the leader of the nearby and closely comparable settlement of Tabunta, when speaking of their relationship to their parental hamlet Mkpot, claimed a slightly greater measure of independence. The formal kinship tie with Mkpot was not denied but was expressed in terms of sharing a common 'goat of the pepper' (a goat given to the lineage group at a marriage) and if a leopard were caught he said he would call the leader of Mkpot to come there, in his own settlement, where a dance of celebration would be held and from where the leopard would be carried forward to the village leader's *aca*, if the latter (he added somewhat tendentiously) 'did not wish to operate upon it here'.

If either of these settlements *were* to acquire independent status as hamlets it seems probable that their genealogical link with their parental groups would be simplified by the omission of the irrelevant intervening names, so that in the case of Tagbotoko, for example,

Tagbotoko would be remembered simply as *mɔ Ɛcu*, the 'son' (or descendant) of *Ɛcu* who moved away from his father's (rump) descent group to found his own group, equal in status to his father's.

Two points arising from this account of actual secessions should be stressed: firstly, the internal composition of these seceded settlements has a close formal resemblance to all residential or community groupings up to the level of a village: the pattern is of an *etɔk*, a residential group, composed of a segmental series of kinship units (here *bɛkɛt*, 'households'; only at the higher levels could they be called *banɛrɛkɛt*, 'lineage groups' – a point we return to later), all ultimately connected through their founder (e.g. Agbotoko) to the dominant descent line shared by whatever wider grouping exists. Secondly, and following on from the first point, the crucial difference between Tagbotoko, the seceded settlement, and the higher residential groupings (hamlet or village) is the difference in what I have termed the 'constitutional' rights of their leaders – in traditional terms, the right to receive and pass forward (or retain) a leopard. Any increase in the size and operational autonomy of such smaller residential groups is then likely to bear upon those rights which define their status, *vis-à-vis* other groups.

It is just conceivable, although unlikely, that Tagbotoko could in time grow sufficiently in size and effective autonomy to claim for itself the independent status of a village. It is more likely that it could achieve the partial independence of a hamlet, which indeed it is not so distant from now. If for some reason the latter proved impossible (following upon the death or depletion of its population) it could still return to its parental hamlet and if its members were of sufficient number they would form there a separate (minor) lineage group. The status which a settlement such as Tagbotoko might eventually claim depends basically upon the growth of its numbers, and thus its ability to assert operational autonomy *relative to* the other settlements and hamlets composing the wider village. Whereas in a 'classical' segmentary system the critical condition in matters of growth is the even expansion of groups, here the critical condition relates rather to *differential* growth rates. We return again to the fact that new settlements – in the traditional society at least – were more likely to be founded by those with claims to wealth, who had more wives and 'whose children were many'. It would seem to be precisely for this reason that the process of hiving off and achieving equal status has occurred predominantly in the lines of leadership succession. The evidence for this is not only genealogical but in the existence of separated village leaders' settlements in a number of present-day villages.[1] When in Tali 1 I discussed with commoner members of the village why the settlements of the chiefly lineage group should be separate from the others (cf. *Figures 8* and *12*) the proverb was quoted: 'The leopard does not lie down with the goat.' The implication was that bɔ Mfɔnjo as 'leopards' were concerned to aggrandize themselves: it was better for them, and safer for others, that they should do so apart, living in their own settlements.

Since the consolidation of settlements at the beginning of this century, changes in residential grouping have occurred not only at the lowest level, by the founding of small new settlements such as we have been considering, but also through the movement of larger, already established (and earlier consolidated) groups. The movements of Talinchang away from the main body of Tali (suggesting a preliminary move towards a claim for further constitutional independence) or of Bara to its former site (when it reverted from being a village section of Tali to a village in its own right) were of this kind. In such movements there is no radical regrouping of allegiances within the communities that have moved: they retain their original identity and composition, and merely 'move up one' in the constitutional hierarchy. In certain cases, however, large-scale residential movement can involve a regrouping of allegiances: a new settlement then emerges formed from previously existing village sections, or sometimes sub-sections, which has compositely a new identity and still has pretensions to advanced constitutional status. Most frequently such moves would seem to occur at the immediate sub-village level and entail the hiving-off of half of a village, which distinguishes itself as 'Upper N——' or 'Lower N——', whichever is the case. The separation of 'Upper' Ebeagwa from 'Lower' Ebeagwa was of this kind. So too was the separation of 'Lower' from 'Upper' Tayo, involving a complex regrouping of ancillary lineage groups in relation to a split in the dominant descent line and a successful attempt to acquire the village leadership (*Figure 31*).

Tayo, a village of the Nkokenok II village group, recognizes *Ajwiɛ* as its ancestral founder. Briefly, the constitutional history is that after *Ajwiɛ*'s death the village leadership should have passed to Tanyi Takum, his 'first-born'. Tanyi Takum, however, relinquished the leadership in favour of his younger full-brother, Achem, although he retained certain formal rights in relation to the presentation of a leopard. At the time the Germans moved Tayo to the main path (then the main route from Mamfe to Bamenda) a son, or descendant, of Achem

[1] Examples are: Okoyong, Obang, Tinto, Ekpaw, Bachu Akagbe, and Tali itself.

was leader, by name Tanyi Aye. He fell foul of the German administration and was imprisoned. During his absence a matrikinsman (manɔ), the son of Achem's twin, Sabi, acted as leader in his stead, being formally recognized as such by the Germans. On Tanyi Aye's return from prison he resumed the village leadership, but died soon after. Another mɔ Acɛm succeeded, by name Tata Tanyi.

In the 1920s and almost certainly as a consequence of Tata Tanyi's succession, a dispute broke out between bɔ Acɛm and bɔ Sabi. Bɔ Sabi then left the former composite settlement and about 1929 moved to their present site of 'Lower Tayo', taking with them bɔ Tabasi and bɔ Acuataŋ, descendants of the 'last-born' son of Ajwie. Tayo was thus residentially divided into 'Upper' and 'Lower' parts and all later village

Figure 31 Sub-village secession in Tayo

Note: The genealogy of Lower Tayo ancestors has been 'stretched' to allow them to be represented separatly.

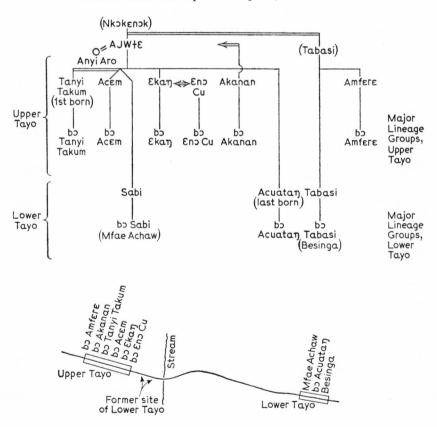

leadership disputes have hinged upon the competition between them. On Tata Tanyi's death the leadership was retained by *bɔ Acem*, going to Nyok Tambe, a son of Tanyi Aye. In 1953, when he died, a further protracted dispute ensued, which was finally resolved in favour of Ashu Arok, a son of the former regent village leader in the time of the Germans and a member of *bɔ Sabi* lineage group. The major contender for Upper Tayo at that time was a leading, influential man from *bɔ Tanyi Takum*, and it is reported that it was then agreed that the right of future succession should go to his own lineage group of *bɔ Tanyi Takum*.

The serial formation of lineage groups within a residential group

In the previous section a distinction was made between new residential groups established by processes of differential growth (e.g. Tagbotoko, which could potentially 'move up' the constitutional hierarchy, eventually to reach village status) and those established by a process of division and regrouping (e.g. the new and rump sub-villages of Tayo). In both cases the developing autonomy of the residential group provides a context for, and precipitant influence in, the formation of new lineage groups, but the process in each case varies slightly.

The formation of lineage groups in the first type of residential growth is the simplest. As Banyang describe this, the descendants of a brother or follower of the settlement founder, or sometimes of a later associate, acquire in time an identity of their own and, within the context of the residential group, come to be recognized as a separate *nɛrɛkɛt*, lineage group. This process is that which is recorded in a great many of the genealogies already cited. We would emphasize, however, that a factor in the emergence of separate lineage groups is the growing autonomy of the residential group itself. Tagbotoko (*Figure 30*) may be conveniently taken to illustrate the point. The need for the members of such a small settlement is to emphasize their own solidarity, especially in relation to their parental lineage group, *bɔ Ɛnɔ Mbi/bɔ Ɛcu*: this they do, as we have seen, by speaking of themselves as *bɔ Tagbɔtoko*, common kinsfolk, *nɛrɛkɛt amɔt*. Were, however, Tagbotoko to gain the status of hamlet, its leader directly responsible to the village leader, the pressure upon them to assert an undivided solidarity would be less, and greater recognition would then be given to the separate kinship clusters within the settlement, which already exist genealogically: they would become indeed *banɛrɛkɛt* within a *nɛrɛkɛt*, (minor) lineage groups within a (major) lineage group. A similar process of social 'precipitation' would seem to occur in the movement of a hamlet to village status, and is suggested by the fact that there is generally a greater number of major lineage groups composing a village than minor lineage groups composing a hamlet. Talinchang, a hamlet of Tali 2, has for example only three constituent lineage groups, yet in size it is little smaller than Ejwengang, a village with at one time seven, now six, lineage groups, and is a great deal larger than Bara, a village with five, formerly six, lineage groups. Talinchang is an extreme example of a hamlet because of its size; but it is its size which is exceptional, not its lineage-group composition, which is basically similar to all the other hamlets in Tali 1 and 2. One would predict that were Talinchang ever to become a village – and the reasons which hold it back are primarily political – kinship clusters now existing *within* the major lineage groups would undoubtedly establish a separate identity for themselves and thus increase the total number of lineage groups making up the new village. Some evidence for this process of lineage-group formation is provided, finally, by the nature of the remembered genealogical links between established lineage groups: in a hamlet or village which the history of the wider group claims to have hived off from the remainder or to be relatively newly established, the genealogy linking its component lineage groups tends to be more complex, the links shown more varied, than the genealogy for a long-established residential group which has maintained its present constitutional status for some time. This is precisely what we would expect if new lineage groups tend to emerge at the time residential autonomy is developed and if over time *all* genealogies tend to become simplified. Again, Ejwengang and Ebeagwa provide examples, in comparison with the longer-established Tali (taking Tali before its split). Another example is Besongabang (in this case an offshoot village much larger than the older 'parental' residential group it seceded from): and within Besongabang, the hamlet of Mbefong may be cited (reputedly the oldest-established section), against that of Besinga (the most recent).

We have been considering so far lineage group formation in the context of on-going residential growth. Settlements, hamlets, and villages not only increase in size or status, however, but sometimes diminish. The process of change in such cases would seem to be reversed: there is a loss of constitutional status, assimilation to a wider residential group, and in this assimilation a tendency for the norms of residential autonomy (the operational corporateness of an ɛtɔk) to be replaced by those of kinship solidarity (the operational corporateness of a nerɛkɛt). To return to our example of Tagbotoko, were this group to *return* to Nsebanga, its parental, hamlet, it would so do as an additional minor lineage group, bɔ *Tagbɔtoko*, to those already established. Bara when it formed part of Tali, Etemetek when it formed part of Eyanchang, both formed additional sections equivalent to major lineage groups in their host villages. Further evidence for such reassimilated residential groups is provided in the place-names irregularly associated with certain major lineage groups of a village, often where the remembered genealogical connection of this group suggests a distant connection or is in some other way irregular (e.g. Nten Era or bɔ Amɛnankɔ of Bara; Nten Ambaw or bɔ Ta Ncɛn of Ejwengang; Besinga or bɔ Tabasi of Tayo).

The formation of new lineage groups in the context of the second type of residential change – typically, the hiving-off of a sub-village – involves the interaction of descent and residential ties in an even more critical way. I shall consider this process in the context of present post-consolidated settlements. In a large consolidated settlement the majority of the male members of a lineage group normally live in close proximity in a distinct section of the settlement but there are usually one or two members who have gone to live more or less permanently with the members of another lineage group in a different part of the total settlement, so that there are, even within a consolidated, composite settlement, a scatter of ties which cut across its sectional divisions (e.g. 15, 16, 17, 32, 33 in the composite central settlement of Tali 1, 4 and 9 in Bara, *Figures 10* and *9*). While the settlement remains united, this scatter of ties does not radically affect lineage group membership: people are at hand and can easily be fetched to take part in a lineage group matter; all are collectively represented in the community council which is common to them. Should a substantial part of the total residential group hive off, however, taking with them (or leaving behind) such small groups of kin, the latter who were formerly part of an inte-grated lineage group in the residentially united village will now acquire a separate identity in the newly established sub-village. Typically such a cross-cutting of residential and descent ties adds to the serial formation of lineage groups in a sub-village – which may become eventually a village.

The Tayo example, already cited, shows us this process at work (*Figure 31*). It is significant here that the new sub-village (Lower Tayo) was formed by groups of kin more closely related to those that were left behind than to those who moved, for it was precisely by moving (or in bɔ Amfɛrɛ's case by not moving) – that is, by establishing themselves as distinct units in the context of a different residential group – that their independent identity from their kinsfolk was confirmed. This 'unmeshing' effect is shown in *Figure 31*, where genealogical ties and residential separation work in opposition to each other.

A further example of cross-cutting descent and residential ties, seen from the viewpoint of the lineage group itself, is *bɔ Tanyi Ako* of Tali. Here the residential separation of lineage group members from the main body of kin had varying consequences according to the order of residential group they attached themselves to, and for one section the emergence of Tali 2 to village status precipitated their own recognition as a new (major) lineage group within it (*Figure 32*).

Figure 32 Genealogical secessions from *bɔ Tanyi Ako*

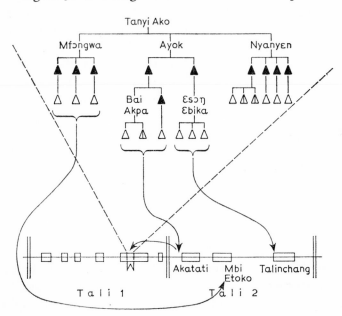

Secessions from *bɔ Tanyi Ako* of Tali have taken place at various times in its history. At one time Bai Akpa (of *bɔ Ayok*) went off with his brother to build a separate small settlement near to the 'head' of Akatati, but after his death his son (who had spent many years working away) returned with his father's brother, now the senior elder of *bɔ Tanyi Ako*, to resume their position in the main settlement. At about the same time, or possibly a little earlier than Bai Akpa's move, Esong Ebika went (by himself) to join his mother's kinsfolk in the minor lineage group of *bɔ Tanyi Esɔŋ* at Talinchang. His three sons continue to live there, occupying houses at the extreme head of the settlement. An earlier secession than either of these, which took place when Tali settlements were still 'scattered in the bush', is traced to Mfongwa, reputedly the 'eldest son' of Tanyi Ako, who went to join the leader of Nchang (now Mfae Nchang) and built his own separate settlement there on the 'Etoko path' (Mbi Etoko) which gave the group its name.

In 1953 relations between these various genealogical sections of bɔ Tanyi Ako had become entangled in the politics of the Tali split. The senior elder of bɔ Tanyi Ako had tried very hard to involve both the sons of Esong Ebika and bɔ Mfɔngwa in the affairs of the (nominally united, parental) lineage group and he had spent much effort in trying to convince the former to return home. Although they resisted this, they did continue to recognize his authority, consulted him in important matters, and attended a number of lineage group functions in the 'home' settlement. Bɔ Mfɔngwa on the other hand were more recalcitrant: the genealogical connection was not denied; its own senior elder assured me, for example, that there could be no question of intermarriage. But he refused to respond to the approaches of the senior elder of the inclusive bɔ Tanyi Ako; he kept clearly away from its lineage group functions and on one notable occasion when visited by him left the powerless, but deeply angered senior elder of bɔ Tanyi Ako with nothing to say beyond the unspoken imprecation of 'We shall see. . . !' (Cɔŋ sɛngɔ). In fact, by this time, bɔ Mfɔngwa had been recognized as a separate and equal section of the effectively independent Tali 2 and when the latter's status was formally agreed to, its former five major lineage groups had become six (see *Figure 16*).

It is a central feature of Banyang social structure that, while the principles of common descent and residential association are interrelated and co-present, in the organization of corporate groups the two principles work in opposition and contradistinction to each other rather than as co-ordinate, parallel principles of group allegiance. Residential independence is qualified by descent solidarity; residential unity is differentiated by descent disparity. I have tried earlier to show how this interaction between the two principles is an essential part of the continuing structure of Banyang social groups, and in this chapter I have been concerned to demonstrate how the same interaction is essential also to the on-going processes of group formation. In the interaction between descent and residence the critical issue is always the degree to which a residential group as ɛtɔk can assert its effective autonomy, ultimately whether it can achieve the status of a village. The dominant descent line acquires its shape, the serial lineage groups fall into place according to how this issue is decided. The issue is a constitutional one involving the recognition or reallocation of fixed rights, not only by the residential group seeking a greater autonomy but also by those with whom it wishes to remain associated (albeit on a different footing). To gain such a 'constitutional' change is in turn a political aim and problem, involving strategy, power, and influence in relation to the decision to be made. The following chapter focuses more directly upon these processes of constitutional politics that form part of a community's movement towards autonomy.

13

The Processes of Constitutional
Politics: The Tali Split

In the preceding chapter I showed how change and growth in the
formation of descent groups occur in relation to the changing status of
residential groups and I argued that it is the latter process – that is, the
growing autonomy of a residential group – that is critical for all other
processes of change in the corporate organization of groups in Banyang
society. In this chapter I attempt to show how the growing autonomy
of a residential group gives rise to the feature of constitutional politics –
the attempt to change or reallocate recognized, 'constitutional' rights –
which has already been noted as a characteristic of Banyang political life.

Most Banyang villages are seen as having acquired at some point in
time a formal autonomy that was not previously theirs. Typically, as
already described, this process of acquiring autonomy entails a 'recognized',
or 'constitutional', hiving-off from a parent village. *Figure 33* shows how
the members of Ndifaw village group see their own village group as
having been formed over time. Similar diagrams, some of which would
show secessions as having occurred in multiple stages, could be produced
for all other village groups. The diagram illustrates the two dimensions of
a village group constitution as it moves over time: thus the continuity of
the group (its continuing political solidarity) is associated with and expressed in its overall genealogy, especially that of the dominant descent
line; change in the relative status of its component parts, in particular the
creation of new, independent villages, is associated with and denoted by
the reallocation or acquisition of rights by those leaders who represent
the newly formed villages. In an earlier chapter (Chapter 3, p. 75) we
emphasized the importance of taking both aspects of the constitutional
history of a village group together and noted how in the statement of this
history the acquisition of independent rights to receive a leopard serves
to modify – and is thus superimposed upon – the fact of a common genealogical relationship.

In the first part of this book a number of examples were given of disputes or stratagems focused upon the issue of village leadership. We were concerned there especially with establishing the *fact* of constitutional politics: that there was not some kind of sociological *deus ex machina* establishing the way in which fundamental political rights were allocated, but that these rights had been acquired or distributed as the end-result of a political process occurring over time. Here we are concerned more

Figure 33 Ndifaw village group constitution over time

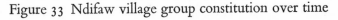

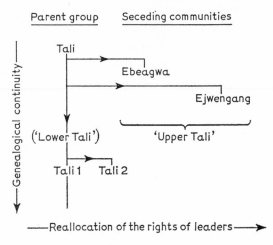

precisely with the nature and forms of this political process. What we suggest as the typical developmental sequence is based upon the differential growth in operational strength of one section of a village (a hamlet or sub-village) in relation to its other sections: this gives rise in the first place to factionalism within the village, which is likely to become most acute over the issue of leadership succession; if then the growth in operational strength continues and if it is not constitutionally accommodated within the village (either by a shared leadership, or more simply by a take-over of the village leadership) it is likely to lead to secession from it and a political battle to obtain a recognized independent leadership which will give to the seceding group a constitutional status equal to that from which it has seceded, i.e. it becomes a village in its own right. This kind of process is already implicit in some of the examples of constitutional politics already given. After discussing some of the general conditions of such a developmental sequence, the present chapter will examine in detail a single case-study of secession, the 'Tali split', which was the last of the series of secessions shown in *Figure 30*.

Village leadership as the focus of political dispute

I have already referred to the high incidence of disputes over village leadership (p. 129) and can here only reaffirm the general observation that such disputes are endemic in Banyang country, being especially evidenced in Upper Banyang villages. Few of the latter villages which I have visited have not been at some time, in the present or recent past, without a dispute concerning leadership succession. An important feature of these disputes is that the candidates contending for the leadership normally represent, and are supported by, sections of the village which have at their lower level the operational status and thus some of the autonomy of residential groups, bɛtɔk, in their own right. Tayo (pp. 290–291) provides a clear example; another is Bara, where the sub-village grouping centred upon bɔ Esɔŋafiɛt and represented by their own leader contended for the succession when the last village leader died (cf. p. 49).

The fact that such disputes should occur is in part made possible by the absence of any clear rules concerning succession. Leadership is not an office which is inherited along with other 'properties' of the deceased man;[1] it is rather a personal attribute which has to be reconferred by the community which owns it (it will be remembered that 'leadership belongs to the community') whenever its holder dies. This does not mean, however, that certain patterns of succession do not operate.

One of the broadest of these was noted by Gorges, who writes that 'In Eastern Banyang and the Mbang Clan the nominee [to a village leadership] is usually a son, in Western usually a brother'.[2] This is offered as a generalization rather than an invariable rule, and Gorges is careful to cite a number of discrepant examples (filial succession among Lower Banyang, fraternal among Upper). In fact, the use of kinship terms is here somewhat misleading and the alternatives are better presented as those between a 'monopolized' leadership, which is held by single descent line or lineage group, and a 'circulating' leadership, which is open to all, or a number, of the descent lines composing a village. Various degrees of limitation are possible in the case of a 'circulating' leadership, and to this extent make it partially 'monopolized' by two or three related descent lines. These are not 'culturally given' norms of succession but constitutional arrangements

---

[1] The discrepancy between the inheritance of formal status, including property, and leadership succession is especially marked among Lower Banyang, who maintain the principle of primogeniture in the former case but not (except sometimes retrospectively, in the early stages of a village genealogy) in the latter. Cf. also the following paragraph above.

[2] Op. cit., para. 173.

locally worked out by particular villages and dependent upon the balance of power within them.

Thus where leadership has been monopolized by a single lineage group or descent line over a number of successions, this is usually associated with the continuing numerical dominance of that lineage group within the village. Where succession circulates between lineage groups, the balance of power is likely to be more unevenly divided, and the more open access to leadership a constitutional embodiment of a political compact between united yet equal partners. It happens among Upper Banyang that the more developed forms of leadership rely upon such sectional dominance within a village: thus the examples that Gorges cites of 'filial' succession among Upper Banyang (Tali, Defang, Takwa, and Ebuensuk) are all villages that have produced powerful leaders, whose own supporting sections have been able to monopolize the leadership over a sequence of successions. (Even this, however, is not entirely true for Takwa, where the leadership has been held in one lineage group for two successive leaders but before that circulated between three lineage groups.) The case of Tayo, already referred to, is also relevant, for here we see how leadership, held for some time in one descent line (bɔ Acɛm), was under pressure passed to a second descent line (bɔ Sabi) on the understanding that it would revert, on the next succession, to a third (and possibly original) descent line (bɔ Tanyi Takum): a 'monopolized' leadership has here been converted to a 'circulating' leadership under political pressure where this constitutional change serves to accommodate and contain what would otherwise appear as a potential threat of secession (cf. pp. 290–291). If they had not been allowed access to the leadership of the conjoint Tayo, bɔ Sabi, the nuclear lineage group of Lower Tayo, would almost certainly have sought independence and a separate leadership in their own right.

A further possibility of constitutional compromise lies in the device we have already noted of distinguishing between the roles of leader, where the greater de facto influence of the operative leader (nowadays the 'European's leader') is weighed against the greater claims to legitimate status of the ritual or 'true' leader (nowadays the 'traditional' mfɔ etɔk or 'community leader') who in fact is usually a somewhat ineffecual figure.

The actual procedure of selecting a new village leader relies upon the 'policy-making' procedures of the corporate community (Chapter 7) and involves most directly the inner council of a village. Although each succession has to be decided as a fresh issue, its discussion is nevertheless constrained by previous decisions and by the agreements which may have been made in order to achieve those decisions. The candidates for the next village leadership are then already likely to be in line before the present leader has died. I have been told by Upper Banyang that a village leader who wishes his own son to succeed him may call together the inner council of the village, or sometimes village group, before his death, and make known his wishes to them, accompanying them with gifts of money and spirits. Such an inner council agreement, however, is dependent upon very much the same 'proving' process as those already discussed (pp. 178, 181), and this procedure by no means precludes later dispute. In the Lower Banyang village of Besongabang I was told that no such prior nomination would be made and that the matter would be taken up and discussed by the inner council once a village leader had died: even so, it was clear that the main candidates for the leadership, and the parties supporting them, would already be known and widely discussed.

It may appear that the decision regarding succession to village leadership is based entirely upon 'political' factors of relative group strength and party representation. This is not so. Personal qualities – initiative, fair-dealing, level-headedness – are also looked for in a village leader, and the claim of individuals or sectional representatives is strengthened or weakened according to their personal qualities and the inner council's assessment of their ability to 'hold the community well'. On the other hand, in a large, politically dominant, lineage group there is usually little difficulty in finding someone suitably endowed, and the representatives of village sections claiming the right of succession have by the nature of things already established to some degree their personal ability in leadership.

The decision regarding succession having been made at the village level (where it is rarely quickly concluded, and sometimes involves a protracted dispute of months and even years), it has then in most areas to be confirmed at the level of the village group, that is, by the most extended order of community grouping recognizing a tradition of united political action. A meeting of the village group should be called and the new village leader presented to it, who in turn should provide the meeting with a goat and wine. Nowadays such confirmatory action is sometimes delayed or omitted (partly no doubt since it is the authority of the administration which serves as the more effective sanction) yet it is still recognized that the wider grouping has this right to sanction what is in effect a transfer of constitutional status within it. So similarly in Upper Banyang villages, but not generally in Lower, the succession of a hamlet leader, decided internally by the hamlet members, requires for its formal completion the further validation of the village council, obtained by the presentation similarly of a goat (cf. the case cited pp. 57–58, although here in exceptional circumstances it was the village group rather than village which confirmed the hamlet leader of Okorobak).

As already described at some length in Chapter 4, the Colonial administration has found itself drawn willy-nilly into village leadership disputes. Its role has been twofold: firstly (by virtue of its own superior authority, although not always formally required to exercise it), its sanction has provided the ultimate confirmation of any individual person's succession to the leadership; secondly (and in consequence of the former role), appeal to the administration has formed one element in the strategy of any contending party to gain recognition of its claims. Since, however, the policy of the British administration has always been to refer such disputes back to the villagers themselves, there has been no radical change in the content or likely progress of the disputes; the administration has become part of and has extended the process of constitutional politics, but its developmental sequence remains substantially the same: compromise within the constitutional framework of a united village (with either a unitary or a dual leadership) or secession and the attempt to obtain an independent constitutional status equal to that of the parent village. (For further details of leadership disputes involving the administration and for secessions recognized by it, see Chapter 4, especially pp. 122–129.)

Possible secession serves always as a potential threat in any dispute over leadership succession. It is not, however, a threat that can easily be put into effect unless the contending faction has succeeded in some degree in building up its effective autonomy over a period of time: this may be done by changes of residence, by a growth in size, and by such institutional aids as the acquisition of association lodges (especially of Ngbe). This growth in operational autonomy may be relative rather than absolute, and in this century has been influenced by the conditions of Colonial rule, which have made it easier for relatively small groups, peripherally attached to a larger, to survive alone. Changes in the source of wealth have also made for a greater levelling of socio-economic status so that individual men can no longer (as they did in the past) monopolize control over large polygynous households, supported by many slaves. Even so, no secession occurs abruptly but is led up to by a cumulative process of internal development and political manœuvring. At this point, however, it will perhaps be more profitable to turn to an actual example of secession and to examine the circumstances leading up to and finally effecting it.

The Tali split: phase I

The Tali leadership dispute and eventual division of the formerly united village into two villages of equal status formed a series of events which overshadowed all other political issues during my early period of field-work in Tali. An account of them is presented to illustrate not only the general features of constitutional politics which we have been discussing but also the interrelationship between such politics and other processes and themes earlier considered in this book. The most important events leading to the split occurred in 1953–1954 and were either directly ob-served by me or recounted to me soon after they occurred. I have, how-ever, tried to set these events in a wider historical context, leading up to and extending beyond this time. Phase I of the history takes us up to the initial resolution of the leadership dispute in March 1954, when it was decided by the assembled representatives of Tali that the 'community' (i.e. the former Tali village) should remain united but 'under two independent chiefs'. Phase II traces the outcome of this somewhat unusual con-stitutional decision which at first did in fact provide a formula by which the operational unity of Tali was re-established; eventually, however, this precarious unity was to give way and what emerged were two separate villages, each with operational autonomy and each with its constitutionally recognized independent leader.

The central theme in this case-study is the relationship it shows between the operational structure of the community – the balance of power between its various parts in terms of their governmental efficacy and the degree of influence wielded by their representatives – and the constitutional norms defining formally recognized statuses and relationships. The process of constitutional politics emerges from a discrepancy in this relationship. As a practical issue it focuses on the question of village leadership but arises basically from the growing corporate autonomy of Tali 2 as a community, ɛtɔk, in its own right. The issue is played out not only in terms of the traditional institutions of the society but also and more especially in terms of the circumstances of the Colonial régime: the administration is constantly involved in the dispute and when it is finally settled lends its sanction to the resolution. The same circumstances help also to create the paradox of this resolution, in which the wider residential grouping is maintained despite the division of constitutional rights regarding leadership. We examine an attempt to support this situation by modern associational means, the 'Chiefs' Council', which, however, finally gives way in the face of disagreement at this wider level.

A number of secondary themes are interwoven with the first: the diffuseness of the political community which allows the operations of government at a number of different levels; the quest for status by individuals on the basis of the residential groups which they represent; the critical balance between unity and division which determines the operational autonomy of a residential group at any level of grouping; the interaction of residential and kinship ties; the relationship between 'inner council', 'council', and 'community' in the decision-making and governmental processes; the role of the administration in the present-day political organization; the role of the associations.

The events themselves are first described as an on-going narrative before brief (and, for our book, concluding) comments are made on the themes that the events illustrate.

In the latter half of the nineteenth century Tali was one of the largest of Upper Banyang villages, its leader, Defang Baimbi, one of the most powerful of all village leaders. Both in Tali and in its neighbouring villages, the power and wealth of Defang are today remembered in extravagant terms. Defang's political influence was almost certainly related to his control of the main market for Upper Banyang, which was a focus for the traffic in slaves, who were brought down from the highland territories lying beyond the borders of Upper Banyang country and passed forward through Banyang country to the eastern Ejagham. Today the size of Tali's remaining 'slave' quarters, especially that associated with the leader's section, Mbinjong, are a mark of its former power and wealth. The influence of Defang stretched, then, beyond his own village group and it is reported that intractable disputes from other villages might be taken to him on Tali market day for his judgement or help. Defang was succeeded by his son Bali (about whom little is heard), Bali by his son Baimbi.

When the first Germans arrived they found Baimbi the established leader. It is reported that 'Ta Njok' passed through Tali on his way to Fontem in Bangwa, where he was killed. Some time later Commander von Besser (remembered simply as 'Commander') arrived in Upper Banyang country. Other villages, the story is told, were then fleeing into the bush to avoid meeting him: Baimbi on the other hand went out of his way to meet and offer hospitality to the German, and, in return, gained the latter's recognition of his status, and support for his local authority over the neighbouring villages. Later, the unity of Tali was also maintained, if not enhanced, by the movement of its settlements to the path (*Figure 11*, p. 43).

It was perhaps inevitable, however, that Baimbi's wealth and influence, which were a concomitant of Tali's size, should eventually give rise to conflict with the administration. Tali members say because of a 'woman palaver', present administrative records because of a case of 'slave-dealing', Baimbi was sent to prison by the Germans:[1] he was not first village leader to be so. Baimbi's place was taken by his immediate follower among the Tali minor leaders, *Nyenti, who became then the officially recognized village head. (For his place in Tali political grouping see below.) Nyenti did not last long: he too was imprisoned on a charge of tax embezzlement (he claimed to have been robbed while travelling to pay it in), and the officially sanctioned village leadership reverted then to Egbemba, a matrikinsman of Baimbi's within the chiefly bɔ Mfɔnjo lineage group.[2] When the British took over from the Germans, Egbemba continued to be recognized and to act as village leader, even after Baimbi's return from prison. Administrative records refer to him occasionally as the 'official' chief, acting on behalf of the 'rightful' chief Baimbi, but it is clear that he enjoyed the support of the majority of Tali, and by the end of his long period of leadership he had so consolidated his position as to be one of the most influential of Upper Banyang chiefs, whose legitimacy of office was unquestioned.

Both before and during the time of Egbemba, Tali's united leadership nevertheless overlaid a complex internal political structure. At the end of the nineteenth century, before the consolidation of settlements, a broad distinction existed between 'Tali' and 'Tali over the Mfu', a distinction that was perpetuated in the regrouping of settlements on the path. Apart from a number of offshoot settlements from the chiefly lineage group which had crossed the Mfu river in the north, 'Tali over the Mfu' consisted mainly of three residential clusters: Akatati (probably the longest established of the sections: it will be recalled that in the time of Defang its leader claimed the ritual right to 'operate' upon a leopard brought to Defang); Nchang (formerly a single hamlet which later expanded into four separate sections, 'Upper' and 'Lower' Nchang, Mfae Nje, and – the most recent to emerge – Mbi Etoko); and finally Talinchang (whose common name with Nchang

[1] The two versions are not mutually exclusive and in either case are closely associated with the traditional prerogatives of community leaders. There is some doubt also as to whether Baimbi was imprisoned on one or two occasions. For the administrative version, which refers to a single imprisonment, see Memorandum by Divisional Officer Mamfe, to Senior Resident, Cameroons Province, 6 February 1931, Buea Archives, Af 18.

[2] Nyenti's brief occupancy of the official headship is generally omitted in accounts of the dispute. It was reported to me by his son and confirmed by Ta Taboko, the senior elder of Tali. It is apparently this which provides the basis for the later claim of Tali 2 that they were given their own 'paper' by the Germans.

suggests a distant association with it). Nchang was the largest of these clusters; it had evidently grown in size and then held the dominant position in this part of Tali. The leader of Nchang was Nyenti, who was recognized as the most influential of the minor leaders of Tali, being regarded as second in status to Baimbi, the overall leader, and having special responsibility as the representative of 'Tali over the Mfu'. In the status terms used to describe his relationship with the village leader, Nyenti was Baimbi's 'orderly', was to him as the 'Secretary' is to the 'Governor'.[1] In this regard he was the logical successor-regent for Baimbi when Baimbi was imprisoned. When Nyenti himself returned from prison (and Egbemba had become village leader) he again acted as Egbemba's main adviser, towards the end of his life assuming the role of senior elder of the village.

It was not until Egbemba died in 1948 that the balance of power between these two halves of Tali emerged as a competition for the village leadership. Nevertheless, before this time there were a number of indications of the way things were moving in this, the 'emergent' half of Tali. Talin-chang, who had least to gain in any claim towards sub-village leadership, moved away from the main part of 'Tali over the Mfu', thus establishing for themselves a greater autonomy in at least the practical, day-to-day affairs. At the time when 'Clan Heads' were recognized in the late 1920s, Taku Nchi, leading elder of Akatati, made a claim for this status. This claim is significant, not only because it has been shown that elsewhere such claims formed part of the strategy of achieving officially recognized leadership, but also because it came from the leader of Akatati, the most likely rival to Nyenti in this half of Tali. In fact the claim proved abortive.[2] Again, not long before Egbemba's death the Divisional Officer records a dispute which arose in 1941 when after 'the recent death of one of the big men' the announcement was made 'that Tali town should be divided into two'. The details of this dispute are not known: it is reported to have aroused the annoyance of the 'Ndifaws of Ejuingang, Ibeagwa and Tali' and appears to have been settled without much question.[3]

[1] On the prevalence of this pattern – where the second in status to the village leader represents the next most important section of the village, the potential opposition to the established group – see Chapter 2, p. 67.
[2] Gorges, paras. 35–37. The dispute arose twice, once after the death of Manyang in Ebeagwa and again at Assessment. On the first occasion the Divisional Officer told Taku Nchi to give a feast to prove his claim, but 'only a few Tali elders attended'. On the second occasion 'Taku Nchi asked whether the Clan Head would not be made President of Atebong Court in addition to Egbe Mba, and on receiving a negative answer immediately withdrew his claim, naïvely admitting that he only wanted more money and power for Tali.' Gorges adds: 'This is a useful indication of what the Clan Headship means to the present-day Banyang.'
[3] Banyang Touring Diary. Entry for 9 October 1941.

At Egbemba's death in 1948 each side of Tali put forward their own nominee for the leadership. The 'established' half proposed another member of the chiefly lineage group, C. T. Bai, son to the late Baimbi: the 'emergent' half of Tali proposed Takum Mfotaw, an older man who had for some time been building up his position as the leader of Akatati. By this time Nyenti had died, and his position had been taken over by his son (of the same name), who had returned home from abroad to do so, but who was still a youngish man and had yet to prove himself in the political affairs of Tali. The latter found it wise therefore to support the claims of Takum Mfotaw of Akatati, who was also supported by all the other sections of 'Tali over the Mfu', including Talinchang, but with the exception of the immediate settlement of Tanyi Tabe, whose leader, Taboko, remained loyal to the traditionalist group. The argument which the emergent faction put forward was that at the time of Egbemba's succession there had been an agreement that when he died the leadership would revert to their own half of the village. Although in this particular case the argument did not carry a great deal of conviction, its terms were plausible enough, for such agreements, as we have already shown, are not infrequently made to resolve disputes over succession. Whatever had in fact taken place when Egbemba took over the village leadership, the traditionalist party denied that any such agreement had been made and felt that their position was strong enough to resist further compromise. At a meeting of the whole village group presided over by the District Officer, it was then their nominee who was declared to have succeeded Egbemba. Faced with an impasse in their claims to the single leadership of Tali, the dissident faction now changed their approach. The claim that they now put forward was to an independent leadership of their own, and for the first time they began to speak of themselves as 'Tali 2',[1] i.e. a separate community of equal status with 'Tali 1'. This new claim was supported by a concerted effort to get the British administration to recognize their rights to a separate leadership. A series of letters and petitions were sent to various levels of the administrative hierarchy: to the Resident, to the Secretary of the Eastern Provinces, and finally to the Commissioner of the Cameroons. The grounds adduced for their claim were a modified version of the original Ndifaw story, supported by what other threads of tradition could be turned to their favour. Ndifaw was now said to have had *four* important sons: Tanyi Tiku (of Ejwengang), Tanyi Takum (of Ebeagwa), Tanyi Nga (formerly of Akatati, but now representing Tali 2),

---

[1] The District Officer notes the use of this name as a new development in his entry for 15 July 1949 in the Banyang Touring Diary.

and the 'youngest', Mfonjo (who legendarily acquired the Tali leadership and founded the chiefly lineage group which had retained it). It was claimed that four 'papers' had been given by the Germans and four official village leaders recognized by them. The questions were put: Who was the youngest son of Ndifaw? Who has the 'key of Tali, the knife and stool'? And finally: Is it possible that a village of this size could be without a chief? After further inquiries the formal reply given by the administration was that it was not their policy to allow villages to become divided and that Tali should remain as a single village under one chief.[1] When, at the beginning of 1950, it had become apparent that these appeals to the administration would not be effective in securing Tali 2's independence, the younger Nyenti changed sides, leaving the dissident faction to join the 'established' group of the (rump) Tali.

Weakened by Nyenti's defection, 'Tali 2' still refused to accept the authority of the 'constitutional' village leader and continued in effect if not officially to operate as an independent village. Already in 1949 'Tali 2' had refused to pay their tax through the village leader and, as the Divisional Officer notes, 'For the purpose of Tax collection Tali has once again become two independent villages'.[2] Tax collection became a yearly issue, but 'Tali 2' always managed to collect and hand in theirs separately, invariably in advance of the rump Tali. Again, in the matters of road clearing and hammock-bridge building 'Tali 2' operated independently of, and usually more speedily than, the rump Tali. Some modification occurred during this time in 'Tali 2's' formal leadership: Takum Mfotaw, although he continued to act as one of the main spokesmen for 'Tali 2', withdrew to the position of senior elder, and a younger man, Abane, took over the role of claimant leader. Known by both sides as *mfɔ Abane*, for one he was '*mfɔ Tali 2*', for the other '*mfɔ Akatati*' (i.e. a mere hamlet leader, a 'Quarter Head').

In July 1953, when I arrived in Tali, the situation was one of stalemate. The dispute had now lasted for five years and dominated all other matters in Tali. Kinsfolk still visited their relatives and there was a certain coming and going on the personal or lineage group level, but in 'community matters' there was a complete rift between the two sides. While the rump Tali continued as before, 'Tali 2' now operated as a single, independent community, regularly meeting to hear and judge cases brought before it. The leading members of both sides would not speak to each

[1] Based on accounts from members of Tali and from correspondence seen which was kept by them.
[2] Banyang Touring Diary. Entry for 7 October 1949.

other and at this level there was a great deal of acrimony. Some months after my arrival, for example, Nyenti, whose defection from Tali 2 was regarded as a major weakening of their strength and who occupied a social island in their midst, was only just able to stop an attempt to set fire to one of his houses made by his immediate rival in Nten Nchang, who had taken his place in 'Tali 2' and was there recognized as 'Quarter Head' for this split section. In the rump Tali, Peter Esong of Kembong was similarly isolated with his followers within Kembong hamlet, having been found guilty of consorting with 'mfɔ Abane' and, suspectedly, of giving away the secrets of his own side.[1] The 'inner council' of the rump Tali (from which Peter Esong had been excluded but which now included Nyenti from the 'overside') was constantly concerned with the way in which 'Tali 2' could be forced to come in line; and, no doubt, the leading members of 'Tali 2' were similarly preoccupied with questions of their own strategy.

On both sides various measures were tried. 'Tali 2' had tried to obtain support from other villages of the village group but were less successful here than the rump Tali. Thus when the 'Ndifaw Clan Union' was (at the second attempt) constituted at a meeting in Ebeagwa village, 'Tali 2' sought to enter it on equal terms with the rump Tali, being supported in this attempt by an emergent faction of Ebeagwa. This attempt, which has already been described (pp. 175–178), was foiled, and 'Tali 2' was forced to remain outside the Union. They then approached villages in Nkokenok II with a request to join their Clan Union. This was refused and they were reduced to forming their own Union, which met (somewhat to the amusement of rump Tali) by rotation in the three 'Quarters' or village sections of Akatati, Mfae Nchang, and Talinchang.

Primarily, however, it was to the administration that both sides looked. The rump Tali believed that their case here was the stronger: 'Tali 2' had defied the administration's ruling and should be punished for doing so. In the past, it was said, they would have gone to fight 'Tali 2': it was now incumbent on the administration to arrest mfɔ Abane and imprison him. Complaints were made by deputation to the District Officer and in the final stages a telegram was prepared to send to the Commissioner of the Cameroons.

'Tali 2', having had their original case rejected by the administration, were more circumspect in their attempt to gain official sanction for their de facto autonomy. In 1953, when the District Officer passed through Tali

[1] See also p. 70. This had cost Peter Esong the 'Quarter Headship', which had been taken by the representative of another minor lineage group in the hamlet.

on tour, the question was raised once again of tax-collection: formal permission was sought for them to collect their taxes separately under *mfɔ Abane*. The D.O. evaded giving formal permission, although he allowed the taxes to be collected separately. More particularly, 'Tali 2' sought to have their case heard by the Banyang Native Authority Council in Bakebe. Their alliances outside the Ndifaw village group placed them here in better stead, so that when (after much reluctance on the part of the rump Tali) their case was finally heard in February 1954, their claim to an independent chiefship was supported by the Council. It was then that the inner council of the rump Tali, refusing to accept the N.A.'s decision, rallied to make its own plea to the administration, claiming that it was solely a matter for the 'clan' and not for the 'N.A.' to decide the 'crowning of a chief'.

Finally, in March 1954, a bare two months later, the dispute was resolved. It had then lasted for six years. At a time when I was absent from Tali, the resolution was prompted by the then Assistant District Officer at a meeting of the members of Tali (not of the whole village group), when he suggested points, including a division in the role of chiefship, that might help to reconcile the disputants. He argued that, with an impending reorganization of local authorities in the Division, a divided and discordant Tali would be placed at a disadvantage. His suggestions were left to be discussed again later by the combined members of Tali and, although not directly accepted, they prepared the way for the agreement that was in fact reached. The form of this agreement as set out by the Headmaster of Tali school (who had interested himself in Tali politics and had been called to act as mediator) is given in Appendix B. As stated there, its essential terms were that '. . . we [the leading members of the two sides of Tali] . . . unanimously resolve to be united under the aegis of two independent chiefs for the ultimate good of our town . . .'. Tali village politics had thus performed a complete *volte face*: instead of being operationally divided under one constitutional chief they now agreed to be constitutionally *united* under *two* chiefs.

This was the situation I discovered shortly afterwards when I returned to Tali. The change in atmosphere was immediately apparent. The two senior elders of the two sides, who when I had left had been bitter enemies, now came to greet me together. (These two men were also the leading signatories of the document referred to above.) Everywhere there was talk of the new-found unity of Tali: it was now a single, united community, *etɔk ɛmɔt*; its members were the common descendants of one ancestor, *bɔ ci amɔt*; all were *bɔ Ndifɔ*. The point was put most vividly at a later meeting of the Executive Committee of the Clan Union (when some parrying was required of the claims of the two other villages to have been consulted over the issue): 'The community was sick – but it did not die!' (*Etɔk ɛme – ɛbɔk ɛgu!*). If any community case (*ndak ɛtɔk*) was now heard in either part of Tali, representatives from the other side were called to take part in the hearing. The 'two independent chiefs' when present at a community meeting sat side by side, as did the two senior elders. A new 'inner council' was formed conjointly from the leading members of the two sides (the two chiefs, the two senior elders, Mr Tataw, and a supporter of the leader of Tali 2), at whose meetings quantities of spirits were drunk with some sense of jubilation. (Nyenti in the meantime was lying low.) Far from being divided, Tali as a community was apparently never more strongly united.

The Tali split: phase II

It is worth asking why exactly this sudden transition had occurred. In the first place the previous stalemate needs to be emphasized: the dispute had gone on for a number of years; the protagonists to the dispute in Tali 2 had in gifts and entertainment disposed of much of their wealth; the leading members of Tali 1 (as we may now call it), with what they believed to be right on their side, nevertheless lacked the sanctions which could effectively enforce it. Secondly, and it would seem almost by chance, the advantage of overcoming this disagreement and of reasserting a united front seems suddenly to have become apparent to both sides: instead of each side separately looking for its friends among the other's opponents, the two by combining outweighed any possible opposition, certainly within the village group, but also potentially, as the A.D.O. had hinted, in the wider local authority context. It is relevant here to say that the residential circumstances of Tali helped to produce the logic of their recombining: secession in the past and even on occasion in the present (e.g. in the case of Tayo) was, or is, usually effected in the first place by residential secession, but Tali 2's size and her strategic position on the road put the possibility of a major change of settlement out of the question. Much of the rancour in the Tali dispute arose indeed from the close proximity of the two series of settlements, which on the interpersonal and everyday level still retained much contact with each other. Since the political rift had not been consolidated through residential secession, it required only the magical wand of a change of front and a formula which both sides could accept to reheal the fracture and re-establish unity – 'the community was sick – but it did not die!' Finally, from both sides' points of view much was to be gained from the agreement and not a lot lost: Tali 2 gained the recognition of their leader's independent and equal status with the leader of Tali 1 (this formal point was insisted upon) but agreed to merge once again with Tali 1 and to establish the conjoint community of the traditional Tali; Tali 1 regained their place of dominance in a reunited Tali but had now to accept their opposite numbers in Tali 2 as partners rather than subordinates. The terms of the agreement were unusual but the fact that a constitutional compromise was effected is entirely in line with the course of other constitutional disputes, whose outcome we have earlier noted as not being without paradox (cf. especially the uncertainty surrounding the formal position of 'official chiefs' referred to in Chapter 4).

The resolution of the constitutional issue, so long in dispute, put an entirely different complexion on Tali's government. 'The community became strong': ɛtɔk ɛtaŋ. A series of potentially disruptive cases were brought to the now combined community (which has been earlier termed the 'supra-village council') which dealt with them effectively, almost summarily. Three of these cases have already been examined in Chapters 6 and 8. It is notable that the conduct of these cases was dependent upon the unity of the combined 'inner council' and that the fines imposed were high – some thought excessive. The central paradox of the compromise agreement still remained, however: if each side of Tali had its own formally independent leader, by what means would the unity of Tali as a whole – 'the united community' – be represented and maintained? To answer this problem, members of Tali turned to the association-form, and constituted a 'modern' association, whose creation and early development I shall describe in some detail.

The original idea of the association came from Mr Ojong, the Headmaster who had acted as mediator, but it was approved of and quickly taken up by the leading men of both sides of Tali: formally named the 'Chiefs' Council' by Mr Ojong, it was also known as the ncɛm or ncɛmti ('union' or 'association') and latterly became the 'Town Council'. In organization it was conceived of as an exclusive group of the leading members of both sides of Tali, who as a body represented and could act on behalf of the combined community: its superiority of status and the authority which it embodied were both emphasized. In its formative stages it was frequently referred to as ntɔ ɛtɔk, 'the heart of the community'.

The inaugural meeting of the Chiefs' Council was held in Taboko's acɔ a month after the dispute had been settled. It was attended by selected representatives of the various sections of the two sides of Tali, by the

Headmaster, and myself. Wine was provided for the meeting. It started late, however, and apart from establishing the group and providing much discussion, it settled only a few of the points regarding the detailed form of the Council. Taboko opened the meeting with a speech emphasizing the need for unity and good sense. The Headmaster then put forward his own proposed scheme (see Appendix B) and this was discussed briefly. In particular the suggestions regarding a central hall and particular dress for the chiefs were approved. The discussion then turned to the matter of appointments, which were filled alternately from both sides of Tali. Little of this discussion was 'open'; most of it was conducted by small groups going off to arrange among themselves whom they thought should occupy the positions available before suggesting these at the general meeting.[1] The final offices (and the persons filling them, where their names have already been mentioned) were: President (Chief of Tali 1); Assistant President (Chief of Tali 2); Patrons or Chiefmakers (Taboko as the senior elder of Tali 1, and Takum as the senior elder of Tali 2); Treasurer (Joseph Enaw); Assistant Treasurer (the chief's *nɛm mu* of Tali 2); Secretary (Mr Tataw); Assistant Secretary (from Tali 2); Chief Whip (Baimberi); Messenger; Steward. As this shows, the leading members of the two sides of Tali, including all the members of the combined inner council, were appointed to the main offices, which were duplicated so that Tali 1 and Tali 2 each had their representatives of equal status, seniority within the status going to Tali 1.

The appointments being made, the discussion became more general and less purposive. The wine was drunk, and at the final throwing of the sediment, an oblation to the dead, Taboko summarized the Council's aims and invoked aid for it. Calling first upon the past village and sectional leaders of Tali by name, but then extending his invocation to all the dead ('those whom I can remember and those whom I cannot remember'), he continued:

> There was a dispute in Tali which lasted for a long time, since Egbemba died. Now this has been settled and the community has come together as one, with one voice. May no one speak against the community or do evil. Tali was always known as having strength. Now it has recovered its strength and no one can surpass it. Today we have met to talk the affairs of the community. We have drunk wine. This is yours (with the

[1] These 'huddle' conferences are a recognized procedure in important discussions. I was told at this time that the Council was a 'thing of the Europeans' (*ɛnyŋ ndek*) and good because of this; nevertheless, matters still had to be arranged privately (*ɛju*).

left hand), may you drink, may all things be peaceful. See our share (with the right hand) who remain on earth. May you raise our right hands, may we live peacefully . . . etc.

At a second meeting, which I did not attend, there was further discussion regarding the Council's constitution and the payments to be made by its members. It was agreed that the two Presidents should provide goats for the meeting and that all other members should give a bottle of brandy or 10s. (I was also to give a goat.) Wine was to be provided in turn. There was some discussion of the laws to be made by the Council. For this meeting the leader of Tali 1 had provided a goat, and wine was also drunk.

By its third meeting it was apparent that the Council was beginning to achieve strength from its formal constitution. There was also, at this time, much talk about it at the informal meetings of the inner council. For its present meeting the leader of Tali 2 had provided his goat. The meeting was again held in Taboko's *acɔ ɛkɛt*, where, by this time, all members of the Council had their own positions according to their status or office. The meeting itself was opened with prayers (said by a Basel Mission convert) but with all members participating. Two cases were then discussed. The first arose from a letter signed on behalf of 'The Ndifaw Clan Union, Executive Committee, Tali branch' and concerned a member of Tali who had failed to accept the judgement of the Clan Union assembly and against whom action was being threatened for 'abusing the community'. The letter apologized for his conduct and asked for his failure to be excused (the original matter, an involved case concerning the wife of a fellow-kinsman, having now been settled). This was discussed generally and it was agreed that if the offender paid a modified fine to the Council it would excuse his action. A second case concerned a member of the Council who was being reported to have spoken against it. He had said (the statement was quoted): 'The heart of the community, the heart of the community, the heart of the community – is what?' (*Ntɔ ɛtɔk, ntɔ ɛtɔk, ntɔ ɛtɔk – bɛ ji?*). He was asked what he meant by this. (Its implication however was to belittle the leading members of the community, especially those who formed the present Council.) The person himself denied having made it and, against the certainty of those present at the meeting, offered to swear his innocence on a cult-agency. One senior elder advised him to admit his guilt but plead drunkenness at the time, but this advice was not accepted. Taboko suggested a 5s. fine (largely a token fine since everyone was certain of the case against him) but discussion finally petered out with the matter never really being settled.

The Minutes, Aims, and By-Laws of the Council were then read and discussed. The Headmaster's proposed Aims (recorded in Appendix B) were accepted and recorded in the book kept by the Secretary. It was agreed that initial entry to the Council should be by 5s. payment (apart from the bottle of brandy) and that this was to be followed by a 6d. subscription for every week. Meetings would be held on Sundays once a fortnight. The laws accepted by the Council were as follows:

1. That no non-member should be allowed to attend a Council meeting. If such a person did enter he would be fined £1.[1]
2. A person who is drunk and misbehaves may be fined 10s.
3. Nothing said in the meeting may be repeated outside. The seriousness of this offence was emphasized and the fine of a 'real goat' (i.e. not commutable) was attached to it.
4. The Chiefs' Council was the superior authority for the whole of Ndifaw. (Thus, specifically, it was ascribed higher status than the Clan Union.)
5. Any case between two members of the Council should be settled within it.
6. Money collected by the Council should be used for its own benefit.
7. No one should be late in attending the meetings. (Fine: 1 jug of wine.)

In general discussion certain other rules were suggested which were not formally accepted. It was suggested thus that any fine awarded by the Council should include one jug of wine; this, however, was refused. Taboko further suggested that if anyone committed bɛnaŋ, 'back-biting', subversive or treacherous talk, and thus injured the present unity of Tali, he should be made liable to the Chiefs' Council where his case would be heard and judged. This proposed law had the support of the meeting but was not, however, incorporated in its written by-laws.

At this meeting there was much talk of the Council as representative of the community. The Council embodied the community. Various actions made or matters discussed had reference to this. Thus it received at this meeting a minor 'animal of the community' which had recently been

---

[1] All meetings of the Council were guarded by the dɛnkwɔ palm-leaf. For its first meetings notice of the meeting was given to its members by written notes; these were collected at the meeting and as 'tickets' served to exclude strangers. Apart from these and at this time, the Council had no other formal sign marking its exclusiveness.

caught by a member of the settlement in which it was meeting. (The meat was cooked and eaten communally at the same time as the goat.) It was said that now that the Council represented Tali, the District Officer's recognition and approval of it should be obtained; the Council should be established, with the administration's approval, as the authoritative body in Tali. It was suggested therefore that copies of its constitution should be sent to the District Officer. The importance of the Council's political role in succeeding to Ngbe was also the subject of one speech. In Banyang life, it was said, there were two things: Mfam and Ngbe. The forefathers had Ngbe, which they had bought and had passed on to those now living. The latter had now found a better association (*ako*), this Council, which would be the means of both strengthening and improving the community. Other matters discussed at this meeting concerned what action should be taken at the forthcoming meeting of the Clan Union to effect Tali 2's entry into it and whether an Ngbe law should be made abolishing the Tali Ekan Society (see p. 268). After the food had been eaten and while wine was still being drunk, the members turned to 'playing Ngbe'. It was thus that the meeting was concluded.

Unfortunately, shortly after this last meeting I was to leave Tali and six months later Banyang country itself. The Council continued to meet regularly, however, discussing community issues, hearing cases brought before it, receiving a few new members (minor leaders or sectional heads) and 'dancing Ngbe'. When I returned to Tali in 1958 the council was still in existence, although much of its initial impetus was lost and its meetings were less frequent. I had fully expected to find that by this time (four years after the original agreement) the rather precarious unity of the combined Tali had given way and that 'Tali 1' and 'Tali 2' had become independent not only by virtue of their separate leadership, but also operationally, as distinct village communities. In fact this was not the case – or, at least, was not so entirely. Tali 1 and Tali 2 had by this time acquired a great deal of practical independence, but mutual consultation between the leading members of both halves still continued (in a way which is unusual between most villages of a village group) and it was formally recognized that for any important meeting in either side of Tali representatives should be sent for from the other side.

As the A.D.O. had foreseen, Tali's ability to remain united (despite its 'two independent chiefs') placed it in a strong position in the wider political scene. When elections were held for the Southern Cameroons' House of Assembly, it was their man who was nominated to stand for the local constituency and who was eventually elected. This was Nyenti, who in 1960 became briefly the subject of a *cause célèbre* in the Cameroons when an inquiry was set up to establish the circumstances in which he had 'crossed the floor' of the House. Later Nyenti was elected to the Federal parliament but after further criticism subsequently withdrew from national politics.

Within Tali itself, the 'united community' became subject to further strains and by 1965 (when I again revisited Banyang country) had in all appearance become finally completely divided. The issue which had forced this final rift was the positioning of 'Tali market'. The original Tali market had ceased to function when German rule was established. Years later, a new (mainly subsistence-foods and petty trade goods) market was set up by the emergent faction of Tali ('Tali over the Mfu', later Tali 2). Tali 1 now claimed that if anyone had the right to a market, it was they, and had established a new market of their own, for which they obtained a government licence, and which was deliberately arranged to take place on the same day as Tali 2's market. A war of attrition had resulted which was then going in Tali 1's favour.

Themes and comments

The Tali split as an example of constitutional politics. Throughout the events that they have been described there is a continuous, if changing, relationship between the operational or politically effective structure of Tali and the constitutional arrangements which give recognition to this structure. What is known of the late nineteenth-century situation in Tali suggests a strong, established core-group, centred upon the large, if ramified lineage group of *bɔ Mfɔnjo*, who had monopolized the village leadership over a sequence of successions. The wider political influence of Defang Baimbi (his reputation as a patron who would settle cases or take up causes; his success in withstanding the Mbo by fighting) would appear to have rested upon a firm power-base within his own, large community. Even so, the political unity of Tali was not without its internal complexities: apart perhaps from the residential secessions that had occurred among the *bɔ Mfɔnjo* themselves (note for example that in *Figure 11*, p. 43), Atemngen, Ebunta, and Tanyi Tabe are all *bɔ Mfɔnjo*), the most important of the emergent internal divisions was that between the major part of the community situated between the Mfu and Mfi rivers and the three main sections 'over the Mfu', centred upon Nchang. The evidence suggests that the latter had grown, or were then growing, in size: Nchang was itself to divide into three, then four, separate sections; the trend of residential secession within the village as a whole was a movement to the 'overside' of the Mfu (for example, all the residential secessions of bɔ Tanyi Ako, previously discussed pp. 295–296, accord with this trend, as do those of bɔ Mfɔnjo, at a different level). 'Tali over the Mfu' were represented by the leader of Nchang, whose position as the informal head of an (operationally autonomous) 'sub-village' underlay his formal recognition as second in status to the village leader. This constitutionally-contained balance of power persisted through the period of German administration and under British administration while Egbemba remained village leader.

Nevertheless, some of the conditions affecting the constitutional unity and its relationship to the operational power structure within Tali were to change during the time of these two administrations. Most notably the person whose status was most closely linked with the constitutional unity of the village and who stood at the head of the hierarchy of personal influence, the village leader, was to suffer a radical reduction in the circumstances which supported his influence: rights over slaves and access to wives. In attempting to use his influence to his own advantage, or arbitrarily, Baimbi, like a number of other village leaders, was removed and punished by the administration. It is interesting to note that Baimbi's successors both, in different ways, were chosen from the internal divisions of Tali already described: for a brief time the leader of Nchang, formerly second in status to Baimbi, represented Tali to the administration, but when he too fell foul of it, Tali's official leader was a son of Ebunta, drawn from one of the secessional groups of bɔ Mfɔnjo. It is difficult not to draw the conclusion that this second choice of successor helped to restore the unity of bɔ Mfɔnjo as the power-base for the constitutional village leader, but widened the potential division between the traditional Tali (rump) and the emergent sub-village 'Tali across the Mfu'. In time the effective informal leadership of the latter group passed from Nchang (now Nten Nchang) to Okorobak.

When Egbemba finally died it was virtually inevitable that the question of his successor should give rise to a dispute. The operational division between the two major sub-groups of Tali now emerged as a factional rivalry between candidates for the village leadership. At this stage the power struggle between the two groups still occurred within a single, commonly accepted constitutional framework: that Tali was one community and should be represented by a single leader. It was only when the contending faction could obtain neither success nor compromise within this framework that they changed the issue, which became one directly of their own constitutional status, i.e. their right to an independent (village) leadership. The political struggle became now explicitly an issue of 'constitutional politics', the attempt of an operationally autonomous community to acquire formal recognition of their *de facto* status.

The absence of compromise on the first issue was consistent with the stalemate which was reached on the second. Yet eventually – after all the stratagems of Tali 2 in their appeals to an external authority, and despite the vengeful wrath of the rump Tali, rendered ineffectual by the same authority – the issue was resolved by a 'political' agreement between themselves, which was itself in the nature of a compromise. What had been compromised upon here was the normal association of an independent village leadership with the effective independence of the village in most political affairs: Tali tried to restore the operational unity of what *had* been the constitutional unit (Tali as a village under a single leader) by formally recognizing the existence of two leaders, each at a different level representing their own community (which we have now, by definition, to call separate villages). Such an agreement was bound to be precarious. This agreement was effective for a time and was institutionally supported by the Chiefs' Council: it established a 'compromise constitution', if such we may call it, within which tangible political gains were made by the combined Tali. Yet the corporate constitutional link for the combined community (which apart from the Chiefs' Council was no more than the asserted recognition of Tali's continued unity) was a slender one, and could hardly be expected to withstand or contain any major division of interest between the two sides. When such a division of interest emerged, the precarious wider link in the 'compromise constitution' broke down and Tali became two villages, with the more usual form of each having its own constitutional leader and each its own operational independence.

In this re-examination of the events described I have dwelt especially upon the changing relationship between the 'constitutional' and 'operational' aspects of Tali's political organization: I turn now to examine how some of the themes earlier discussed in this book are also evidenced in the constitutional politics of the Tali split.

The diffuseness of the political community. In writing the narrative of these events I have felt some difficulty in translating the term ɛtɔk, which moved like the political action itself, between different orders of residential grouping. In terms of the distinctions earlier made, three levels of grouping were directly involved: sub-village, village, and supra-village. In the development of the events, Tali 2 (at first 'Tali over the Mfu') acquired effective autonomy as a sub-village; it claimed and achieved constitutional recognition as a village; the combined Tali then operated together as a supra-village, before eventually its two parts became separated once more, not only constitutionally but also operationally, as villages. The flexibility (and instability) of these orders of grouping are an inherent characteristic of Banyang political system, in both concept and operation. The paradox of 'a united community under two independent chiefs' would not have been possible as a solution were not the concept of an *ɛtɔk* an elastic one, a strong element of contingency determining the level of residential group involved in political action at any one time.

Despite the contingency of political action and the diffuseness of the political community, certain rights and statuses were recognized as having critical and continuing importance. It was indeed over the legitimacy – or legitimization – of these rights that the major contest took place. They concerned pre-eminently the ultimate independence of a community leader, an *mfɔ ɛtɔk*: whether (in my own terminology) he could claim to be a village leader. In modern circumstances, which have further singled out the 'village head' or 'village chief' as having a special status, the contest became more explicitly and directly concerned with the status of this man. (At one point Taboko observed that in the past the dispute would not have occurred over the leadership as such but over some incidental matter: past stories confirm this but show also that the 'incidental matter' would have related to the issue of leadership.) The traditional rights to, and presentation of, the 'animals of the community' were not directly involved in the events, although the emergent Tali 2 in claiming legitimacy for its village leader did in fact attempt to trace his claims back to the past – in terms of 'Ndifaw's sons' and of the veiled rights associated with the possession of 'the key of Tali, the (leopard) knife and stool'. More directly, the collection of tax as a present-day index of village leadership was involved. This follows, as I have attempted to show earlier (pp. 127 f.), a common pattern whereby a claimant village leader has usually in the first stage of securing independent status sought at least the tacit approval of administration by fulfilling the tax-collecting task normally associated with village leadership.

What was unusual in the intitial resolution of the Tali dispute was that the recognition of a new 'independent chief' did not *divide* Tali politically, but went with a reaffirmation of its unity. It was as though the issue of status could be treated separately from that of corporate community grouping: this was a *political* compromise *constitutionally* ratified in a way not dissimilar from earlier divisions in the rights of leadership between the effective status and the ritual office. But as in those earlier compromises the essential point had been won.

The quest for status. Abane, Takum Mfotaw, Nyenti, his rival in Nten Nchang, and Peter Esong of Kembong were all involved at different levels and in various ways with an attempt to improve or extend their status, either as *bafɔ* or *bo ɛtɔk*, either 'leaders' or 'persons of the community', and in some cases both. In this quest all relied upon the support of their immediate residential group, and the part they played was conditioned by the place and strength of this group within the wider residential configuration. At the same time and at the lower levels much also depended upon the way a minor leader played his hand, above all upon whose side he opted for. There were two 'crossings' of side (one perhaps partial: an attempt to play it both ways). Both cases involved a splitting of the supporting hamlets (Nten Nchang and Kembong) and the emergence of a new, separately based leader to replace the defector. The terms of the dispute's settlement did not immediately determine whether Nyenti or his rival should emerge pre-eminent. In fact Nyenti lay low for a time, and then with the support of Tali 1 was readmitted to the conjoint 'inner council' and confirmed as the sectional representative or 'Quarter Head' of Nten Nchang in Tali 2. It was this which led his rival into such extreme opposition to the corporate power and authority of the community which we have already traced (pp. 239–240).

The balance between unity and division determining the operational autonomy of a residential group. The most dramatic example of the significance of this balance is the change that was effected at the resolution of the dispute. Both before and after this, however, a gradual alteration in balance was occurring: in this gradual emergence of 'Tali over the Mfu', later Tali 2, much depended upon the quelling of possible divisions within their own ranks. Thus in my first formal encounter with him and his council, the leader of Tali 2 insisted (as the members of the rump Tali had not) that there were no *bɛtɔk* within Tali 2: it was all *one ɛtɔk*, undivided. Yet the defection of Nyenti and his followers had already by this time weakened their case and the slight havering of Talinchang was also evident. (At this very meeting, for example, its representative had failed to attend and – at *mfɔ Abane*'s instigation – a special messenger was sent to fetch him.)

We need not further comment on the unity of the conjoint Tali that so effectively strengthened its governmental authority. Even here, however, the established leaders were not without their potential opposition, whose murmurings of protest have been briefly reported (pp. 187, 261).

The interaction of residential and kinship ties. This theme is the least fully evidenced in the events as they have been described. It is relevant, however, that Tali 2 never denied their kinship connection with the remainder of *bɔ Ndifɔ*: in their re-framing of the genealogical charter they were indeed able to make capital out of the status of Mfonjo as the remembered 'last born' son of Ndifaw, who was in this way antedated by their own claimed founder-ancestor, Tanyi Nga. Their secession was a secession as a *residential* group, an *ɛtɔk*: thus in the movement of individuals between the two sides (Joseph Enaw, a member of the inner council of the rump Tali, very regularly visited his mother in Akatati; others similarly visited their kinsfolk), it was generally said of such visits that if they concerned 'matters of the lineage group/of kinship' (*barak anɛrɛkɛt*) they were quite permissible: what one could *not* discuss were 'community matters' (*barak ɛtɔk*). The cross-cutting of community and descent ties was however relevant in two cases. One concerns the emergence of *bɔ Mfɔngwa* as a major lineage group in Tali 2, which has already been described. The other, which I have not earlier referred to, was an occasion in 1951 when a member of Mpomba killed a leopard and the leader of Mpomba called their 'kinsmen' in Talinchang to join with them in its presentation to the leader of (the rump) Tali. Talinchang responded to the invitation, and were later admonished by the rest of the emergent Tali 2 (who had stayed away) for doing so.

The relationship between 'inner council', 'council', and 'community'. Questions of strategy were the predominant concern of both sides' inner council (this certainly was true for the rump Tali and I presume it was true also for the emergent Tali 2). When a public action or decision was required, the matter was referred to the council, whose 'voice' was taken to be binding upon the community they represented.

The role of the administration. After Egbemba's death when the formal office held by him in the Native Authority had been disposed of elsewhere (to Fontem of Ebeagwa, who became President of the Appeal Court), there was no official reason why the administration should be concerned in the question of his successor as village leader. Yet again and again the administration was brought in, in the hope that it would sanction a change or would enforce the rights of the legitimists. Nevertheless, the presence of the administration served to extend and complicate the 'normal' process of constitutional change, rather than radically alter it. Playing the dispute back in the first instance to the people themselves, the officers of the administration accepted the majority view and the traditional order. Yet the administration's very presence had reduced the sanctions which had helped to maintain just this order: under the Colonial régime the leaders of Tali had been reduced in wealth and power; nor could the issue of the dispute ever be put to the test of fighting, as the members of the rump Tali claimed would have occurred in the past. Under the shield of administrative authority, Tali 2 could emerge as a separate autonomous unit, gaining if not direct, then vicarious, sanction for its existence by the fulfilment of the tasks officially expected of villages (collection of taxes, maintenance of roads, bridge-building). Ultimately, since the administration *would* not punish what the legitimists of Tali saw as the usurpation of their rights, and since the legitimists themselves *could* not, the only way forward was some kind of compromise. Significantly, too, this was suggested by an officer of the administration and was offered with the carrot of an advantageous position in the local authority structure. The Tali members wanted to get the best of both worlds: they retained the larger communal grouping which would give them an advantage in the modern context of government but still operated the constitutional norms of leadership to give them their two 'independent chiefs'. The problem was to maintain over time the effective corporateness of the conjoint Tali *without* a single, constitutionally sanctioned leader.

The role of associations. The 'Chiefs' Council' (or 'Town Council') was formed to meet this problem – or, at least, an aspect of it. It provided thus a single, authoritative body with superior powers in Tali (it claimed in the whole of the Ndifaw group). Much was indeed claimed for it and for a time, by its overlapping membership with those who were the leaders of the two sides of Tali, it did embody the power and authority of the combined community. I was able to observe this association only in its early stages and am unable to say how its own collapse was involved in the breakdown of political co-operation between Tali 1 and Tali 2. In its form and purpose it was closer to the Clan Unions than to Ngbe, but nevertheless had some of the exclusiveness of the latter and its meetings tended, far more readily, to flow over into convivial and recreational occasions enhanced by participation of the leading members of the combined community. It remained, however, an association organized for a specific group and for an explicit (if not altogether precise) purpose, and to this extent resembled the Clan Unions. It resembled them also in its primary function: to consolidate and give some formal expression to the political unity of a residential grouping wider than the communities recognizing a single leader. We have already spoken of the precarious 'compromise constitution' which united the two parts of Tali. The Chiefs' Council, by an adaptation of the associational form, provided at a different level a further 'constitutional' form and context for the continued corporate political unity of the combined community. Yet ultimately this 'constitution' (like those provided by the Clan Unions for the village groups) depended upon the continued political solidarity of the particular group it represented, and upon the continued acceptance of the particular policy it embodied: by its very nature it lacked the 'segmental' potentiality of Ngbe or the traditional associations. When eventually the solidarity broke, the policy changed, the association itself foundered.

Appendix A

Two texts relating to the Clan Unions. The first is from the Minute Book of the Ebeagwa Secretary and is an account of the Ndifaw Clan Union which was written by him but was later read to and approved by the Ebeagwa village Committee.

NDIFAW CLAN UNION

History

This Union was inaugurated in the year 1953 on 1 and 2 January. Its first general meeting was held in the premises of Chief C. T. Baiyee of Mbinjong Quarters, Tali. In its first attempt the three important villages of Edjungang, Ebeagwa and Tali were fully represented. Through some misunderstanding between the two young men, the villages of Edjungang and Ebeagwa caused the activities of the Union to be at a standstill. Not till 4 September was it possible for another general meeting to be held at Ebeagwa. From this time onwards successful meetings continued to be held monthly in the three centres.

A. AIMS

1. To promote mutual understanding and unity among the indigenous citizens of the clan.
2. To provide a channel through which all matters affecting the clan can be presented constitutionally to the Government.
3. To inculcate pride; spirit of loyalty among members; sympathy and understanding between Government and the Clan as a whole.
4. To strengthen the financial background of the clan.
5. To settle disputes, other than criminal, arising between members of the Clan.

B. There is a monthly contribution of 3*d.*, 6*d.*, or 1*s.* paid by each member of the Union.

1. Pay your 3*d*., 6*d*., or 1*s*. monthly without failure.
2. Make sure that your payments are entered in the Cash Book.
3. Attend all General Meetings and Social Functions of the Union.
4. Encourage all who are not in the Union to join the Union.
5. Remember that Unity is Strength.
6. Be honest, punctual, and efficient in whatever you may be given to do.
7. Remember that no Union can continue to serve the best interests of its members or even exist without the financial backing of its members.
8. Fulfil your obligations honourably and faithfully and leave the rest to God.

C. BY-LAWS

[*Not listed*]

D. CONSTITUTION

The Union comprises all the citizens of the three villages making up the Ndifaw Clan. It consists of two bodies, namely the Committee and the General Assembly. The Committee is made up of 21 members chosen from the three important branches of the Union. This body undertakes to fish out all matters affecting the Clan and bring such matters to the General Meeting for discussion. It has the right to leave out any matter or matters that it considers unimportant to the general welfare of the Union.

The following offices have already been opened: President and Vice, Secretary and Assistant, Treasurer and Assistant, Members, Spokesmen, Scrutinizers, and Messengers. This body and the Committee form the official organ of the Union, but no final decision can be given by them unless it is backed by the majority of the General Assembly.

The second text is a copy of Tanyi Nkongo Clan Federation By-Laws signed by its General Secretary and Chairman and dated 20 May 1952

TANYI NKONGO CLAN FEDERATION BY-LAWS, TAKWAI, MAMFE

1. Committing adultery with any of the clan member's wife, fine will be inflicted apart from any other action that the owner may wish to proceed with. £7 10*s*. 0*d*. fine.

2. No intermarriage within or outside the clan with women who have divorced marriage with members of the clan federation.

3. All necessary assistance or help should be rendered to any person from the clan by any member of the clan who is attacked with illness or enemies found within or outside the clan.

4. Any lady who is from the clan and prostituting and comes home to make any invitation for any dance, no member of the clan should attend to the invitation nor should any other village attend for such an invitation. It shall be lawful for any member of her family who is a member of the clan to stand for such celebration of her behalf. It shall be unlawful for any other village to attend such a prostitute's invitation.

5. It shall be unlawful for prostitutes to move with shoes or head ties on within the clan. This encourages married wives to become prostitutes. A breach of this law is punishable with a £5 fine.

6. Prostitutes are not allowed to attend any dance within the clan nor is it lawful for any member of the clan knowing her as such to dance with her. Such a prostitute will be fined 10s. and such a member 5s.

7. Any person who tells out our clan discussed matters to non-members of the clan shall be punished with the fine of £1.

8. Any person who intends to speak in the meeting's house should give a warning by ringing the meeting's bell, neglect of this is a fine of 3d.

9. Fighting is not allowed during time of meetings. A breach of this law shall be a fine of 10s. on both parties.

10. Using insultive words against any person in the meeting shall be a fine of 2s. 6d.

11. Talking unreasonably during the trial of any matter in the meeting shall be punished with the fine of 6d.

12. Wilful damage of property in the meeting house shall be punished with a fine of 10s. This does not include the cost of the article damaged.

13. Refusing to carry out orders of the clan federation shall be punished with the fine of 7s. 6d.

14. Insultive behaviour in the public during the period of meetings shall be punished with the fine of 5s.

15. Using slang or insultive words unreasonably on married wives will be punished with a fine of £2 when found guilty during trial.

16. Nobody from outside Tanyi Nkongo is allowed to hunt within their bush without the knowledge of the village head. Anyone caught

committing a breach of this law, all meat, fish, etc. will be claimed from him and would also be fined £5. If he refuses the fine the case will be transferred to the Native Court bound to pay the Tanyi Nkongo Nyamkpes and Tui societies in court.

17. All animals which belong to the native laws and customs are strictly prohibited if anyone kills it and fails to bring it to the V/H. A breach of this law Nyamkpe and Tuis societies will claim him and bound to pay £3 10s. 0d. or if he refuses to pay such a fine, the case will be transferred to the native court.

18. Anybody who is not a subject of Tanyi Nkongo who comes to hunt or do fishing in any of these three villages, a person whom he dwells in his house must report to the village head that he has a stranger. Any animal that he kills first belongs to the villagers. If the person fails to report that he has a stranger to the village head, he will be bound to give a goat or a fine of £1.

19. If any lady has retired from prostitution or comes home to join marriage with any of our clan member, the man must bring such a lady before the meeting for an introduction, and give to the father of the lady the sum of 13s. for starting marriage in the presence of the meeting. Any lady who does not follow our instructions and feels to take her own steps, she shall be fined £5 and the Tanyi Nkongo clan Nyamkpes and Tuis societies will claim her to pay such fine for going against the above by-law.

20. A man who has been a member of the clan Federation and refuses to come to the meeting again will be fined £1. If he comes in and goes out again he will be fined £1. And so it would go on till the end of his life.

21. Any stranger who wishes to make any of our three villages his station, he would be allowed and would give to the villagers a goat and sufficient palm-wine for making peace in his stay in the village. Whenever such a stranger intends to leave the town or village all things that he has like farms or houses would only belong to the villagers and never to be sold by him in any way.

22. Nobody is allowed by the clan Federation to claim any area of our land as his belongings without the knowledge of the village head or villagers.

23. Anybody who writes any letters for any married wife without the knowledge of such a wife's husband shall be punished with a fine of 15s. each.

After the by-laws have been prepared by special members of a joint committee, Nyampke and Tui Societies were put to guide and stamp them to be followed within the clan.

The above by-laws shall be enforced by any member of the clan when a breach of the above by-laws is committed in his views. In enforcing the by-laws and actions or anything whatsoever befalls upon the person acting, it shall be the duty of the whole clan to stand on his behalf for aid.

This was suggested and was to the consent of the whole clan Federation. The aim of this is to bring UNITY, CIVILIZATION, AND TO AVOID PROSTITUTION AND OTHER BAD HABITS IN THE COUNTRY.

'UNITED WE STAND AND DIVIDED WE FALL'

Signed by four representatives of Takwai, Mambo, and Bara Villages. Copies forwarded to the District Officer Mamfe and Banyang Native Authority.

Appendix B

Texts relating to the Tali dispute and Chiefs' Council. The first is a report by Mr Ojong, Headmaster of Tali School, to the Assistant District Officer, Mamfe District.

SETTLEMENT OF THE TALI CHIEFTAINCY CASE, 28 MARCH 1954

Consequent on the meeting that was held on 21/2/54 the A.D.O. who presided over the meeting of the Chieftaincy case between Tali One and Tali Two authorized me to preside over a second meeting of the two groups of people and issue an accurate statement of fact with the following terms of reference in relation to his advice to the people:

1. That the people should consider the advisability of uniting Tali into one main group and by tradition, the Chief by right of blood, descended from the house of the late Chief, should be called the first Chief and invariably should be vested with supreme executive powers in the administrative functions in the whole of Tali. That the other new Chief of Tali should be recognized by his people and the people of the traditional Chief, but in the exercise of power the second Chief has right only over his own people and shall be called a Sub-Chief and shall automatically play second fiddle to the traditional ruler in the administration of the town and in public Councils.

2. That the people of Tali should take his advice seriously into mind as their long-standing quarrel would bring them no material prosperity, but that a turn of mind from enemies to friends would surely land them on becoming a united well-ordered group of men capable of tackling its own affairs when the existing system of Native Administration would be reformed.

DECISION TAKEN AT THE FINAL MEETING OF THE PEOPLE OF TALI

With some deviation from certain points, following the foregoing pattern of advice laid down by Mr A. A. Atta, the A.D.O. in charge of Mamfe Division on 21 February 1954, and which we partly consider to be the only true solution to end our long chieftaincy strife which has now lasted for six years, we the undersigned persons, chief-makers, supporters, and chiefs of the two sections of Tali village, do hereby, in the presence of our Headmaster, Mr P. T. Ojong, the president appointed by the A.D.O., on this 28 March 1954, unanimously resolve to be united under the aegis of two independent Chiefs for the ultimate good of our town and henceforth, Mr Abane Fotow, newly installed, shall act as an independent Chief to Chief Tabi Baiye who had hitherto been the only man holding the reins of chieftaincy in Tali. Following this decision therefore, whenever a Chief dies his people have the independent right to elect a new Chief with full executive powers as the late Chief.

1. Tabokoh Banyu, His Mark	2. Takem Fotor, His Mark
3. A. ABANDA	4. Oben Kebua, His Mark
5. W. B. ABANGE	(Spokesman)
7. ABANE – Chief	6. Ayuk Tanyi, His Mark
9. Baiyee Ayuk, His Mark	8. Mbong Nchang, His Mark
11. JOHN EGBE	10. Tambe Ndakor, His Mark
13. C. T. BAIYEE – Chief	12. Baya Ayuk, His Mark
15. Tambe Anike, His Mark	14. Baiyee Nyo, His Mark
	16. D. B. EBUNTA (Spokesman)

Proposals concerning the Tali Chiefs' Council drawn up by Mr Ojong, Headmaster of Tali School

THE PROPOSED CHIEFS' COUNCIL

I. AIMS

(a) The aims of a Chiefs' Council in Tali are to foster co-operation between members of the two sections of Tali in matters consciously conceived and which aim at strengthening the social, educational, and economic background of the whole village.

(b) The Council will stand forth to aid the two chiefs in constructional advice in the execution of their official duties and to settle all disputes that may arise between the two parties, taking due care to avoid further family split such as happened and nearly deterred the progress of the whole of Tali.

(c) In the course of events, the Council will endeavour to recommend a specific kind of traditional costume that will be worn by our two chiefs on all state occasions as well as that there shall be chiefs' attendants to help them in carrying their little effects whenever they are going out for state duties.

(d) The Council will define clearly the relationship between the two chiefs and their subjects and how a chief should behave in order that he may gain the respect of his people.

(e) The Council will arrange for the erection of a central town hall where state matters will be discussed in common.

(f) As in all practical purposes, a basic subscription will be imposed on every member for the efficient running of the Council.

2. MEMBERSHIP

Only men of sound moral background and intelligence will be chosen for the Council, these being drawn from the two sections of Tali on an equal representative scale. To begin with, about seventeen men will constitute the Council: six men from each section of Tali and three nominated members – strangers – to represent certain communal interests in Tali which are not otherwise adequately represented. This altogether will make up a total of seventeen members, including the two chiefs.

3. SECRETARIAT

Officers will be elected by the people themselves, namely: a President, Assistant President, Honorary Secretary, Assistant Honorary Secretary, Treasurer, Assistant Treasurer, Chief Whip, and a Messenger.

4. DISCIPLINE

In all Council sessions order will be maintained by the Chief Whip and if a member is found whose conduct is likely to cause a breach of the peace that member may be fined, suspended, or in repeated acts of of offence the member is expelled through the unanimous sanction of the whole Council.

Bibliography

Works referred to in the Text

ANDERSON, H. O. 1929. *Preliminary Assessment Report on the Banyang Tribal Area*. TS.

ARDENER, E. and others. 1960. *Plantation and Village in the Cameroons*. London: Oxford University Press.

ARDENER, S. 1953. 'The Social and Economic Significance of the Contribution Club among a Section of the Southern Ibo.' *WAISER Conference Proceedings*, Sociology Section.

BARNES, J. 1954. *Politics in a Changing Society*. Manchester: Manchester University Press.

BARTH, FREDRIK. 1959. *Political Leadership among the Swat Pathans*. London: Athlone Press.

BOHANNAN, LAURA. 1952. 'A Genealogical Charter'. *Africa* 22: 301–315.
— 1958. 'Political Aspects of Tiv Social Organization', in *Tribes Without Rulers*, John Middleton and David Tait (eds.). London: Routledge.

BOHANNAN, P. J. 1957. *Justice and Judgement among the Tiv*. London: Oxford University Press for International African Institute.

CHILVER, E. 1963. 'Native Administration in the West Central Cameroons 1902–1954', in *Essays in Imperial Government: Presented to Margery Perham*, Kenneth Robinson and Frederick Madden (eds.). Oxford: Basil Blackwell.

CHILVER, E. M. & KABERRY, P. M. 1960. 'From Tribute to Tax in a Tikar Chiefdom.' *Africa* 30: 1–19.

CRABB, D. W. 1965. *Ekoid Bantu Languages of Ogoja, Eastern Nigeria*, Pt. I. Cambridge: Cambridge University Press.

D'ENTRÈVES, A. P. 1967. *The Notion of the State*. Oxford: Clarendon Press.

DIKE, K. O. 1956. *Trade and Politics in the Niger Delta 1830–1885*. Oxford: Clarendon Press.

EASTON, DAVID. 1959. 'Political Anthropology', in *Biennial Review of Anthropology 1959*, B. J. Siegel (ed.). Stanford: Stanford University Press.

EVANS-PRITCHARD, E. E. 1940. *The Nuer*. Oxford: Clarendon Press.

FALLERS, LLOYD. 1963. 'Political Anthropology in Africa'. *European Archives of Sociology* **4**: 311–329.

FORDE, D. 1964. *Yakö Studies*. London: Oxford University Press for International African Institute.

FORTES, M. 1945. *The Dynamics of Clanship among the Tallensi*. London: Oxford University Press for the International African Institute.

FORTES, M. & EVANS-PRITCHARD, E. E. (eds.). 1940 *African Political Systems*. London: Oxford University Press for International African Institute.

GIERKE, O. 1900. *Political Theories of the Middle Ages* (trans. by F. W. Maitland). Cambridge: Cambridge University Press.

GLUCKMAN, M. 1955. *The Judicial Process among the Barotse of Northern Rhodesia*. Manchester: Manchester University Press.

GOLDIE, H. 1890. *Calabar and its Mission*. Edinburgh.

GORGES, E. H. F. 1930. *Banyang Tribal Area Assessment Report*. TS.

GREENBERG, J. H. 1955. *Studies in African Linguistic Classification*. New Haven, Connecticut: Compass Publishing Co.

GULLIVER, P. H. 1963. *Social Control in an African Society*. London: Routledge.

HARRIS, R. 1965. *The Political Organization of the Mbembe, Nigeria*. London: HMSO.

INTERNATIONAL AFRICAN INSTITUTE. 1956. *Linguistic Survey of the Northern Bantu Borderland, Vol I*. London: Oxford University Press for International African Institute.

ITTMAN, J. 1935–36. 'Kenyang, die Sprache der Nyang.' *Zeitschrift für Eingeborenen-Sprachen* **26**: 2–35; 97–133; 174–202; 272–300.

JONES, G. I. 1956. 'The Political Organization of Old Calabar', in *Efik Traders of Old Calabar*, D. Forde (ed.). London; Oxford University Press for International African Institute.

KRIGE, E. J. & J. D. 1943. *The Realm of the Rain-Queen*. London: Oxford University Press for International African Institute.

LIENHARDT, G. 1958. 'The Western Dinka', in *Tribes Without Rulers*, John Middleton and David Tait (eds.). London: Routledge.

LYNCH, D. 1946. *The Concentration of Economic Power*. New York: Columbia University Press.

MCFARLAN, D. M. 1946. *Calabar: The Church of Scotland Mission 1846–1946*. London: Nelson.

MAIR, LUCY. 1962. *Primitive Government*. Harmondsworth: Penguin.

MAITLAND, F. W. 1898. *Township and Borough*. Cambridge: Cambridge University Press.

MANSFELD, A. 1908. *Urwald-Dokumente*. Berlin: Dietrich Reimer.

MIDDLETON, J. & TAIT, D. (eds.). 1958. *Tribes Without Rulers*. London: Routledge.

OTTENBERG, S. 1955. 'Improvement Associations among the Afikpo Ibo.' *Africa* **25**: 1–28.

PARKINSON, J. 1907. 'A Note on the Efik and Ekoi Tribes of the Eastern Provinces'. *J. Roy. Anthropol. Inst. 37*: 261–267.

PARTRIDGE, C. 1905. *Cross River Natives*. London.

PERHAM, M. 1937. *Native Administration in Nigeria*. London: Oxford University Press.

RUEL, M. 1960. 'Migration in Two Southern Cameroons Tribes: (2) The Banyang of Mamfe Division', in *Plantation and Village in the Cameroons*, E. Ardener and others. London: Oxford University Press.

— 1962. 'Banyang Settlements: Part I: Pre-European Settlement. Part II: Change of Settlement and Later Developments'. *Man* **62**, 175 and 196.

— 1962. 'Genealogical Concepts or "Category Words"? A Study of Banyang Kinship Terminology.' *J. Roy. Anthropol. Inst.* **92**: 157–176.

— 1964. 'The Modern Adaptation of Associations among the Banyang of the West Cameroon.' *Southwestern Journal of Anthropology* **20**: 1–14.

— 1965. 'Witchcraft, Morality and Doubt.' *Odu* University of Ife Journal of African Studies **2**: 3–26.

SMITH, M. G. 1960. *Government in Zazzau, 1800–1950*. London: Oxford University Press for International African Institute.

— 1968. 'Political Organization', article under entry Political Anthropology in *International Encyclopaedia of the Social Sciences*, Vol. 12, pp. 193–202. Macmillan and the Free Press.

SOUTHALL, A. W. (1956). *Alur Society*. Cambridge: Heffer.

STASCHEWSKI, F. 1917. *Die Banyangi*. Baessler-Archiv Beiheft VIII.

SWABEY, M. H. 1937. *Intelligence Report on the Kembong Area*. TS.

SWARTZ, MARC J., TURNER, VICTOR W. & TUDEN, ARTHUR (eds.). 1966. *Political Anthropology*. Chicago: Aldine.

TALBOT, P. A. 1912. *In the Shadow of the Bush*. London: Heinemann.

— 1926. *The Peoples of Southern Nigeria*, 4 vols. London: Oxford University Press.

WADDELL, H. M. 1863. *Twenty Nine Years in the West Indies and Central Africa*. London: Nelson.

337

WEST CAMEROON GAZETTE, No. 10, Vol. V. 1965.

WESTERMANN, D. & BRYAN, M. A. 1952. *Languages of West Africa.* London: Oxford University Press for International African Institute.

WILLIAMS, G. 1957. *Salmond on Jurisprudence* 11th Edn. London: Sweet and Maxwell.

ZINTGRAFF, E. von. 1895. *Nord Kamerun.* Berlin: Paetel.

Documents Where these were consulted at the Buea Archives Office the reference there is given in brackets.

Annual Report on the Ossidinge Division. 1916. (Ce 1916/2.)

Annual Report on the Mamfe Division. 1929, 1931, 1932, 1933, 1934, 1935, 1936, 1937, 1938, 1940, 1942, 1943, 1947. (Ce 1929/1 etc.)

Banyang Touring Diary.

Correspondence relating to Assessment Report. (Af 18.)

Jahresbericht 1937, von Rev. E. Peyer, Fotabe. Archives of the Basel Mission, Basel.

Proposals for the Federation of the Banyang, Bangwa, Mundanis and Mbo Clans of the Mamfe Division, July 1950.

Index

Aba riots, 106

aca (LK; *acɔ* UK), 'meeting house'. *See* settlement patterns

administrative functions, 140, 186–9; failure of office treated as a community offence, 188–9

African Political Systems, xi, xii

Agbotoko. *See* Tagbotoko

age-groups, 205, 206–10, 261, 262

ako (LK; *akoŋ* UK). *See* association

Alur, xiii

ancestral spirits, 63, 95, 152, 177, 203n, 314

Angbo (association or sub-association), 202, 223

'animals of the community', xiv, 23f, 49f, 195, 238, 248n, 316–17, 321. *See also* leopard, python, crocodile

ankwɔ, 'he should pay'. *See* -*kwɔ*

Anyang, 2, 9, 10, 13

Ardener, S. G., 260n

Are, 119, 119n. *See also* Mbinjong

'articulation', as a function of descent, xvii, 74–5, 77

Arusha, xi, 162n

Asae, 79n

Ashu (leading elder, Tinto 1), 122n

Ashum, 119, 122

association(s) (*ako, akoŋ, ba-*), 146, 191, 195–6, 197f, 205, 209, 213, 241, 260n, 270, 317; types of, 199–205; modern, 60, 185, 199, 205, 259f, 313f; young men's, 137, 205, 209, 210, 260, 268–9; women's, 203–5; membership of, 200, 223, 226–8, 245, 315; lodge organization, 199–200, 213, 228–30, 242, 255–9; former, listed, 202, 203; constitution, xix, 199, 242, 315–17; 'grades', 200, 206–7, 210–11, 218f, 228, 243; rule of secrecy, 200, 245–6, 316; transferability of status, 209, 229, 255, 257; masked dancer, 201–2, 211–13, 214; governmental role of, 140–1, 272, 324; authority of, 201, 209, 215, 242, 249, 316; in relation to community structure, xix, 196, 218, 255, 273; political role of, xviii–xix, 181, 273, 317; as 'polities',

xix, 250f, 257–8, 273. *See also* age-groups, Angbo, 'Band', 'Bank', Basinjom, Clan Unions, Chiefs' Council, Eja, Ekan, Mbia, Mbokondem, Ngbe, Tui

Atebong, 11n, 106, 259

authority: of community distinguished from authority of lineage group, 133, 152f; acceptance of, a condition of group membership, 136, 165; balance between formal and effective, 194; transmuting of power to, 248n; difference between Ngbe and Clan Unions', 273

autonomous political action, as characteristic of Banyang residential groups, xiii–xiv, 22, 133, 162, 184f, 254, 256; in formation of new groups, 277, 289, 292, 293, 296, 298, 303–4, 320

Awanchi, 10, 183. *See also* Kendem

Ayok Etayak village group (*bɔ Ayok Ɛtayak*), 52, 83, 87–93, 99–100, 113–14, 183, 281, 286, *Figures 18, 19*

Ayundep, 29

Bachu Akagbe (Badshu Akagbe; *also bɔ Ncuɔmbirɛ*), 64, 79, 106, 108, 124, 173, 281 282–5, 290n, *Figure 29*

Bachu Ntae, 118, 124, 128n

Bacui (Kɛcui), 10, 10n

bafɔ. *See* leaders

Baimberi, 37, 243, 260, 314, *Figure 8*

Bakebe, 59, 65, 107, 111, 117n, 119, 122, 172–3, 203, 214n

Balundu, 200, 251

Bamenda, 11, 105n, 113n, 271

Bamileke, 11

'Band' (modern association), 175, 259, 259n, 268

Bangwa, 4, 5–7, 9n, 11, 112n, 184, 188, 200, 213–14, 217

'Bank' (modern association), 260–1

Banyang (sing. Manyang): country and population, 1, 5, 10, 15, 16; mode of livelihood, 10–11, 15–16; differences between Upper and Lower, 2, 5n, 9, 28,

senta, 'open compound'. *See* compound

serial assimilation, of lineage groups, 279, 292–6

settlement change, 16, 22, 26, 33f, 41, 43, 118, 286, 290, 305–6, *Figures 6, 7, 11*

settlement patterns, 7, 22, 26f, 278, *Figures 3, 4, 5, 8, 9, 30, Plates 2, 3*; 'meeting house' or 'bottom house' as the focal point of settlement, 28, 29–30, 30n, 34, 255

'slaves', 4, 12–13, 55, 61, 69, 120, 145, 149, 151, 166f, 194–5, 255, 305, 306; as unit of reckoning, 57, 149, 167, 195

Smith, M. G., xi, xii

social change, 14–16, 116f, 303; formation of descent and residential groups, xix–xx, 275f. *See also* Colonial administration, associations, settlement change

Staschewski, F., 27, 29, 34–5

status: status-system of a community 68–70; quest for, 305, 322; (associational) status-categories, 225–6, 242–3. *See also mu ɛtɔk, nɛm mu*

sub-village, as an operationally distinct residential group, 45, 47, 139, 143, 151, 290–1, 319, 321, *Figures 1, 31*

Sumbe, 128

supra-village, 21, 25, 45, 144, 170, 194, 313, 321, *Figure 1*

Tabe Aru. *See* Okorobak

Taboko, xx, xxi, 37, 37n, 39, 58, 70, 99, 137–40, 143, 146, 153–4, 169, 306n, 313–14, 321, *Plate 4*

Tagbotoko (Agbotoko) breakaway settlement, 93, 286–9, 291, 293, *Figures 20, 30*

Tainyong Clan. *See* Tayong village group

Takwa (Takwai), 11, 33n, 48, 68, 162, 184–5, 213, 236, 269–70, 301, 328f

Talbot, P. A., 2, 8, 11n, 13n, 14, 14n, 210n, 223n, 234n, 241n, 250n, 251n

Tali (Tali 1, Tali 2), xx, 5, 7, 9, 9n, 11, 15, 27, 29, 34, 39, 41, 43f, 47, 53f, 57n, 62, 79, 81, 83, 86, 90, 96, 99, 104, 109, 115, 121, 125, 128–9, 136, 142f, 147–8, 151, 158n, 160, 166f, 174f, 187, 192, 194f, 202, 204f, 213, 215, 217–18, 224, 226n, 228, 230, 237, 239–40, 256, 258f, 271–2, 277, 280n, 290, 290n, 292–3, 295, 301, *Figures 11, 12, 16, 17, 33*; derivation of name, 62; case of the Tali split, 304–25, 332–4

Tallensi, xiii

tancoko mɔ, 'youngest child', 56, 57n, 124, 175n, 291

Tanyi Ako. *See bɔ Tanyi Ako*

Tanyi Nkongo village group (*bɔ Tanyi Nkoŋo*), 11, 33n, 44, 48–9, 53, 147, 162, 181, 263n, 269f, *Figure 13*

Tanyi Tabe, 37, 37n, 45, 47, 137–8, 142, 153–4, 217, 260, 308, *Figure 8*

*Tataw, N. A., 41, 70, 138, 146–7, 171, 177, 209, 264n, 312, 314

tax collection, 103, 107, 111f, 123, 128, 288, 306; as an index of a leader's status, 113–14; involvement in constitutional politics, 113n, 116, 127, 309, 310, 321

Tayo, 290–1, 294, *Figure 31*

Tayong village group (Tainyong), 53, 123–4, 126, 269, 271

theft, 137, 139

'things of the community', 59f, 120f, 260n, 309; 'Chief's regalia', 126; tax regalia, 127

Tinto village group, 13, 34, 108, 117n, 119f, 127, 173, 290n, *Figure 21*

Tiv, xiii, xv, 78

trade and trading routes, 5, 9, 11–12, 250, 253, 254, 255, 305, 318

Tui (association), xix, 188, 190, 199, 201, 213–15, 258, *Plate 8*

village, as an order of residential grouping, xiv, xvii, 20, 21f, 78, 143, 194, 207, *Figures 1, 2*; constitutionally defined, 24; as administrative unit, 103, 107, 118; use of terms Village, Village Head, Village Council by Colonial administration, 105f; role in fighting, 182, 184

village cults, 63–5. *See also* Mfam

village group, as an order of residential grouping, xv, 20, 21f, 144, 193, *Figures 1, 2*; constitutionally defined, 25

Waddell, H. W., 250, 250n, 253, 253n

Warri Province, 106, 106n

were-animals, 50. *See also* witchcraft

Westermann, D., 2

witchcraft, 170, 170n, 205, 210f

women's associations. *See* associations

Yakö, 241n, 258n

Yoruba, 258n

Zintgraff, Count E. von, 13, 13n, 27, 59